GROWTH
WITH
SELF-MANAGEMENT

GROWTH WITH SELF-MANAGEMENT

Yugoslav Industrialization 1952–1975

JOHN H. MOORE

Hoover Institution Press
Stanford University
Stanford, California

Hoover Institution Publication 220

International Standard Book Number: 0–8179–7201–3
Library of Congress Catalog Card Number: 79–2464
Printed in the United States of America

Designed by Elizabeth Gehman

To
Sue, John, and Matthew

Contents

Figures

Tables

Preface

This study is an outgrowth of interest in workers' self-management that dates to a visit in 1968–69 to the University of Virginia by Professor Aleksander Bajt of the University of Ljubljana. Professor Bajt sparked my interest in the institutions of self-management and encouraged me to continue my studies of the system. Later he was most helpful in arranging visits to Yugoslavia for research and discussion. I stand greatly in his debt, although I know he will find much in this study with which to disagree.

I am greatly indebted to the National Fellows Program of the Hoover Institution at Stanford University. The bulk of the quantitative research and preliminary writing of this book was done during 1975–76 under the sponsorship of the Institution's National Fellows Program. Without that year, the book would never have been undertaken. The Hoover Institution also provided a research grant to support my work during the summer of 1977. Earlier I spent two terms as Senior Associate Member, St. Antony's College, Oxford University, under the auspices of the Sesquicentennial Fellows Program of the University of Virginia. During that time, I was able to do extensive background research into the institutions of self-management, work which, although not directly discernible in this book, nevertheless forms an essential part of its background.

Work on the book was supported in a number of other ways. I owe much to the Thomas Jefferson Center Foundation of Charlottesville, Virginia, and, indirectly, to the Earhart Foundation and the Scaife Family Charitable Trusts. If the book would never have been undertaken without the National Fellows Program, it would never have been written without the help of the Thomas Jefferson Center Foundation. The Thomas Jefferson Center Foundation, along with Stanford University and the University of Virginia, supported the computer work done for the study. The foundation also provided comfortable office facilities and the superlative secretarial assistance of Mrs. Carolyn Southall and Mrs. Anne P. Hobbs. The work load was lightened greatly by the excellent assistance of Mrs. Rebecca Strode, research assistant of the Foundation. I was also aided significantly by the excellent Yugoslav collection of the Alderman Library at the University of Virginia and by the library's staff, especially Angelika Powell.

Parts of this study, in different forms, have appeared elsewhere. The industrial production index and measurements derived from it were the basis for my article, "Industrial Production in Yugoslavia," which appeared in the 1977 Joint Economic Committee publication, *East European Economies Post-Helsinki*. The index of structural change, described in appendix E and reported in chapter 6, was separately published in the March 1978 issue of the *Review of Income and Wealth* under the title "A Measure of Structural Change in Output." A paper based on the work in chapters 6 and 10, entitled "Yugoslav Regional Development Policy, 1952–71," was published in *Revue de l'est*. I am grateful for permission to use these materials in this book.

The book was completed at the Law and Economics Center of the University of Miami School of Law. I am deeply grateful to the center and its director, Henry G. Manne, for providing me with the opportunity to complete the work. Mrs. Joanne Davis of the Law and Economics Center typed the final draft with remarkable speed, precision, and understanding of the problems of putting together such a manuscript.

My greatest debts are intellectual. During my studies of Yugoslavia, many people have contributed to my understanding of the country and the economics of self-management and industrial growth. At various times, and in a variety of ways, Professors Roland McKean and Paul Shoup of the University of Virginia, Svetozar Pejovich of the University of Dallas, Eirik Furubotn of Texas A. & M. University, Milorad Drachkovitch of Stanford University, Eugene Zaleski of the Centre national de la recherche scientifique, and Ljubiša Adamovich of the University of Belgrade all were very helpful to me.

Three other individuals stand out in my mind for their many contributions, direct and indirect, to this book. I have already mentioned Aleksander Bajt, without whose stimulation and encouragement I would not have begun studying the Yugoslav economic system. Over the years, Professor S. Herbert Frankel of Oxford University has contributed in countless ways to my understanding of the power and limitations of economics in explaining the behavior of the human animal and to helping me keep economic matters in perspective. Finally, perhaps the greatest debt is owed to my teacher and former colleague, Professor G. Warren Nutter of the University of Virginia. The stamp of his work and example, no doubt imperfectly reproduced, is deeply impressed throughout this book.

Finally, I am deeply grateful to my wife, Sue Corbett Moore, for her steadfast willingness to join me in all endeavors and for her constant encouragement during what has been an unduly long period of preparing this manuscript.

PART ONE

Prelude to Measurement

CHAPTER ONE

Continuity and Change in Workers' Self-Management

During World War II, Yugoslavs fought two wars, one against the Nazi occupation and the other among themselves. In 1945, Tito and his Partisans emerged as the winners of both conflicts. It was only natural, in view of Tito's background, that the fledgling communist state joined forces with the Soviet Union, and the early postwar Yugoslav society and economy were patterned closely after the Soviet model. Relations between the two states soon soured, and in 1948 Stalin expelled the defiant Yugoslavs from the Cominform.

Caught in the no-man's-land between the communist and capitalist camps, Tito faced the most basic of problems: survival. Politically, survival required an ideological departure from Stalinism, a new approach to the communist state arguably superior to the Soviet system. The solution to this problem was workers' self-management. Like many socially revolutionary ideas, including the Bolshevik revolution, this one did not result from analysis of the properties of a socialist system organized in that particular way. According to Djilas, the idea of a system based on worker control of industrial enterprises occurred to him while he was rereading Marx in an effort to discover an ideological basis for claiming that the Yugoslav system was superior to Stalinism.[1] Nothing was known about the economic characteristics of the system, nor could reliable predictions be made about its operation.

Workers' self-management was, in short, experimental; it was adopted above all for political reasons. Because it was experimental, frequent changes in the institutions defining it inevitably occurred as the economic characteristics of the system became evident. But because the system was inherently politicized, changes also occurred for political reasons, and reactions to unforeseen economic properties were strongly colored by the political implications of proposed modifications in the system. In this Marxist state, politics and economics were—and still are—intimately intertwined. Appreciation of this fact is important to understanding the development of self-management, as the brief survey later in this chapter and the discussions in subsequent chapters show.

Workers' self-management was the chosen solution to the problem of political survival. Physical survival was another matter. Yugoslavia was perceptibly threatened from both ideological sides, and defense of the state necessarily assumed primary importance. Physical security required a strong industrial base; hence, the objective of rapid industrialization, never far from the thoughts of communists in those days, became even more urgent. But this objective often conflicted with the ideology of workers' self-management, and the subsequent history of Yugoslavia can be understood better if the problems of reconciling these two objectives are recognized. In fact, one of the most important functions of workers' self-management may have been legitimization of a Yugoslav version of forced-draft industrialization.

The aim of this book, however, is not to analyze Yugoslav history in this light, although insight into the nature of the conflict is one of the book's by-products. Its purpose is more modest: namely, to measure and analyze Yugoslavia's success in generating industrial growth during the first twenty years or so of workers' self-management. Industrial growth has been a relatively neglected facet of the experience of self-management. Western scholars generally have been preoccupied with other concerns—how a self-managed firm operates, the income distribution generated by the system, and the implications of property rights for investment decisions and managerial incentives.

Previous discussions of industrial growth have been based on the official Yugoslav index of industrial production, which is, for reasons discussed below, unsuitable for many purposes. This book develops a new sample index of industrial production, methodologically comparable to indexes commonly used in the West. Much of the following analysis is based on that index, on a new index of structural change in output, and on comparisons with other countries based on these measurements.

The period covered by this study begins in 1952, a year which can reasonably be taken to mark the inauguration of self-management in Yugoslavia. During that year, at the Sixth Party Congress, Tito set the country on its new path, formalizing the direction in which policy had been moving since the Cominform expulsion and, especially, since Djilas' discovery in 1950 of the idea of self-management. The system, if an institutional framework undergoing such constant revision can be called that, underwent continuous change after its inauguration. For that reason, no single date can be singled out as signifying the beginning of the system. The year chosen here can be said, however, to mark a watershed between the old and new systems.

CONTINUITY AND CHANGE

It is impossible to understand the Yugoslav system of workers' self-management without appreciating the continuous change that has characterized it. The well-known Yugoslav economist Branko Horvat gives a graphic description of the environment in the early years:

> In the fourteen years covered [1952–65], every three days brought a regulation issued at the level of the Administration or Parliament. In addition, the Federal economic secretariats and banks produced rules, orders, instructions, decisions, and solutions (245 in 1965). When we take into account the regulations of the republics and localities, and subtract holidays and vacations from the time available, it follows that every working day brought some administrative surprises. However, this does not exhaust all the possibilities for administrative pressure. State bodies, the National Bank, and the Social Accounting Service also have their internal regulations; they also change and, by the nature of things, even faster and more often than legislative acts.[2]

A detailed history of these developments would require a book longer than this one and would, by itself, cast little light on the modifications important for the analysis of the development of industrial production. But some discussion of the changes, especially those crucial to the economic system, is important for understanding the nature of self-management and the discussion in this book.

Decentralization in the Early Reforms

Decentralization of economic decision making and enterprise autonomy are often said to be the hallmarks of worker self-management in Yugoslavia. In fact, it is incorrect to speak of these two as if they are merely opposite sides of the same coin. Their political import is different, and the government treats them differently. Formal authority to make decisions has been progressively decentralized. The actual autonomy of an enterprise in the sense of the power to implement its own choices has, however, remained closely constrained, except for the years immediately after the 1965 reforms. That exception led to a growth of enterprise power, independent of the government, which proved unacceptable to the leadership. The result was the reforms of 1971 (essentially reaffirmed in the 1974 constitution) in which—while formal decentralization proceeded—the autonomy of the enterprise was again reduced.

In 1958, for example, the concept of income distribution was changed. Prior to 1958, enterprises possessed only the right to decide on the distribution of the "profit" remaining after payment of material costs, depreciation, a number of taxes and other obligatory payments, and—most importantly—wages. In 1958, they were granted the formal right to decide on the disposal of enterprise income, including the payment of wages (or personal incomes).[3] Thus, an enterprise could determine the disposal of all its income after meeting its business and fiscal obligations. But this formal right was illusory. At the same time, the government established a system of minimum personal income payments and highly progressive taxes on payments over the minimum that effectively eliminated the scope of decision open to an enterprise.[4]

Similarly, the 1961–65 Five-Year Plan provided for the formal relinquishment by the government of its control over the distribution of enterprise net income. Also, most of the progressive taxes that had constrained actual enterprise autonomy in this respect were replaced by proportional taxes.[5] By the end of 1961, however, most of the power of an enterprise to decide the distribution of its income had been eliminated by anti-inflationary measures. The remaining power was effectively eliminated by the establishment in April 1962 of rules restraining income distribution and a network of government commissions to oversee their enforcement.[6] There was further retrenchment in 1963, including the blocking of certain enterprise investment funds, the placing of ceilings on increases in personal incomes, and the further extension of price controls.[7]

The 1965 Reforms: Decentralization and Reaction

Genuine devolution of authority to the enterprises took place only after the 1965 reforms, and then it was the result of a movement motivated by both economic and political factors. During the debates over disappointing economic performance in the early sixties, reformers gained the ascendancy. They argued that existing economic problems stemmed from government control of investment. According to their argument, banks, which administered investment funds, had little incentive to make economically sound investment choices. Enterprises were confident of being rescued if their plans failed and thus were not motivated to exercise restraint in proposing projects. According to the reformers, this led to excessive aggregate investment and poor investment choices (including "political" factories), both of which fueled inflation. Government attempts to control inflation, largely through price controls, only worsened the situation. The controls distorted relative prices; since the prices of consumer goods were controlled less stringently than the prices of materials and producer goods, consumer goods enterprises tried to expand. This created strong demands for materials, which were in relatively short supply because of their low prices. Market operations were hamstrung; signals were distorted; costs could not be calculated; unprofitability went unpenalized; and efficiency unrewarded.

This economic argument and the movement to decentralization—or "deétatization," as it became known—received support within Yugoslavia. In large part, support for the movement was politically motivated. During the previous decade, there had been a certain devolution of political authority. Local and republican governments had gained power during those years, and de-étatization appeared to promise further extension of their power. The reformist movement gained support from regional (i.e., ethnic) interest groups, which opposed centralism because of fears of strengthening Serbian nationalism and which saw the reform and de-étatization as a means of retaining some degree of autonomy. Pressure behind the movement for reform was also generated by economic groups that, quite apart from their own views about the larger questions of efficiency and growth, were naturally inclined to favor reforms that would increase their own power. Even within the party there were those who favored decentralization.[8] Thus, a coalition formed by persons with different reasons for supporting de-étatization measures emerged in both the economic and political spheres. This coalition was not unopposed, but in the end it persuaded Tito that acceptance of at least some of the reformers' views was necessary not only for economic reasons, but also for the survival of Yugoslavia as a coherent nation. Although the reforms of 1965 focused on the economy, they were, thus, the product of many considerations, most of which were unique to Yugoslavia.

The victory of the reformers was frustrated at the outset of the reform by those interests that stood to lose economic or political power and influence. But the opponents not only opposed the economic reform itself, they also transgressed party discipline by their resistance to official party policy.[9] Yugoslav leaders perceived their resistance as evidence of an intraparty group capable of opposing the party line, and this breach of discipline was the cause of the ouster and disgrace in 1966 of Ranković, Tito's old comrade-in-arms. This and related disciplinary moves effectively squelched resistance to the reform, and, for a time, the real autonomy of enterprises expanded.

But this expansion was short-lived. If its inception can be dated from the year of Ranković's removal, within five years it was swallowed up by the reaction against the nationalism, the regionalism, and the technocratic elite that it, along with the other measures of the reform movement of the mid-sixties, spawned. The endorsement of de-étatization and the resulting devolution of economic and political authority led to a further erosion of the authority of the central party organization, which, especially in its manifestation in Croatia, seemed to threaten the unity of the country. But Croatian nationalism was only one element, albeit the most important one, of a whole range of what was viewed as excessive localization of authority.

The tale of the reaction against the reforms goes beyond the time span of the bulk of this study, but it merits a brief description. In the economy, enterprises and banks had become centers of independent power of a magnitude that the central party evidently could not tolerate. The first action taken against the movement came in late 1971 with the forced resignation of the leaders of the Croatian independence movement. This was followed by the nationwide purge of liberal leaders during the next year, clearly signifying the reversal of the de-étatization movement. With these moves, Tito successfully reasserted the central party's control over the economic and political life of the country and effectively ended, at least for the time, the movement to greater local autonomy.

From the economic point of view, this meant that the autonomy of enterprises was again reduced. Initially, this was accomplished without substantive legal change. Later, with the promulgation of the 1974 constitution, the power of enterprises was formally reduced by the redefinition of an enterprise as a mere legal front for a collection of basic work units (BOAL) and by the readoption of the pre-1964 procedure for selecting an enterprise director, who again was to be chosen from a list proposed by a committee half of whose members were appointed by the local communal assembly.[10] In essence, the system returned to the situation that had existed before 1965. The central party's authority and control over economy and polity were reasserted.

The fate of the 1965 reforms illustrates the great importance of political factors for economic institutions in Yugoslavia. It also demonstrates that government control over enterprise decision making was never fully relinquished, but remained a constant factor modifying the behavior of the enterprise management and therefore the outcome of the operation of the economic system. The lines from the government to enterprises ran through a variety of channels and were drawn with varying degrees of tautness at different times, but they were never entirely severed.

Selection of Enterprise Directors

One such line was the power to influence the selection of enterprise director, the individual who has dominant influence in an enterprise. This power was exercised to differing extents by the communal assembly, itself influenced by the central government and the party. Until 1965 and again after 1974, the commune had significant power in the selection process, by virtue of membership on the committee that either selected the director (until 1965) or compiled the list from which the director was chosen by the enterprise (after 1974). Earlier there had been barely concealed direct control over the enterprise in the form of communal influence over decision making and, in 1956, the establishment of party "aktivs" in factory subunits.

Control of Enterprise Income Distribution

Until 1965, the government retained direct and indirect control over the disposition of net income, perhaps the most important power available to a self-managed enterprise. It relinquished that power afterwards for only a short time. Control was exercised in two principal ways: by taxation of income, which reduced an enterprise's scope for choice and effectively removed the decision of the overall level of investment from its authority, and by the use of direct controls on the amounts that could be paid out as personal incomes. The importance of taxation before the 1965 reform was revealed by the magnitude of the numerous taxes and compulsory deductions that enterprises were obliged to pay from their incomes. Possibly the most important provision of the 1965 reform was its reduction of taxes, which increased the discretionary authority of enterprises. In the years immediately before the reform (1961–64), more than half of national income—according to the Yugoslav definition of gross sales less depreciation and cost of purchased materials—generated in industry and mining was taxed away from the enterprises. Enterprises allocated about 40 percent of their aftertax income to their internal funds and the remainder to wages.[11] Such heavy taxation of receipts implies substantial reliance on government sources of investment finance and corresponding centralized control over investment decisions in the early sixties.

After 1965, taxation was reduced. Taxes accounted for roughly 40 percent of the income generated by enterprises, leaving the balance at the disposal of the enterprises.[12] Although enterprises were still constrained by various rules about uses of the remaining funds, the tax reductions increased their actual autonomy, the real power that they could wield.[13] The enterprises reacted by increasing both personal income payments and payments to their internal funds. The increase in the former was proportionately greater, however.[14] Given greater discretion, enterprises opted for increased wage payments. This result is consistent with the theory of investment choice in the self-managed enterprise[15] and suggests one reason why, after the reform, enterprises became so dependent on banks for investment finance.[16] In fact, in the six years following the reform, industrial and mining enterprises paid an average of only about 17 percent of national income produced into their internal funds, including their business funds. This level allowed only a relatively small increase in the decentralization of investment finance that the reformers had sought.

Although the tax reductions of 1965 thus provided enterprises with greater latitude in allocating income, their investment decisions remained subject to the influence of outside organizations. Before the reform, the government, through the General Investment Fund (GIF), dominated the overall level of investment and, to a large extent, the allocation of investment funds among alternative uses. As chapter 8 shows, after the reform, the banking system assumed this dominant position, and the government's direct role was reduced to its administration of the Fund for the Accelerated Development of Underdeveloped Regions (FAD). Indirectly, however, the government still exercised considerable power over investment levels and general policy through certain provisions in the 1965 reform of the banking system.[17]

Restraints on the Operation of the Market

Formal models of self-management often assume that enterprises function in a smoothly operating, although possibly imperfectly competitive, market system. With respect to the market in Yugoslavia, the important question is not whether it conformed, more or less, to a model of perfect competition, but rather to what extent it was allowed to function at all.

The most pervasive and consistent interference with the operation of the market was the control of prices, administered partly to influence the direction of economic development and partly in a futile effort to contain inflationary forces. During the period preceding the 1965 reform, the extent of price control widened in industry and mining. In 1958, price ceilings (which effectively established legal prices) were in effect for goods representing 31 percent of the value of production, but by 1962 the figure had risen to 67 percent.[18] In March 1965, immediately before the reform, the government imposed a general price freeze that affected factory, wholesale, and retail prices of industrial goods as well as prices of services and trade margins.[19] A major element of the 1965 reform was an attempt to adjust prices to conform to the world market prices,[20] but the central authorities still did not allow prices to respond to market forces. The new prices were generally frozen, and controls were removed only gradually. As of September 1965, immediately after the announcement of the new prices, products representing about 70 percent of the value of industrial production were subject to price controls; eighteen months later, the fraction was still over 50 percent.[21]

Throughout the period, the general policy was to hold down prices of the products of processing industries and of producer goods, while allowing higher prices for final manufactured goods. Prices of consumer goods were restrained more than those of other final products.[22] The result was a distorted set of price signals that made rational calculation by enterprise directors impossible. The general price freeze led to predictable attempts to evade the controls or to gain exemptions from them;[23] these evasions and exemptions created further distortions in the price system.

Besides price controls, extensive and complex controls on foreign trade and foreign exchange impeded the operation of the market.[24] The government gradually dismantled from 1950 to 1953 the centralized administration of foreign trade of the pre–self-management period, but at the same time established controls over enterprise activity in foreign trade that survived throughout the period, albeit with intermittent relaxations and partial reforms. The domestic price policy, the attempt (at least through 1965) to isolate the domestic economy from the world market, the effort to use the foreign trade sector to stimulate industrial growth, and the endeavors to control the persistent balance of trade deficit led to a set of rules, regulations, and restrictions too diverse and disparate to be called a system (and too complex and extensive to be described in detail here). The controls included, however, a multiple exchange-rate system, the requirement that exporting enterprises sell foreign exchange received in trade (above "retention quotas" of varying levels) to the National Bank at fixed, below-market rates, subsidies and premiums for exports of those goods favored in the development policy, and tariffs and import subsidies rigged for the same purpose.

The 1965 reform contained an ambitious program for reforming foreign trade policy, including tariff reductions, devaluation of the dinar, the discontinuance of the multiple exchange-rate system and import subsidies, and the gradual elimination of administrative intervention in imports. But the trade deficit persisted and widened. Domestic monetary restrictions, rather than decreasing import demand as intended, reduced domestic production, adversely affecting exports. The liberalization of import trade led to a faster than intended growth of imports. The effect of the devaluation was smaller than anticipated and was quickly exhausted. These negative developments in foreign trade led to the readoption, in effect, of many of the features of the earlier system. By 1968, export premiums and subsidies exceeded in value the prereform levels.[25] According to Yugoslav writers, the reform in foreign trade accomplished none of its objectives, and the intended liberalization was stillborn.[26] The same problems persisted.[27]

The complex price and foreign trade controls constituted a formidable obstacle to the operation of the market. The toleration accorded the resulting distortions and irrationalities demonstrated that the government was unwilling to accept the consequences of permitting a free market to work. This is consistent with the general pattern of administrative interference in the operation of the system as a whole, showing that hoary communist commitments to central direction of the economy die hard and raising suspicions about the depth of the commitment by the government and party to a market-directed system of worker self-management.

Other Institutional Impediments

In addition to administrative hindrances, the operation of the market in Yugoslavia was impeded by other institutional factors and by the ubiquitous nationality problem. The most important institutional fact is that enterprise bankruptcy, although legally provided for, in fact rarely occurred.

First, an important fact should be realized: there is little incentive under workers' self-management for individuals to establish new enterprises. In doing so, they lose all rights to the founding capital once the enterprise is set up and operating, retaining only the usual right to share in the income stream. If founders were guaranteed leading positions in the enterprises that they established, this loss might be partly compensated. But there is no certainty that founders will occupy positions guaranteeing them a reward commensurate with the loss of capital and the effort involved in establishing the enterprise. For these reasons, it is likely that most new enterprises are the creations of government units. The motivation for local and regional governments to form enterprises is fairly clear: enterprises provide employment in their areas and funds for financing various social services,[28] both of which are politically desirable for local leaders.

These same factors provide a strong incentive for governments to keep enterprises afloat. Until 1965, the possibility of actual failure was remote. Banks were not subject to profitability constraints—indeed, their incentives were tied to the volume of credit they granted—and therefore they were always prepared to rescue inefficient enterprises. In principle, the 1965 banking reform was intended to remedy this by making autonomous economic entities of the banks. The reform, however, proved ineffective; the banks remained, to an important extent, creatures of the government. Furthermore, undoing earlier irrational decisions supporting political factories and other inefficient enterprises would have entailed politically intolerable increases in visible unemployment, particularly during a time when measured unemployment was already a highly sensitive issue.

For these reasons, failure was never a serious concern for most Yugoslav enterprises. One of the most important consequences was that enterprises had little incentive to avoid excessive investment programs. Indeed, to the extent that local goverment influenced investment decision making, the same forces that encouraged the founding of new enterprises also stimulated additional investments. This was one of the key arguments of the economic reformers in the debates preceding the 1965 reforms.[29]

A self-management system with an effective mechanism for the exit of inefficient firms is not inconceivable. But it seems likely that the political and ideological forces that would lead to the adoption of such a system would also create powerful pressures causing exactly the same response to inefficiency as occurred in Yugoslavia. It is also true that part of the explanation for the refusal to permit failing enterprises to submerge is to be found in circumstances peculiar to Yugoslavia, particularly the way in which political power devolved onto the local communal governments and the existence of regional interest groups in the country. But, whatever the prospects elsewhere and whatever the explanation for the lack of business failure in Yugoslavia, the fact remains that failure was rare. The workings of the system, especially the rate of investment, must be viewed from this perspective.

Finally, the nationality question and its corresponding ethnic connotations limited the efficacy of the market. One disappointing aspect of regional policy was that out-migration from the less developed areas was smaller than expected; the planners expected migration to relieve the pressure of surplus population on the developing industrial sectors of the backward regions. But measured unemployment in the less developed areas rose, becoming a serious problem by the end of the period covered by this study.[30] In retrospect, it is surprising that the planners assigned such weight to migration in view of the ethnic and religious differences of the country. But, regardless of the wisdom of the regional policy, its failure in this respect illustrates the fact that the operation of the labor market, imperfect as it might be as a result of the nature of the self-managed firm and the reluctance of its members to expand membership, was also impeded by ethnic suspicions and hostilities unique to Yugoslavia.

Localism rooted in regional interests also impeded capital flows. According to one well-known Yugoslav economist, this was one of two factors accounting for sluggishness in interregional capital flows. The second major factor, he argues, was the system of price controls, which had the same effect because the more profitable economic branches (those with relatively higher controlled prices) tended to be located in regions that were relatively rich in capital resources.[31] Thus, the price control system and the regional singularities of Yugoslavia combined to exacerbate the capital flow problems inherent in a socialist economy. These factors combined with the absence of constraint on investment to produce a highly unsatisfactory structure of capital investment. On the one hand, the low prices for semifinished goods and materials and the impediments to interregional capital flows created bottlenecks in processing industries.[32] On the other hand, excessively high rates of investment in industries producing relatively high priced goods and in political factories generated excess capacity and the proliferation of uneconomically scaled plants.[33]

Continuity in Self-Management

This abbreviated and necessarily incomplete survey of change and constraint in self-management highlights some of the properties of the system and its relation to Yugoslav political reality. Despite this welter of change, some aspects of the system did remain constant.

First, rights of ownership in enterprises remained fundamentally unchanged. It is true, however, that if the term "property rights" refers to the bundle of rights pertaining to the use and disposal of physical assets, many of the changes just described affected these rights in various ways. In that sense, there were many changes in property rights after 1952.

But in a more fundamental sense, the principle of ownership in the means of production was not changed. That principle—the right to use—means that the workers in an enterprise, acting through their workers' council and managing board, have the right to use the assets of their enterprise and enjoy the income they produce, but not the right to reduce the capital of the enterprise. According to Yugoslav ideas, the capital "belongs" to the society as a whole; the members of an enterprise are granted the right to use it, not to use it up. The members of an enterprise were constrained by an enormously complex set of rules and regulations and by the difficulties of effectively controlling the managerial staff of a large organization. Furthermore, the income left at their discretion was restricted by numerous obligatory payments specified by law. Finally, although the workers were obligated to maintain the capital of their enterprises at no less than its beginning level (it is not clear how this can be verified in a system with no capital market and persistent inflation), they could and did sell individual capital assets. Except for these qualifications, the basic principle has not been altered.

Second, the institution of the workers' council remained fundamentally unchanged. In all but the smallest enterprises, workers' councils were elected by the workers, and, in larger enterprises, the councils in turn selected managing boards. The workers' council had authority to select a director for the enterprise and to request his removal and, in principle, had ultimate authority over the operations of the enterprise.[34] Again, the details of the arrangements within enterprises changed after 1952. The rules for participation of representatives of other organizations—notably the commune—in the selection of enterprise directors were modified. Workers' councils at different levels of the enterprise were provided. Regulations governing the organization of workers' councils in enterprises formed by the merger of existing enterprises had to be established after mergers were permitted in 1965. But the basic principle—that the enterprise is supposed to be a type of cooperative, with ultimate authority lying in its members, the workers—remained intact.[35]

CHAPTER TWO

Economic Policy and the Transition to an Industrialized Economy

With the adoption of self-management, the Yugoslav government abandoned the use of Soviet-style administrative planning. It did not, however, give up central economic planning entirely. Plans were drawn up by elaborate procedures, adopted into law, and published in the *Official Gazette* of the Yugoslav parliament. But the role actually played in the economy by the Yugoslav planning system and the efficacy of the system in implementing economic policy are questionable.

The plans were not legally binding on any individuals and did not (as a general rule) contain directives to specific economic entities to perform any concrete actions.[1] Quantitative specifications of targets grew less frequent as time passed; performance in meeting targets, when specified, was not good. The 1957–61 Five-Year Plan was deemed fulfilled after only four years, which was considered evidence of excellent economic performance, but which also indicated inaccurate planning. The subsequent 1961–65 Five-Year Plan was abandoned after only one full year because of its obvious infeasibility. Actual economic policy probably resulted as much from reactions to immediate events as it did from the implementation of predetermined economic plans. This has been the experience in the Soviet Union[2] and surely would come as no surprise in Yugoslavia.

Because the plans were so vague and the attitude toward them so cavalier, questions may be raised about their function. Some of these questions are discussed more fully in chapter 8. However, one function of the plans is clear. They served—especially the five-year plans—as official announcements of intended development policies. Moreover, the policy actually carried out was broadly consistent with the plan statements.

The underlying strategy was based on high rates of investment, a commitment to heavy industry, and the exploitation of known natural resources. In fact, so far as the relative emphasis on different industrial branches is concerned, the strategy could have been derived from analyses of the postwar economy that were drawn up during the war by associates of the government-in-exile.[3] The strategy was augmented and complicated by foreign trade policy, the regional question, and the complexities of the relations among the central government, the regional governments, and the industrial enterprises.

The general policy objective was modernization—the transformation of Yugoslavia from a backward, agrarian, traditional economy to a modern, industrialized one. Later in this chapter, data are presented that show the extent of the change that occurred during the first twenty years of workers' self-management. Initially, modernization was rapid and extensive, but due to deceleration in the pace of industrialization, it later slowed. The reasons for this slackening are complex and not matters of economic alone. Their full analysis is beyond the scope of this book, but one cause seems to have been a conflict between tradition and ideology in rural areas, a conflict that created a dilemma for the leadership.

INDUSTRIALIZATION POLICY

The five-year plans of this period did not ignore the nonindustrial sectors of the economy, nor were noneconomic aspects of Yugoslav society overlooked. Plans were made for the development of agriculture, transportation and communications, forestry, and trade, as well as for industry. The so-called broadening and strengthening of socialist relations in the country—which, in effect, meant extending socialist property ownership and buttressing the system of self-management—were consistently given precedence in the plans.

But these other aspects of economic development must have been secondary to the main issue of industrialization, the sine qua non for development. Without industrialization, the country would remain defenseless in a world which, especially after the Cominform break, was perceived to be extremely hostile to Yugoslav independence. Without it, the ideologically important system of self-management would remain stillborn; to remain in the predominantly agricultural economy of the early fifties would be to retain the system of property relations that existed in agriculture, a system based on private property despite the abortive collectivization efforts of the party. Without it, personal incomes, according to Marxist theory, could not be expected to rise over the long run.

There is little doubt about the primacy of industrialization in economic policy. The planned rate of growth of the industrial sector was above that for the economy as a whole in all three five-year plans of the period studied. Only one other sector—construction, whose growth was necessarily closely tied to that of the industrial sector—ever had a higher planned growth rate, and that was in the ill-fated 1961–65 plan.[4] The industrial sector consistently received the major share of planned investment funds, and its planned share rose steadily throughout the period.[5] The only apparent subordination of industrialization was in the 1966–70 Five-Year Plan, which gave highest priority to increasing the standard of living. Even that probably reflected the determination to industrialize; according to the planners, higher living standards had first priority because higher incomes were necessary to raise labor productivity and, hence, increase the rate of growth of national income.[6] In other cases, plan provisions that seemed to be directed at nonindustrial development actually had industry-related purposes. For example, the 1957–61 plan stipulated increased provision of social services. However, the emphasis was on social services that would increase industrial productivity—especially training schools and preventive health care—as well as on housing and community services.[7] Utilitarian objectives in schooling and training can also be found in subsequent plans.[8]

There were common themes in the postwar industrialization policy, although the means employed in executing the policy varied considerably in details, and different branches and product lines were favored at different times. The thrust of the policy is more readily understood in the light of some background on prewar economic development.

Prewar Development

Despite the depression, there was significant industrial development in Yugoslavia before the war. Electric power production in 1939 (the last year for which accurate data are available) was about 1.5 billion kilowatts (higher than in 1947) and had been growing at annual rates of about 25 percent since 1935. Steel production tripled between 1932 and 1939, the textile industry was growing rapidly, a nonferrous metals industry had been founded, which included aluminum as well as copper production, and a chemicals industry of considerable size existed. Besides these newer branches of industrial activity, more traditional industrial lines—food products, wood and timber products, and building materials—were also well established.[9]

Just before the war, industrial employment totaled nearly 400,000 (omitting construction employment). Although much of this employment was probably in small-scale plants, the scale of operations in many was larger than that of mere cottage industries, as the data in table 1 indicate.[10] Employment was dominated by food, tobacco, textiles, and lumber and wood products, which together accounted for some 60 percent of the total. These were all traditional Yugoslav industries, based largely on readily exploited raw materials and emphasizing traditional production patterns. (Textiles and clothing are a partial exception. They grew fairly rapidly in the 1926–39 period.) The newer, more modern branches—mining and metallurgy, chemicals, electric power, and paper and printing—were as yet in nascent stages, accounting for just under one-fourth of employment.

TABLE 1

PREWAR INDUSTRIAL EMPLOYMENT IN YUGOSLAVIA, 1938

Branch	*Employment* Thousands	*Employment* Percentage of Total[a]	Number of Employees per Firm
Textiles and clothing	94.6	24.8	223.1
Lumber and wood products	75.8	19.9	171.1
Food and tobacco	60.4	15.8	64.6
Mining and metallurgy	58.5	15.3	170.1
Building materials	29.1	7.6	61.8
Leather and leather products	28.4	7.4	295.8
Paper and printing	15.1	4.0	143.8
Chemicals	11.9	3.1	55.9
Electrical power	7.8	2.0	31.0
Total	381.6	100.0	

SOURCE: Nicholas Mirkovich, ed., *Jugoslav Postwar Reconstruction Papers*, mimeographed (New York: Yugoslavia, Office of Reconstruction and Economic Affairs, 1943), 4: 5–6.

[a]Details may not add to total because of rounding.

Indeed, in many ways Yugoslavia was a country awaiting development. This lack of development can perhaps be ascribed to the political turbulence that characterized its history as a nation. As of 1939, production was in the doldrums, with plants often operating well below capacity.[11] Besides this unutilized productive capacity, the country had an abundance of natural resources, especially minerals (whose exploitation began in earnest only after 1930),[12] hydroelectric power sources, and timber. It had a large unskilled labor force, but a shortage of skilled manpower. The economy was highly centralized, with the government dominating large segments of industry, and there had been considerable reliance on foreign capital to finance development. In 1939, Yugoslavia remained predominantly agricultural and had to be considered a backward and largely preindustrial country. But, like Russia in 1913, it was not without an industrial base.[13] Opportunity for rapid development existed.

As in Russia, however, war interrupted the course of history and economic development and destroyed or damaged much of the base that had been built. Material losses were great, especially in transportation.[14] These losses were partly compensated by reparations and relief,[15] which formed an important resource in the First Five-Year Plan.

Human losses were devastating, proportionally the greatest of any of the countries involved in the European war. UNRRA estimated that approximately 1.7 million persons, about 10 percent of the prewar population, died as a result of the war. These losses were concentrated among males and younger age groups. In 1931, males formed 49.5 percent of the population; in 1948, 48.1 percent. In 1931, persons aged 20–34 constituted 25.5 percent of the population; in 1948, only 20.9 percent.[16] The consequences of the human loss were permanent, of course, and provided additional motivation for improving the education and training of the population.

In summary, Yugoslavia in 1946 was a country abundantly endowed with natural resources, with a brief, but not unsubstantial, experience of industrial growth and a history of centralized control over industry and dependence on government and foreign financing of that industry. But it had suffered considerable losses in the war. The first efforts to promote rapid industrialization were made through a system of directive planning patterned after the example of the Soviet Union. After 1948 and the rupture of relations with the Cominform, a new approach was sought. The development of self-management, with its professed decentralization of authority, required a new approach to planning. Formulating the new approach took time, and it was not until 1957 that the Second Five-Year Plan—the first of the self-management era—appeared.[17]

General Development Strategy

The development policies of the self-management period were consistent with the possibilities and limitations of Yugoslav resources. The general policy might have been adopted by any postwar government; the exceptional aspect of what was done is not to be found in the policy, which was far from novel, but in its mode of implementation. It was a dual strategy based on heavy industry and exploitation of natural resources.[18] Industrialization—indeed, modernization in general—demands energy, and increasing energy production was always given top priority. Different branches of energy production were emphasized at different times, but one or more of them—electric power, coal, natural gas, or petroleum—was always stressed. (Petroleum production had barely begun before the war, with an annual output of no more than 500 tons. During the German occupation, annual output increased to about 150,000 tons, an indication of the extensive petroleum resources existing in the country.)[19] Generally next in priority were ferrous and nonferrous metallurgy, commonly viewed as essential to development, and in Yugoslavia based on relatively generous ore endowments.

This combination of the commitment to heavy industry and the exploitation of natural resources was reflected in the high priority given to chemicals. The development of heavy industry would lead to strong demand for chemicals; the production of inorganics could be based partly on mineral resources and that of organics partly on developing petroleum extraction. Further examples of the dual strategy were found in timber and wood products and in building materials: industrialization would entail extensive construction, and Yugoslavia has always had abundant timber, stone, and other raw materials for construction.

The end result of the industrialization process was supposed to be (and, in fact, turned out to be) the development of manufacturing industries, especially those manufacturing capital goods. Both electrical and nonelectrical machinery and equipment were given relatively high priority in all plans. The plans did not specify Marxist Group A and Group B products, but the actual plan priorities ran roughly along these lines, which was part of the reason for the emphasis on capital goods. The government also hoped that a substantial increase in capital goods exports could be achieved.

In contrast with these high-priority branches of industry, textiles, leather, food, tobacco, paper, and rubber were either not mentioned among the priority items or given relatively low priorities. Except for rubber, these branches were more or less traditional in Yugoslavia and principally produced consumer goods. Part of the reason why consumer goods were ignored was that Yugoslav economic expansion entailed very high investment rates. Such investment was made possible by limiting the share of real wages in national income, and this was reflected in the low priorities given to consumer goods.

Foreign Trade and Development

Foreign trade policy was closely linked with industrialization policy.[20] There was a complex system of multiple exchange rates (or a set of tariffs, subsidies, and tax rebates equivalent to such a system) meant to aid industrialization and to insulate the domestic economy, which was supposed to remain a controlled socialist state, from the outside world. The aim of the foreign exchange system was to stimulate exports of high-priority industries, especially manufactured goods, and discourage exports of agricultural products and raw materials. Imports of machinery and equipment and raw materials were favored by the system, while imports of consumer goods were restrained.

Imports of machinery and equipment were encouraged not only to augment domestically produced capital goods, but also to obtain advanced technology, especially from the West. Even after the Comecon blockade was lifted in 1955, the bulk of machinery and equipment imports was obtained from Western Europe and the United States.[21] Concern about the continued willingness of Western trading partners to finance this exchange was undoubtedly one of the major reasons for the protracted discussion and debate over methods for reducing the balance of trade deficit, which was persistently high throughout the period. From some points of view, continuing the deficit would not have been a bad thing; as some Yugoslav economists observed, the deficit amounted to a fairly important source of finance for the industrialization program.[22]

Regional Policy

The industrialization of the economy as a whole was complicated by the simultaneous effort to improve the economic positions of the less developed regions of the country. Accelerating economic development in these regions and narrowing the gap in per capita national income between them and the other regions were separate, explicit parts of Yugoslav policy beginning with the 1957–61 plan.[23] The main method used in attempting to accelerate development in the less developed regions was to transfer investment funds to them from the other parts of the country. Because the recipients of these funds apparently used them less efficiently than the donors,[24] there is some evidence that such transfers lessened the rate of overall industrial growth.

On the other hand, price and foreign trade policies tended to favor general industrialization and the more developed regions. Price policy tended to maintain relatively high prices for manufactured goods and low prices for agricultural products and raw materials; foreign trade policy favored exports of manufactured goods and imports of raw materials. Since production in the less developed regions was most advanced in raw materials and agricultural products, this worked against the less developed and in favor of the more developed regions. Some Yugoslav writers argue that the investment transfer program, on the one hand, and price and foreign exchange programs, on the other, more or less canceled each other out, leaving the less developed regions no better off than they would have been without any regional policy. Again, the general industrialization policy was at odds with the regional policy.

Perhaps the two did result in no net difference for either regional or overall growth; if so, their implementation was mere waste motion. It seems more likely, however, that the price and foreign trade policy, along with the commitment to general industrialization, had priority and that the relatively inefficient use of investment funds by the less developed regions was unexpected.

Decentralization

Apart from the complications brought about by regional policy, the formula for industrialization was unexceptional. High rates of investment in heavy industry and the branches supporting it, price and foreign trade policies favoring these sectors, and exploitation of natural resources are all unremarkable as government development policies.

It should be emphasized, however, that it was a centrally determined policy. Much has been made of the decentralized nature of the system of workers' self-management, and it is true that under this system much decision-making authority was delegated to enterprises. In fact, the decentralization of management, in the sense of the central government's not directly supervising the operation of individual enterprises, is one of the features that distinguishes the economy of the self-management era from the prewar economy, in which government ownership and direct operation were common.

But the central government did not relinquish its overall control of the system, and it conceived the development policy. The sharp readjustments that occurred when economic reforms in the sixties gave workers and citizens more freedom of choice clearly demonstrated that the lines for development chosen by the government were not those the populace would have chosen.[25] Had they been under a regime that permitted them such freedom, development of measured output might have been less rapid and almost surely would have been in different directions. As it was, the industrialization policy led to far-reaching changes in Yugoslav society and its economy.

TRANSITION TO AN INDUSTRIALIZED ECONOMY

Changes in the structure of national income illustrate the impact of the development policies followed during the first twenty years of workers' self-management. The data in table 2 show the composition of national income, defined by Yugoslav concepts, for various years during that period. Although instructive, these data must be used with caution.

Difficulties in Interpreting Yugoslav National Income Data

The difficulty in using the data, especially when making international comparisons, arises from the Yugoslav definition of national income, which is derived from Marxist notions of material product. As a result, many service activities included in Western definitions of national income are regarded as nonproductive and are therefore excluded from Yugoslav data on national income. These activities are financed largely by taxes on the incomes of enterprises in the "productive" sector. Those incomes, including taxes, constitute total national income as computed by the Yugoslavs; thus, aggregate national income according to the Yugoslav definition is not very much different from what it would be under the Western definition.[26] However, the difference in accounting methods makes an important difference in the distribution of national income. In comparison with similar data for Western countries, the shares of the "productive" sectors are overstated.

Unfortunately, the extent of the overstatement cannot be calculated precisely sector by sector on the basis of available data. Only rough aggregate estimates can be made. Payments to the "nonproductive" sector from the "productive" sector represent the principal source of income for the former sector. Those payments averaged 30 percent of the social product realized in the productive sector during the period from 1952 to 1971, implying that the overstatement of the shares of the productive sectors shown in table 2 is substantial.

On the other hand, aggregate data for shares of social product produced in the productive sector and paid to the nonproductive sector show essentially no change over time, so that, except for one additional problem, the trends of the

TABLE 2

SECTORAL DISTRIBUTION OF NATIONAL INCOME
Selected Years
(Percentage)

	Share in National Income[a]				
Sector	1952	1956	1961	1966	1971
Industry and mining	21.5	26.5	29.0	33.6	36.1
Agriculture[b]	34.3	33.3	29.5	25.9	20.7
Forestry	3.4	2.4	1.6	1.3	1.0
Construction	10.7	7.3	9.3	8.9	9.3
Transportation and communications	5.6	6.1	6.5	6.2	6.8
Trade and catering	17.2	16.7	18.1	18.8	21.1
Handicraft[c]	7.3	7.7	6.0	5.3	5.1
Total	100.0	100.0	100.0	100.0	100.0

SOURCES: SZS, *Statistički godišnjak SFRJ 1971* (Belgrade: SZS, 1971), p. 119; idem, *Statistički godišnjak SFRJ 1972* (Belgrade: SZS, 1972), pp. 98–99.

[a]Calculated from data on national income in 1966 prices. Details may not add to totals because of rounding.

[b]Includes fishing.

[c]"Productive" part only.

shares of the productive sector shown in table 2 can be taken to represent changes in the structure of output.[27]

The additional difficulty involves an index number problem. As industrialization proceeded, relative prices of industrial products fell. The measured structure of output therefore varies depending on the prices in which it is measured. For example, the share of industry and mining in the 1954 national income is 42.8 percent if measured in 1954 prices, 35.6 percent if measured in 1960 prices, and 22.5 percent if measured in 1966 prices.[28] If output were consistently measured in 1952 prices instead of 1966 prices, the 1971 share of industrial output would be larger than it appears in table 2, and a different change in structure (in the sense of a different percentage change in the industrial and other sectoral shares) would be observed. There is no logical ground for choosing among alternate price bases for measurement of structural change, just as there is no logical basis for the resolution of the index number problem in general.[29] Data such as those in table 2 are useful in discerning trends, but the absolute sizes of the numbers or changes in them have limited meaning. Thus, comparisons with similar data for other countries are hazardous.[30]

Large-Scale Industry and Agriculture

With these qualifications in mind, the data in table 2 reflect the transformation rendered by industrialization—as well as by other facets of economic policy and exogenous factors—during the first twenty years of workers' self-management.

The most striking changes were the decline in the shares of agriculture and forestry and the increased share of industry and mining. This shift reflects the rapid growth of industrial output and the much slower growth of agricultural output.[31]

According to these data (in 1966 prices), it was only sometime after 1961 that the share of industry and mining exceeded that of agriculture. Nevertheless, the shift toward industry was substantial, especially in comparison with the structure of the economy before the war. Based on calculations using official index numbers for industrial and agricultural output, the share of agriculture before the war was substantially more than twice that of industry and mining; according to the table 2 data, by 1971 the share of industry and mining was about 1½ times greater than that of agriculture.[32]

Rapid industrialization is also reflected in changes in the sectoral distribution of the so-called economically active (*aktivno*) population. This category of employment, rather than employed personnel (*zaposleno osoblje*), must be used in measuring aggregate employment changes. The Yugoslav definition of employed personnel includes only those persons employed in the social sector, thereby omitting private agriculture, still by far the dominant part of agricultural employment in the country, as well as all other privately employed (including self-employed) persons. The data in table 3 are taken from census data for the distribution of economically active people; these data include all persons, whether they are employed in the social sector or elsewhere. The absolute value of the share of industrial employment is probably understated by these figures.[33] Even so, the share of industry and mining more than doubled over that period, while the share of agriculture fell by about one-third.

In 1971 there remained, however, a surprisingly high proportion of agricultural employment. This fact, which surely indicates redundant labor in rural areas, probably resulted from a combination of factors: the limitation on the size of private landholdings (ten hectares), the unwillingness of the peasants to give up their private holdings and join collectives or agricultural enterprises, and the persistence of traditional methods. Here, as in the Soviet Union, agriculture has been a problem in development policy; ideology conflicts with efficiency. Efficient agricultural production can hardly be expected when the bulk of output comes from holdings of ten hectares or less, but the state has been unwilling to increase the size of private holdings allowed, and the peasants unwilling to join large-scale collectives (which have their own efficiency shortcomings in any case). The agricultural dilemma remains one of the factors inhibiting economic development.

The situation in the countryside was an impediment to another objective of the party and the government, the strengthening of so-called socialist social relationships. One important aspect of this objective was growth in the share of output

TABLE 3
ECONOMICALLY ACTIVE POPULATION BY SECTOR, CENSUS YEARS
(Percentage)

Sector	Census Year[a] 1953	1961	1971
Industry and mining	8.0	13.6	17.7
Agriculture, forestry, and fishing	66.8	56.9	44.6
Construction	2.6	3.8	4.5
Transportation and communications	2.1	3.0	3.6
Trade and catering	3.1[b]	3.7	5.9
Handicraft[c]	4.7	4.5	4.9
All others[d]	12.8	14.4	18.8
Total	100.0	100.0	100.0

SOURCES: SZS, *Popis stanovništva 1953* (Belgrade: SZS, 1959), vol. 2, xliv; idem, *Popis stanovništva 1961* (Belgrade: SZS, 1965), vol. 3, part 1, pp. 3, 104; idem, *Popis stanovništva 1971* (Belgrade: SZS, 1974), vol. 3, part 1, pp. 11, 23.

[a]In 1953, the economically active population of Yugoslavia, defined to exclude pensioners, invalids receiving support, student stipendiaries, and the like, was 7,849,000; in 1961, 8,340,000; and in 1971, 8,890,000.

[b]Includes banking and insurance.

[c]Includes craft organizations in the social sector and private shops, both producing goods for sale and supplying personal services.

[d]Includes government, school, scientific, cultural, health, and other activities. In 1953, personal services were partially included in this category.

produced in the social, as opposed to the private, sector. According to national income data, the share of private production in national income fell from about 34 percent in 1952 to 28 percent in 1961 and to just under 20 percent in 1971.[34] These figures probably understate the actual share of private activities in Yugoslavia, at least in comparison with corresponding Western national income data, because they do not include the value of "nonproductive" services supplied through the private market.

The persistence of the private sector was due mostly to agriculture; in 1952, the private sector contributed nearly 85 percent of national income produced in agriculture and in 1971, still accounted for over 75 percent.[35] The decline in the share of the agricultural sector, with its relatively large private share, accounted for the bulk of the decline in the share of all privately produced output. Peasant resistance to abandoning private farming and joining collective or state farms was the major reason for the failure to reduce the share of private output.

The Decline of Small-Scale Industry

At the beginning of the period of self-management, there was a substantial small-scale industry sector in Yugoslavia. In common with experience elsewhere, modernization of the industrial sector substantially reduced the importance of small-scale industry. From an economic point of view,[36] the enterprises included in small-scale industry functioned at an uneconomically small scale of operations. Replacing these firms with enterprises in the worker-managed sector probably improved the overall efficiency of production in manufacturing.[37] Exploitation of these potential scale economies may partly explain the rapid early industrial growth rates, although reliable estimates of the importance of scale economies in Yugoslav industrial growth do not exist.[38]

It is difficult to quantify the importance of the decline of small-scale industry to modernization or to estimate possible biases in production indexes—including both the official index and the sample indexes in this book—without knowing the output of the handicraft sector. Data published in statistical yearbooks for handicraft sector social product and national income cannot be used for this purpose because coverage in the social product accounts includes a number of nonindustrial activities and the conceptual basis for these accounts differs from that underlying the production indexes.

Measuring biases in the industrial production indexes presents further problems. Reporting of handicraft sector output has been selective and sporadic. For example, although shops and cooperatives making food products were an important, but declining, part of the handicraft sector during this period, recent statistical yearbooks do not provide any data about food products output in this sector. Continuous series for handicraft sector production can be assembled for only a handful of goods, and the price or value-added data needed to construct weights seem to be entirely unavailable. Thus, it is not possible to construct a methodologically comparable production index for small-scale industry. The importance of the decline of small-scale industry must, therefore, be inferred from some alternative indicator.

One such indicator is employment. As the data in table 4 show, between 1954 and 1971 handicraft sector employment in organizations that made items also produced in the industrial sector declined absolutely for the sector as a whole and for most individual branches. Except for paper products (included in "All others" in table 4), all handicraft branches showed relative declines in employment; in food and leather products, the declines were particularly large.

These employment data must be interpreted with some caution because there are differences in definition and coverage for which adjustment cannot be made. First, data on handicraft sector employment include owners of private handicraft shops, employees of those shops, and members of handicraft cooperatives,[39] while the figures for industrial sector employment include only members of self-managed enterprises. Second, neither set of employment figures can be adjusted for hours worked because the necessary data are not available. The bias introduced, if any, is unknown. Third, the branch subdivisions and even the sector totals undoubtedly conceal differences in the distribution of employment among product lines and types of employment. For example, in some handicraft branches the 1971 data (but not the 1954 figures) give the number employed in

TABLE 4

HANDICRAFT SECTOR EMPLOYMENT IN MANUFACTURING, 1953, 1961, AND 1971

Branch	*Handicraft Sector Employment (number of workers)*			*Handicraft Sector Expressed as Percentage of Total Manufacturing Employment*[c]		
	1953	1961[a]	1971[b]	1953	1961	1971
Fabricated products, total	326,894	322,684	263,457	34.0	22.3	14.7
Leather products	45,994	27,883	15,831	71.6	46.5	24.1
Food products	36,635	13,318	24,259	47.5	12.9	16.4
Textiles	67,852	58,511	45,589	47.3	27.4	16.1
Metal products	71,019	82,210	58,164	41.8	29.2	16.3
Wood products[d]	65,890	57,824	39,394[e]	37.7	33.8	22.6
Electrical products	6,238	13,333	11,452	31.6	20.8	10.7
Stone, clay, and glass products[e]	5,440	10,420	10,617	8.3	8.7	8.6
Chemicals[f]	1,201	3,496	2,675	5.6	5.8	2.5
All others	26,625	55,689	55,476	11.9	14.8	13.0

SOURCES: SZS, *Popis stanovništva 1953* (Belgrade: SZS, 1959), vol. 2, p. lxxiii; idem, *Popis stanovništva 1961* (Belgrade: SZS, 1965), vol. 3, part 1, p. 104; idem, *Statistički godišnjak FNRJ 1957* (Belgrade: SZS, 1957), p. 111; idem, *Statistički godišnjak SFRJ 1972* (Belgrade: SZS, 1972), p. 91; idem, *Statistički godišnjak SFRJ 1973* (Belgrade: SZS, 1973), pp. 186–87; and Branimir Marković, *Kretanje narodnog dohotka, zaposlenosti i produktivnosti rada u privredi Jugoslavije 1947–1967* (Belgrade: SZS, 1970), p. 45.

[a]Individual branch employment is taken as the number of economically active persons in each branch.

[b]Individual branch employment is the sum of employed personnel in social sector handicraft shops and total employed personnel in private handicraft shops. The total for fabricated products is the sum of the individual items.

[c]Percentages are calculated for annual average employment data in the industrial sector and the absolute figures in the table. For the individual branches, industrial employment categories are combined to be consistent with the products included in the handicraft sectors listed.

[d]Includes building of small boats.

[e]Includes nonmetals and building materials.

[f]Includes rubber products.

services, presumably repair services; in metal and electrical products, the proportion of such employment was high,[40] probably substantially higher than in the industrial sector. Similar shortcomings in comparability probably exist in the composition of output.

Despite these shortcomings, the data show a marked decline in small-scale industry. The decline was especially marked in the food and leather products branches, "traditional" branches which together employed about 12 percent of all industrial workers in 1954. In these two branches, it is especially clear that output shifted from small-scale to large-scale industry. To a lesser extent, the same was true of textiles and wood products.

These output shifts are very important in interpreting indexes of consumer goods produced in the industrial sector alone. At the beginning of the period studied, a substantial share of consumer goods output was produced in the handicraft sector; quantities produced in the industrial sector were relatively small.

Therefore, indexes measuring consumer goods output produced in the officially designated industrial sector have artificially small output bases.

In those handicraft branches in which employment grew—metal products, electrical products, and paper products—repair and other services were important. In the Yugoslav economy, as in the Soviet Union, the emphasis was on raising levels of physical output, with maintenance services having much lower priority. Small-scale operators apparently stepped in to meet demand in Yugoslavia, where the work was legal as long as employment restrictions were observed.

The paper products branch, in the handicraft sector accounts, includes bookstores and printing along with other paper products. Bookstores are not included in the paper products or printing and publishing branches of Yugoslav industry, so the employment data in table 4 are overstated to that extent.

Although the data do not suffice to quantify the bias in the production indexes due to the omission of figures on the decline of small-scale industry, it is obvious that the higher the rate of growth of products in the industrial sector relative to the handicraft sector and the larger the share of handicraft sector output in the total in the base years, the greater the resulting bias in the index of industrial production. Government policy clearly favored the industrial sector and there is little doubt that growth rates were higher in that sector than in the handicraft sector. At the same time, the employment data indicate that the handicraft sector share of output was large in 1952.

There are, therefore, two implications in the decline of small-scale industry. On the one hand, it represents the successful outcome of the government's modernization policies. On the other, its omission from the measurement of the production of manufactured goods causes overstatement of industrial growth as measured by the official and sample production indexes, insofar as these indexes are supposed to measure growth in capacity to product fabricated goods.

PART TWO

Measurement

CHAPTER THREE

Methods of Measuring Growth

Method necessarily precedes measurement, and the choice of method depends on the purpose of the measurement. For some purposes, official Yugoslav indexes are satisfactory. However, the official industrial production index is based on methods and procedures that render it incomparable with indexes commonly compiled and published by many Western countries. To assess the pace of Yugoslav industrial growth by comparing rates derived from the official index with the rates implied by Western indexes therefore produces misleading results. Sample indexes were compiled for this study to provide a measure of industrial growth comparable to Western indexes.

The methods and procedures used in constructing the official index and several sources of incomparability and bias in it are described in the first part of this chapter. The last part deals with the methods used in calculating the sample index.

THE YUGOSLAV INDUSTRIAL PRODUCTION INDEX

The official Yugoslav industrial production index is compiled and published by the Federal Institute of Statistics (Savezni zavod za statistiku; hereafter, SZS). According to SZS, the index is equivalent to a value-added index with annually changing weights. It is calculated by linking together a series of annual relatives. Each annual index is calculated in two stages. First, an annual relative is calculated for each industrial branch as the weighted sum of the annual relatives of the products included in the branch. Second, these relatives are aggregated using a second set of weights.[1]

There are several sources of incomparability and potential bias in this procedure. First, the practice of linking annual relatives and the weights used are open to question. Second, the procedure by which data for both weights and output are obtained makes it hard to interpret the official index and to construct sample indexes. Third, once assembled, the data may be manipulated by the compilers for political purposes.

The Reporting System

The output data and weights in the official and sample indexes depend partly on the so-called product nomenclature. The nomenclature is a periodically updated list of products of the industrial sector, published by SZS. Many, if not most, of the items listed actually refer to groups of products. For example, one item in the 1969 nomenclature is ''rolled sheets of aluminum alloys,'' a category obviously including many different individual products. The range of heterogeneity is broad: crude petroleum, cold-rolled steel sheets, copying machines, steel screws, television sets, Vitamin C, sugar, and office cabinets were among the items each forming a single entry in the 1969 nomenclature.[2]

SZS production data are derived from monthly and annual reports submitted by industrial enterprises. Each enterprise, in its annual report, is supposed to report the output of every product that can be assigned a place in the nomenclature as that product emerges in the enterprise's production processes. For example, copper concentrate, crude copper, electrolytic (refined) copper, and rolled copper wire are all listed in the nomenclature for the nonferrous metals industry. If an integrated firm were to purchase ore and process it completely to rolled copper wire, it should, in principle, report the production of each intermediate product as it emerged during the production process. These reports are supposed to be made whether the enterprise sells the product, either to a final consumer or to another enterprise for further processing; processes the product further itself (as in the example); or uses the product directly as part of the compensation of its member workers (as might happen, for example, if a steel firm used part of its output for building recreational facilities for its members).

Output is reported on a product, rather than on an establishment, basis. For many purposes, Yugoslav enterprises are classified in industrial branches on the basis of their principal activity, in a way similar to that familiar in United States practice. Physical output data are not reported in the same way. Enterprises are supposed to report the output of every identifiable item they produce, even if that product is not classified in the same industrial branch as that in which the enterprise itself is classified. For example, if an electrical products firm were to develop facilities for producing wire from refined copper as a step in the production of electric motors, it should, in principle, report the production of that wire, even though the wire is counted as output of the nonferrous metals branch of industry, not the electrical products branch.

Sources of Distortions in the Data

These methods of reporting output mean that the reliability of the production data (and, it will be seen, the data used for the official weights) rests on the reliability of the reports by enterprise managers. This system may create certain biases in the data. Furthermore, there are indications of distortions after the data are reported by enterprises.

Production is reported at many stages of fabrication; as a consequence, there is double counting of output. Therefore, either the weights used should be good approximations to value added or the index should be based on subsets of products chosen at specified stages of fabrication. The Yugoslav index for industry is comprehensive; officially published subindexes (production equipment, reproduction materials, and consumption goods) do not correspond to different stages of fabrication. Furthermore, the weights used in the official index bear only a tenuous relation to value added.

Variability in the accuracy of reporting is likely to result from the organization of the system. It is up to enterprise managers to report production; how carefully they do so can be expected to vary from one individual to another, depending on a number of factors.[3] Mere random variability should not be expected; Yugoslav planning and development policies probably introduce a bias in favor of more comprehensive reporting in high-priority branches of industry. The extent of variability is also influenced by factors affecting the costs of monitoring reporting. Greater accuracy and wider product coverage can be expected in branches with fewer enterprises,[4] in branches in which a larger proportion of output is produced by enterprises classified within those branches instead of by enterprises outside them, and in branches with greater product uniformity. Consideration of these factors for the 1961 indexes suggests that reporting was probably most accurate in energy and metallurgy, was somewhat less accurate in chemicals and electrical products, less still in metal products, and least in building materials, food products, and textiles.[5] Accuracy in reporting output of new products would be affected by the same factors.

Branch shares in total industrial output and relative branch growth rates may be biased according to the completeness of reporting, and these biases depend on the factors affecting product coverage. Between 1953 and 1971, important increases in the number of enterprises took place in the electric products, chemicals, and printing and publishing branches. These increases would tend to raise monitoring costs and thereby reduce accuracy and coverage. Important declines in numbers occurred in the coal and food products branches.[6] The proportion of output reported for a given branch that was produced by enterprises classified within the same branch probably increased in the process of industrialization, but whether this had any differential effects among branches is conjectural.[7] Moreover, the degree of product uniformity most likely declined in branches producing highly fabricated goods, especially metal products, electrical products, and chemicals; relatively fewer new products were introduced in the textiles, wood, and food products branches. These changes suggest that coverage deteriorated in electric products, chemicals, printing and publishing, and, to a lesser extent, metal products; coverage may have improved in coal and food products.

In addition to these technical problems, other practices may have caused distortions in the output data. Yugoslavia's revisionist position and its insistence on its own interpretation of Marxist doctrine make good economic results particularly important. There is an incentive to overstate production, and there are no statistical agencies independent of the state to provide outside checks on the official data. Official data have reported poor performance, but Yugoslav data display characteristics similar to many well-known peculiarities of Soviet statistics, suggesting that the statistical service engages in some of the same practices.[8]

For example, output series are added and dropped, usually without explanation. In some cases, the reasons for dropping series are obscure. For example, oxygen production simply disappeared from one source after 1962. Reports of the production of salonite slate products were discontinued in 1961, and calcium cyanamide reports ceased in 1969. In other cases, there are hints of why series are dropped. The production of chromium ore was reported by grade of ore until 1969; for 1970 and 1971, only total production was given. As it happens, during the years leading up to 1969, there was a steady decline in the share of higher-grade ores in total production, which raises suspicions about the motivation for the change.

Sometimes it is clear that series are added because the items involved are new products. Clothes washing and drying machines were first reported and probably first produced in 1957, steam turbines in 1956, and compressors in 1963. The production of several types of electrical equipment may fall in this category. Electric irons apparently were first produced domestically in 1959, electric phonographs in the same year, and television receivers in 1957. A number of similar examples can be drawn from chemicals. Vitamin C was first reported in 1961; oxytetracycline and chlorotetracycline in 1963, and several types of plastic materials, including aminoplasts, polyesters, polyvinyl acetate, polystyrol, and polyethylene were reported only after 1961.

Not all series that begin in the middle of the period studied in this work can reasonably be supposed to correspond to new series. Gunpowder production was first reported in 1959, but it is hard to believe that it was not produced earlier. Certainly the fact that bread production was not reported in the industrial statistics until 1964 cannot be taken to mean that production of bread was zero before then. (In this case, the most likely explanation is that a large proportion of bread was produced outside the industrial sector in the earlier years [in the handicraft sector, by private producers, or at home]; the figures for the industrial sector might have seemed too small and were simply suppressed.)

This apparent selectivity in reporting is one indication of possible distortions. Ambiguity in the specification of output series is another potential source of distortion. Ambiguity is most serious in product lines in which considerable aggregation takes place. For example, pumps are aggregated and reported in tons; the same is often true of metal and woodworking machines, tractors, diesel and electric locomotives, metal furniture, and other products of the metal industry. Radio receivers are reported in numbers of units, but neither the size nor the type of receiver is specified. Batteries are reported in tons. Certain types of clothing and other finished textile products are reported in square meters; again, no breakdown that would allow more precise measurement of the output is provided. In some cases, supplementary data that alleviate the problems caused by this aggregation are given, but the data are often fragmentary and incomplete. Some aggregation of this type is inevitable; full description of the output of the industrial sector would be literally impossible. But at the same time, aggregation can conceal important changes.

Because of insufficiently detailed specification, changes in productive output and capacity may be hidden behind unknown product quality changes. Canned vegetables, for example, are reported in tons; not only the mix of vegetables included but changes in product quality also remain unknown. Similarly fabric production is reported in thousands of square meters; fineness of weave and other quality indicators are not generally given. In some cases, the problem is complicated by the use of conventional units; in textiles, for example, yarn production is given in thousands of effective tons, and in building materials the output of bricks is reported in millions of standard units. The methods for converting crude outputs to the conventional units are not given in standard sources.

Questions raised by selectivity and ambiguity are further complicated by changes in the coverage of published product series. Much of this necessarily is unknown since there usually is no way to detect it. But considerable change must have occurred during the period of this study since the number of entries in the nomenclature, and hence the fineness of detail in which products were classified, grew markedly over the period of this study.[9] In some instances, the published data clearly show changes in coverage, but there is no fully satisfactory means of dealing with these changes even where they are known to have occurred.

A change in coverage apparently took place, for example, in reporting the production of silver. Until 1963, this series was designated anodic silver (*anodno srebro*); after that it became refined silver (*rafinirano srebro*). The two series do not dovetail. To construct a single series for silver, one must take the ratio of anodic to refined silver during years in which the two series overlap to represent the ratio for the whole time period. Another example is found in rolled-lead products. Coverage of this series was broader after than before 1957, but no information about the change in coverage is given in the basic source. In this case, the only link available is 1958, when output under both coverages is available in different editions of the source. For the years before 1958, output under the broader coverage must be estimated by assuming that the relation between the broader and narrower coverages was the same as it was in 1958. Steel railroad tracks, an important product in ferrous metallurgy, provides another, more clear-cut example. Until 1963, production data were given for rails plus accessories, with no finer breakdown. After that date, the sources list both output of rails and the broader category. To estimate output of rails—the more precise coverage—in the years prior to 1963, one must assume that the ratio of the two series after 1963 provides a reliable estimate of their ratio in earlier years.

Other cases are less manageable than these, which present problems familiar to those who study output statistics of communist countries. For the years 1957 through 1963, for example, a series for extruded and pressed products of copper and copper alloys was reported. For the years before and after, there seems to be no way to reproduce this series from the subseries that seem to constitute it. Cases of this sort are unusual, but in a number of cases some estimating method must be devised to provide continuous series with comparable coverages.

The reasons for the changes in coverages are largely a matter for speculation. In many cases, series were disaggregated in ways that are clear enough; the desire to provide additional detail was probably the reason in many instances. In other cases, however, less, rather than more, detail was provided, and links were left unspecified.

No set of output statistics is free from some problems of this sort. However, the existence of motive and opportunity for tinkering with the data and certain peculiarities observed in them suggest some manipulation. Nothing can be done about this except to take note of it.

The Official Weights

The method used in constructing the official index was described in some detail in a 1957 SZS publication.[10] From 1952 through 1969, the weights for individual products and for branches of industry were based on the sum of wages and depreciation; after 1969, they were based on the Yugoslav concept of national income. However, because the index for any given year was calculated with the use of weights derived from data collected two years earlier, the wage-plus-depreciation formula was in effect through 1971.

The relation of the sum of wages and depreciation to value added is more tenuous in Yugoslavia than in a capitalist system. First, depreciation rates typically were below those required to maintain the real value of capital.[11] Second, wages (or personal incomes, as the Yugoslavs prefer to call them) were a residual.[12] The size of the residual depended on many factors, including turnover-tax rates, rates of deductions charged against enterprise earnings, and the impact of price controls. The influence of these factors was not uniform across industrial branches, and the weighting system based on them is distorted in an unknown way.

The methods used for cumulating and assigning weights to product groups and industry branches are a further source of distortion. Weights for product groups were compiled from the financial reports of enterprises that reported production of the products in question. The procedure required arbitrary assignments of costs by enterprises and entailed unknown variations in the coverage of the products involved. Branch weights were obtained from the wage and depreciation data for the branches as a whole, and it is not clear whether they were the sum of the weights obtained for the products included in the branch.

The final peculiarity of the Yugoslav weighting system is that the weights are changed every year.[13] Annual changes in weights are required for some indexes,[14] but their use causes difficulties in making comparisons with commonly used fixed weight indexes. Furthermore, certain well-known interpretations of the movement of fixed weight indexes are lost when moving weights are used.[15] The combination of moving weights with the method of computing branch weights seems to be a source of upward bias in the Yugoslav index.[16]

THE SAMPLE INDEXES

The sample indexes are based on physical production data taken from official Yugoslav sources.[17] The coverage in the sources expanded during the period studied, and so did the quantity of price data from which the weights were derived. For these reasons, larger samples are possible for the later than for the earlier years; for the first decade, limitations on availability of both output and price data restrict the sample size for any fixed weight index. Of course, the output data used in the sample indexes are subject to the limitations and qualifications just noted. Further discussion of sample sizes and coverage is contained in the next chapter.

The Sample Index Weights

Several sets of weights were calculated, all intended to provide estimates of value added in production. One set of weights is based on producer prices for specific, individual industrial products.[18] In many, if not most, cases, prices were given for individual products. As a result, the weights derived from them had to be imputed to broader product classes in the construction of the index since the nomenclature groups in which output data were classified generally included more than one product. The sample indexes based on these weights are called "imputed weight" indexes.

The second set of weights is based on unit values of industrial products. Unit values were calculated from Yugoslav data for realized sales values and physical quantities sold.[19] The unit-value data provide greater detail than the price data. Furthermore, they are organized more or less along the lines of the nomenclature; hence, it is possible to determine which products are included in individual product groups. For example, in the calculation of the 1961 unit-value weight for starch products, sales and delivery data were given for three types of products included in that classification. The unit value computed from these data corresponds to a base-year output-weighted average of the unit values of the three types.[20] Weights based on unit values can be assigned to output series with more confidence than the price-based weights because the information about the products included in the output classes is better.

Sample indexes based on these weights are called "direct weight" indexes. This term is used only to differentiate between indexes. The indexes based on unit values are not true direct weight indexes because the weights sometimes were used to weight output series containing more products than those included in the data used to calculate the weight.

On the whole, the unit-value weights are probably more reliable than the price weights. Unfortunately, unit values can be calculated beginning only in 1959; thus, there is no alternative to the use of price weights for the construction of a Laspeyres index with a 1952 base.

The weights were developed in three stages: (1) the basic information on price or unit value was obtained; (2) the turnover tax was eliminated; and (3) an estimate of value added was obtained by multiplying the resulting figures by estimates of the ratio of value added to gross value (net of turnover tax) for the product groups in which the item in question was classified.

The turnover tax was eliminated because Yugoslav enterprises may sell their products on the market, rather than delivering them to a state trading network. Consequently, there is some question about the incidence of the turnover tax and therefore of how to treat it when using product price or unit value to estimate product cost and value added. Incidence depends on the elasticities of supply and demand for the product in question. Different estimates of these elasticities produce different estimates of the incidence, thereby leading to different conclusions on the treatment of the tax in computing weights. Clearly, the smaller the supply elasticity and the greater the demand elasticity, the more heavily the turnover tax is shifted to factors of production (at least in the short run).[21] According to the conventional theory of the self-managed firm, supply elasticities are relatively low.[22] Furthermore, there was inflation during much of the period studied, and the government continuously intervened in the market, notably by setting ceiling prices. With excess demand for a product, a seller in effect faces an infinitely elastic demand curve. For these reasons and in the interests of simplicity and consistency, it was clearly best to assume that turnover tax was borne entirely by factors of production. Therefore, the turnover tax was deducted in toto from the price or unit value when calculating product cost.[23]

After the turnover tax was removed from price or unit value, the resulting figure was adjusted to provide an estimate of value added. At this point, some aggregation of the output series was unavoidable because the data for the adjustments were not available on a product-by-product basis. The adjustment data were obtained from the series of statistical bulletins on the performance of enterprises in the social sector that SZS began publishing in 1961.[24] These bulletins contain financial information about industrial enterprises, including the so-called social product (*društveni proizvod*), the turnover tax paid (*porez na promet*), and the costs of purchased materials and services (*materijalni troškovi*). The sum of social product, costs of materials, and purchased services corresponds to the gross value of sales of the enterprise; hence, the ratio of social product (net of turnover tax) to the sum of itself and materials cost can be taken as the ratio of value added to product price or unit value (net of turnover tax). The available data permitted the calculation of this ratio for a number of groups of products in all but one industrial branch.[25] The net prices or unit values of those products belonging to the available subgroups were then multiplied by the appropriate ratios to obtain the final weights.

CHAPTER FOUR

Growth of Industrial Production, 1952–1975

Yugoslav industrial output grew at a rapid, but diminishing pace between 1952 and 1975. According to the official index, the average annual growth rate over the whole period was 10.0 percent. Growth at this rate corresponds to a ninefold increase in output over the period.

According to the sample indexes, this is an overstatement. The highest average annual growth rate implied by the sample indexes is 8.9 percent; other variants give annual rates ranging down to 8.4 percent. These growth rates correspond to an output expansion of about sevenfold, roughly 80 percent of that implied by the official index. These growth rates are consistent with those experienced by other countries, as is shown in more detail in chapter 6.

The growth patterns of industry branches reflect the industrialization policy and prewar industrial development already described. Growth tended to be slower in branches relatively well developed before the war than in newly developing branches. Two factors help account for this: the general tendency for established industries to grow more slowly than new ones and the tendency in development policy to favor new branches. These factors gave rise to wide discrepancies in growth rates among branches.

There was substantial retardation in growth rates during the period. During the first years, retardation was gradual but noticeable. Around 1960, the slowdown became more marked, but there is evidence of a stabilization or a possible reversal of the retardation after 1971. Retardation can be seen most clearly by considering two subperiods, 1952–61 and 1961–71, and by comparing average annual growth rates; rates in the second subperiod are about four percentage points below those in the first subperiod, regardless of which index is used for the calculations.

INDUSTRIAL GROWTH MEASURED BY THE SAMPLE INDEXES

Several variants of the sample index along with the official index are presented in table 5; average annual growth rates calculated from these indexes for the period as a whole and for several subperiods are shown in table 6. The variants have different coverages because of limitations in the availability of the data required to compute the indexes. Generally speaking, as the point of observation recedes into the past, information about quantity of output and price or unit value diminishes. The sample index based on 1952 product prices has the most limited coverage (159 series for different products or sets of products), mainly because 1952 product price data are sparse. Unit values for 1961 can be calculated for a much larger number of products; indeed, coverage of the direct weights index was restricted not by lack of information on weights, but by lack of data on physical production. As a result, the 1961 unit value index had a product sample about twice as large (401 series) for the first decade as the 1952 product price index. For the 1971–75 subperiod, enough data are available to expand the sample to 442 series.

Because unit values were not available until 1959, only one index with 1952 weights could be compiled, and only one Laspeyres index is available for the first decade of the period. The indexes based on 1961 prices and unit values are Paasche indexes for the first and Laspeyres for the second part of the period.[1]

The sample indexes are reasonably robust. Changes in base year, weights, and sample all cause differences in measured growth rates, but the general range of the growth rates is well confined. Analysis of aggregate growth is presented in the next section and further discussion of retardation in the last section of this chapter. Possible reasons for the discrepancies between official and sample indexes are examined in the following chapter.

GROWTH BY INDUSTRIAL BRANCHES

The data compiled in Yugoslav statistics and used in computing the official and sample indexes pertain to what Yugoslav national income accounts term the industry and mining sector. That sector and the indexes measuring its growth correspond to the sector called industry in the U.S. accounts, not to manufacturing. The difference between industry and manufacturing in the U.S. classification is that mining and electric power are included in industry, not in manufacturing. In the Yugoslav system, electric power generation is shown as a separate branch of industry and mining. Mining activities are distributed among the branches of industry that process the ores and other raw materials extracted in mining; extrac-

TABLE 5

INDEXES OF INDUSTRIAL PRODUCTION IN YUGOSLAVIA, 1952–75

Year	Official Yugoslav Index (1)	1952 Imputed Weights[a] (2)	1961 Imputed Weights[b] (3)	1961 Direct Weights[c] (4)	Moving Weights[d] (5)
1952	100.0	100.0	100.0	100.0	100.0
1953	111.1	102.4	104.5	107.6	102.4
1954	126.3	118.4	118.3	121.6	118.4
1955	147.0	140.0	136.9	140.6	140.0
1956	162.1	154.6	149.4	153.8	154.6
1957	189.2	179.9	172.0	180.8	179.9
1958	209.8	200.0	187.4	200.5	200.0
1959	237.7	217.3	205.5	226.1	217.3
1960	274.3	245.4	232.3	258.6	245.4
1961	294.0	260.2	250.0	275.0	260.2
1962	314.0	281.6	274.4	302.2	284.5
1963	362.7	324.0	311.0	344.4	326.8
1964	421.1	366.9	350.6	398.2	380.2
1965	454.8	389.2	371.5	423.0	404.6
1966	474.4	408.6	392.6	436.6	417.4
1967	473.0	403.6	389.6	428.3	412.0
1968	503.3	420.4	406.3	446.0	433.2
1969	560.2	458.3	440.0	489.0	476.2
1970	611.2	489.0	467.3	518.4	506.7
1971	674.2	522.0	504.3	560.6	549.2
1972	726.8	564.4	533.5	591.4	584.0
1973	770.4	597.7	562.0	617.3	609.6
1974	852.8	653.2	615.0	680.2	672.3
1975	900.6	677.1	636.1	713.9	705.6

SOURCES: Col. 1: SZS, *Industrija 1975* (Belgrade: SZS, 1976), p. 10. Cols. 2–5: See appendixes A and B for description of sources. Methods are described in chapter 3.

[a]Weights derived from 1952 product prices; 1952 product sample.

[b]Weights derived from 1961 product prices; 1952 product sample.

[c]Weights derived from 1961 product unit values; 1952 product sample.

[d]For 1952–61, weights derived from 1952 product prices; 1952 product sample. For 1961–71, weights derived from 1961 product unit values; 1961 product sample. For 1971–75, weights derived from 1971 product unit values; 1971 product sample.

tion of coal, iron ore, petroleum, natural gas, nonferrous metal ores, and nonmetallic mineral ores all are reported as part of the output of the industry branches that use them. In addition, Yugoslav branches contain different groups of products than the corresponding U.S. branches.[2]

Branch Growth Rates

Two aspects of industrial growth are discernible in the pattern of the rates of growth of individual branches of industry (according to the Yugoslav classification) shown in table 7: (1) the effects of the industrialization policy followed, and

TABLE 6

ANNUAL RATES OF GROWTH, YUGOSLAV INDUSTRIAL PRODUCTION
SELECTED PERIODS, 1952–75

	Average Annual Growth Rate[a]				
Period	Official Index	1952 Imputed Weights Index	1961 Imputed Weights Index	1961 Direct Weights Index	Moving Weights Index
1952–75	10.0	8.7	8.4	8.9	8.9
1952–57	13.6	12.5	11.5	12.6	12.5
1957–61	11.6	9.7	9.8	11.1	9.7
1961–66	10.0	9.4	9.4	9.7	9.9
1966–71	7.3	5.0	5.1	5.1	5.6
1971–75	7.5	6.7	6.0	6.2	6.5

SOURCE. Calculated from table 5.

[a]Calculated between terminal years by the compound interest formula.

TABLE 7

ANNUAL GROWTH RATES, YUGOSLAV INDUSTRIAL BRANCHES[a]
(Percentage)

	1952–75		1961–75		1971–75	
Branch	Official Index	Sample Index[b]	Official Index	Sample Index[c]	Official Index	Sample Index[d]
Electric power production	12.4	12.5	10.4	10.6	7.6	8.4
Coal and coal products	4.0	4.2	1.9	1.9	2.6	2.2
Petroleum and petroleum products	15.0	14.0	11.2	10.8	6.0	5.5
Ferrous metallurgy	11.0	10.2	7.5	6.6	8.2	6.4
Nonferrous metallurgy	8.1	8.2	7.1	7.6	8.7	12.5
Stone, clay, and glass	12.0	10.7	9.4	8.8	6.2	7.1
Metal products	10.6	11.9	8.1	9.1	9.0	8.7
Electrical products	16.3	16.4	12.1	11.6	10.0	8.3
Chemicals	16.8	10.4	14.9	8.4	10.9	5.2
Building materials	8.2	7.0	7.4	8.6	8.2	7.8
Lumber and wood products	8.3	7.1	7.5	4.4	6.3	3.1
Paper and paper products	13.0	11.6	10.7	8.1	6.1	4.4
Textiles and textile products	8.1	5.7	7.2	4.6	7.2	4.9
Hides and leather products	8.2	8.7	6.4	7.8	6.8	7.7
Rubber products	11.2	13.1	10.2	12.8	9.0	9.5
Food products	10.2	7.7	7.3	6.0	5.4	5.0
Printing and publishing	n.a.	10.1	n.a.	7.4	n.a.	4.2
Tobacco products	4.0	4.6	5.7	6.0	6.1	6.4

SOURCES: SZS, *Industrija 1975* (Belgrade: SZS, 1976), p. 10; and data underlying table 5.

[a]Calculated as annual averages between terminal years by the compound interest formula.

[b]1961 direct weights index with 1952 product sample.

[c]1961 direct weights index with 1961 product sample.

[d]1971 direct weights index with 1971 sample.

(2) the importance of older, traditional branches of industry in overall growth. In turn, the effects of several strands of the industrialization policy can be observed: the emphasis placed on energy production, the stress on exploiting natural resources, and the attempt to develop new branches with material bases in newly exploited natural resources. For example, petroleum and petroleum products and electric power production are among the leading branches in both indexes.[3] The petroleum branch includes extraction of crude oil and natural gas, two industries that expanded rapidly, reflecting both the policy of rapid development of energy supplies and the objective of exploiting the previously almost untapped reserves of oil and gas. The rapid growth of electric power production is also due to the energy policy, as well as to Tito's predilection for electrification.[4] In contrast, the coal industry, which had been relatively well developed at the beginning of the period and falls into the set of "traditional" industries, grew very slowly, the energy policy notwithstanding, because of the substitution of other fuels in industry.

The electric products branch is an example of the conjuncture of high priority in the development policy and the development of a new branch. According to the sample index, its growth rate for 1952–75 was the highest of all branches. Beginning with a very small base (in 1952, it accounted for only about 3 percent of social product originating in the industrial sector), it exhibited very high growth rates in the early years. As the branch matured, however, there was a sharp retardation in the measured rate of growth, as seen in the growth rates in the later periods—a pattern to be expected in a branch in which there was rapid introduction of new products. The chemicals branch is another example of a branch emphasized in the development policy that had a small initial base, although in this case there is considerable divergence between growth rates according to the official and sample indexes.[5]

Other branches illustrate some of these same points. At first glance, the relatively slow growth of the metal products branch may be surprising. However, the growth rate for the branch as a whole obscures very rapid growth in some parts of it. Some parts not highly developed at the outset (particularly transportation equipment and machinery) were given relatively high priority in the development policy. Similarly, the very rapid growth of the paper products branch seems surprising. However, development policy emphasized exploiting timber resources and developing industries based on wood. Paper production benefited from this emphasis. The wood products branch itself grew rather slowly, probably due to its relatively high level at the beginning of the period studied.[6] Rubber products also grew very rapidly, no doubt a reflection of the emphasis on transportation equipment in the industrialization policy.

Among the branches that were relatively important in Yugoslav industry in 1952, ferrous and nonferrous metallurgy were consistently given high priority in the development policy. Although neither exhibited unusually high growth rates over the period as a whole, both maintained relatively rapid growth. Furthermore, growth in nonferrous metals retarded less than almost any other branch during the last few years of the period. This was due largely to increases in production of aluminum, zinc, and ferroalloys.[7] The building materials branch also exemplifies the emphasis on developing branches with indigenous raw materials bases. This branch maintained a fairly steady growth rate while most branches exhibited retardation; its rank according to growth rate rose steadily throughout the period. Much of this growth was due to increases in production of wood-based materials, especially plywood and particle board.

Finally, note should be taken of the performance of branches that were reasonably well developed at the beginning of the period, but did not receive high priority in the industrialization policy, particularly food products, textiles, and tobacco. Together, these three accounted for about one-third of the value of social product generated in the industrial sector in 1952, and textiles were, by this measure, the largest single branch. All three branches were near the bottom in measured growth. Even so, the growth rate for food products almost certainly overstates the growth rate of production of processed food as a whole because of the displacement over the period of food produced in the handicraft or small-scale sector by food produced in the industrial sector. It should also be noted that the overall growth rate for textiles conceals some important divergences among components of the branch.

Growth Rates for Revised Product Groups

In certain branches, the Yugoslav classification scheme groups activities that might better be considered separately. Tables 8, 9, and 10 present growth rates for mining and industrial activities classified by a scheme intended to clarify some aspects of industrial growth obscured in the official classification.[8]

The main purposes in regrouping the data were to separate mining from the industrial branches and to divide metal products into components. The first was accomplished completely; all mining series were separated from the original branches and recombined into a single index, which shows (see table 8) that mining grew slowly throughout this period. The relatively slow growth of mining was due mostly to the slow growth of coal and nonferrous metal ores, as shown by the data in table 9. The growth rate of iron ore was also slightly below the industrial average. On the other hand, the mining of nonmetallic minerals (quartz sand, stone, and flour; crude fireclay; crude magnesite; crude feldspar; and crude barites) and the extraction of crude oil and natural gas grew at very rapid rates. The influence of the extent of development of a branch of activity at the beginning of the period is evident; coal mining, nonferrous metals mining, and iron mining all were relatively well developed in the prewar Yugoslav economy. The policy of exploiting previously untapped petroleum resources—a policy

TABLE 8

AVERAGE ANNUAL GROWTH RATES OF REVISED INDUSTRIAL GROUPS[a]
(Percentage)

Group	1952–75	*Period* 1961–75	1971–75
Mining[b]	5.9	4.1	4.1
Electricity and processed fuels[c]	12.9	10.5	6.4
Ferrous metallurgy[d]	10.1	6.6	6.8
Nonferrous metallurgy[e]	8.8	8.2	13.1
Building materials[f]	7.0	6.3	5.0
Transportation equipment[g]	16.8	10.6	8.1
Agricultural equipment[h]	10.9	9.4	15.3
Intermediate producer's goods[i]	11.3	7.9	7.8
Other machinery, tools, and equipment[j]	12.5	10.4	10.3
Chemicals[k]	9.7	7.8	4.4
Textiles and allied products[l]	4.5	2.2	-0.4
Clothing and footwear[m]	9.3	9.2	7.9
Food and allied products[n]	7.0	5.7	3.8

SOURCE: Calculated from data underlying column 4 of table 5.

[a]Calculated between terminal years by the compound interest formula.

[b]Includes coal, crude oil, and natural gas; iron, nonferrous metals, nonmetallic minerals, and quarrying.

[c]Besides electricity, includes fuels derived from coal, petroleum, and natural gas.

[d]Obtained from the Yugoslav ferrous metallurgy branch by removing ferrous ore mining and adding steel castings from the metal products branch.

[e]Obtained from the Yugoslav nonferrous metallurgy branch by removing nonferrous ore mining and adding nonferrous castings from the metal products branch.

[f]Obtained by combining the stone, clay, and glass products branch (less mining of nonmetallic minerals) with the building materials branch (less quarrying) and adding fasteners (rivets, screws, and nails) from the metal products branch, a number of products of the lumber and wood products industry (sawn timber, veneer, plywood, solid parquet flooring, and wood impregnation), and roofing felt.

[g]The sum of a number of items from the metal products branch (steam locomotives, motor locomotives, freight and other special coaches, other railroad coaches, tubs, mine cars, other miscellaneous cars, trucks and light trucks, buses, bodies for trucks and other vehicles, spare parts for motor vehicles, and bicycles) with tires and tubes for motor vehicles and bicycles from rubber products.

[h]The sum of agricultural tools, agricultural machinery and equipment, and tractors, all from the metal products branch.

[i]The sum of several items from rubber products (pipes, sanitary wares, and rubberized canvas), metal products (armatures, steel ropes, barbed wire, chains, fittings and accessories, metal utensils, metal packing materials, electrodes, and roller bearings), two from electrical products (cables and insulated conductors), wooden containers and boxes, several items from paper products (newsprint, kraft paper, wrapping and other packing paper, cigarette paper, other paper, and cardboard), and several from hides and leather (sole leather, other leather for footwear, technical ready-made goods, pigskin for manufacturing, lining leather from kips, and furs).

[j]The sum of a number of items from the metal products branch (boilers for central heating, equipment for steam heating, cutting tools, pumps, steam boilers not for central heating, water turbines, steam turbines, building machinery and equipment, metal and woodworking machinery, ventilation and air conditioning equipment, refrigeration equipment, balances, and clocks) and a number from electrical products (rotating machines—all sizes, accessories for rotating machines, transformers for meters, switchgear, distribution equipment, cinema projectors and capacitors, telephones, telephone exchanges, installation materials, electric light bulbs, lamps, accumulators, and primary cells).

[k]Obtained by adding three series from lumber and wood products (tanning materials, colophony and turpentine, and matches) to the Yugoslav chemicals branch.

[l]Obtained by removing clothing from the Yugoslav textiles branch.

[m]Clothing from the textiles branch plus leather footwear from the hides and leather products branch plus rubber footwear from the rubber products branch.

[n]Food products branch plus tobacco products branch.

TABLE 9

AVERAGE ANNUAL GROWTH RATES: SELECTED MINING BRANCHES[a]
(Percentage)

Branch	1952–75	*Period* 1961–75	1971–75
Coal mining	3.6	1.8	2.7
Crude oil and natural gas	15.7	8.8	7.8
Iron ore	8.8	6.6	8.2
Nonferrous metals	4.8	4.0	3.5
Nonmetallic minerals	9.3	4.8	2.8

SOURCE: Calculated from data underlying table 8.
[a]Calculated between terminal years by the compound interest formula.

TABLE 10

AVERAGE ANNUAL GROWTH RATES: INDUSTRY AND MANUFACTURING[a]

Sector	1952–75	*Period* 1961–75	1971–75
All industrial products	8.6	7.1	6.4
Mining	5.9	4.1	4.1
Electric power production	12.5	10.6	8.4
Manufacturing[b]	8.8	7.2	6.5

SOURCE: Calculated from data underlying table 8.
[a]Calculated between terminal years by the compound interest formula.
[b]All industrial products less mining and electric power production. This grouping is intended to approach the U.S. manufacturing sector, but is not identically defined or fully comparable to it.

whose implications extend from the rapid growth rate of the extraction of the crude materials to the rapid growth of the chemical industry, the development of artificial fibers, and the rest of petroleum-related industrial development—is also clearly seen.

Output data from the metal products branch were used to calculate growth rates (table 8) for transportation equipment, agricultural equipment, other machinery, tools, and equipment,[9] and partly for intermediate producers' goods. By a substantial margin, transportation equipment was the fastest growing subgroup in the metal products category. The outputs of trucks, buses, railroad vehicles, and even bicycles grew very rapidly. On the other hand, for the period as a whole, agricultural equipment grew considerably less rapidly than transportation equipment and also less rapidly than other types of machinery. Tractors grew faster than the average for this group (at a little more than 12 percent per year for the twenty years), but agricultural tools and other machinery and equipment grew more slowly. From these data it appears that the output of agricultural machinery and equipment grew only slightly more rapidly than industrial output as a whole. Given the extremely low level of mechanization in agriculture at the beginning of the period,[10] the relatively low rate of growth of agricultural machinery and equipment indicates a correspondingly low priority for agricultural mechanization. Whether the faster growth in the most recent period means a reversal of this policy is unknown.

The removal of mining from the basic metals branches shows that actual output of ferrous and nonferrous products grew faster than the Yugoslav definitions of branches indicate. The difference in ferrous metallurgy, however, was small because the growth rate for mining was only slightly lower than for the branch as a whole and because the weight of mining in the branch was relatively small. The impact on nonferrous metallurgy is considerably greater—and for opposite reasons. Nonferrous ore mining grew more slowly than the nonferrous metals branch, and mining was a relatively important part of the branch.[11]

Some additional details are worth brief emphasis. The growth rate of the revised chemicals branch is marginally below that of the original branch, apparently because of the inclusion of certain chemical products classified elsewhere in the Yugoslav scheme. The removal of clothing from the textiles branch reduces the measured rate of growth of the branch, especially in recent years, indicating that clothing output in industry grew faster than the average for the branch as a whole. Comparison of the growth rate for the original textile branch with those for the revised textiles and allied products group and the clothing and footwear group suggests that clothing was a relatively small part of the original textile branch at the beginning of the period. In turn, part of the reason why the base for clothing in the industrial sector (i.e., in the textiles branch of industry) was small in 1952 is that a substantial fraction of the clothing output was produced not in the industrial, but in the handicraft sector. The rate of growth of the revised clothing and footwear branch is relatively high, partly for that reason and partly because of the rapid growth of rubber footwear. Finally, the inclusion of tobacco products in the food and allied products branch reduces the measured rate of growth in comparison with the original food products branch.

What impact does the removal of those activities considered nonmanufacturing (mining and electric power) have on the growth rates? The growth rate for the index entitled "All Industrial Products" in table 10 was calculated from an index for only those products included in the revised product groups; hence, it is not fully comparable with the growth rates for industry as a whole that are reported in table 5. Nevertheless, the effects of removing nonmanufacturing activities can be seen here. Although mining grew more slowly than industry as a whole, electric power production grew faster; the net effect of their removal is to increase the growth rate slightly for those products that are considered manufacturing products in the United States, in comparison with the growth rate for all products included in the Yugoslav index.

RETARDATION OF GROWTH

The growth rates for the subperiods shown in tables 7, 8, and 9 all point to steady retardation in the rate of growth of industrial production. The pattern is shown graphically in figure 1. The first signs of hesitation in the rate of industrial production can be seen around 1961–62, immediately after the inauguration of the 1961–65 Five-Year Plan and the first economic reforms. These difficulties apparently were partly responsible for the decision to abandon the plan and begin work on a seven-year plan, intended to span 1964–71, and meanwhile to resort to a series of annual plans. Growth revived briefly after 1962, but slowed again in 1965 and 1966, concurrent with the major reforms of those years. An actual decline in production in 1967 was followed by a period of steady growth, but at a lower pace, which lasted through the end of the period analyzed here.

The period surrounding the major reforms, 1964–67, thus exhibited relative

FIGURE 1

INDUSTRIAL PRODUCTION INDEX NUMBERS

All Industrial Products
(1952 = 100)

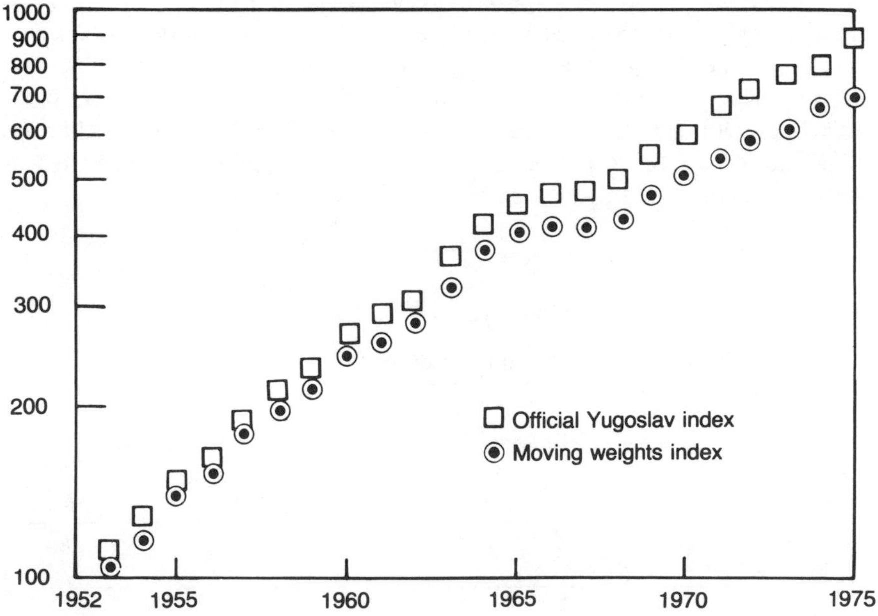

SOURCE: Table 5.

stagnation in growth of output (see table 11). Beginning in 1967, industrial output expanded again at a steadier, but significantly lower pace. By either the official index or the moving weights sample index, the average annual rate of growth in the last eight years was more than four percentage points lower than that during the first twelve years of the period. It is tempting to infer from this that the reforms, by altering the organizational forms and incentives in the self-management system, substantially reduced the capacity of the system to generate industrial growth. This inference is, however, premature and oversimplified. The breaks in the pattern of growth that occur roughly contemporaneously with the reforms were accompanied by substantial changes in the composition of output. Because the reforms included extensive price reforms, it is possible that the reductions in growth rates during the reform period resulted from a restructuring of output caused by changes in relative prices. This possibility is discussed at greater length and further evidence presented in chapter 7. The lower, but steady growth rate of the postreform period is probably due less to any change in the capacity of the system to generate growth than to other factors, including the natural tendency to slowing of growth in a maturing economy.

The pattern of declining growth rates occurred in all but one industrial branch (defined according to the Yugoslav classification). In table 12, declines are measured in two ways: as the absolute decline (in percentage points) between the growth rate through 1964 and that from 1967 through 1975 (the years of stagnation around the reforms are omitted to avoid measuring from troughs or peaks); and as a relative reduction, calculated by expressing the absolute decline as a percentage of the growth rate during the period before the reforms. Only the building materials branch grew more rapidly after the reforms. In every other branch, growth rates declined; in every branch except nonferrous metals, the declines exceeded 20 percent. There seems to be no simple relation between proportional declines in growth rates and first-decade growth rates.[12]

TABLE 11

AVERAGE ANNUAL GROWTH RATES OF YUGOSLAV INDUSTRIAL OUTPUT, SELECTED PERIODS[a]
(Percentage)

	Period		
Index	1952–64	1964–67	1967–75
Official Yugoslav Index	12.7	4.0	8.4
Moving Weights Index	11.8	2.7	7.0

SOURCE: Table 5.

[a]Calculated between terminal years by the compound interest formula.

TABLE 12

DECLINES IN GROWTH RATES, 1952–64 and 1967–75[a]

Branch	Absolute Decline[b]	Percentage Decline[c]
All industrial branches:		
Official index	4.4	34.2
Sample index	5.1	41.8
Electric power production	4.6	30.9
Coal and coal products	4.8	65.5
Petroleum and petroleum products	9.7	54.6
Ferrous metallurgy	5.0	37.7
Nonferrous metallurgy	1.0	11.0
Stone, clay, and glass	4.8	34.7
Metal products	7.8	44.4
Electrical products	14.7	59.9
Chemicals	11.8	68.8
Building materials	-1.0	12.1[d]
Lumber and wood products	7.2	63.5
Paper and paper products	10.1	67.1
Textiles and textile products	5.1	56.0
Hides and leather products	5.8	48.1
Rubber products	3.3	22.5
Food products	5.6	50.6
Printing and publishing	7.2	51.8
Tobacco products	3.7	55.6

SOURCES: Table 6 and data underlying table 7.

[a]Except where noted, declines are measured according to a linked sample index using 1961 unit-value weights and the 1952 sample for 1952–61; 1961 unit-value weights and the 1961 sample for 1961–71; and 1971 unit-value weights and the 1971 sample for 1971–75.

[b]Average annual growth rate for 1952–64 minus that for 1967–75.

[c]Absolute decline as percentage of average annual growth rate for 1952–64.

[d]Increase.

INTERNATIONAL COMPARISONS

One reason for calculating the sample index of industrial production for Yugoslavia was to facilitate comparisons with growth in other countries. By international standards, industrial growth in Yugoslavia from 1952 to 1971 was rapid. However, if Yugoslavia's initial stage of development is considered, its growth rate is unremarkable.

When the growth in Yugoslav manufacturing output is compared with that in other countries (measured by U.N. compilations of production indexes reported by member countries), Yugoslavia ranks near the top. Table 13 compares Yugoslavia and some noncommunist countries that reported output during a contemporaneous period and whose indexes are methodologically similar to the

TABLE 13

GROWTH OF MANUFACTURING OUTPUT: SELECTED COUNTRIES, 1953–71
(Percentage)[a]

Country	Average Annual Growth Rate	Country	Average Annual Growth Rate
Republic of Korea	15.7[b]	Federal Republic of Germany	7.1[j]
Japan	13.8[c]	Austria	7.1[k]
		Netherlands	6.7[l]
Yugoslavia	9.8[d]	France	6.6[m]
Israel	9.6[e]	India	6.2[n]
Mexico	9.0[f]	Denmark	5.5[o]
Venezuela	8.2[g]	Canada	4.9[p]
Philippines	7.2[h]	Luxembourg	3.5[q]
Italy	7.1[i]	United States	3.5[r]

SOURCES: Yugoslavia: Calculated from table 5 (moving weights index). All others: United Nations, *Statistical Yearbook, 1972* (New York: U.N., 1973), pp. 154–67; and idem, *1972 Supplement to the Statistical Yearbook and the Monthly Bulletin of Statistics* (New York: U.N., 1973), pp. 69–102.

[a]Calculated between terminal years by the compound interest formula. Because of differences in weight bases and coverages, as well as remaining methodological differences, the growth rates in the table are not fully comparable. All countries included report an arithmetic index using some form of value-added weights, and coverage is approximately the same as that of Yugoslavia. The succeeding footnotes specify the most important differences in coverage and weight bases.

[b]1970 weights.

[c]Excludes printing and publishing; 1970 weights.

[d]Index calculated by deducting mining and electric power production from industry and mining in the direct weights (1961 base) sample index.

[e]Excludes repair of clocks and watches; 1968 weights.

[f]Excludes nonferrous basic metals and furniture; 1950 weights.

[g]Excludes leather footwear, basic metals, and machinery; 1957 weights.

[h]Excludes basic metals; 1965 weights.

[i]Excludes printing and publishing, repair shops, and some miscellaneous categories; 1963 weights, adjusted to 1965 base.

[j]1958 weights.

[k]Excludes sawmills, printing and publishing, and coal products; includes stone quarrying, clay, and sand pits; 1964 weights.

[l]1963 weights.

[m]Excludes clothing and wood products; 1962 weights.

[n]1970 weights.

[o]Excludes sugar factories and refineries; 1955 weights.

[p]1949 weights.

[q]Excludes paper and paper products; 1970 weights.

[r]1967 weights.

Yugoslav sample index. According to these figures, only the Republic of Korea and Japan had distinctly higher growth rates than Yugoslavia; Israel, Mexico, and Venezuela were in the same general range as Yugoslavia. The sample of countries is restricted, however. If comparable data were available for other countries, Yugoslavia would probably rank lower on the list. For example, Egypt, Nicaragua, Panama, Ecuador, Syria, and Turkey all reported manufacturing indexes showing higher rates of growth over this period than did Yugoslavia, but the coverages of the indexes or the time periods for which data were reported were so different that including the actual growth rates in table 13 would have been misleading.[13]

The results shown in table 13 require qualification because there were wide variations in the 1952 levels of development of the countries listed. Although there is no fully acceptable way to compare international output levels, per capita electric power production, although subject to qualifications,[14] can be used to establish orders of magnitude. In 1952, per capita electric power production in Yugoslavia was about 161,000 kilowatt hours, a level on the same order as those in Mexico (198,000), Venezuela (136,000), and Panama (110,000), countries that also had growth rates approximating that of Yugoslavia. Yugoslavia's 1952 per capita electric power production was smaller than Japan's (604,000), which had a much higher growth rate, and Israel's (416,000) which had a slightly lower growth rate. On the other hand, measured by per capita electric power production, Yugoslavia in 1952 was more highly developed than the Republic of Korea (31,000), Philippines (47,000), and India (22,000) and recorded a lower rate of output growth than Korea and a higher growth rate than the Philippines and India.[15] If the initial stage of development and the subsequent rate of growth of manufacturing output are negatively correlated[16] and if per capita electric power production can be taken to measure stage of development, the Yugoslav record appears to be unexceptional by the standards of the noncommunist countries in the postwar period.

Comparison with other European communist countries and the Soviet Union is more difficult. The methods used in the official production indexes for these countries differ significantly from those of the sample indexes and the official Yugoslav index. Neither measure of Yugoslav output, in other words, provides a measure of growth fully comparable with the official indexes of the other bloc countries. Western calculations of sample indexes for the Soviet Union and the bloc countries provide estimates of growth rate methodologically more nearly comparable with the indexes of this study. Unfortunately, precisely contemporaneous estimates are not available, and minor methodological differences remain. Consequently, divergences in absolute magnitudes between growth rates measured by different indexes are subject to a considerable margin of error.

With the exception of Hungary, all official indexes are weighted with gross-value weights, a practice that causes well-known distortions.[17] The impact of these distortions on the indexes cannot be assessed without detailed study of the industrial structure in each country, a task beyond the scope of this work. Generally, if fast growing product lines are also those in which there is relatively extensive double-counting of output or if there is a general tendency to vertical disintegration of industry over a given period of time, a gross-weighted index will rise faster than the appropriate net-weighted index. Without more detailed study, the existence and magnitude of biases for the individual countries are unknown. However, it is generally believed that these indexes are biased upward.

The Hungarian industrial production index weights outputs by the sum of wages and depreciation, which would approximate the appropriate measure, value added, if wages and depreciation were properly calculated. Because of the absence of a capital market in Hungary and imperfections in the workings of the labor market, the weights used probably differ from "true" value-added weights. Nevertheless, the Hungarian index is probably less susceptible to the upward biases of the gross-weighted indexes.

The differences in weighting systems are further complicated by differences in the base years adopted by each country and by differences in the coverages of the indexes; these disparities are summarized briefly in the notes to table 14. These inconsistencies and the fundamental differences in weighting systems render precise comparisons impossible.

Nevertheless, Yugoslav growth may be compared qualitatively to growth in the bloc and the Soviet Union on the basis of table 14. When differences in weights and initial stages of development (measured again by per capita electric power production) are taken into account, Yugoslav growth approximates the general pattern, no more and no less. By the crude measure of initial development level, Bulgaria and Romania started at about the same level as Yugoslavia; their measured growth rates according to official indexes are higher, but probably are biased upward because their indexes employ gross weights. The Western estimates are consistent with this view. Poland and the Soviet Union had measured output growth rates about equal to Yugoslavia's. But, again, there is likely an upward bias in their growth rates because of the gross weights used in their indexes. The more comparable Western index for Poland and the U.S. index for the Soviet Union indicate that growth proceeded more or less consistently with the initial level of development. Measured by per capita electric power production, Czechoslovakia and East Germany were significantly further advanced in 1952 than Yugoslavia; when the likely bias in their official indexes and the Western estimates are considered, their growth rates relative to Yugoslavia's also fit the pattern. Hungary's growth rate based on both its official index and the Western measurement is more nearly comparable to Yugoslavia's and is consistent with its initial stage of development relative to Yugoslavia's. On the whole, these data show that Yugoslavia's growth rate, measured by the sample indexes, does not deviate significantly from the general pattern in East Europe.

The assessment of industrial growth in the first twenty years of self-management may be extended in another direction. Based on per capita electric power production, the Soviet Union was in approximately the same stage of development in the early or middle 1930s as Yugoslavia was in 1952.[18] It is instructive to compare the growth of production in the Soviet Union for a twenty-year period beginning in the 1930s with Yugoslavia's during 1952–71. Any twenty-year

TABLE 14

MANUFACTURING GROWTH RATES AND ELECTRIC POWER PRODUCTION IN SOVIET BLOC COUNTRIES AND YUGOSLAVIA, SELECTED PERIODS

Country	*Average Annual Growth Rates*[a] *(Percentage)* From Official Indexes 1953–71[b]	From Western Estimates 1950–71[c]	1952 Per Capita Electricity Production (kwh/person)
Bulgaria	12.6[d]	8.3[k]	189.4
Romania	12.1[e]	7.8[k]	177.9
Poland	9.4[f]	5.2[k]	479.6
Czechoslovakia	8.1[g]	4.2[k]	948.1
German Democratic Republic	7.6[h]	3.5[k]	1,261.7
Hungary	6.6[i]	3.8[k]	444.0
USSR	9.8[j]	8.0[l]	593.0
Yugoslavia	10.5	9.2[m]	160.7

SOURCES: For all official indexes except that of Yugoslavia, see sources cited in table 13. Official Yugoslav index from table 5. Western estimates for USSR from Rush V. Greenslade and Wade E. Robertson, "Industrial Production in the U.S.S.R.," in *Soviet Economic Prospects for the Seventies,* ed. U.S., Congress, Joint Economic Committee (Washington, D.C.: Government Printing Office, 1973), p. 280. Western estimates for other East European countries (except Yugoslavia) calculated from Thad P. Alton, "Economic Structure and Growth in Eastern Europe," in *Economic Developments in Countries of Eastern Europe,* ed. U.S., Congress, Joint Economic Committee (Washington, D.C.: Government Printing Office, 1970), pp. 49–50; and Alton et al., "Economic Growth in Eastern Europe," mimeographed (New York: Research Project on National Income in East Central Europe, 1978), pp. 6–11. Western estimates for Yugoslavia from table 5. Electric power production from United Nations, *World Energy Supplies, 1951–1954* (New York: U.N., 1957), pp. 124–35. Population data from U.S., Bureau of the Census, *Statistical Abstract of the United States, 1954* (Washington, D.C.: Government Printing Office, 1954), p. 955.

[a]Calculated between terminal years by the compound interest formula.

[b]Except for Romania (1953–70) and East Germany (1953–67).

[c]Except for USSR and Yugoslavia, which are 1953–71.

[d]Gross output weights; 1954 base for 1960 and earlier, 1962 base for 1961 and later.

[e]Excludes publishing, includes fishing and logging; gross output weights; 1955 base for years to 1965, 1963 base for 1965 and later.

[f]Includes fishing and repair services; gross output weights; 1956 base for 1956–60, 1960 base for 1961–70, and 1971 base for 1971.

[g]Excludes publishing; gross output weights; 1954 base through 1960, 1960 base for 1961–67, and 1967 base for 1968 and later.

[h]Excludes publishing; includes fishing; gross output weights; 1955 base for 1955–67, 1967 base for 1968 and later.

[i]Weights are sum of wages and depreciation; 1954 base for 1949–57, 1958 base for 1958–61, 1962 base for 1962–67, and 1966 base for 1968–71.

[j]Excludes publishing; includes logging, fishing, maintenance and repair of passenger cars and household machines and appliances, repair of footwear and knitted goods, film processing, dry cleaning and dyeing, and secondary processing of nonferrous metals; gross output weights; 1963 base.

[k]For a succinct discussion of the methodology employed in these indexes, see Thad P. Alton, et al., "Statistics on East European Economic Structure and Growth," mimeographed (New York: Research Project on National Income in East Central Europe, 1975), pp. 58–60, 68–73. The growth rates were calculated from indexes formed by linking the Alton group's indexes for 1950–67 and 1965–77 at 1965.

[l]The growth rate is calculated from the Central Intelligence Agency index for civilian industrial production, whose coverage approximates that of indexes for Yugoslavia. The CIA index weights individual products by July 1, 1967 or later prices and aggregates industry branches by 1968 value-added weights.

[m]Index calculated by deducting mining and electric power production from industry and mining in the direct weights 1961 base sample index.

period beginning in the thirties is interrupted by the Second World War; thus, Soviet growth must be measured for subperiods not including the war. A production index for the Soviet Union methodologically similar to the sample indexes can be obtained from Nutter's work.[19] However, differences in coverage and weighting systems remain.[20]

Given the imperfections of the comparisons, the growth rates shown in table 15 again suggest that the rate of industrial growth in Yugoslavia during the early stages of development was of the same general order as that in the Soviet Union over roughly the same developmental stages. In both cases there was pronounced retardation of the growth rate, and the absolute magnitudes of the growth rates were so nearly the same that no definite conclusion about differences in them is warranted. Later it will be seen that Yugoslavia in fact implemented a set of industrial development policies that were, despite the institutional differences between the two countries, similar to those of the Soviet Union. For this reason, the similarity in generating industrial growth is not surprising.

TABLE 15

YUGOSLAV AND SOVIET INDUSTRIAL GROWTH RATES, SELECTED PERIODS
(Percentage)

	Average Annual Growth Rate[a]
Yugoslavia	
1952–61	
Imputed Weights[b]	11.2
Direct Weights[c]	11.9
1952–71	
Imputed Weights[b]	9.1
Direct Weights[c]	9.5
Soviet Union[d]	
1928–37	
Laspeyres	11.6
Paasche	10.1
1950–55	
Laspeyres	10.3
Paasche	7.7

SOURCES: G. Warren Nutter, *The Growth of Industrial Production in the Soviet Union* (Princeton: Princeton University Press, 1962), p. 113; and table 5.

[a]Calculated between terminal years by the compound interest formula.

[b]1952 weights and sample.

[c]1961 weights and sample. Because of differences in weight type and sample this index grows faster than the imputed weights index. The faster growth does not represent a counterexample to the Gershchenkron effect.

[d]Growth rates are calculated from Nutter's index for all civilian products.

CHAPTER FIVE

Sample versus Official Measurements

The sample indexes indicate significantly lower rates of industrial growth than the official index. Plainly, the differences in measured growth must result from differences in either coverage, weights, or means of calculation of the indexes. This chapter discusses these possible sources of discrepancies for the period 1952–71, as well as the inaccuracies in measurements of growth arising from output data.

COVERAGE

The most obvious differences between the official and sample indexes are in their coverages. The official index aims at comprehensive coverage. The sample indexes, of course, do not. They are based on output samples whose size varies with the availability of data for outputs and product weights. The data in table 5 suggest that coverage may explain the observed differences in growth rates: sample size and growth rate seem to be directly related.

However, coverage is not the only difference among the sample index variants. Types of weights, base years, and periods covered also differ and make it difficult to draw conclusions about the effect of sample size alone. For example, comparison of the 1952–71 growth rates of the 1952 imputed and 1961 direct weights indexes does not yield unambiguous implications about the effects of coverage because the base years and weight types of the two indexes are different.

Comparison of the 1961–71 growth rates generated by the 1961 imputed and 1961 direct weights indexes is more meaningful. This comparison eliminates the base year difference, leaving only differences in weight type and sample size. If the weight difference does not create systematic bias in growth rates, the comparison gives a good indication of the effect of sample size since the direct weights sample is about twice as large as the imputed weights sample. Yet the difference in growth rates between the two indexes corresponds to a difference in measured growth rate of only about one-tenth of a percentage point, or 2 percent.

The difference in weight type can be eliminated by comparing 1961–71 growth rates of imputed weight indexes with weights from different years. An experiment was performed in which the rate for this period according to the 1952 imputed weights index was compared with that according to an imputed weight index with 1961 weights. The sample using 1961 weights was about one-third larger (208 series). Besides the increase in sample size, there was also a difference in the weight base year; so the growth rates are not fully comparable.[1] This shortcoming aside, the change from the 1952 to the 1961 coverage with imputed weights resulted in an increase in the measured rate of growth from an annual average of 7.2 percent to 7.7 percent, an increase of a little under 7 percent.

These results suggest that the restricted coverage of the sample indexes was a contributing factor in the slower growth rates obtained from them. Would further expansion of the sample size raise the growth rates of the sample indexes to that of the official index? Evidence bearing on this question can be obtained from the physical growth rates of some products excluded from the 1961 direct weights index because data for calculating weights were not available. If weight data had been available to incorporate these products in the sample index, the sample size would have been increased by about 40 percent (to 460 series).[2] The average annual growth rate for the direct weights index between 1961 and 1971 was 7.4 percent; what would it have been if these products had been included?

Without data for weighting the additional series, no conclusive answer can be given. However, median physical growth rates can be ascertained for the additional series in each industry branch (see table 16). In six of the eighteen branches, the median growth rate of the unweighted products appears to be significantly greater than the sample index growth rate for that branch. In seven others, the opposite seems to be the case. In the remaining five branches, either no new series were available or the difference between the unweighted products median and the sample index growth rates was insignificant.

The analysis can be carried one step further by taking the median growth rate for products excluded from a branch to represent the growth rate for excluded products from that branch as a whole. These median growth rates can then be combined with the branch growth rates measured by the sample index by use of an appropriate weighting scheme.[3] The result is an estimate of the growth rate for industry that would have been obtained if the sample index had included the products for which weights were unavailable.

Needless to say, this result must be viewed with considerable caution. The result indicates that coverage of the sample index is adequate. If it is assumed that the omitted products should be weighted at 25 percent of the total[4] (which implies that the sample index coverage represents only three-fourths of value added in industry, surely an underestimate), then the 1961–71 average annual growth rate rises to 7.7 percent. This results in an increase in the growth rate of about 4

TABLE 16

MEDIAN GROWTH RATES OF UNWEIGHTED PRODUCTS BY INDUSTRY BRANCH, 1961–71

Industry Branch	*1961–71 Growth Rates* Median for Products in Branch (Percent per year)	As Fraction of Growth Rate Measured by 1961 Direct Weights Index[a]
Electric power production	(b)	1.00
Coal and coal products	3.22	1.99
Petroleum and petroleum products	(b)	1.00
Ferrous metallurgy	2.36	0.36
Nonferrous metallurgy[c,e]	5.26	0.88
Nonmetallic minerals products[c]	11.73	1.24
Metal products[d]	11.71	1.42
Electrical products[d]	18.41	1.53
Chemicals[c,d,e,f]	8.25	0.86
Building materials	7.71	1.02
Wood and wood products	9.31	1.84
Paper and paper products[c,e]	15.13	1.35
Textiles and textile products[c,d]	5.30	0.94
Hides and leather products	3.57	0.48
Rubber products	9.71	0.72
Food products[c,d,e]	4.01	0.60
Printing and publishing	5.06	0.57
Tobacco products	(b)	1.00

SOURCE: Data from appendix B.

[a]The ratio of the median growth rate of the products excluded from the index to the growth rate for the branch as measured by the 1961 direct weights, 1952 sample, index.

[b]No change in product coverage between the 1961 unit weights index and the 1971 physical output data.

[c]Growth rates for 1962–71 included in those from which median was derived.

[d]Growth rates for 1963–71 included in those from which median was derived.

[e]Growth rates for 1964–71 included in those from which median was derived.

[f]Growth rates for 1965–71 included in those from which median was derived.

percent, proportionally smaller than the increase noted in the earlier discussion of the 1952 and 1961 imputed weights indexes. These results indicate that the difference in product coverage for included branches between the official and sample indexes accounts for little of the difference in their rates of growth.

Branch Coverage

The shipbuilding branch was excluded altogether from the sample indexes because of the extreme heterogeneity of output, because work in progress commonly formed a relatively large share of annual production, and because output was frequently measured in terms of inputs, especially labor. If shipbuilding grew faster than the industrial average, its omission could cause part of the difference. In fact, according to the official index, shipbuilding output did grow marginally faster than the industrial average, increasing at 10.7 percent per year between 1956, when it was first recorded, and 1971.[5] However, its weight in overall industrial production was small (2.2 percent of the total in 1960 and 1.8 percent in 1970);[6] hence, its exclusion would not make a significant impact on measured rates of growth.

Treatment of New Products

The third, and probably most important, difference in coverage lies in differences in the treatment of new products. In the sample indexes, new products are introduced when the base year, and with it the product sample, changes. But this is not the only way in which new products enter the sample indexes. The definitions of the Yugoslav product nomenclature are broad enough to include products that fit the description, but nevertheless are new. The aggregated production data used to calculate the sample indexes provide no information about the extent of new product inclusion, and there seems to be no way to estimate the importance of these inclusions.

In the official index, new products are introduced more or less continuously. Not only is all production that can be squeezed into the existing nomenclature reported; each year products that correspond to expansions in the listing in the nomenclature are added to the product set. The nomenclature has expanded continuously: the number of items listed rose by a factor of nearly five between 1957 and 1972.[7] This expansion resulted partly from additional detail in the specifications of existing products and partly from the introduction of new products.

It can be shown that an index constructed by linking a series of annual relatives (the official Yugoslav method) where coverage expands between pairs of years exhibits a more rapid rate of growth than a fixed sample index whose coverage is constant if the new series added to the linked index grow more rapidly, on average, than the series covered initially.[8] If the expanded coverage were due entirely to new products and if, as is typical, the output of new products grew in their early production periods more rapidly than the average, this would imply an upward bias in the official index, compared with the sample indexes.

But the expanded coverage did not result entirely from the introduction of new products. Although there is abundant evidence that new products, at least initially, did grow much more rapidly than average,[9] the data do not permit a conclusive answer to the question of whether, over the years, new products consistently grew more rapidly than established ones. Consequently, it cannot be firmly concluded that the treatment of new products is the cause of the higher growth rates of the official index. However, it appears that it was an important factor.

It is arguable whether the Yugoslav index or the fixed weight indexes used in this study treats new products more appropriately. New products are produced output and represent an expansion of productive capacity; their exclusion means that the fixed weight indexes understate the true growth in productive capacity. There is no conclusive rebuttal to this objection since there is no fully satisfactory way to treat new products in a production index. The Yugoslav method may appeal to some because it includes new products. On the other hand, in doing so it sacrifices internal year-to-year comparability and, perhaps more importantly, comparability with the fixed weight indexes used in other countries. Whether the Yugoslav index overstates or understates the "true" growth in productive capacity cannot be known. It does appear, however, that it overstates growth in productive capacity in comparison with that of other countries when growth is measured by more conventional means.

DIFFERENCES IN BRANCH WEIGHTS

Branch weights are not employed directly in the sample indexes. The industrial growth ratio was calculated each year by aggregating branch value-added sums for that year and dividing by the corresponding base year sum. This procedure is equivalent to calculating the growth ratio as the weighted sum of the branch growth ratios, using the base year branch value-added sums as weights. Thus, another possible cause of the differences between the official and sample indexes lies in differences in branch weights.

The data in table 17 show, for 1952 and 1961, the official weights,[10] the value-added weights implied in base year branch sums, and, for comparison, branch shares in social product originating in industry and mining according to official data. All weights or shares are expressed on the basis of a total of 10,000, the convention used in the official weights.

Although there are substantial discrepancies between the official and sample branch weights and between both of them and the corresponding social product shares, it is doubtful that much of the difference between the official and sample indexes results from the branch weights. Although some relatively fast growing branches seem to be underweighted in the sample indexes, some relatively slow growing ones are underweighted in the official index. For example, to judge by social product shares, in the 1952 weight set, metal products, electrical products, and chemicals appear underweighted in the sample index (based on 1952 imputed weights), but textiles appear underweighted in the official index. Both 1952 weight sets overstate the relative importance of electric power production, but this relatively fast-growing branch is more overweighted in the sample index than the official index.

The net result of these and other differences in branch weights can be seen by

TABLE 17

OFFICIAL, VALUE-ADDED, AND SOCIAL PRODUCT WEIGHTS

	1952			1961		
	Official (1)	Value-Added (Imputed) (2)	Social Product (3)	Official (4)	Value-Added (Direct)[a] (5)	Social Product (6)
Electric power production	460	865	261	647	302	458
Coal and coal products	1,400	1,267	807	879	656	506
Petroleum and petroleum products	300	159	178	193	298	455
Ferrous metallurgy	760	672	468	514	588	516
Nonferrous metallurgy	800	884	674	478	696	472
Stone, clay, and glass	500	108	408	431	256	266
Metal products	1,400	639	1,607	1,758	1,665	1,747
Shipbuilding	0	0	117	222	0	179
Electrical products	250	110	288	433	478	522
Chemicals	440	201	404	460	492	571
Building materials	400	434	159	393	424	400
Lumber and wood products	900	608	885	825	922	682
Paper and paper products	250	89	217	140	220	236
Textiles and textile products	1,000	2,508	1,964	1,142	1,635	1,112
Hides and leather products	230	335	240	259	240	212
Rubber products	60	129	75	83	86	185
Food products	600	296	492	645	750	675
Printing and publishing	100	0	75	237	172	275
Tobacco products	150	697	678	114	122	382
Others[b]	0	0	2	29	0	148
Total[c]	10,000	10,000	10,000	10,000	10,000	10,000

SOURCES: Col. 1: SZS, *Indeks fisičkog obima industriske proizvodnje: Metodologija i ponderacioni sistem* (Belgrade: SZS, 1957), p. 10; Col. 2: Calculated from data underlying the index numbers in table 5; Col. 3: Calculated from SZS, *Statistički godišnjak FNRJ 1957* (Belgrade: SZS, 1957), p. 131; Col. 4: SZS, *Industrija 1963* (Belgrade: SZS, 1964), pp. 5–6; Col. 5: See Col. 2; Col. 6: Calculated from SZS, *Statistički godišnjak SFRJ 1963* (Belgrade: SZS, 1963), p. 111.

[a]1961 sample.

[b]Includes films, mining exploration (in national income accounts), and miscellaneous branches.

[c]Details may not add to totals because of rounding. In 1961, the official weights attributed a total of 118 to "other unclassified products." This is not included in the 10,000 total.

computing industrial growth rates using alternate branch weights. This was done by weighting branch growth rates from two versions of the sample index with alternate branch weights to produce overall growth rates for industry. The results show that differences in branch weights are not a major cause of the observed differences between sample and official indexes. On the contrary, with the exception of the direct weights index growth rates weighted by 1952 official weights, growth rates measured by the 1952 imputed weights and 1961 direct weights sample indexes either are not significantly different from or are actually higher than the rates that result from an index calculated by using either the 1952 official branch weights or the 1952 branch social product shares (see table 18).

Comparison of the 1961 weight sets cannot be summarized readily. If 1961 social product shares are taken as a reference, both sets of weights are more closely clustered around those shares in 1961 than in 1952, but significant discrepancies remain.[11] In both indexes, by this standard of comparison, some fast-growing branches are relatively overweighted and some underweighted, and the same can be said of slow-growing branches.

Repeating the experiment just described for the 1961 weight sets gives slightly different results. In this case, the use of 1961 Yugoslav social product weights produces growth rates for 1961–75 estimated as weighted averages of branch growth rates. The resulting rates are slightly higher than those estimated by the sample indexes (see table 19). On the other hand, weighting sample index branch growth rates by the official Yugoslav weights produces growth rates for industry as a whole that are essentially identical with those recorded by the sample indexes.

The use of social product shares as a reference should not be taken to suggest that the sample indexes would be improved if the sample branch growth ratios were aggregated by means of social product shares. The most important objection to using social product shares as branch weights is that the data upon which the shares are based include the turnover tax, which was eliminated from the product weights in our indexes. Turnover-tax rates varied widely among products, and their inclusion would distort social product shares based on data unadjusted for these variations.[12] It was not possible to adjust the social product

TABLE 18

AVERAGE ANNUAL GROWTH RATES FOR INDUSTRY, 1952–75, ALTERNATE BRANCH WEIGHTS

	Sample Index Branch Growth Rates	
Branch Weights	Imputed Weights Index[a]	Direct Weights Index[b]
1952 Official Weights	8.5	8.8
1952 Social Product Shares[c]	8.1	8.5
Sample Index Weights	8.7	8.4

SOURCES: Growth rates calculated as weighted average of branch growth rates obtained from the indexes shown. Branch growth rates were obtained from table 6. Weights were taken from table 17.

[a]1952 imputed weights index with 1952 product sample.

[b]1961 direct weights index with 1952 product sample.

[c]Social product is national income (Yugoslav definition) plus amortization. The shares are based on social product according to the organizational (i.e., principal activity) definition.

TABLE 19

AVERAGE ANNUAL GROWTH RATES FOR INDUSTRY, 1961–75, ALTERNATE BRANCH WEIGHTS

Branch Weights	Sample Index Growth Rates Imputed Weights Index[a]	 Direct Weights Index[a]
1961 Official Weights	7.1	7.1
1961 Social Product Shares[b]	7.6	7.5
Sample Index Weights	6.9	7.1

SOURCES: See table 18.

[a]With 1961 product sample.

[b]Social product is national income (Yugoslav definition) plus amortization. The shares are based on social product according to the organizational (i.e., principal activity) definition.

shares for turnover tax (or for other shortcomings of the social product data) on the basis of available data.

THE OFFICIAL COMPUTATION PROCEDURE

The official index is calculated by linking a series of annual growth ratios, each computed using a different set of weights. There is evidence of a strong positive correlation between the rate of growth in a branch of industry and the weight assigned to it in the index; the faster a branch grows, the more rapidly its weight grows. Intuitively, this suggests that the annual change in branch weights causes upward bias in the official index.

This correlation between branch growth rates and weights results from the way in which branch weights are derived. Roughly speaking, they are the sum of wages and depreciation in a branch expressed as a proportion of total industry wages and depreciation and therefore should be roughly correlated with branch growth rates. Empirically, the correlation turns out to be striking. Regressions between annual rates of changes in branch weights and relative annual growth rates of branches, with one exception (1966–67), consistently show a positive and usually highly significant relation.[13] The fact that branches with the highest relative growth rate receive the most rapidly growing weights suggests an upward bias in the index.

Unfortunately, this intuition cannot be proved algebraically. Even if there is a positive correlation between the growth rates of output in individual branches and the growth rates of the corresponding branch weights (which is, incidentally, the opposite of what would happen in the construction of an index with weights based on relative production costs),[14] an annually linked index may grow more or less rapidly than a fixed weight index.[15] It is easy to construct arithmetic examples in which an annually linked index grows faster than a fixed weight index and in which very large differences in values accumulate over a number of years. Thus, the positive correlation observed suggests that the method of calculating the official index causes it to increase more rapidly, but without more conclusive evidence, this must remain only a speculation.

AMBIGUITIES IN THE OUTPUT DATA

The defects, discussed in chapter 3, in the production data on which both the official and sample indexes are based raise questions about the accuracy of all indexes of Yugoslav industrial production.

The sample indexes are based entirely on production in physical units, most often weights, but also volumes, numbers, areas, or kilowatts. The official index is based almost entirely on physical units as well, but some series are estimated on the basis of hours of labor or value of output.[16] In the sample indexes, the units of measurement are particularly troublesome in metal products, where the most common measure of the output of complex machinery and equipment is the weight of the products. The sample index value-added weights are expressed in dinars per ton or kilogram; if production costs per ton or kilogram change systematically because of changes in the kinds of machinery produced and the weights are not adjusted to reflect these developments, the measurement of output could be biased.

Production costs can change for many reasons apart from changes in factor supplies or technology: machines can become more sophisticated or be produced with greater precision, both of which entail higher costs per unit of weight. There is little evidence that could form the basis for a judgment on such questions.

Another possible source of changes in production costs when those costs are expressed in terms of dinars per unit weight is change in average size of the products involved. If other factors remain the same, it is likely that costs per ton fall when the number of units per ton falls and vice versa; adding weight to a machine—given the same production technology, degree of sophistication, and precision—ordinarily would involve only using heavier materials in it, without other changes in costs. There are some data that give a rough idea of changes in sizes of machinery and equipment; these data are fragmentary, however, and generally do not cover the entire period from 1952 to 1971.

For types of machinery for which data are available, there is little suggestion that the units of measurement introduce net bias.[17] In transportation equipment, average size for most items rose. This would tend to produce an upward bias in a fixed weight index where output is measured in tons.[18] Most types of metal- and woodworking machinery also became larger in average size, as did much of the machinery used in the textile, leather, building materials, and construction industries.[19] In agricultural machinery, more individual items for which data are available decreased in average size than rose, but the quantitative significance of this is unknown.[20] The underlying data are neither complete enough nor sufficiently detailed to allow firm conclusions or to justify attempts at quantification, but there is little reason to suspect that a fixed weight index would consequently be biased downward. Even if the sophistication or quality of the machinery were systematically related to size, the fact that average size apparently changed in both directions would tend to reduce any resulting bias.

These questions may also be important in instruments and precision machinery. Unfortunately, much less information is available for these product groups. Items from them included in the sample indexes usually are measured in numbers of units.[21] In most cases for which data are available, the average unit size of these products fell; a base year weight might understate production costs in these cases.

Electrical products is another branch in which units of measurement may create bias. Again, few data are available to determine whether these units are a substantial cause of net bias. For rotating machinery, measurement is in numbers of units; the available data suggest that underweighting in a fixed weight index could result.[22] Data for most household electric appliances are less complete than those for other goods and generally pertain to shorter periods, which sometimes terminate before 1971. The available information gives no clear indication of bias in either direction.[23] There is little reason to suspect, however, that an overall bias is introduced in the electrical products branch by the units of measurement, at least on the basis of the available information.

Questions about units of measurement arise in a number of additional cases. In the timber and wood products branch, veneer, plywood, and parquet flooring are entered in the sample index in cubic meters; in each case, information about square meters per cubic meter would be useful in judging whether systematic bias is thereby introduced. The textiles branch presents many similar problems, such as the use of conventional, but undefined, units ("effective tons" for yarn and thread) and square meters for fabrics without specification of weave. The ferrous and nonferrous metallurgy branches contain similar examples (for example, steel profiles and extruded aluminum products are measured in tons). Unfortunately, data that could provide insight into the possible biases introduced by these units of measurement are not available.

CHAPTER SIX

Regional Industrial Growth

Unifying the disparate peoples of Yugoslavia has been the dominant domestic challenge of Yugoslav politics since the country's formation. It is a problem that transcends economics, but economic policy has played a major role, negatively and positively, in its history. The communist government viewed economic policy as a key element in the effort to curb the unremitting centrifugal forces of the Yugoslav polity. However, the objectives of regional economic policy often conflicted with the policy for nationwide industrialization. When that happened, regional objectives usually gave way. Yugoslav economists, especially those from the backward areas of the country, have come to question whether economic policy, taken as a whole, actually bestowed net benefits on the less developed regions.

Resolution of this issue is not one of the objectives of this study. Evidence bearing on the question is, however, a natural by-product of the measurement of industrial growth. The evidence is consistent with the views of Yugoslav economists who express disappointment wth regional economic policy, even in the narrow context of the specific objectives established in the economic plans. The failures of regional policy are discussed in more detail in chapter 10. In this chapter, sample index numbers and growth rates derived from them are presented and compared with official indexes.

Politically, Yugoslavia is a federation consisting of six republics: Serbia, Croatia, Slovenia, Bosnia-Hercegovina, Macedonia, and Montenegro. Two autonomous provinces, Vojvodina and Kosovo, lie within Serbia. There are great social and cultural differences among the regions and great disparities in economic development.

Regional economic development became a separate, explicit part of Yugoslav policy beginning with the 1957–61 Five-Year Plan.[1] Broadly speaking, the objectives were twofold. First, the pace of economic development in the less developed regions was to be raised relative to that elsewhere. Second, and partly as a result, the gap in per capita national income between these areas and the other regions was to be reduced. The policy intended to achieve these aims was based on rapid industrialization of the less developed areas.[2] Substantial transfers of investment funds from the more advanced parts of the country were to be the major vehicle for implementing this policy.

The government's specification of the regions to be considered less developed was sensitive because of the economic benefits that accompanied that designation. By and large, the designations followed political boundaries rather than lines defined by economic considerations, and generally speaking they were at the level of republics or autonomous regions rather than at more detailed levels. Designations varied in different periods, but Macedonia, Montenegro, and Kosovo were consistently designated as less developed after explicit classification began in the 1957–61 plan. Bosnia-Hercegovina was treated irregularly but was included in the less developed group more often than not.[3] Accordingly, these four areas are considered the less developed regions for the purposes of the discussion in most of this chapter.

The classification in the plans is open to criticism. For the purpose of studying industrial production, different and readily defended designations can be made. For example, if the share of national income produced in industry and mining is the criterion for classifying initial level of development, Bosnia-Hercegovina was more developed industrially in 1957 than either Serbia proper or Croatia, and Vojvodina was less so than Macedonia or Kosovo. Some tests using this alternative measure of level of development are reported later in the chapter.

Growth rates calculated from the sample production indexes indicate that the regional development program had mixed success in stimulating higher growth rates in the less developed regions during the period ending in 1971. It had even less success in reducing interregional differences in per capita growth rates because of more rapid growth of population in the less developed areas. There is little evidence of a strong relation between initial levels of industrial development and subsequent rates of growth of industrial production. What evidence there is suggests that more detailed study may reveal the expected inverse relation, but no statistically significant relation has yet been found.

More importantly, there is little evidence that output of crude materials grew much faster in the less developed regions. This result contradicts the assertions of Yugoslav economists that production of manufactured goods was relatively neglected in the less developed regions.

These conclusions are based on measurements made according to the sample indexes, but similar patterns of growth rates are observed in the official index. Generally, the sample index implies slower growth rates than the official index. The most important discrepancies between the indexes concern Kosovo and Bosnia-Hercegovina. The official index implies a considerably higher growth rate for Kosovo than the sample index; the sample index a higher rate for Bosnia-Hercegovina.

REGIONAL GROWTH IN INDUSTRIAL PRODUCTION

Separate output data for Kosovo, Vojvodina, and Serbia proper are not available before 1956. Up to 1956, therefore, only the growth of industrial production in the less developed republics—Macedonia, Montenegro, and Bosnia-Hercegovina—can be measured separately by the sample indexes. In any event, the most interesting period for regional growth begins when regional policy became explicit in 1957. The indexes in this chapter include a measurement of growth in the republics[4] beginning in 1952 and a separate index with a 1957 base for the six separate republics and the two autonomous provinces. This second index has a somewhat different sample than the indexes reported in chapter 4 and therefore is not fully comparable with them. The index numbers for the republics shown in table 20 were calculated by linking the 1957-based and the 1952-based indexes at 1957. Growth rates calculated from these index numbers are presented in table 21.

For 1952–71, the less developed republics (ignoring the autonomous provinces) grew more rapidly than the others. Montenegro, Macedonia, and Bosnia-Hercegovina, in that order, were the fastest growing republics; Slovenia, Croatia, and Serbia (the aggregate) were the slowest. Superficially, this result coincides with the objectives of the regional policy.

But closer examination raises doubts about the policy's efficacy. First, ordering the republics by growth rates produces a ranking roughly inversely correlated to initial level of industrial development. This raises the possibility that the high growth rates of the initially relatively underdeveloped areas may reflect the small industrial bases from which they started. This possibility is examined more closely later in the chapter. Second, regional policy was not explicit until 1957; thus conclusions about its success or failure should be based on developments after 1957.

The data in the last three columns of table 21 bear on this question. With these data, analysis of the Serbian conglomerate on the basis of its constituents—Serbia proper, Kosovo, and Vojvodina—is possible. Here the results according to the sample indexes are less conclusive and less favorable to the regional development program. For 1957–71, two republics consistently classified as less developed, Macedonia and Montenegro, had the highest rates of growth observed. But Bosnia-Hercegovina grew less rapidly than Serbia proper and at about only the same rate as Vojvodina. Neither Serbia proper nor Vojvodina was designated as less developed. Industrial output in Kosovo, according to the sample indexes, grew more slowly than any of the other areas of Yugoslavia for this whole period. Despite its having been industrially the most backward part of the country at the initiation of the regional policy, its growth rate was lower than those of Croatia and Slovenia, the most advanced republics.

TABLE 20

INDEXES OF INDUSTRIAL PRODUCTION:
REGIONS OF YUGOSLAVIA, 1952–71[a]

	Region								
Year	Serbia (Total)	Serbia Proper[b]	Kosovo[b]	Vojvodina[b]	Croatia	Slovenia	Bosnia-Hercegovina	Macedonia	Montenegro
1952	100.0	–	–	–	100.0	100.0	100.0	100.0	100.0
1953	108.1	–	–	–	109.4	111.2	109.5	104.0	96.3
1954	120.8	–	–	–	124.4	124.3	125.7	141.8	103.6
1955	137.7	–	–	–	140.5	142.0	158.6	163.4	125.7
1956	147.6	–	–	–	148.2	151.2	186.3	190.5	146.8
1957	186.8	100.0	100.0	100.0	170.6	170.9	214.5	219.3	170.1
1958	211.9	115.5	96.7	110.5	183.2	180.7	242.3	289.6	218.6
1959	236.3	130.7	103.3	128.9	205.9	204.4	278.4	303.7	251.5
1960	271.5	149.0	122.6	153.4	237.1	234.9	314.9	340.0	366.1
1961	285.5	160.3	102.6	162.4	254.1	250.4	340.4	362.0	466.9
1962	321.2	179.0	125.7	181.3	274.8	266.2	361.5	394.3	537.5
1963	379.7	209.6	146.4	220.0	304.1	288.1	415.7	461.6	690.9
1964	448.5	250.5	159.4	263.6	347.8	322.6	480.0	533.9	875.1
1965	475.3	262.5	174.2	287.5	369.9	331.4	522.3	599.4	932.9
1966	494.5	271.1	183.7	304.6	387.3	331.9	530.3	642.7	974.1
1967	476.2	264.6	183.6	285.8	377.7	331.4	523.4	646.5	980.9
1968	479.3	270.9	186.2	273.2	394.1	359.2	546.2	726.4	1,095.9
1969	529.9	300.8	200.9	298.2	421.1	401.3	583.1	775.1	1,268.2
1970	552.2	317.2	218.9	299.8	437.1	434.4	622.5	833.7	1,314.8
1971	610.7	348.9	233.5	328.8	475.5	451.9	693.5	908.7	1,213.0

SOURCES: Calculated from same sources as for table 5; see appendixes A and B.

[a]Direct weights index, 1952 samples.

[b]Data are separately available for most series for Serbia proper, Kosovo, and Vojvodina beginning only in 1956. The indexes are started at 1957 to coincide with the first year of the Second Five-Year Plan.

The results for 1961–71 cast a slightly more favorable light on regional policy. For this period, Montenegro, Macedonia, and Kosovo had the highest rates of growth. Growth in Bosnia-Hercegovina was slower, and it ranked behind Vojvodina and Serbia proper as well as the first three. However, during the 1961–65 Five-Year Plan only certain parts of Bosnia-Hercegovina were designated as less developed and hence eligible for the investment fund transfers that were the main part of the program. Thus, the relatively slow growth of Bosnia-Hercegovina during this period could be dismissed as evidence of weakness in the policy because the policy was not directed toward this region.

During the last subperiod shown in table 21, there is little to differentiate the less developed from the more developed regions. Of the less developed regions, Macedonia emerged as the fastest growing of all parts of Yugoslavia. But the second most rapidly growing area was Slovenia. Compared with 1961–71, the growth rate in Kosovo during 1966–71 fell very sharply, and output grew more slowly there than in Serbia proper or Bosnia-Hercegovina, both more developed at the outset than Kosovo. If these results are considered together, there is little evidence even at this aggregate level of analysis that regional policy was highly effective.

TABLE 21

AVERAGE ANNUAL GROWTH RATES OF INDUSTRIAL PRODUCTION: REGIONS OF YUGOSLAVIA, SELECTED PERIODS[a]
(Percentage)

Region	Period				
	1952–71	1952–57	1957–71	1961–71	1966–71
Yugoslavia	9.5	12.6	8.4	7.4	5.1
Less developed areas					
Macedonia	12.3	17.0	10.7	9.6	7.2
Montenegro	14.0	11.2	15.1	10.0	4.5
Bosnia-Hercegovina	10.7	16.5	8.7	7.4	5.5
Kosovo	–	–	6.2	8.6	4.9
Other areas					
Serbia, total	10.0	13.3	8.8	7.9	4.3
Serbia proper	–	–	9.3	8.1	5.2
Vojvodina	–	–	8.9	7.3	1.5
Croatia	8.6	11.3	7.6	6.5	4.2
Slovenia	8.3	11.3	7.2	6.1	6.4

SOURCES: For Yugoslavia, calculated from the direct weights index, table 5. Others calculated from table 20.
[a]Calculated between terminal years by the compound interest formula.

GROWTH OF PER CAPITA OUTPUT

The objectives of regional development policy extended beyond simply achieving higher growth rates in the areas designated less developed. Besides accelerating economic development in the backward regions, the policy was intended to reduce differences in developmental levels between them and the rest of the country.[5] Since one of the indicators of the level of development was national income per person,[6] evaluation of the policy must include measurement of per capita growth rates.

For this purpose, regional industrial growth rates were adjusted by means of estimates of population growth rates. The results (table 22) show that the differences in aggregate industrial production growth rates between the less developed and the other regions virtually disappear when population growth is considered. Population grew at annual rates of less than 1 percent during 1957–71 in the areas not designated as less developed. In contrast, it rose at significantly higher rates in the less developed republics, reaching more than 2 percent per year in Kosovo.[7] Adjustment to per capita growth rates has little effect on area rankings; per capita industrial output grew somewhat more rapidly, on the whole, in the less developed areas. The main exception was Kosovo, whose extremely high rate of population growth pushed it further down in the rankings.

But the differences are small. Regional development policy was based on rapid industrialization of the less developed areas. The failure to accelerate per capita industrial output growth in these areas relative to the rest of the country doomed the objective of reducing gaps in per capita national income.

INITIAL STAGE OF DEVELOPMENT AND GROWTH

Interregional differences in growth rates could have been the result of different levels of development at the beginning of the period. Small industrial bases often are associated with rapid measured rates of growth; high growth rates in the early stages of industrialization may reflect economies of scale or initially increasing returns to capital (in the aggregate). The sheer arithmetic of the growth calculations also favors units with small bases.

Under different conditions, light could be cast on the reasons for observed interregional growth rate differences by estimating aggregate production functions for the republics and provinces. However, the regions of Yugoslavia are too closely knit in the national economy to make the estimation of separate aggregate production functions sensible.[8] Furthermore, in view of the quality of the data at the regional level, it is hard to justify the use of highly sophisticated estimation techniques. However, two kinds of less sophisticated evidence are relevant to

TABLE 22

ESTIMATED ANNUAL AVERAGE RATES OF GROWTH:
OVERALL AND PER CAPITA INDUSTRIAL PRODUCTION
(Percentage)

Region	*Period and Measure*					
	1957–71		1961–71		1966–71	
	Overall[a]	Per Capita[b]	Overall[a]	Per Capita[b]	Overall[a]	Per Capita[b]
Yugoslavia[c]	8.4	7.3	7.1	6.1	4.8	3.9
Less developed areas, total	9.1	7.5	7.9	6.3	5.6	4.1
Other areas, total	8.2	7.4	6.9	6.2	4.6	4.0
Less developed areas						
Macedonia	10.8	9.4	9.6	8.0	7.2	5.6
Montenegro	15.0	13.8	10.0	8.9	4.5	3.5
Bosnia-Hercegovina	8.8	7.4	7.2	5.9	5.4	4.2
Kosovo	6.2	3.6	8.6	6.0	4.9	2.3
Other areas						
Serbia proper	9.3	8.5	8.1	7.2	5.2	4.4
Vojvodina	8.9	8.2	7.3	6.8	1.5	1.1
Croatia	7.6	7.0	6.4	5.8	4.1	3.6
Slovenia	7.2	6.4	5.9	5.1	5.9	5.2

SOURCES: Average annual growth rates of industrial production from data underlying table 20. Population growth rates from SZS, *Demografska statistika 1971* (Belgrade: SZS, 1974), pp. 30–32.

[a]Calculated between terminal years by the compound interest formula.

[b]The overall rate reduced by the average annual growth of the population, calculated between terminal years from estimated annual average populations by the compound interest formula.

[c]Growth rates for Yugoslavia in this table are not fully comparable to those in earlier tables because of differences in sample.

this question: retardation of growth and the correlation of growth rates with initial stages of development.

Was there a sharper retardation in growth rates in the less developed regions? Retardation was general throughout Yugoslavia; in every region, the 1966–71 growth rate was smaller than that for 1957–71 (see table 21). Retardation was also steady; all regions except Kosovo show a smaller rate of growth for 1961–71 than for 1957–71, and all except Slovenia had slower growth rates in 1966–71 than in 1961–71.[9] The regional pattern is broadly consistent with the general, steady retardation in industrial growth rates experienced in Yugoslavia as a whole.

However, declines in growth rates do not appear to be strongly related to overall growth rates. The difference between the 1957–71 and 1966–71 growth rates expressed as a ratio of the 1957–71 growth rate can be used as one measure of the degree of retardation; the larger the ratio, the greater the degree of retardation. According to this measure (calculated from table 22), there is no evidence that growth retarded more sharply in the less developed regions. For example, the proportional declines in growth rates in both Serbia proper and Croatia exceeded those in Macedonia, Bosnia-Hercegovina, and Kosovo.[10]

To test for correlation of growth rates and initial development levels, a measure of the initial level of industrialization is needed. The ratio of national income produced in industry and mining to total national income produced in each region in 1957 is an intuitively appealing possibility. But there is a difficulty with this measure. Yugoslav national income accounting procedures generally cause this ratio to be higher than it would be if Western methods were used. More to the point here, the procedures may cause systematic interregional bias.

The overstatement of the share of industry and mining arises because "nonproductive" activities—education, government, personal services, etc.—are not directly accounted for in national income. If, as is typically the case, the share of these services in national income (Western definition) were to rise as economic development proceeds, the share of industrial production (along with other "productive" sectors) as measured in the Yugoslav national income accounts would rise faster than it would in Western-style accounts because the services are, in effect, included with the productive sectors. If the same relation between national income level and share of nonproductive services also held across republics and provinces in Yugoslavia, the share of industry and mining in the advanced areas would be overstated relative to the backward regions. No attempt has been made to determine whether such a relation exists in Yugoslavia, but the data for share of industry and mining in national income should be viewed with this possible bias in mind.

Figure 2 is a scatter diagram for the republics and autonomous provinces showing proportional retardation in growth rates and the proportion of national income originating in industry and mining in 1957. The visual impression of a

FIGURE 2

GROWTH RATE RETARDATION
AND INITIAL LEVEL OF INDUSTRIALIZATION

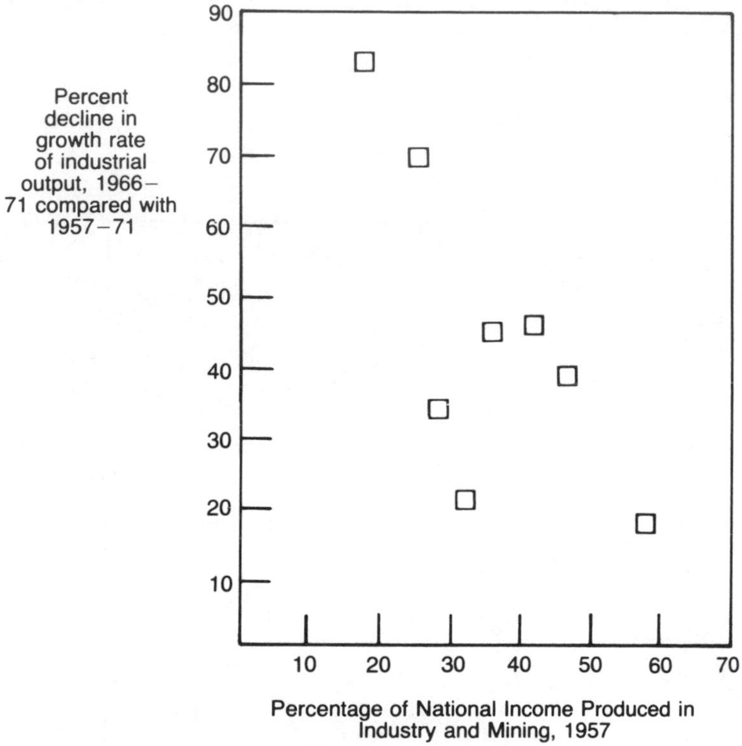

SOURCES: Table 22, and SZS, *Statistički godišnjak FNRJ 1959* (Belgrade: SZS, 1959), p. 331.

negative correlation that is consistent with a negative relation between initial degree of industrialization and subsequent growth rate retardation is only weakly confirmed by simple linear regression of the two variables. In such a regression, the coefficient had the expected negative sign, but was not statistically significant.[11] If the possible bias in the independent variable is taken into account, the apparent relation becomes weaker still. The evidence suggests, but does not conclusively prove, that rate of growth and initial level of industrialization were negatively related during the period studied.

Rather than a correlation between initial industrialization level and growth retardation, a direct relation between initial development and later industrial growth rates can be explored. Using the same measure of initial industrialization, a test of this relation also leads to equivocal results. The inconclusive—although still suggestive—visual impression given by the scatter diagram of figure 3 is consistent with a regression of the growth rates for 1957–71 on the 1957 shares of national income produced in industry and mining. Once again, although the relevant coefficient was negative, it was not statistically significant.[12]

FIGURE 3

INITIAL LEVEL OF INDUSTRIALIZATION AND GROWTH RATE

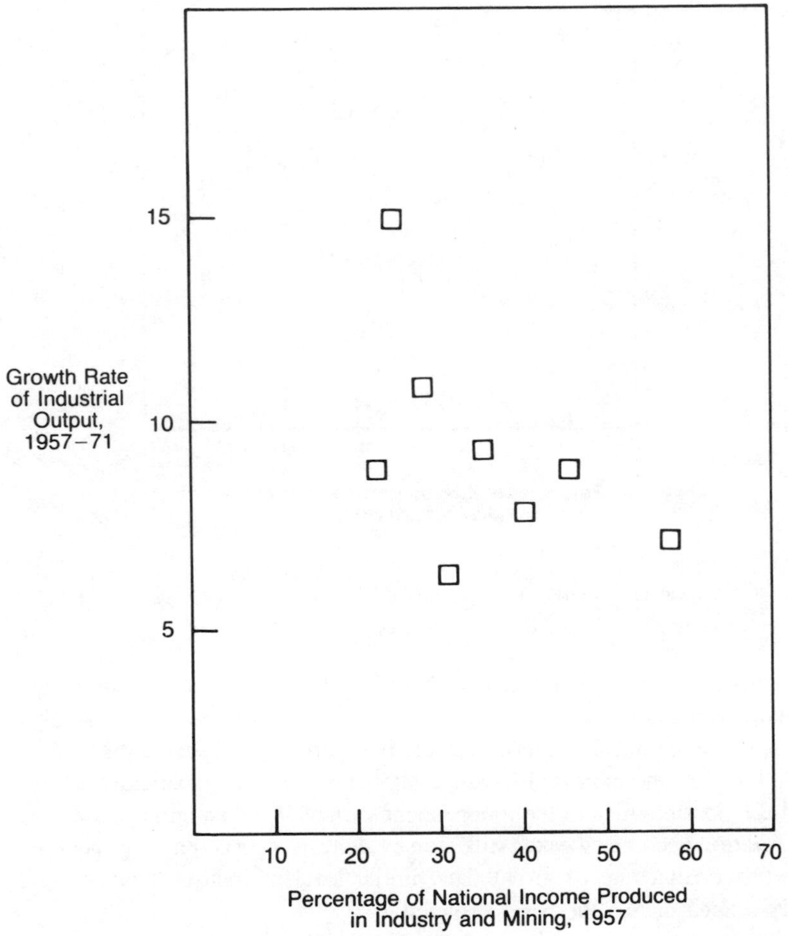

SOURCES: See figure 2.

GROWTH OF RAW MATERIALS AND MANUFACTURED GOODS OUTPUT

Dissatisfaction with the nature and results of regional development policy provoked a lengthy and elaborate effort by Yugoslav economists to diagnose the causes of the perceived failure of the policy. Major aspects of that discussion are summarized in chapter 10. One important point in the debate was the assertion that industrial development in the relatively backward area (as defined in the plans) was slower than it would otherwise have been because the policy emphasized the wrong kinds of output. Specifically, it was argued that the policy overemphasized production of primary goods, including the output of the extractive industries, the production of energy and raw materials, and the development of transportation.[13] Whether investment policy favored these lines of production is discussed in chapter 10. It is shown here that, at least as far as industrial output data are concerned, this criticism has little merit. (Because of limitations on the scope of measurement in this study, the question of the development of transportation services is omitted.)

If there were excessive emphasis on the production of energy, raw materials, and other primary goods in the less developed regions, one would expect to see relatively higher growth rates of those products in the backward areas. In particular, these products should grow more rapidly relative to manufactured goods output in the less developed areas than elsewhere. Quite apart from the general drawbacks of the official industrial production indexes, they cannot be used to investigate this question. The official index is subdivided in a number of ways, but none is fully suitable for this purpose, and none of the subindexes is readily available at the republic or autonomous province level.[14] Accordingly, a set of special indexes was calculated for crude materials and for manufactured goods.

The first index is intended to measure the production of crude materials and energy in the republics and autonomous provinces, beginning in 1957. A sample of products was chosen to represent the types of goods supposedly overemphasized in the less developed areas. This sample included products from twelve of the eighteen industrial branches.[15] From the twelve branches, crude products—those with low degrees of fabrication, ores, and the like—were selected for the new index. For example, quartz sand and crude fireclay (among others) were selected from the nonmetallic minerals branch; sawn timbers from the timber and wood products branch; and yarns and fibers from textiles. The outputs of electric power and other energy sources were also included.[16] Outputs for these products in the reference years of 1957, 1961, 1966, and 1971 were weighted by 1961 direct weights to provide index values for the output of crude materials.

Manufactured goods were defined as the residual resulting from excluding crude materials, as defined here, from total industrial output. The index for manufactured goods was calculated by subtracting the weighted output of crude

TABLE 23

AVERAGE ANNUAL GROWTH RATES OF CRUDE MATERIALS AND MANUFACTURED GOODS: REGIONS OF YUGOSLAVIA, 1957–71[a]

(Percentage)

Region	1957–71		1961–71		1966–71	
	Crude Materials[b]	Manufactured Goods[c]	Crude Materials[b]	Manufactured Goods[c]	Crude Materials[b]	Manufactured Goods[c]
Less Developed Areas						
Macedonia	7.1	10.9	7.4	9.7	4.2	7.3
Montenegro	10.2	21.1	8.0	11.5	2.2	6.0
Bosnia-Hercegovina	6.4	10.3	5.0	8.4	4.0	6.1
Kosovo	6.7	5.1	11.4	3.5	5.8	2.6
Total	6.8	10.8	6.7	9.4	4.3	7.0
Other Areas						
Serbia proper	6.6	10.1	6.1	8.6	5.2	5.2
Vojvodina	5.9	10.4	5.6	8.0	−0.3	2.3
Croatia	6.1	8.2	4.8	6.9	2.3	4.7
Slovenia	2.6	8.6	1.5	7.0	0.4	7.2
Total	5.3	9.1	4.5	7.6	2.3	5.2

SOURCES: Calculated from data underlying table 20.

[a]Calculated between benchmark years by the compound interest formula.

[b]Includes electric power, mining of crude ores, timber cutting, yarns, leather, and other crude materials. See appendix D for full listing.

[c]Products included in sample index for region but not in raw materials.

materials from the weighted output of all industrial products and converting the result into an index.[17]

The results of these calculations, presented in table 23, provide little support for the critics of the regional program. Superficially, it appears that crude materials production grew slightly more rapidly relative to the output of manufactured goods in the less developed areas. In 1957–71, for example, the ratio of the growth rate for crude materials to that for manufactured goods in the less developed regions as a whole was 0.63; the same ratio for the developed regions was 0.58. Kosovo provides the most extreme example of relatively rapid growth in the output of crude materials; it is the only region in which production of raw materials grew faster than the production of manufactured goods.

But the aggregate ratios for the regions are misleading because of the heavy influence of extreme values. The very low growth rate of crude materials production in Slovenia, for example, exerts a strong influence on the relatively advanced group of regions. Croatia and Serbia proper both have, for 1957–71, higher ratios of crude materials to manufactured goods growth rates than either Montenegro or Bosnia-Hercegovina, and both of the latter have higher ratios than Vojvodina. Thus, closer examination of the relative growth rate reveals little correspondence between classification as a less developed region and relatively rapid growth in output of crude materials.

This, of course, does not vindicate regional policy; manufactured goods output might have risen more rapidly than it did had the investment policy been different. But these measurements show, not unexpectedly, that relatively rapid growth in crude materials output is not incompatible with advanced levels of industrialization and continued rapid growth in output of manufactured goods.

COMPARISON WITH THE OFFICIAL INDEX

Agreement between the sample and official indexes is less than complete, as the data collected in table 24 reveal. The differences notwithstanding, there are substantial areas of consistency between the two indexes. The sample index usually shows lower growth rates than the official index. Both the sample and official indexes show steady and generally uniform retardation in growth rates for all regions of the country, except for the previously noted cases of Kosovo and Slovenia. According to both indexes, the rate of growth of industrial production in Macedonia was at or near the top of the set of growth rates throughout the period, and that of Montenegro, after being near the top in 1957–71 and 1961–71, fell off sharply in 1966–71. According to both indexes, growth in Croatia and Slovenia, although rapid in absolute terms, was slow relative to growth in other regions—except for the pace of growth in Slovenia in the last subperiod. On all these points regarding the pattern of growth, there is close agreement between the sample and official indexes.

TABLE 24

AVERAGE ANNUAL GROWTH RATES BY REGION:
OFFICIAL AND SAMPLE INDEXES[a]
(Percentage)

Region	*1957–71* Sample	*1957–71* Official	*1961–71* Sample	*1961–71* Official	*1966–71* Sample	*1966–71* Official
Montenegro	15.1	15.9	10.0	11.4	4.5	4.9
Macedonia	10.7	14.0	9.6	13.6	7.2	12.7
Serbia proper	9.3	10.1	8.1	8.6	5.2	7.8
Vojvodina	8.9	9.6	7.3	8.8	1.5	6.4
Bosnia-Hercegovina	8.7	8.5	7.4	7.3	5.5	5.4
Croatia	7.6	9.0	6.5	8.5	4.2	6.7
Slovenia	7.2	8.7	6.1	8.3	6.4	8.4
Kosovo	6.2	11.6	8.6	13.1	4.9	8.4

Period and Index

SOURCES: Growth rates according to the official index calculated from SZS, *Industrija 1973* (Belgrade: SZS, 1974), p. 11. Sample index growth rates from table 21.

[a]Calculated between terminal years by the compound interest formula.

The most important differences concern the growth rates for Bosnia-Hercegovina and Kosovo. Bosnia-Hercegovina is the only case in which the sample index shows a higher rate of growth than the official index; one result is that it ranks higher among the regions according to the sample index than according to the official one. The reasons for the lower rate recorded by the official index must lie in the growth rates of individual items or branches of industry and in the weights assigned to them. The official index implies growth rates that are low relative to the sample index in electric power, ferrous metallurgy, metal products, chemicals, and textiles.[18] It is difficult to understand why the official index shows such a low growth rate for electric power (slightly less than 6 percent per year, 1957–71); its principal components, hydroelectric and thermoelectric power, grew in physical terms at annual rates of 11.7 and 14.9 percent, respectively, over the period.[19] In the other branches, not enough is known about the coverage of the official index to make meaningful comparisons with the sample index. The cause of the differences, then, remains clouded.

In the case of Kosovo, the patterns exhibited by the growth rates of the sample and official indexes are much the same, but the discrepancies in the absolute values of the growth rates are larger than in any other region. (The growth rate for 1961–71 reflects, in part, the fact that output in 1961 was so unusually small that the base value for the calculation is artifically low; see table 20.) The discrepancies probably are due to the fact that Kosovo's industrial base was extremely small in 1957. In that year, according to official national income statistics, Kosovo produced less than 2 percent of Yugoslav industrial output (in contrast, Bosnia-Hercegovina produced about 15 percent).[20]

Data for a branch-to-branch comparison in Kosovo are separately available beginning only in 1963, limiting that comparison to the last part of the period.[21] This limited comparison suggests that small bases and possible upward bias arising from the Yugoslav index methodology (see chapter 4) are the reasons behind the discrepancies. According to the official index, the two fastest growing branches in Kosovo (1963–71) were chemicals and petroleum and petroleum products. Both of these had extremely small bases,[22] and in both the influences of new products and the weighting system would have been strong.

CHAPTER SEVEN

Changes in the Structure of Output

The growth of industrial production in Yugoslavia was accompanied by substantial change in the composition of output. Most studies of industrialization do not consider changes in output structure, but its importance in assessing growth is evident. It is especially important for Yugoslavia because of the insight it provides on the impact of economic reform on the industrial sector.

The pace of structural change varied during the period covered by this study. It was most rapid from 1952 to 1957; least rapid from 1971 to 1975; and moderately higher following the reforms of the mid-sixties. There is evidence of a tradeoff between the growth rate of output and the speed of structural change; that is, more rapid structural change seems to have been obtained at the price of reduced rates of growth.

The higher rates of structural change were associated with economic reforms, which entailed, among other things, price reforms and greater reliance on market forces. In the years after 1965, structural change was generally more important relative to sheer growth in output than it had been in earlier years. This suggests that the slowdowns in the absolute rates of growth resulted from adjustments of disequilibria caused by preexisting fixed prices and related rigidities in the economy. In fact, when structural change and absolute growth are considered simultaneously, economic performance appears steadier than is suggested by the rather violent fluctuations in growth rates. A combined index of development, based on the assumption that growth and change are parts of the same process of development, exhibits a relatively steady, but declining pattern over the whole period. The combined index moves more steadily, in particular, than either the annual growth relatives or the annual indexes of structural change in output.

Limited international comparisons taking structural change into account confirm that Yugoslavia's postwar industrialization was in line with experience in other countries, athough comparisons of this sort are difficult. Oddly enough, Japan's pace of growth and rate of change in output composition were very nearly the same as Yugoslavia's over the first twenty years studied.

STRUCTURAL CHANGE IN YUGOSLAV INDUSTRIAL OUTPUT

Structural change in Yugoslav industrial output was measured by combining a special index with the 1961 direct weights index using the 1961 sample.[1] Consequently, the samples in the output and structural change indexes were identical. Indexes were calculated for subperiods and year-to-year changes.

Table 25 presents the results for the period as a whole and for certain subperiods; table 26 records year-to-year changes. The subperiod with the most extensive structural change was the first, from 1952 to 1957, a period during which there was no five-year plan. As the data in table 26 show, the first year in this subperiod, 1952–53, had the most rapid structural change of any year in the entire period. (If the structural change index is recalculated for 1953–57, omitting 1952, its value falls substantially.) The next subperiod, 1957–61, corresponds to the first four years of the originally projected Second Five-Year Plan. Originally intended to extend through 1962, this plan was deemed to have been fulfilled in four years instead of five because of the rapid industrial growth that occurred in that time. The structural change index reveals that this rapid growth was accompanied by a relatively slow pace of structural change, the slowest of any subperiod except the last.

The next two subperiods, 1961–66 and 1966–71, correspond to the five-year plans of the reform period. Both of these plans, especially the 1966–71 plan, called for the weakening of the role of the central government relative to local plan executors, particularly the enterprises. The reforms included a shift of responsibility for investment credit allocation to the banking system in 1963–66, foreign trade reforms in 1961 and 1965, a price reform and temporary adoption

TABLE 25

GROWTH RATES AND STRUCTURAL CHANGE: YUGOSLAV INDUSTRIAL SECTOR, SELECTED PERIODS

Period	Average Annual Growth Rate, Percent[a]	Index of Structural Change[b]
1952–75	8.9	53.5
1952–57	12.6	32.2
1957–61	11.0	15.5
1961–66	9.7	16.8
1966–71	5.1	18.8
1971–75	6.2	13.6

SOURCES: Calculated from output and value-added data derived from official Yugoslav sources. See appendixes A and B.

[a]Calculated between terminal years by the compound interest formula from 1961 direct weights index.

[b]The angle whose cosine is calculated by the formula discussed in appendix E.

TABLE 26

ANNUAL GROWTH RATES AND OUTPUT STRUCTURE CHANGE:
YUGOSLAV INDUSTRIAL SECTOR

Second Year of Pair	Percent Increase in Industrial Output[a]	Index of Structural Change[b]
1953	7.6	24.0
1954	13.0	13.0
1955	15.6	14.3
1956	9.3	12.3
1957	17.6	10.1
1958	10.9	8.9
1959	12.7	7.5
1960	14.4	6.6
1961	6.3	6.4
1962	9.9	8.3
1963	14.0	7.7
1964	19.1	7.0
1965	6.2	5.3
1966	3.2	11.5
1967	-1.9	12.3
1968	4.1	8.8
1969	9.6	9.0
1970	6.0	10.6
1971	8.2	6.6
1972	5.5	12.3
1973	4.4	7.2
1974	10.2	7.0
1975	4.9	6.4

SOURCES: See table 25.

[a]Calculated from 1961 direct weights index with the 1961 sample.

[b]The angle whose cosine is calculated by the formula discussed in appendix E.

of freely fluctuating prices in 1965, and a reduction in taxes on enterprises (which led to their having a greater share of their net income to disburse as wages or retain for investment) in 1964–65.[2]

The immediate impact of the reforms during the first year or so of each of the respective five-year subperiods was to strengthen market forces, previously held in check by a variety of regulatory constraints. In fact, the 1961–65 Five-Year Plan was abrogated after its first year of operation, and for the remainder of the period only annual plans were issued. Similarly, there were important reversals of the reforms of the 1966–70 Five-Year Plan after its second year of operation; a general freeze was imposed on the newly freed prices in 1968, and the shares of income left at the disposal of enterprises retreated after reaching a peak in 1967.

Structural change in both of these subperiods proceeded at higher rates than in the 1957–61 Five-Year Plan; furthermore, change in the early parts of both subperiods was generally greater than that later on, as the data in table 26 indicate. Although it was not linear, there seems to have been an inverse relation between growth rates and structural change over these groupings of years. In the 1966–71 subperiod, whose beginning was marked by a sudden and unprecedented relaxation of central control, very rapid structural change occurred throughout the six years. Growth rates in this period were relatively low. In the 1961–66 period, structural change was less rapid, and growth rates higher.

After 1971, the central government reasserted its authority, and reversed much of the decentralization that had taken place during the preceding decade. The last four years of the period studied were characterized by less rapid change in the composition of industrial output than had occurred during the reform years and by a moderate increase in the rate of growth of output.

Structural Change and the Rate of Growth

The importance of structural change relative to growth in capacity to produce the base year commodity bundle can be represented by a composite measure denoted as ρ.[3] The larger ρ is, the more important structural change relative to growth in the base year capacity. Movement of this measure underlines the apparent inverse relation between structural change and growth rate, as shown in figure 4.

FIGURE 4

STRUCTURAL COMPONENT OF ANNUAL TOTAL CHANGE IN OUTPUT, 1952–75[a]

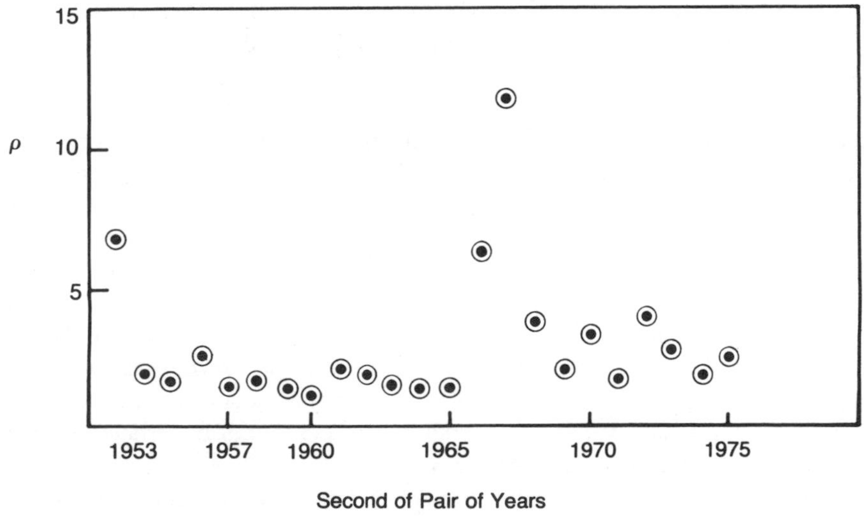

[a]See appendix E for definition and description of ρ.

The first year of the self-management period, 1952, was, it is plain, a year of important structural change, probably as a result of the initiation of the new industrialization drive. Up to the beginning of the 1957–61 Five-Year Plan, structural change diminished in importance and, as can be seen, was relatively unimportant during that five-year plan. With the beginning of the next five-year plan in 1961, there was a temporary upswing in the relative importance of structural change; at the same time, there was a corresponding temporary setback in growth rates. The reason for the more rapid structural change is not entirely clear, but one hypothesis is that the reforms adopted at that time partially released previously restrained market forces, causing restructuring of the output mix. However, the reforms in this direction were short-lived, and so was the greater relative importance of structural change.

The more extensive reforms of the mid-sixties followed, reaching their peak intensity around the time of the inauguration of the 1966–70 Five-Year Plan. As noted, the reforms included in this plan and other concurrent legal changes had the effect of increasing the importance of market forces relative to administrative restrictions for the allocation of resources. These resulted in a large increase in the rate of structural change and a corresponding or, at least, simultaneous decline in the rate of growth of output, as measured by a Laspeyres index. In the years after 1971, the adjustment process seems to have continued, as the relative importance of structural change remained high. The erratic behavior of the index shown in figure 4 during this part of the period is intuitively consistent with a continuing adjustment, suggesting that industrial sector disequilibrium prior to 1965 was extensive.

This suggests that prior to the reforms, as was true prior to the adoption of the 1957–61 Five-Year Plan, there was substantial disequilibrium in the industrial sector, the result of years of price, foreign exchange, and output controls. It appears that readjustment of output composition was the cause of the sharp reductions in growth rates experienced at this time. This interpretation is superficially consistent with the view commonly held in Yugoslavia that the reforms caused the slowdown.

However, this view may be misinformed. To see why, a measure of the combined effects of output growth and structural change (denoted here as γ) is useful. In the process of economic development, change in the structure of output—which is not costless—and growth in output may be considered alternate uses of resources, resources that can either be used to increase the rates of production of the existing set of products or to support changes in the structure of output. If so, this third measure can be used as an indicator of the overall performance of the system in generating economic development.

The values of γ, plotted in figure 5, suggest that the performance of the sixties was viewed by the Yugoslavs with, perhaps, more alarm than was appropriate. It is true that there was a secular decline in overall industrial development (i.e.,

FIGURE 5

ANNUAL TOTAL CHANGE IN OUTPUT, 1952–75[a]

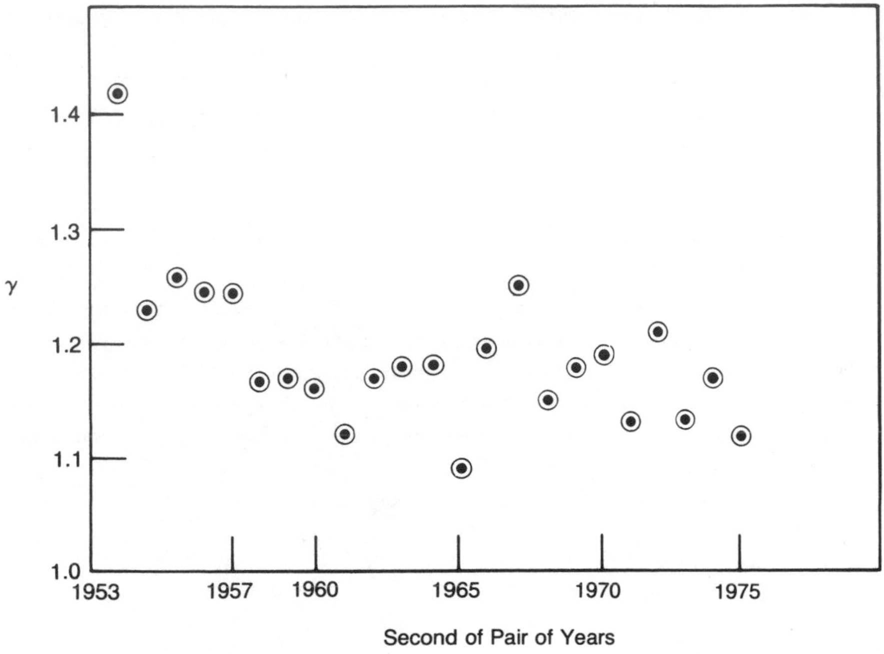

[a]See appendix E for definition and description of γ.

combined growth and structural change) over the entire period, but this can occur in any developing economy.[4] On the other hand, except for 1964–65 (which was not singled out by Yugoslavs as a particularly bad year), there was no precipitate decline in the index during the 1962–71 decade. From this point of view, what was seen by Yugoslav economists and politicians as the disastrous consequences of the reform in the first two years of the fourth plan might have been only an adjustment in the structure of output, a reaction to prior constraints that might well have been expected. Overall, performance was neither much better nor much worse than in the two preceding plan periods. The single-minded focus on measured rates of growth of output might have led to an incorrect interpretation of the situation and possibly to incorrect policy measures.

Much of what has just been said rests on the presumption that there is a trade-off between structural change and growth in capacity to produce the base year output bundle. That trade-off could exist if it were more costly than it would otherwise be to produce a given rate of measured growth in output when that growth is also accompanied by structural change. For this to be true, changing the output mix must be costly.[5] This relation is only a working hypothesis, and it can be tested with Yugoslav data for the first twenty years of the period.

A simple relation between a production index (λ) and the structural change index (θ) should not be expected. During the period, there was secular retardation in the pace of economic development, reflected by the combined measure (γ) of growth and change; since γ is proportional to the product $\lambda\theta$, retardation in γ indicates that the relation between λ and θ shifts over time. The shift could be taken into account by a variety of specifications; one reasonable specification that allows for a shift is $\lambda\theta^{\beta_1} = e^{-(\beta_0+\beta_2 t)}$, or

$$\log \lambda = -\beta_0 - \beta_1 \log \theta - \beta_2 t$$

This specification of the relation between λ and θ is inadequate for Yugoslavia because of the existence of business cycles. Yugoslav economists were among the first in communist countries to recognize, date, and try to measure cycles in economic activity.[6] To account for cyclical swings, two dummy variables were included in the test equation, taking values of unity in those years in which, according to Horvat's dating, cyclical extremes occurred.[7]

The regression results were as follows (equation [1]):

$$(1)\ \log \lambda = 0.24 - \underset{(3.85)}{0.045} \log \theta - \underset{(9.68)}{0.0048t} - \underset{(1.29)}{0.020T} + \underset{(5.69)}{0.045P}$$

In this equation, λ, θ, and t are defined as indicated in the preceding paragraph, and P and T are dummy variables for peak and trough years. All variables have the expected signs, and all except the dummy variable for troughs are significantly different from zero at the 95 percent level. Approximately 67 percent of the variance in year-to-year changes is explained by the equation.[8] Thus, when secular changes in growth rates and cyclical movements in output are considered, the expected relation between growth in output and structural change emerges clearly. For this limited experience with industrialization, it appears that there is an inverse relation between growth in output and changes in the composition of output.

INTERNATIONAL COMPARISONS OF STRUCTURAL CHANGE

International comparisons of the extent of structural change must be viewed with caution. In comparing two countries, differences in the index can result from differences in base year output mix as well as differences in structural change

TABLE 27

STRUCTURAL CHANGE IN INDUSTRIAL OUTPUT:
YUGOSLAVIA AND SELECTED COUNTRIES[a]

Country	Period	Index of Structural Change	Annual Industrial Growth Rate[b] (percent per year)	Base Year Coefficient of Variation
Yugoslavia	1952–66	22.6	11.1	0.786
	1952–71	30.6	9.5	
Japan	1950–64	29.1	15.5	0.783
	1950–69	31.2	9.4	
Federal Republic of Germany	1955–69	19.0	6.1	0.940
	1955–73	24.1		
United Kingdom	1951–65	13.5	3.3	0.656
	1951–70	17.2		
United States	1950–64	13.4	4.7	0.808
	1950–69	16.9		

SOURCES: Yugoslavia: SZS, *Industrija 1971* (Belgrade: SZS, 1972), p. 10; and idem, *Privredni bilans Jugoslavije 1952–1962* (Belgrade: SZS, 1963), pp. 42–49. Japan: Bureau of Statistics, *Japan Statistical Yearbook 1971* (Tokyo: Bureau of Statistics, 1972), pp. 244–45. Germany: Statistiches Bundesamt, *Statistiches Jahrbuch für die Bundesrepublik Deutschland 1974* (Stuttgart: Statistiches Bundesamt, 1974), pp. 230–34. United Kingdom: Central Statistical Office, *Annual Abstract of Statistics, 1961* (London: Her Majesty's Stationery Office, 1961), p. 133; and idem, *Annual Abstract of Statistics, 1968* (London: Her Majesty's Stationery Office, 1971), p. 153. United States: Bureau of the Census, *Statistical Abstract of the United States, 1968* (Washington, D.C.: Government Printing Office, 1968), p. 719; and idem, *Statistical Abstract of the United States, 1971* (Washington, D.C.: Government Printing Office, 1971), pp. 686, 690–94.

[a]Based on branch indexes of industrial production weighted according to measures of net output in industry.

[b]According to official indexes, except for Yugoslavia, which is calculated from the direct weights index (table 5). Growth rates were calculated between terminal years by the compound interest formula.

over time, and unwarranted conclusions might be drawn about relative changes in the two countries. For that reason, the data presented in table 27 comparing structural change in several countries must be interpreted with caution.

Specifically, structural change in a country's output, as measured by its structural change index, will be over- or understated in comparison with a second country's as the coefficient of variation of its base year output is greater or smaller than that of the second country's base year output (see notes 13 and 14 to appendix E). Base year output mix coefficients of variation are shown in the last column of the table to facilitate interpretation of the structural change indexes.

By coincidence, the extent of variation in base-year output mix was almost exactly the same in Japan in 1950 as it was in Yugoslavia in 1952; hence, the structural change measures are almost precisely comparable.[9] A comparison of similar fourteen-year periods shows that during 1950–64 Japan had a higher growth rate than Yugoslavia in 1952–66 and, according to the index of structural change, also experienced more rapid structural change. Over longer periods

(1950–69 and 1952–71), growth rates were lower in both countries; the reduction was proportionally larger in Japan than in Yugoslavia. Over corresponding nineteen-year periods, the extent of structural change in the two countries was almost equal, as were the growth rates for the entire period.

Comparisons with the other countries shown in table 27 are less easily made because of the greater differences in base year variations of output mix. Next to Japan, the United States presents the most nearly comparable base year output variety. In comparison with Yugoslavia, the United States had a considerably smaller rate of growth of industrial output and a substantially smaller degree of structural change. This pattern of growth reflects the size and maturity of the U.S. industrial sector.

The coefficients of variation show that, in comparison with Yugoslavia, the index for West Germany overstates structural change by about 8 percent (of the index value), and the index for the United Kingdom understates its degree of change by about 1 percent.[10] West Germany, with a smaller rate of growth than Yugoslavia, also shows less structural change, and the extent of its structural change relative to Yugoslavia's is overstated by the data because of the larger variation in the composition of its base year bundle of output. The United Kingdom, with the smallest annual growth rate, shows a small degree of structural change; in this case, as noted, the change is understated relative to Yugoslavia because of the smaller variation in the vector composition of base year output.

In summary, the first 23 years of workers' self-management saw a transformation in the structure of industrial output that was rapid by world standards. To the extent that structural change is tantamount to modernization, this fact reflects the success of the industrialization policy. Of course, not all change represents desirable progress, and it is not necessarily true that structural change corresponds to modernization. Finally, the Japanese experience indicates that the Yugoslav economic system and its methods of planning and plan implementation were not unique in their power to generate growth and change.

PART THREE

Analysis and Appraisal

CHAPTER EIGHT

Industrialization Policy and Investment in Industry and Mining

The growth of Yugoslav industrial output must be attributable to a combination of expansion in the rates of use of productive factors and changes in the efficiency with which they were used.[1] Given adequate data, the importance of increases in the physical inputs could be measured. Subsequently, estimates of the importance of other factors—technical change, education of the labor force, economies of scale, etc.—could be made by the well-known residual technique. But the data are not adequate,[2] and a less sophisticated approach to analysis of the sources of growth must be used.

Factor productivity is discussed at greater length in the next chapter, and some rough estimates based on the available data are made. These estimates, together with observations of investment rates and extensive discussion of the matter by Yugoslav economists, lead to the conclusion that the very high rates of investment sustained throughout the period studied were a major factor in the rapid industrialization of Yugoslavia.

Aggregate investment rates (investment expressed as a percentage of national product) were much higher in Yugoslavia than in, for example, the United States and were remarkably stable during the first twenty years of self-management. In the industrial sector, investment rates were higher at the beginning than at the end of the period, but the earlier rates may have been abnormally high. A definite cyclical pattern is visible in investment rates, with a period of about ten years between peaks. There is, however, no apparent relation between this crude cycle and the Yugoslav business cycle. There was a clear decline in the ratio of net to gross investment in industry and mining during the twenty years studied here, a decline that may partly explain the retardation in the industrial growth rate.

Patterns of investment expenditures and capital stock growth rates were examined to see if investment policy was consistent with statements on industrialization policy in the five-year plans. Broadly speaking, investment did follow plan dictates. Energy production, particularly electric power, received high priority in investment fund allocation throughout the period. Investment policy seemed to favor more highly fabricated products; raw materials and semifabricates were relatively neglected. This policy coincided with a movement away from the "traditional" branches of Yugoslav industry to newer, more modern branches, although the coincidence was not complete.

During 1957–71, the industrial capital stocks of Montenegro, Macedonia, and Kosovo grew at rates substantially above those of the more advanced areas. Bosnia-Hercegovina's capital stock growth rate was, however, below that of the other republics and autonomous provinces, with the exception of Slovenia. This regional differential in investment rates effectively reallocated capital stocks. This may have been intentional, the result of the investment fund transfer program that formed the core of regional policy. But the less developed areas began with small capital stocks, and differential growth rates might have occurred without any explicit transfer program.

About one-third of investment finance was provided from enterprise funds, including amortization. The balance was provided by social investment funds (principally the General Investment Fund) until 1963, when this fund was abolished as part of a general banking reform. After 1963, most of the balance was provided by the commercial banks, with a smaller, but substantial, share coming from the Fund for the Accelerated Development of Underdeveloped Regions. Because of extensive mergers of commercial banks and probable central control of their activities, the reforms may have had little impact on decentralizing control of the flow of nonenterprise investment funds.

THE MAGNITUDE OF AGGREGATE INVESTMENT

Table 28 compares Yugoslav and U.S. investment rates. For a variety of reasons, it is difficult to produce fully comparable investment data and ratios of investment to other economic aggregates for these two countries, and the ratios shown in the table should be viewed only as general indicators of relative investment rates. In the two sets of U.S. estimates, government investments are not included in definition 1, but are, at least to an important degree, in definition 2. Yugoslav investment data include government investments; hence, the second U.S. definition is more nearly comparable.[3]

Yugoslav investment rates were much higher than U.S. rates, regardless of the definition used. Gross investment rates were about twice and net investment rates about three times as high as the U.S. rates. The greater disparity of net investment is due to two factors: (1) depreciation is necessarily small relative to gross investment when there is a high rate of net capital formation; and (2) depreciation is chronically understated in Yugoslavia, which makes the Yugoslav gross ratios in the table smaller and the net ratios larger than they would otherwise be.[4] If the Yugoslav trade deficit is subtracted from social product (to give an aggregate conceptually the same—except for the difference arising from Marxian accounting—as U.S. net national product), the investment ratios become even larger. Under this definition, which relates investment expenditures to domestic output, the gross ratio ranges between 29.9 percent (1966) and 41.5 percent (1963), and the net between 21.7 percent (1966) and 31.8 percent (1961). By any of these measures, Yugoslav investment rates were very high; moreover, they remained remarkably constant over the period studied here.

Sectoral Investment Rates

The constancy in aggregate investment rates, however, masks considerable variation in sectoral investment rates (see table 29). Although the ratio of total investment to total net social product was more or less constant over the twenty years, there was an apparent secular decline in the ratio for industry and mining. This appearance is somewhat deceptive, however. For gross investment, rates in the first three or four years of the period were substantially higher than in the subsequent fourteen or fifteen years, and the low ratio for 1971 may be only a fluke. For most of the period—including all of that encompassed by the five-year plans after self-management was inaugurated—the gross investment rate remained reasonably stable.

Reservations about extreme values aside, however, the evidence is consistent with a downward trend in investment rates for industry and mining. Simple regression of the gross investment rate on time for the entire twenty years indicates the existence of a long-term downward trend in the rate.[5] The same is true for net investment ratios,[6] although, as with the gross rates, the downward trend is accentuated by abnormally high rates in the early years. Furthermore, there was a marked drop in the net investment rate after 1966, evidently a one-time downward shift that resulted from a change in the amortization rules. After 1966, central determination of depreciation rates was abandoned, minimum rates laid down, and enterprises permitted to set their own rates subject to the minima.[7]

Investment rates for the economy as a whole tended to be higher than in the industry and mining sector. This relationship is displayed graphically in figure 6. The industry rate was higher until 1956, but then dropped below the rate for the entire economy and remained below it for the rest of the period. The decline in the ratio for industry and mining was reflected in a reduction in the sector's share in total investment expenditures. From a peak of 65.4 percent in 1952, the industry and mining share fell to 34.8 percent in 1957; subsequently, it fluctuated between 30 and 40 percent. The decline between 1952 and 1957

TABLE 28

TOTAL INVESTMENT AS PERCENTAGE OF NATIONAL PRODUCT: YUGOSLAVIA AND UNITED STATES

	Yugoslavia		*United States*			
			Definition 1[c]		*Definition 2*[d]	
Year	Gross Investment[a]	Net Investment[b]	Gross Investment	Net Investment	Gross Investment	Net Investment
1952	33.6	22.5	15.1	7.9		
1953	35.5	24.6	15.4	7.6		
1954	36.4	24.6	15.8	8.4		
1955	32.1	21.1	16.8	8.2		
1956	31.9	20.3	17.0	8.1		
1957	30.1	21.2	16.5	7.3		
1958	32.0	23.6	15.3	5.8		
1959	33.1	25.3	15.9	6.6		
1960	34.8	27.4	15.5	6.1	19.5	8.8
1961	37.5	29.3	14.7	5.2	18.4	7.6
1962	38.4	29.7	15.1	5.3	19.7	8.6
1963	37.7	28.7	15.1	5.3	19.6	8.5
1964	36.5	27.3	15.3	5.6	19.6	8.6

1965	29.6	21.5	15.8	6.2	20.6	9.7
1966	29.0	21.0	15.5	6.2	20.8	10.1
1967	32.1	22.2	15.0	5.4	19.4	8.4
1968	34.5	24.3	15.1	5.6	19.6	8.8
1969	34.3	24.1	15.5	5.8	19.7	8.7
1970	36.2	26.2	14.8	5.0	18.4	7.4
1971	34.7	24.9	15.3	5.6	19.0	8.0

SOURCES: Yugoslavia: Social product and amortization from SZS, *Statistički godišnjak SFRJ 1963* (Belgrade: SZS, 1963), p. 109; idem, *Statistički godišnjak SFRJ 1972* (Belgrade: SZS, 1972), p. 105; and idem, *Statistički godišnjak SFRJ 1973* (Belgrade: SZS, 1973), p. 121. Investment data from SZS, *Statistički godišnjak SFRJ 1963*, p. 114; and idem, *Statistički godišnjak SFRJ 1973*, p. 262. United States: Estimates 1 derived from net national product, amortization, and investment data in U.S., Council of Economic Advisers, *Economic Report of the President, 1975* (Washington, D.C.: Government Printing Office, 1975), pp. 264f. Estimates 2 derived from gross domestic product, gross capital formation, and capital consumption data in Organization for Economic Cooperation and Development, *National Accounts of OECD Countries, 1960–1971* (Paris: OECD, n.d.), pp. 50, 57.

[a]Gross investment (based on data originally reported by Služba društvenog knjigovodstva) divided by social product *(društveni proizvod)* less amortization, converted into percentages.

[b]Gross investment less amortization, the total divided by social product less amortization, converted into percentages.

[c]Gross private domestic investment (less capital consumption allowances, for net investment) divided by net national product, converted into percentages.

[d]Gross capital formation (corporate, government, households, and others; less capital consumption for net investment) divided by gross domestic product less capital consumption, converted into percentages. Data for 1952–59 are not available.

TABLE 29

INVESTMENT IN INDUSTRY AND MINING AS PERCENTAGE OF NATIONAL PRODUCT[a]

Year	Gross Investment[b]	Net Investment[c]	Year	Gross Investment[b]	Net Investment[c]
1952	44.4	33.5	1962	32.0	21.5
1953	44.8	33.0	1963	31.9	20.7
1954	39.3	26.9	1964	30.0	19.4
1955	33.8	21.9	1965	25.0	15.4
1956	29.4	14.5	1966	26.1	15.3
1957	24.6	14.4	1967	25.8	10.7
1958	22.0	12.2	1968	29.4	14.0
1959	23.3	14.1	1969	26.0	9.9
1960	26.6	18.1	1970	25.7	10.9
1961	31.4	21.9	1971	20.7	6.3

SOURCES: Social product and amortization data from SZS, *Statistički godišnjak SFRJ 1963* (Belgrade: SZS, 1963), p. 109; and idem, *Statistički godišnjak SFRJ 1972* (Belgrade: SZS, 1972), p. 105. Investment data from SZS, *Statistički godišnjak FRNJ 1955* (Belgrade: SZS, 1955), p. 259; idem, *Statistički godišnjak FRNJ 1956* (Belgrade: SZS, 1956), p. 249; idem, *Statistički godišnjak FRNJ 1957* (Belgrade: SZS, 1957), p. 301; idem, *Statistički godišnjak FRNJ 1958* (Belgrade: SZS, 1958), p. 216; idem, *Statistički godišnjak FRNJ 1961* (Belgrade: SZS, 1961), p. 236; idem, *Statistički godnišjak FRNJ 1962* (Belgrade: SZS, 1962), p. 228; idem, *Statistički godišnjak SFRJ 1967* (Belgrade: SZS, 1967), p. 252; idem, *Statistički godišnjak SFRJ 1968* (Belgrade: SZS, 1968), p. 253; idem, *Statistički godišnjak SFRJ 1970* (Belgrade: SZS, 1970), p. 247; idem, *Statistički godišnjak SFRJ 1971* (Belgrade: SZS 1971), p. 247; and idem, *Statistički godišnjak SFRJ 1972* (Belgrade: SZS, 1972), p. 256.

[a]Investment expenditures based on data of Služba društvenog knjigovodstva. These data are not fully comparable with the investment data collected and reported by Savezni zavod za statistiku. See chapter 8, note 3 for further explanation.

[b]Gross investment expenditure divided by social product produced in industry less amortization reported for industry, converted into percentages.

[c]Gross investment expenditure less amortization, the sum divided by social product produced in industry less amortization reported by industry, converted into percentages.

resulted largely from increases in the shares of agriculture (from 4.1 to 10.2 percent) and housing and community services (from 5.2 to 14.3 percent).[8]

Cyclical swings in investment rates appear to be visible in figure 6. The period of the cycle shown, however, bears no immediately apparent relation to the periods of the cycles in economic activity that have been studied by Yugoslav economists.[9]

Whatever the long-term trend of gross investment in industry and mining, there was—because of the relatively small initial capital stock and rapid rates of investment—a downward trend in the ratio of net to gross investment in the sector (see table 30). In contrast to the trends in gross and net investment, the downward movement in this ratio is statistically significant.[10] This reduction in the ratio of net to gross investment is one of the reasons why retardation in the

FIGURE 6

INVESTMENT EXPENDITURES AS PERCENTAGE OF NET SOCIAL PRODUCT

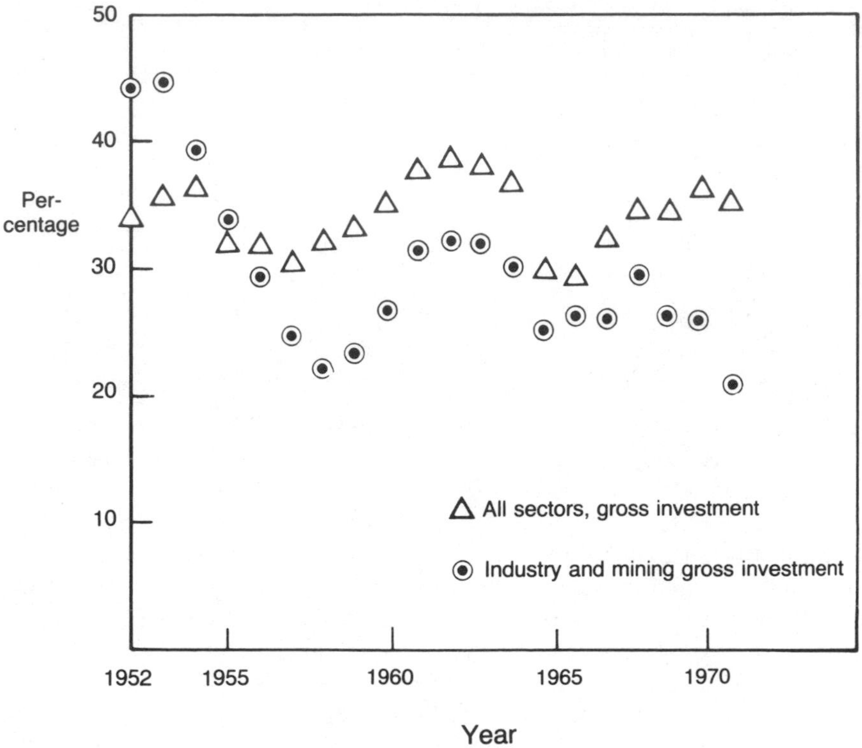

SOURCES: Tables 28 and 29.

rate of growth of the industrial output occurred. Any attempt to reverse this downward trend will more than likely encounter difficulties, and the retardation will continue.

INVESTMENT ALLOCATION IN INDUSTRY AND THE INDUSTRIALIZATION POLICY

The industrialization policy was implemented principally through allocation of investment resources. The information in the five-year plans about industrialization policy and its priorities is largely qualitative and difficult to assess.

TABLE 30

NET INVESTMENT AS A PERCENTAGE OF GROSS INVESTMENT:
INDUSTRY AND MINING, 1952–71

Year	Percentage	Year	Percentage
1952	75.6	1962	68.3
1953	73.6	1963	64.6
1954	68.4	1964	64.3
1955	64.8	1965	61.1
1956	53.8	1966	58.0
1957	58.4	1967	41.0
1958	53.4	1968	47.3
1959	59.0	1969	37.1
1960	67.2	1970	41.4
1961	68.8	1971	28.6

SOURCES: See table 29.

Moreover, the plans were not faithfully followed. In order to ascertain the policy actually carried out, it is necessary to infer investment decisions by analyzing the outcome.

This procedure presumes that the authorities had effective control over investments. Since enterprises could and did invest their own resources and were not legally required to adhere to the centrally determined plan, this presumption is only partially correct. The central authorities retained effective control of the bulk of investment resources, however, and, through a system of allocations, matching requirements, and other methods too complex to describe here, exercised considerable influence over the investment choices of enterprises. Undoubtedly there was slippage between the intentions of the authorities and the results achieved in investment allocation. But to take the position that the actual allocation was independent of their intentions is to imply that central government policy had no effect on the outcome. That is surely untenable. There is evidence (presented below), in fact, that the authorities strongly influenced investment allocation throughout the economy and, in particular, in the industrial sector.

The discussion in this section is limited to investment fund allocations and capital stock growth rates in officially defined industry branches. This is not the only dimension of economic policy, of course; investment and capital growth could also be analyzed, for example, in terms of levels of production, of groupings relevant to foreign trade considerations, or of consumer goods versus producer goods, all of which, at least partially, cut across branch lines. The plans themselves go beyond industrial branches in discussing policy. However, to reclassify investment and capital stock data on lines other than those adopted here would require the use of assumptions unwarranted by the quality of the data.

Investment Allocations as Indicators of Priorities

The allocation of investment resources provides one way—admittedly incomplete—of assessing industrialization policy. The branch distribution of investment expenditures shows the relative drain on investment resources represented by each and thus provides a rough means of appraising the priorities of the policymakers. For convenience, investment expenditures (see table 31) are grouped by years to approximate the periods of the five-year plans as well as the initial period when there was no plan. Convenience is achieved at a price, however. Yugoslav investment outlays generally are reported in nominal terms, and there is no fully satisfactory way to deflate these figures.[11] For that reason, the distributions in table 31 had to be calculated by summing nominal investment outlays by branch over the years concerned and then dividing by total nominal investment expenditures for the period. The resulting distributions are not the same as would be obtained from an appropriately deflated series of investment figures. But in the absence of the required data, the distribution based on nominal figures seems adequate for the purpose at hand.

If priorities are judged by commitment to expend investment funds, then the first priority, whether measured in terms of gross or net investment, clearly was the production of electric power. This is consistent with Tito's emphasis on electrification, noted earlier, and is reflected in the rapid growth of electric power production seen in the measurements of output growth. More broadly, four branches—electric power, ferrous metallurgy, nonferrous metallurgy, and chemicals—consistently accounted for at least 40 percent of both gross and net investment; the share of these four branches rose as high as 55 percent of gross investment (1952–56, by the calculations shown in table 31) and 78 percent of net investment (1966–71). Relatively high shares of gross investment went to metal products throughout the period, although the net investment share generally ranked lower because of relatively high amortization rates. Two important consumer goods branches, textiles and food products, also accounted for relatively large shares of investment expenditures during part of the period.

These data provide information about the rationing of available investment funds among branches and thus about willingness to commit scarce resources. They are not, however, fully satisfactory for assessing the intentions of the policymakers. Insofar as the policy is assessed at the level of the branches of industry, policy priorities could be better expressed in terms of intended relative rates of growth; the higher the priority, the faster the branch was intended to grow. From this point of view, assessing policy would require knowledge of the intended rates of growth of noncapital factors and of expected technological change in each branch; investment decisions represent only one aspect of the overall policy. Merely knowing the percentage distribution of investment funds

TABLE 31

DISTRIBUTION OF NOMINAL INVESTMENT EXPENDITURES,
SELECTED PERIODS
(Percentage of Total Investment Funds Expended)[a]

Industry Branch	Gross Investment				Net Investment			
	1952–56	1957–60	1961–65	1966–71	1952–56	1957–60	1961–65	1966–71
Electric power	23.6	24.0	20.5	24.9	30.7	24.5	23.0	39.6
Coal and coal products	8.1	10.3	5.6	4.2	7.0	9.2	2.8	1.4
Petroleum and petroleum products	3.5	3.6	4.0	3.4	2.8	2.3	2.6	–3.3
Ferrous metallurgy	16.3	4.2	11.6	12.2	20.0	2.6	14.2	19.5
Nonferrous metallurgy	8.5	7.5	5.2	9.6	8.7	7.7	3.5	11.9
Nonmetallic minerals	6.1	2.7	2.5	2.3	6.8	1.4	2.7	2.3
Metal products	6.6	8.1	10.0	7.5	2.2	5.4	9.2	0.7
Shipbuilding	0.6	1.2	0.9	1.0	–0.1	0.9	0.7	0.7
Electric products	2.4	1.8	3.2	3.0	2.5	1.3	3.5	1.3
Chemicals	7.0	6.3	8.6	7.7	7.5	6.0	9.1	7.3
Building materials	1.1	3.1	2.6	3.8	0.6	3.9	2.0	4.8
Timber and wood products	3.2	4.0	3.8	3.4	1.2	3.7	3.3	1.6
Paper and paper products	2.6	3.8	5.3	2.2	3.1	5.0	6.6	0.8
Textiles and clothing	3.9	6.5	7.2	5.1	2.2	6.7	7.2	1.1
Hides and leather products	0.5	1.4	0.9	0.9	0.2	1.6	0.8	0.8
Rubber and rubber products	0.3	0.7	0.9	0.6	0.1	0.9	1.0	0.2
Food and food products	4.8	8.7	5.2	5.8	4.1	10.2	5.5	6.6
Printing and publishing	0.6	1.1	1.4	1.8	0.2	0.8	1.4	2.1
Tobacco products	0.5	1.0	0.7	0.7	–0.0	1.2	0.8	0.7

SOURCES: See table 29.

[a]Details may not add to 100 because of rounding.

is of little use even in this limited respect because it is the relation of investment to the existing capital stock (along with the other factors) that is important in forming expectations about growth.

Capital Stock Growth Rates and Industrialization Priorities

The information necessary to assess expected growth rates along such detailed lines is not available, however. As a substitute, the growth rate of the real capital stock in each branch may be taken to indicate priorities in the actual development policy.[12] This extreme simplification is justifiable on two major grounds. First, as noted above, the Yugoslav authorities exercised control of economic policy principally through the investment channel. Control over other factors, in particular labor, was largely indirect. In the case of labor, for example, some measure of control was exercised over relative wages (early in the period) and over education and training programs. Thus, capital investment was the main direct policy instrument, and intended growth rates of capital stocks must have served an important function in promoting differential rates of growth among industry branches.

The second justification for focusing on capital stock growth rates is empirical. Experiments with a simple model of growth by industry branch, in which the influence of changes in labor employment by branch is considered,[13] produce rankings of branches by expected rates of growth that are almost identical with rankings by capital stock growth rates.[14] Thus, these growth rates appear to provide a reasonable substitute for the purpose at hand.

Table 32 shows growth rates of capital stocks by industry branch listed in order of their capital stock growth rates for the period 1957–61. The rankings in other subperiods are, it will be noted, considerably different, suggesting an unexpected volatility in priorities. Moreover, there is little correlation between the rankings in different subperiods. A large shift might have been expected between the rankings of 1952–56 and those in subsequent periods due to the adoption of the 1957–61 Five-Year Plan and the possible changes in policy it embodied. But the shift between those two periods was not much different from that between the subsequent two pairs of periods.[15]

The pattern suggests continuous change in policy, an evolution in which the adoption dates of the five-year plans have little significance. In turn, this suggests that those plans were not so much statements of important, intended changes in policy as position statements with forecasts based on the continuation of current policy and expectations about future exogenous developments. Seen from this perspective, the otherwise woeful-looking record of experience with the five-year plans takes on a different light. Economic plans with targets that are supposed to be fulfilled can be attacked with reason if targets are not met. But

TABLE 32

AVERAGE ANNUAL GROWTH RATES OF CAPITAL STOCKS BY BRANCH OF INDUSTRY, SELECTED SUBPERIODS[a]
(Percentage)

	Period			
Branch	1952–56	1957–61	1961–65	1966–71
Paper and paper products	18.3	15.3	19.2	7.9
Chemicals	11.5	13.5	14.8	9.9
Nonferrous metallurgy	14.0	10.9	6.3	6.8
Hides and leather products	5.1	10.5	9.0	8.7
Electric power	21.1	10.1	9.8	9.8
Rubber and rubber products	4.4	9.8	11.7	8.0
Ferrous metallurgy	18.1	9.7	5.3	5.6
Food and food products	0.0	9.6	10.2	5.6
Electric products	24.8	8.5	13.5	11.9
Coal and coal products	7.0	8.3	5.3	5.1
Timber and wood products	4.0	8.2	9.4	7.1
Petroleum and petroleum products	11.3	8.2	11.3	18.2
Printing and publishing	3.0	8.1	14.1	11.3
Textiles and clothing	3.8	7.4	10.6	8.2
Metal products	7.9	6.8	9.9	6.3
Tobacco products	2.8	6.2	3.7	7.3
Nonmetallic minerals	6.8	6.0	8.2	6.5
Building materials	5.8	5.4	5.7	7.0
All branches	10.4	9.0	9.3	8.3

SOURCE: Calculated from SZS, *Osnovna sredstva društvene privrede SFRJ, SR i SAP 1952–1971* (Belgrade: SZS, 1973), pp. 102–5. The data from which the calculations were made were expressed in 1966 values.

[a]Calculated between terminal years by the compound interest formula.

Yugoslav plans may have had little to do with actual policy, which was, in the event, dictated to an important degree by what was occurring in the economy as the result of developments beyond the effective control of the authorities.

There were shifts in the ranks of most branches between subperiods, but certain changes were apparently systematic. Petroleum and petroleum products had the steadiest and most clear-cut rise, beginning with the 1957–61 period; in contrast to the generally falling capital stock growth rate for industry, petroleum's growth rate steadily rose. This increasing emphasis was reflected in its high rate of growth and in the rapidly expanding production of chemicals based on petroleum products during the sixties. Although the movements were not as consistent, the priorities accorded to textiles and to printing and publishing also seem to have risen during the period.

On the other hand, there was steady deterioration in the positions of the "traditional" Yugoslav industrial branches: coal and coal products, and ferrous and nonferrous metallurgy. The declines in the output growth rates of the first two branches, noted in chapter 4, seem to have been the result of deliberate government policy. Despite occasional pronouncements in the five-year plans to the contrary, the results of the planners' actions indicate that these branches received steadily less emphasis.

The outlines of actual industrialization policy are seen in the consistently high rates of capital growth in certain branches of industry. On the whole, capital stocks grew rapidly in the electric products, chemicals, paper, and rubber products branches, as well as in that favored source of energy, electric power. One surprise, in view of its high rate of growth of output, is the relatively low position of metal products. However, the metal products branch was already well established at the outset of the period; a rather large proportion of its output is in such capital intensive products as castings, forgings, and the like, which were already in production at the beginning of the period. Machinery and equipment were the most rapidly growing products in this branch, and these are items whose production is likely to have been somewhat less capital intensive.[16] Another curious case is nonmetallic minerals, where again a relatively low rate of capital stock growth was accompanied by a relatively high output growth rate. Low capital stock growth rates were also recorded in building materials, timber and wood products, and tobacco—all "traditional" branches having relatively low rates of growth.

The outlines of industrialization policy that can be traced from the patterns shown in table 32 are consistent with the industrialization strategy sketched earlier and fit the constraints and opportunities that faced postwar Yugoslavia. There was strong emphasis on energy production, first and foremost through electric power generation. Later, petroleum and natural gas production received stronger emphasis not only as primary energy sources but also as sources of materials for the chemicals branch. The emphasis gradually shifted from production of raw materials and semifabricates—the coal and ferrous and nonferrous metallurgy branches, as well as part of the metal products branch—toward more highly fabricated products—the electric products and chemicals branches, as well as those parts of metal products in which highly fabricated goods were produced. "Traditional" branches were largely neglected in the quest to modernize the industrial sector. It seems likely, although not certain, that these other branches were less subject to central government influence in investment decisions.[17]

Capital Stock Growth Rates and "Linkages"

Do these investment allocation decisions conform to other development criteria? Some U.S. economists[18] note a correspondence in Soviet investments to the linkages first advanced by Hirschman as a means of analyzing development.[19] These authors argue that development is stimulated by investments in those branches of industry with high linkages. The theory is that this creates demand for goods produced in other branches and supplies of goods used in still other industries. For the Soviet Union, these economists have tested investment policy by comparing a ranking of industries according to Hirschman's linkages[20] with one according to share of industrial investment.[21] Finding a high correlation, the authors judge Soviet development policy to have been well informed and recommend its adoption elsewhere.

As has been seen, Yugoslav industrial production grew at rates fully consistent with its stage of development at the beginning of the self-management period, that is, at rates comparable to those achieved in the Soviet Union at similar stages of growth. In retrospect, was Yugoslav investment policy also well informed according to the linkages criterion? It is not possible to answer this question by using Hirschman's rankings of industries by linkages because his definitions of branches differ from those used in Yugoslavia. However, linkages for Yugoslav industry can be calculated from input-output data for certain years.[22] Such calculations were carried out for 1955, 1962, and 1966, and the branches ranked according to total number of linkages. This ranking was then compared with one in terms of capital stock growth rates, and rank correlation coefficients calculated. The results are presented in table 33. These data provide little or no support for the hypothesis that the relatively rapid pace of Yugoslav industrial growth was due to an investment policy that favored branches with high linkages. The results cast doubt on the importance of the linkage hypothesis in explaining economic growth in Yugoslavia and, more generally, on the value of investment policies following those lines for other countries.

TABLE 33

RANK CORRELATION COEFFICIENTS: INDUSTRY BRANCHES RANKED BY LINKAGES AND CAPITAL STOCK GROWTH RATES, SELECTED PERIODS

Year of Linkage Calculation	Period of Measurement of Capital Stock Growth Rate	Rank Correlation Coefficient
1955	1957–71	−0.048
1962	1961–65	0.155
1966	1966–71	−0.149
1966	1952–56	0.292

SOURCES: 1955 linkages calculated from SZS, *Međusobni odnosi privrednih delatnosti Jugoslavije u 1955. godini* (Belgrade: SZS, 1957), table 3–1. 1962 linkages calculated from SZS, *Međusobni odnosi privrednih delatnosti Jugoslavije u 1962. godini* (Belgrade: SZS, 1966), table 3–1. 1966 linkages calculated from SZS, *Međusobni odnosi privrednih delatnosti Jugoslavije u 1966. godine* (Belgrade: SZS, 1969), table 4–1. Capital stock growth rates calculated from SZS, *Osnovna sredstva društvene privrede SFRJ, SR i SAP 1952–1971* (Belgrade: SZS, 1973), pp. 102–5.

INVESTMENT BY REGION

The policy for accelerating economic growth in Yugoslavia's backward areas was implemented mainly through the transfer of investment funds. The purpose of the investment fund transfer program presumably was to accelerate industrial growth in the designated areas relative to the rest of the country by accelerating the relative growth rates of capital stocks in backward areas. Table 34 shows the results of this policy, beginning in 1957 when it was first explicitly articulated.

Bosnia-Hercegovina is included in the set of less developed areas even though its position in the regional development policy was ambivalent. It was not included in the group of less developed regions in the 1957–61 Five-Year Plan and only parts of it were included in the 1961–65 plan. Only in the 1966–70 plan was it included in its entirety.[23] Relative to the other regions consistently designated as less developed, it had a large industrial sector at the outset,[24] and its stock of fixed industrial capital was large relative to those of the other members of the less developed category (see table 34). Apparently, the republic owed its designation as less developed—insofar as it received it—to relatively low per capita income; in 1957, it ranked just above Macedonia and significantly below the lowest of the regions not specified as less developed (Serbia proper). Even so, per capita income produced in the industry and mining sector in 1957 was higher in Bosnia-Hercegovina than in either Serbia proper or Vojvodina.[25]

These difficulties regarding the position of Bosnia-Hercegovina must be kept in mind when interpreting the data in table 34. For example, the 1957–71 annual capital stock growth rate for the less developed areas including Bosnia-Hercegovina was 9.6 percent, only about one percentage point higher than that for the rest of the country. If Bosnia-Hercegovina is excluded, the annual growth rate for the rest of the members of the less developed group is 14.3 percent. The ambivalent position of the republic is shown by the erratic pattern of its capital stock growth rates and by the fact that the size of its industrial capital stock fell relative to capital stock in the rest of the country. Of course, the data in table 34 are at a high level of aggregation. Since only parts of the republic were eligible for development assistance in the 1961–65 period, further disaggregation might show the results of the policy more clearly as far as the affected areas were concerned, results which might be obscured in the aggregate. The same could be said, however, of those parts of Serbia (excluding Kosovo) which were, from time to time, designated as less developed.[26]

Otherwise, the results of the development policy are easy to see. Growth rates of industrial fixed capital were, during 1957–71, highest in Montenegro, Kosovo, and Macedonia; as a result, their capital stocks grew relative to the rest of the country. The other side of this coin is that growth rates of fixed capital in the

TABLE 34

GROWTH RATES AND DISTRIBUTION OF FIXED CAPITAL IN INDUSTRY AND MINING, BY REGION

Region	*Average Annual Growth Rate of Fixed Capital Stock*[a] *(percentage)*				*Distribution of Fixed Capital Stock (percentage)*			
	1957–61	1961–65	1966–71	1957–71	1957	1961	1966	1971
Less Developed Regions								
Macedonia	20.5	14.9	8.5	12.0	3.0	4.4	5.0	5.1
Montenegro	39.7	16.7	4.2	16.7	1.0	2.7	3.3	2.7
Kosovo	11.7	24.6	12.9	14.8	1.6	1.7	2.7	3.3
Bosnia-Hercegovina	7.5	9.1	8.0	7.6	19.6	18.5	17.0	16.7
Total[b]	11.4	12.0	8.2	9.6	25.1	27.4	28.0	27.8
Other Regions								
Serbia proper	11.2	11.7	9.5	9.9	20.5	22.2	22.4	23.7
Vojvodina	9.8	19.6	7.2	10.8	5.9	6.1	8.1	7.7
Croatia	7.7	10.0	8.1	7.9	26.8	25.5	24.3	24.1
Slovenia	5.2	8.9	7.7	6.8	21.7	18.8	17.2	16.7
Total[b]	8.2	11.1	8.3	8.5	74.9	72.6	72.0	72.2
Yugoslavia	9.0	11.4	8.3	8.8	100.0	100.0	100.0	100.0

SOURCE: Calculated from SZS, *Osnovna sredstva društvene privrede SFRJ, SR i SAP 1952–1971* (Belgrade: SZS, 1973), pp. 102–3, 108–9, 114–15, 120–21, 126–27, 132–33, 138–39, 144–45, 150–51, 156–57.

[a]Calculated between terminal years by the compound interest formula.

[b]Details may not add to totals because of rounding.

most developed republics—Slovenia and Croatia—were relatively low; hence, their capital stocks fell relative to that of the other regions. Would this general outcome have occurred even without the development policy, given the initial levels of development and base capital stocks and an overall economic environment conducive to growth? (The reallocations shown in table 34 might reflect substitution of centralized for local investment funds, in this interpretation.) Clearly the Yugoslav authorities did not think so, or at least they were motivated to take explicit policy steps instead of relying on spontaneous developments.

FINANCING INVESTMENT

To understand the financing of investment in Yugoslavia, it is necessary to understand the development and reforms of the investment system over the period studied. Until 1960, investment was dominated by the funds of the central General Investment Fund (GIF).[27] These funds were administered through specialized banks, notably the Yugoslav Investment Bank, which acted as agents for the allocation of credits.[28] Neither the business banks nor the specialized banks had the authority or the assets to finance investments.

The first step in reforming the banking system was taken with the Law on Banking of 1961,[29] in which the business and specialized banks were given the authority to grant investment credits. However, the banks lacked the necessary assets, and this step had little practical importance.[30]

At the end of 1963, the GIF was abolished and its funds transferred to the specialized banks, which were given the responsibility of administering the funds in accordance with the national economic plan.[31] At the same time, it was suggested that other government units holding investment assets transfer their funds to the specialized banks as well, but there was little compliance with this suggestion. Of the assets transferred from the GIF, the bulk went to the Yugoslav Investment Bank, with lesser amounts going to the Agricultural Bank and the Foreign Trade Bank.[32] This change left the specialized banks in the position previously occupied by the GIF; investment credit decisions were now dominated by the specialized banks.

The next important set of changes came in 1965 with the adoption of new laws on banking.[33] These statutes created a new relationship between the business banks of the country and the National Bank. This relationship superficially resembled that between commercial and central banks in capitalist systems, but there were important differences.

The law provided for the formation of banks by enterprises, government units, and other working organizations (but not by individuals). One proviso allowed mergers between existing banks, and an extensive merger movement resulted. The law further established the principle that the banks were to make their own investment and other credit allocation decisions. It specified that the banks were to be run like other economic organizations in the economy, although there were important differences in the management structure of the banks in comparison with other enterprises. Furthermore, at this time the assets of the republic, provincial, district, and communal social investment funds were transferred to the commercial banks, where they were treated as state capital, that is, in the same way as federal funds (i.e., they remained under the control of the federal government).[34]

The transfer of the GIF and other government assets to the specialized banks left them in an overwhelmingly dominant position regarding investment loans viv-à-vis the commercial banks. For the government, purportedly seeking decentralization in investment decision making, this meant that further modifications were required if improvements in investment allocation were to be realized. Therefore, in 1966 certain amendments to the banking law were adopted.[35] The most important of these was the provision that the GIF assets which had been transferred to the specialized banks were now withdrawn and placed in a federal investment fund. The federal secretary of finance was empowered to enter into contracts with the specialized banks concerning the use of these funds for extending loans to the commercial banks. In effect, the specialized banks reverted to the position of being agents for the central government. At about the same time, the republics, provinces, and other lower-level government units whose investment funds had been transferred to the commercial banks were given the option either of withdrawing these funds and then contracting with the banks about their use or of leaving them with the commercial banks. About half of the initial amount of capital transferred to the banks in 1965 was removed as a result of this option.[36]

In the five years following the 1966 amendments, the share of federal funds in the total investment credits granted through the banking system declined, and the share of the commercial banks' own funds increased. In 1969, further changes, which presumably were meant to reflect this fact, were made.[37] The most important was the specification of steps to be taken to liquidate, over an unspecified period of time, the capital of the federal investment fund by applying its assets against the expenditures of the federal government. At the end of this process, the influence that the federal government exercises by means of its direct control over investment assets will be eliminated. However, by 1970 relatively little change had occurred in this respect, and the influence exerted through the centralized funds was still considerable.[38]

Furthermore, even when (and if) the process is completed, the federal government will retain great influence and control. Čobeljić outlines five ways in which the government can exert control over investment credit: it can free specific sectors from some of their obligations; it can ease the acquisition of credit for the sake of expanding productive capacity; it can supplement on its own some parts of investment credit; it can extend the period of repayment; and in some cases it can participate directly in the investment programs of enterprises.[39] These powers were surely retained by the federal government through its control of the National Bank.

The process of reform just described would appear to signify an important decentralization in decision making about investment allocations, which was the avowed intent of the reforms. From a strictly legal point of view, this certainly occurred. Instead of banks being only a creation of the government, as they had been before the reforms, they could now be formed by nongovernmental units, namely, enterprises. The banks had the power to make investment loans on their own account and were empowered to use their funds as they saw fit, within rather broad limits. The GIF, which had dominated investment credit, ceased to exist. Its assets were to be used by the commercial banks, after they were allocated to these banks by the specialized banks acting as the agents of the federal government.

But from a more pragmatic point of view, the reforms seem to have been less significant. The federal government retained much of its power over the use of the former GIF assets through the authority given the federal secretary of finance to supervise their allocation to the commercial banks. Furthermore, those portions of GIF loans still outstanding were to be repaid to the banks. However, banks were not free to use these funds as they wished; the central government retained the power to designate these funds for purposes of its own choosing.[40] Under the new rules, the governing bodies of the commercial banks consisted of representatives of their depositors. Since the government had deposits in every important bank, it automatically had a channel through which it could influence bank decisions.

The government's hand was further strengthened by certain administrative provisions in the law. It exerted direct control over the banks through appointments of directors and management boards.[41] Just as the technical expertise and broad, detailed knowledge of industrial enterprise operations made a director the dominant figure in enterprise decisions, the same factors made a bank's director the dominant figure in bank operations. Moreover, he was the chairman of the bank's credit committee, which, until after 1971, was composed entirely of bank employees with no representatives from the bank's investors or debtors. Thus, effective control over a bank's investment decisions remained under the dominant influence of the director.

Under the new law, the National Bank was to work closely with the commercial banks, even to the extent of supervising their work. In this, as in its other responsibilities, the National Bank was directly responsible to the Federal Assembly and the Federal Executive Council. Commercial banks were obliged to use not only the capital obtained from federal and other government funds, but also the capital accumulated by themselves in conformity with the credit policy laid down by the Federal Assembly, the Federal Executive Council, and the National Bank.[42] Sanctions for failing to adhere to these rules included the refusal to grant further credit and the revocation of credits previously granted. The 1965 laws provided for a Council of Banks, supposedly an advisory body to all banks, presided over by the governor of the National Bank. One of its duties was to coordinate the implementation of the credit and other banking policies that were specified in the plans of the central government.

In addition to these means of central control, later developments in the implementation of regional development policy added to the central government's power to control investment finance. In 1965, the Fund for the Accelerated Development of Underdeveloped Regions (FAD) was established as a vehicle for transmitting investment subsidies (in the form of preferential loans) to the less developed areas.[43] Funds from this source, soon a relatively important part of total investment,[44] were under the direct control of the central government.

Finally, the ability of the federal government to control the investment process was facilitated in a possibly unforeseen way by the workings of the 1965 banking laws. Banks took full advantage of the merger provisions, with the result that, according to a study made by the World Bank, by 1968 almost all investment credits outstanding in the economy were concentrated in ten banks.[45] The contrast with the situation before the reform is interesting. Prior to the reform, the GIF constituted about two-thirds of all social investment funds, the republic investment funds another quarter (or slightly less), and the funds of other government units the balance. The only other source of investment funds of any importance was the funds of the enterprises themselves. After the reform, the share of enterprise funds, after a small rise in the first few years, returned to about the same level as before the reform, or perhaps a little lower. This left the banks and the federal government in the same position, relative to total investment finance, as the social investment funds had occupied before the reform. Thus, the federal government and ten banks controlled what had previously been controlled by the federal government, six republics, two autonomous provinces, and a number of lower-level government units. Given the small number of commercial banks, their position relative to the Yugoslav National Bank, and the mandated responsibilities of the National Bank, the central government lost little real control over the allocation of nonenterprise investment funds.

For this reason, the sum of government and bank funds represents investment sources predominantly under the control of central government economic policy and its creators. Table 35 presents the sources of investment funds for the twenty years studied in this work, according to this organizational scheme. The nominal effect of the reforms of the 1960's is obvious in the drop in the share of direct

TABLE 35

SOURCES OF INVESTMENT FINANCE:
INDUSTRY AND MINING, 1952–71
(Percentage)

	Government and Bank Funds			
	Direct Government[a]	Bank	Total	Enterprise Funds[b]
1952	86.9	0	86.9	13.1
1953	76.2	0.3	76.5	23.5
1954	72.0	0	72.0	28.0
1955	68.1	0	68.1	31.9
1956	64.2	0	64.2	35.8
1957	56.7	0	56.7	43.3
1958	64.6	0	64.6	35.4
1959	65.8	0	65.8	34.2
1960	61.6	0	61.6	38.4
1961	62.6	0	62.6	37.4
1962	62.1	2.7	64.8	35.2
1963	54.7	11.2	65.9	34.1
1964	19.5	50.3	69.8	30.2
1965	3.6	62.7	66.3	33.7
1966	4.2	53.8	58.0	42.0
1967	16.5	53.2	69.7	30.3
1968	15.2	54.7	69.8	30.2
1969	16.4	53.9	70.3	29.7
1970	16.2	53.3	69.5	30.5
1971	15.6	52.8	68.4	31.6

SOURCES: SZS, *Statistički godišnjak FRNJ 1955* (Belgrade: SZS, 1955), pp. 259f; idem, *Statistički godišnjak FRNJ 1956* (Belgrade: SZS, 1956), p. 250; idem, *Statistički godišnjak FRNJ 1957* (Belgrade: SZS, 1957), p. 302; idem, *Statistički godišnjak FRNJ 1958* (Belgrade: SZS, 1958), p. 216; idem, *Statistički godišnjak FRNJ 1959* (Belgrade: SZS, 1959), p. 217; idem, *Statistički godišnjak FRNJ 1960* (Belgrade: SZS, 1960), p. 235; idem, *Statistički godišnjak FRNJ 1961* (Belgrade: SZS, 1961), p. 239; idem, *Statistički godišnjak FRNJ 1962* (Belgrade: SZS, 1962), p. 231; idem, *Statistički godišnjak SFRJ 1963* (Belgrade: SZS, 1963), p. 265; idem, *Statistički godišnjak SFRJ 1964* (Belgrade: SZS, 1964), p. 275; idem, *Statistički godišnjak SFRJ 1965* (Belgrade: SZS, 1965), p. 276; idem, *Statistički godišnjak SFRJ 1966* (Belgrade: SZS, 1966), p. 261; idem, *Statistički godišnjak SFRJ 1967* (Belgrade: SZS, 1967), p. 255; idem, *Statistički godišnjak SFRJ 1968* (Belgrade: SZS, 1968), pp. 256–57; idem, *Statistički godišnjak SFRJ 1969* (Belgrade: SZS, 1969), p. 255; idem, *Statistički godišnjak SFRJ 1970* (Belgrade: SZS, 1970), p. 249; idem, *Statistički godišnjak SFRJ 1971* (Belgrade: SZS, 1971), p. 248; and idem, *Statistički godišnjak SFRJ 1972* (Belgrade: SZS, 1972), p. 257.

[a]Includes GIF, FAD, budget, and a set of other, less important government funds.

[b]Includes amortization and the enterprise business fund.

government finance in 1963–65 and its subsequent effective replacement by bank financing. Prior to the reform, direct government financing of investment was dominated by the GIF. Budgetary allocations played a small role, constituting 5 percent or less of total government-controlled investment funds. The increase in the direct government share after 1966 probably reflects, in large measure, the influence of the FAD.

The sum of direct government and bank funds as sources for investment finance and consequently the share of enterprise funds is notably constant after 1957.[46] If anything, the reforms of the 1960s seem to have resulted in a gradual decline in the share of enterprise funds in total investment finance in industry and mining. Whether this signifies increasing reliance by enterprises on borrowed funds that were not under the control of the central government is a question beyond the scope of this study.

CHAPTER NINE

Productivity in Industry and Mining

In any study of economic growth, and especially in Yugoslavia with its high investment rates, the impact on productivity of capital formation stands high on the list of issues to be examined. For Yugoslavia, the data that relate to this question unfortunately are limited in quantity and quality, and assessment of productivity change is correspondingly restricted.

In the face of these unavoidable limitations on analysis, two approaches are used. First, single-factor average productivities are calculated and discussed. Second, a study of total factor productivity by Branko Horvat, a prominent Yugoslav economist, is analyzed and implications about changes in factor productivity drawn from it. Together, these analyses indicate that increases in productivity, initially very rapid, declined sharply in later years. There is a suggestion in the analysis of the productivity study that economies of scale in industry were one reason for the rapid rate of industrial growth.

High investment rates led to rapid growth in the stock of industrial fixed capital, which exceeded the relatively rapid growth of labor employment. The capital-to-labor ratio therefore rose very rapidly throughout the first twenty years of self-management, apparently leading to a very rapid increase in output per person engaged. The annual average rate of increase for this crude measure of productivity over the period 1952–71 was around 4 percent, by world standards a very high rate if such comparisons can usefully be made on the basis of existing data. There are no periods as long as twenty years in either U.S. or Soviet experience over which output per person increased at such high rates. Although high on average, the rate of increase was not sustained consistently; it accelerated until the mid-sixties and then fell sharply, along with the rate of growth of output.

Capital productivity followed a similar, but less spectacular pattern. Average and incremental capital-output ratios fell after 1952 and continued to fall until the mid-sixties. Then the incremental ratio increased sharply to levels above those at the beginning of the period. The average ratio rose correspondingly. By 1971, the average capital-output ratios had returned to roughly the same level as in 1952.

Thus, both partial productivities rose until the middle of the second decade of the period studied and then began to fall or at least to grow less rapidly. The reductions in the rate of growth of output and of factor productivities may have been connected with the economic reforms and other institutional factors in the second decade. The slowing was not, however, due to a reduction in the growth rate of industrial fixed capital, which continued to rise at high rates throughout the sixties. Some Yugoslav analysts have argued that the rate of capital investment was excessive, resulting in idle capacity, an observation consistent with rising capital-output ratios. Whatever the reasons, performance in the latter part of the period indicates that the policy of heavy investment and rapid increases in the industrial labor force—a Yugoslav version of forced-draft industrialization—reached the limits of its effectiveness within fifteen years of its inception.

Estimating changes in total factor productivity or technological change by means of the Abramowitz residual approach is impractical because of data limitations. An example of the main alternative to this approach, the estimation of aggregate production functions, can be found in a study by Branko Horvat. He calculated that technological change accounted for about 40 percent of the total growth rate of output between 1954 and 1967, with the growth of factor inputs accounting for the balance. It is highly probable, however, that these estimates are biased upward due to unmeasured qualitative changes in the inputs, especially labor.

Analysis of the likely biases in Horvat's estimates leads to two important conclusions: (1) he overstates the importance of rising factor productivity, which he credits with about 4.4 points of the total annual growth rate of 10.4 percent in social product; and (2) the rapid increase in industrial output probably was due partly to economies of scale in the industrial sector.

The period Horvat chose for his estimates appears to have been crucial to the stability of the parameter estimates, which form the basis for the calculation of technological change. Beginning in 1964 or 1965, a significant shift in production relations, which lasted at least until 1971, appears. It is almost certain that reestimation of the production function for the last part of the period 1952–71 would lead to significantly different parameter estimates, with correspondingly different estimates of technological change.

DATA FOR PRODUCTIVITY ANALYSES

As is only too often the case in studying Yugoslav industrial development, the discussion of productivity change must begin with a critique of the data. The empirical investigations reported in this chapter are based on Yugoslav data for numbers of persons engaged and for the fixed capital stock in industry and mining. The lack of more detailed data prevents all but the most rudimentary refinements of the crude input data series. More importantly, the crude series contain important weaknesses that limit the reliability and comparability of productivity estimates. The limitations are especially serious for purposes of international comparisons, for reasons that become apparent in the following discussion.

Labor

The data for numbers of persons engaged are those reported by the Yugoslav statistical service (and others) for employed personnel. This category of workers was defined in 1962 as those persons whose regular or customary occupation was with a workers' collective (i.e., a self-managed firm).[1] Later, the definition was refined by including in this category all persons who were members of workers' collectives.[2] Without having to keep a regular schedule with an enterprise, an individual thus could be included in the category of persons employed; persons working part-time, temporarily, or seasonally were counted along with full-time, permanent, regular workers. At times, even workers belonging to workers' collectives but working outside the country evidently were included.[3] There is obviously no presumption that the series represents the number of full-time equivalents in the industrial sector. Moreover, no data that would permit adjustment of the reported series or even provide a quantitative means of estimating the bias in it appear to exist.[4]

Even qualitatively, little can be said about likely bias in the employed personnel series because of the lack of appropriate data. Seasonal employment variations can be ignored because all estimates in this chapter pertain to changes from year to year. Part-time and temporary workers could be a source of error, however, if there were important year-to-year fluctuations in their proportions in the count of employed persons or if there were steady trends in those proportions. If there were important year-to-year fluctuations, they should be reflected in year-to-year fluctuations in the average number of hours worked per employed person. For the limited period for which data are available, no such fluctuations are evident (see table 36). Around the time of the reforms in 1962–64, however, a downward trend appears in the average number of hours worked, a trend not offset by increases in paid time allowed for vacations or sick leave.[5] This trend could result from an upward movement in the proportion of part-time or temporary workers, whose annual work time would be less than that of regular full-time workers and would thus reduce the average. The downward trend could also result from a growing proportion of enterprise members working abroad but counted as employed persons according to the definitions discussed above. In either case, the series for the number of persons employed would be an upwardly biased estimate of the number of full-time equivalents employed in industry and mining. In turn, this would cause a downward bias in measures of the growth

TABLE 36

AVERAGE NUMBER OF HOURS PER EMPLOYED PERSON PER WEEK: YUGOSLAV INDUSTRY AND MINING SECTOR, 1962–70

	Hours of Work per Week[a]		
Year	Regular Time	Overtime	Total[b]
1962	39.9	1.0	41.0
1963	39.7	1.4	41.1
1964	40.2	1.4	41.5
1965	39.0	1.2	40.2
1966	38.1	1.2	39.2
1967	38.1	0.9	39.0
1968	37.9	0.9	38.8
1969	37.4	0.9	38.3
1970	36.5	1.2	37.6

SOURCES: Calculated from data in SZS, *Statistički godišnjak SFRJ 1963* (Belgrade: SZS, 1963), p. 102; idem, *Statistički godišnjak SFRJ 1964* (Belgrade: SZS, 1964), p. 107; idem, *Statistički godišnjak SFRJ 1965* (Belgrade: SZS, 1965), p. 111; idem, *Statistički godišnjak SFRJ 1966* (Belgrade: SZS, 1966), p. 104; idem, *Statistički godišnjak SFRJ 1967* (Belgrade: SZS, 1967), p. 99; idem, *Statistički godišnjak SFRJ 1969* (Belgrade: SZS, 1969), p. 101; idem, *Statistički godišnjak SFRJ 1970* (Belgrade: SZS, 1970), p. 94; idem, *Statistički godišnjak SFRJ 1971* (Belgrade: SZS, 1971), p. 92; and idem, *Statistički godišnjak SFRJ 1972* (Belgrade: SZS, 1972), p. 96.

[a]Calculated from monthly averages assuming a 52-week year since annual vacations and other paid absences are included elsewhere in the data. Paid sick leave is also excluded from the data reported in the table.

[b]Details may not add to totals because of rounding.

rates of average labor productivity and would create potential difficulties in statistical estimates of total factor productivity.[6] However, the available data are not sufficient to adjust the series for number of persons employed, and it is therefore necessary to use the series as is, bearing appropriate qualifications in mind.

Capital

Ideally, productivity analyses should be carried out using flow data for capital and labor. Generally speaking, neither is available, and some assumption must be made about the relation between stocks and flows in order to transform the size of the stock into a corresponding flow of services.[7] As just noted, the data available are inadequate for transforming the stock of labor into flows. Hence, the measurements and estimates of this chapter are based on the assumption that the flow of labor services is proportional to the number of employed persons according to the Yugoslav definition of that term. Similarly, the unavailability of suitably detailed data necessitates the assumption that the flow of capital services is both directly proportional and in constant proportion to the size of the capital stock measured in gross terms.[8]

To use capital stock is to assume that it is a meaningful aggregate. As a socialist economy, Yugoslavia has no capital market per se (apart from a market for used capital equipment), raising an immediate suspicion about the meaning of capital aggregates. The chronic price controls and artificial depreciation procedures in force in the Yugoslav economy arouse further concern about measurements of capital stock. More fundamentally, the Cambridge controversy gives rise to a deeper and more radical skepticism about the theoretical foundations of capital aggregates in any economy.[9]

The source of the capital stock data used in the first part of this chapter is a special study carried out by the Federal Institute of Statistics.[10] It was chosen from several alternatives because it provides the longest continuous and most comparable coverage of any of the available series and covers the period 1952–71, which accounts for most of the period studied in this book. The methods used by SZS in making these capital stock estimates depart from the perpetual inventory method commonly used for this purpose.[11] Instead, the authors of the SZS study began with the purchase values of fixed capital assets in use at the end of each year and then deflated them by means of various price indexes. In this process, the purchase dates of assets carried on enterprise books and of the several capital revaluations that occurred during the period were taken into account. A number of other adjustments were made in attempting to deal with organizational changes that affected the aggregation of enterprise data and with other methodological difficulties.

The entire process was based on the valuation of capital goods according to acquisition prices; these prices were not generally market-clearing prices and, it can be argued, surely were different from the prices that would have been observed in a market economy with a functioning capital market. Therefore, the estimates of the capital stock rest on an artificial foundation. Moreover, even the most careful process of deflation is unlikely to produce as precise an estimate of the capital stock as a well-executed perpetual inventory procedure. Thus, the skepticism arising from theoretical grounds is augmented by reservations about the procedure actually used in calculating the capital stock in constant prices, a further reason for regarding the empirical results that involve capital inputs with suspicion. There appears, however, to be no better alternative.

PARTIAL PRODUCTIVITY MEASURES

Figure 7 plots the growth of fixed capital stock and the number of persons engaged in industry and mining together with the 1961 direct weights index of industrial production. Visual inspection of the figure reveals that the capital stock (which here includes both plant and equipment) grew more rapidly and more steadily than the number of persons employed. The paths followed by output and by the number of persons engaged were similar throughout the period, while the pattern shown by capital stock—with steady, although slowly retarding, growth—differs from both after 1964 or 1965. These observations necessarily cause the

FIGURE 7

GROWTH OF OUTPUT, EMPLOYMENT, AND CAPITAL STOCK IN INDUSTRY AND MINING, 1952–71

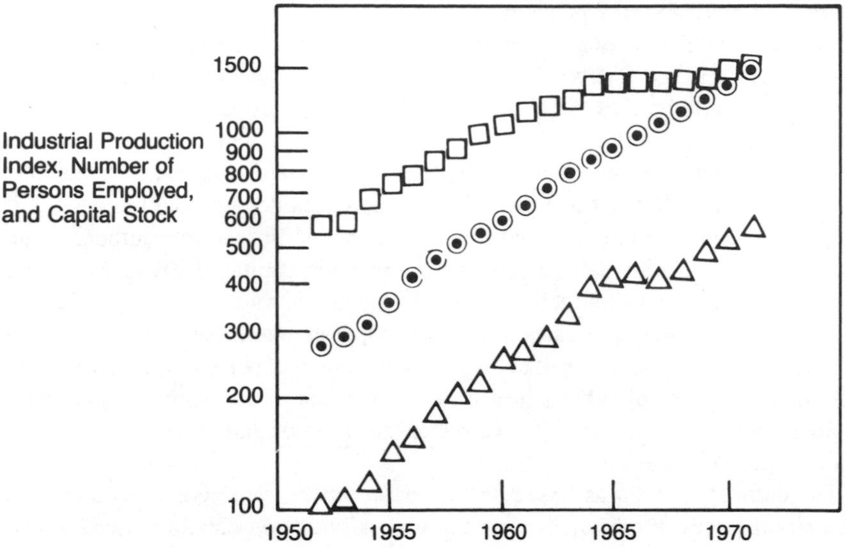

LEGEND: △ Production Index (1952 = 100)
◉ Capital Stock in 1966 Prices, New Dinars (Scale × 10^{-9})
□ Persons Employed, Thousands (Scale × 10^{-3})

SOURCES: Production index is the moving weights from table 5. Number of persons employed is taken from Branimir Marković, *Kretanje narodnog dohotka, zaposlenosti i produktivnosti rada u privredi Jugoslavije 1947–1967* (Belgrade: SZS, 1970), p. 46; SZS, *Statistički godišnjak SFRJ 1969* (Belgrade: SZS, 1969), p. 95; idem, *Statistički godišnjak SFRJ 1970* (Belgrade: SZS, 1970), p. 89; idem, *Statistički godišnjak SFRJ 1971* (Belgrade: SZS, 1971), p. 87; and idem, *Statistički godišnjak SFRJ 1972* (Belgrade: SZS, 1972), p. 91. Capital stock data from SZS, *Osnovna sredstva društvene privrede SFRJ, SR i SAP 1952–1971* (Belgrade: SZS, 1973), pp. 102–3.

average productivities of the two factors to exhibit different patterns over various subperiods.

Average Labor Productivity

The simplest measure of labor productivity is output per person engaged. Three estimates of average labor productivity growth rates, calculated by this simple measure, are presented in table 37. The underlying measures are methodologically different. The official labor productivity index is the quotient of the official index of industrial production and an index of the number of persons employed in industry and mining—i.e., it is the ratio of two indexes, both of which have

TABLE 37

OUTPUT PER PERSON ENGAGED, INDUSTRY AND MINING: ANNUAL AVERAGE GROWTH RATES, SELECTED PERIODS[a]
(Percentage)

	Source of Calculated Growth Rate		
Period	Official Labor Productivity Index[b]	Federal Institute of Statistics Study	Sample Index[c]
1952–71	4.9	–	3.9
1952–56	3.1	2.9	2.3
1957–61	4.0	3.6	3.7
1961–65	6.6	6.4	5.9
1966–71	5.1	–	2.6

SOURCES: Official index: *SZS, Statistički godišnjak FNRJ 1959* (Belgrade: SZS, 1959), p. 137; and idem, *Statistički godišnjak SFRJ 1972* (Belgrade: SZS, 1972), p. 170. Federal Institute of Statistics study: Branimir Marković, *Kretanje narodnog dohotka, zaposlenosti i produktivnosti rada u privredi Jugoslavije 1947–1967* (Belgrade: SZS, 1970), p. 46. Sample index: direct weights index number calculations (see sources to table 5) and labor data from Marković, *Kretanje narodnog dohotka*, p. 45; SZS, *Statistički godišnjak SFRJ 1969* (Belgrade: SZS, 1969), p. 95; idem, *Statistički godišnjak SFRJ 1970* (Belgrade: SZS, 1970), p. 89; idem, *Statistički godišnjak SFRJ 1971* (Belgrade: SZS, 1971), p. 87; and idem, *Statistički godišnjak SFRJ 1972*, p. 91.

[a]Calculated between terminal years by the compound interest formula.

[b]The index with 1957 = 100 was linked to that with 1970 = 100 at 1957.

[c]Estimates of productivity change were made by dividing the 1961 direct weights sample index by an index of number of persons engaged. The latter index was calculated from data for average annual employment in industry and mining.

shortcomings. The growth rates shown under the heading "Federal Institute of Statistics Study" were calculated from a special labor productivity study conducted under the auspices of SZS.[12] The author of that study calculated output per worker by dividing national income originating in the industry and mining sector by the number of persons employed in the sector. His estimates of average labor productivity differ from those of the official index partly because his measure of output is different (in fact, it grew slightly more rapidly than the official index during the period he studied) and, possibly, partly because of differences in his estimates of the number of persons employed.[13]

The third set of growth rates was calculated from the 1961 direct weights index by dividing it by an index of number of persons engaged.[14] Like the official index, it is thus the quotient of two indexes, both of which are open to criticism. For reasons already dwelt on at length in earlier chapters, the sample index provides a measure of the growth of output that is more comparable to standard Western measures than the official index, so that productivity measures based on it may be more meaningful for comparative purposes. But the difficulties with the employment index, discussed above, still remain.

According to the sample index estimate, average labor productivity—measured as output per person engaged—grew at an average annual rate of about 4 percent during the first twenty years of self-management. According to estimates based on the official index, the rate of growth was about one percentage point higher than this. This difference corresponds closely to the difference in measured rates of growth of output over the period; hence, differences in the growth rate of the number of persons employed according to the different measures used must have been small. The period of the SZS study extends only to 1967. Through 1967, the growth rate according to the SZS study was slightly lower than that shown by the official index and somewhat higher than that implied by the sample index estimate.[15] This difference is probably due to differences in the measures of output.

The rates of increase in output per person engaged appear to be remarkably high. Differences in definitions and measurement of both output and employment, as well as basic index number problems, obviate full comparability between countries. Similar productivity measures for the United States and the Soviet Union, however, show generally lower growth rates and fewer, if any, periods of comparable length of such sustained growth. Kendrick's study of productivity in the United States shows no twenty-year periods among his "key dates" in which output per person in mining or manufacturing grew at rates as high as 3.9 percent. The maximum twenty-year rates (of the key dates) were 3.1 percent (mining) and 2.6 percent (manufacturing). Nutter's study of Soviet industry reveals still less capability for long-term sustained growth in output per person engaged. The maximum annual growth rate for productivity measured this way over a similarly long period, for Nutter's benchmark years, was 2.7 percent for 1933–55. Even at that, 1933 was a trough year.[16] The higher Yugoslav growth rates calculated on the basis of the sample index are unlikely to be biased upward by the output measure. Any bias presumably arises from the employment index and would, as noted, tend to cause a downward bias in the growth rate of labor productivity.

The rapid growth in average labor productivity over the period as a whole was not steady. The subperiods in table 37 represent, first, the period prior to the 1957–61 Five-Year Plan (i.e., the first medium-term plan of the self-management period) and, second, the periods originally intended to have been included in the subsequent plans. The path followed by average labor productivity was the same regardless of which index is used to measure it. It rises steadily through the 1961–65 Five-Year Plan and then falls substantially. The growth rate measured by the productivity index based on the sample index falls more sharply than that based on the official index largely because the sample index records a sharper retardation in the rate of growth of output during the 1966–71 Five-Year Plan. The pattern indicated by the growth rates during the subperiods chosen for the table is representative of the movement of average labor productivity for the entire period. It is not an artifact of the particular endpoints chosen; in experiments in fitting curves to productivity indexes, the author of the SZS productivity study found that a parabola gave the best fit.[17]

The rapid growth of average labor productivity was accompanied by and surely due in large measure to rapid increases in the amount of capital per worker, as shown by the growth rates in table 38. To put the rates of growth in perspective, Kendrick's indexes for employment and capital input may be used to calculate growth rates of the U.S. capital-labor ratio.[18] According to these data, sustained rates of growth of this ratio as high as those recorded by Yugoslav industry and mining are rare in U.S. history over twenty-year periods, existing—if at all for mining and manufacturing combined—only before the turn of the twentieth century. Between 1877 and 1899, the annual average growth rate of the capital-labor ratio in manufacturing was about 3.7 percent, but it was only 2.4 percent in mining.[19] By U.S. standards, the capital-labor ratio growth rates for Yugoslav industry (which combines mining with manufacturing) in the first twenty years of self-management appear to be unprecedented.

The growth rate of the capital-labor ratio actually accelerated steadily during the period, with especially rapid increases in the last decade. This resulted, of course, from the more rapid retardation in the growth rate of the number of persons employed compared with the growth rate of the capital stock, especially after 1965.

Average and Marginal Capital Productivity

The high rates of growth of capital stock and of the capital-labor ratio suggest rising capital-output ratios. Calculation of average and incremental capital-output ratios indicates that they rose substantially only toward the end of the twenty-year period. Three measures, two based on official output data and one on the

TABLE 38

AVERAGE ANNUAL GROWTH RATES OF FIXED CAPITAL PER WORKER: INDUSTRY AND MINING, 1952–71[a]
(Percentage)

Period	All Fixed Capital[b]	Equipment
1952–71	3.7	3.6
1952–56	1.4	0.9
1957–61	1.7	1.4
1961–65	4.0	4.2
1966–71	5.7	6.2

SOURCE: Calculated from data for labor from same sources as table 36, and for capital from SZS, *Osnovna sredstva društvene privrede SFRJ, SR i SAP 1952–1971* (Belgrade: SZS, 1973), pp. 102–3.

[a]Calculated between terminal years by the compound interest formula.

[b]Includes buildings, equipment, and "other" types of fixed capital. The latter category was well below 10 percent of the total throughout the period.

TABLE 39

AVERAGE AND MARGINAL CAPITAL-OUTPUT RATIOS, INDUSTRY AND MINING: INDEXES, SELECTED PERIODS

Ratio	Index Numbers, 1952–56=100		
	1957–61	1961–65	1966–71
Average Capital-Output Ratio			
1961 direct weights index	91	85	95
Official output index	89	83	86
Social product index	90	83	83
Incremental Capital-Output Ratio			
1961 direct weights index	81	77	164
Official output index	85	83	119
Social product index	89	78	106

SOURCES: Calculated by formulas given in notes 20 and 21, chapter 10. See table 5 for sources of 1961 direct weights and official indexes. Social product: SZS, *Statistički godišnjak SFRJ 1971* (Belgrade: SZS, 1971), pp. 98–99; idem, *Statistički godišnjak SFRJ 1973* (Belgrade: SZS, 1973), p. 119. Capital stock: SZS, *Osnovna sredstva društvene privrede SFRJ, SR i SAP 1952–1971* (Belgrade: SZS, 1973), pp. 102–3.

1961 direct weights index, are shown in table 39. These measures require some explanation.

Annual incremental capital-output ratios can be calculated readily, but they are subject to rapid and extreme year-to-year oscillations that tend to obscure underlying trends. To avoid cumbersome and unnecessarily detailed explanation of these annual movements, the annual ratios were averaged over subperiods. These averages are not, however, simple averages of the annual ratios in the subperiods; instead, they are calculated from changes in output and capital for each subperiod taken as a whole.[20] In other words, each subperiod is treated as a unit of time, and an incremental capital-output ratio is calculated for that unit. The subperiods correspond to those already used in connection with the partial labor productivity measures. Average capital-output ratios can be calculated easily for each year, and their year-to-year fluctuations are less violent than those of the incremental ratios. For the sake of comparability with the incremental ratios, however, averages for the same subperiods were calculated and are reported in table 39.[21] Because of differences in the measures of output, the absolute values of the ratios are not comparable; hence, the results are reported in the form of index numbers.

The estimates of the partial productivity of capital show that the rise in capital-output ratios occurred as expected but apparently not until later in the period, during the 1966–70 Five-Year Plan. This is reflected in both average and incremental ratios. Through 1965, both measures of capital productivity indicate that output per unit of capital was rising. After 1965, the reverse was true, no matter which index of output is used for the calculations (the only exception is to be found in the average capital-output ratio calculated with social product as the measure of output).

TOTAL FACTOR PRODUCTIVITY IN YUGOSLAV INDUSTRY

Technological change is commonly analyzed by the familiar residual technique. In this method, weighted growth rates of productive factors are subtracted from the corresponding growth rate of output; the residual is the component of growth not explained by the growth of productive factors.[22] This unexplained component has been attributed to many causes—better educated workers, improved working conditions, better organization of industry, economies of scale, and, very often, technological change. This collection of sources of unexplained growth is also subsumed in the portmanteau term: total factor productivity change.

The crucial practical problems in applying the residual approach lie in measuring and weighting the productive factors. Measurement is constrained largely by the availability of reliable data. In a market economy, the weighting issue usually is resolved by assuming that factor markets are in competitive equilibrium so that each factor's share in output can be used as its weight.[23]

In applying this method to Yugoslavia's industrial sector, difficulties are encountered in both measurement and weights. The available data are not adequate for disaggregation of the productive factors to levels of detail finer than the gross levels already used in this chapter. Data on the educational, age, sex, and training characteristics of the labor force are available only for fragments of the period. The capital stock can be disaggregated to plant and equipment, but data on its age and other pertinent characteristics are not available.

But even if disaggregation of the physical series were possible, the problem of weighting would remain. Given the available Yugoslav data, there is no satisfactory solution to this problem. Even at the highly aggregated level of detail used so far, specification of weights raises serious difficulties. There is no capital market and thus no market-determined income share for capital. Imperfections in the labor market cast doubt on the use of reported labor incomes as the basis for calculating labor's factor share;[24] it is more realistic to view the income received by a worker as the residual remaining after a complex set of administratively determined taxes and obligatory contributions levied on enterprise earnings have been deducted, a residual that probably reflects a mixture of wages and the return to capital. For these reasons, estimates of the residual, even at the highest level of aggregation, are inevitably based on an arbitrary assignment of weights.[25] Thus, this approach to the problem appears to be ruled out.

Horvat's Estimates of Technological Change

The principal alternative method used in studying factor productivity is the estimation of an aggregate production function in which some term—a constant term or an explicitly formulated expression—is interpreted as a measure of technological or total factor productivity change. This approach has been applied to the Yugoslav industrial sector by Branko Horvat.[26] Horvat bases his analysis on several variants of the Cobb-Douglas production function, in each of which technological change is estimated in some manner. Two general properties of the Cobb-Douglas function should be noted before undertaking specific discussion of Horvat's results.

First, as used by Horvat (and others), technological change is represented by a term inserted into the production function that reflects change in output that is not captured in the other inputs and is not mere random error; this change is interpreted as measuring neutral, disembodied technological change. Data necessary to estimate functions with embodied, nonneutral technological change do not exist; hence, in studying Yugoslav growth there is no practical alternative to this characteristic of the function. It should be noted again, however, that the technological change variable does not merely measure technological change in the sense of a shift in the production functions. Other factors affecting the productivity of inputs are estimated along with technological change per se.

Second, the Cobb-Douglas specification implies that the elasticity of factor substitution is unity, an assumption that might be important in estimating technological change. As Weitzman has shown, if the elasticity of substitution is less than 1.0, a growth rate of capital greater than the growth rate of labor tends to produce a reduction in the rate of growth of output even if the rate of technological change is not declining.[27] The greater the rate of growth of capital relative to that of labor, the more important this effect is, and the more a Cobb-Douglas procedure underestimates the rate of technological change.

For the Soviet Union, Weitzman thinks this is important. In the period he studied, capital grew at an annual rate of about 10.8 percent, while labor grew at about 2.6 percent, a difference of 8.2 percentage points.[28] Furthermore, Weitzman's estimated elasticity of substitution for the Soviet industrial sector is significantly less than 1.0 (specifically, 0.40).[29] In the Yugoslav industrial sector during the period of this study, the divergence between growth rates of capital and labor was smaller; the average annual growth rates were 9.3 and 5.4 percent, respectively, a difference of 3.9 percentage points.[30] Thus, although nothing is known about the elasticity of substitution in Yugoslav industry, at this level of analysis the lower divergence in input growth rates should reduce concern about possible downward bias in the estimate of the technological change parameter. This would be true even if the elasticity of substitution were significantly less than 1.0.

Horvat used Yugoslav data for labor, capital, and output to estimate several variants of the production function. He identified three distinctive postwar periods: 1945–48, the "postwar reconstruction period"; 1949–55, the "command economy"; and 1955–67 (the last year covered by his study), the "self-management period." He estimated production functions only for the last of these periods; it seems likely that his parameter estimates were sensitive to this choice of period, for reasons noted below. He used his parameter estimates (shown in table 40) for two purposes. First, by seeing whether paid-out factor shares—calculated by the methods criticized in note 25 to this chapter—were in the same proportions as those implied by the production function, he sought to establish the degree of competition in the Yugoslav economy. Second and more to the point, he estimated the extent of technological change in the industrial sector, directly and indirectly. He concluded that the industrial sector was, in fact, competitive because the shares paid to factors were roughly the same[31] as those implied by his production function estimates. He then used the factor shares, based on the parameter estimates, to measure technological change and the contributions of factor inputs to the observed growth of output during the 1955–67 period as well as during earlier periods.

These estimates were made by subtracting from the growth rate of output the weighted growth rates of the factor inputs. The weights were the factor shares, which he assumed to have been constant throughout the period (and, indeed, for the entire period from 1911 to 1967).[32] Some of the results pertinent to the period of the present study are reproduced in table 41. According to these estimates, technical change (or that set of causes of growth included in that term) was an important source of the growth of output from 1955 to 1967. Indeed, on average, it accounted for over 40 percent of the total growth. The remainder, according to Horvat's estimates, was due to sheer growth in the use of productive factors.

TABLE 40

HORVAT'S AGGREGATE PRODUCTION FUNCTION ESTIMATES: INDUSTRY AND MINING, 1955–67[a]

Equation	Estimate	R^2
1.	$\frac{\Delta q}{q} = 4.18 + \underset{(0.080)}{0.501} \frac{\Delta k}{k}$	0.797
2.	$\ln q = 0.849 + \underset{(0.042)}{0.413} \ln k + \underset{(0.001)}{0.043} t$	0.999
3.	$\ln Q = 1.081 + \underset{(0.041)}{0.587} \ln R + \underset{(0.071)}{0.390} \ln K + \underset{(0.004)}{0.042} t$	0.9997

SOURCE: Branko Horvat, "Tehnički progres u Jugoslaviji," *Ekonomska analiza* 3 (1969): 38.
[a]Standard errors of coefficients are shown in parentheses.

TABLE 41

TECHNICAL CHANGE IN YUGOSLAV INDUSTRY AND MINING, 1954–67: RESIDUAL ESTIMATES BY HORVAT

	Increase in Output Attributed to Technical Change	
Year or Period	Percent Per Year	As a Percentage of Total Change in Output
1956	3.44	35.4
1957	3.49	20.2
1958	5.45	46.1
1959	5.47	46.8
1960	5.04	37.0
1961	4.91	70.3
1962	3.88	52.9
1963	4.49	28.8
1964	4.33	27.0
1965	4.47	53.5
1966	3.48	54.2
1956–66[a]	4.36	–
1954–67[b]	4.44	43.1

SOURCE: Branko Horvat, "Tehnički progres u Jugoslaviji," *Ekonomska analiza* 3 (1969): 44, 48.

[a]Simple average of the annual percentage changes.

[b]Derived from average annual growth rates for output, capital, and labor, calculated between terminal years by the compound interest formula.

Possible Biases in Horvat's Estimates

These are interesting results, with important implications for the evaluation of the Yugoslav economic system. At the same time, they illustrate the problems surrounding the use of this technique in the Yugoslav economy.[33] Consider the data used by Horvat. The capital stock data were Vinski's estimates of the stock in 1962 prices;[34] this calculation of the stock implies an average annual growth rate between 1952 and 1967 of 8.8 percent, while that implied by the SZS series used earlier in this chapter is 9.4 percent. The labor input series used by Horvat was the number of persons employed, the same series used in the calculations of labor productivity in this chapter. Output was measured by data for social product in industry evaluated at 1962 prices. For 1955–67, this series grew at an average annual rate of about 10.3 percent, compared with a corresponding rate over that period of about 9.8 percent for the 1961 direct weights index.

Horvat attempted to adjust the capital and labor inputs to account for cyclical movements in the intensity of their use. He performed linear extrapolations of output per person engaged and calculated the average capital-output ratio between cyclical peaks. He then adjusted the inputs to the levels they would have had if the relevant productivities had been the same in the off-peak years as they were in the peak years.[35] This procedure generally results in adjusted factor usages smaller than actual ones. In the case of labor, the adjustment has little impact on the growth rate. However, for 1955–67, the adjustment results in a reduction of the average annual growth rate of capital by about one percentage point per year. Altogether, then, Horvat's adjusted capital stock has an average annual growth rate nearly two percentage points less than that of the capital stock used in the calculations in this chapter.

If, along with this understatement of the capital growth rate, the output index overstates the rate of growth of production, an obvious bias is built into estimates of technical change made by the residual method. This bias might account for as much as 0.5 percentage point per year (of the approximately 4.4 percent for 1955–1967).

A more interesting bias may arise from the parameter estimates. It is well known that unmeasured qualitative changes in the independent variables of a regression, if correlated with those variables, cause bias in the parameter estimates. In estimations of aggregate production functions, measurements of factor inputs are often problematic for this reason. Bias in the parameter estimates resulting from this problem would directly affect Horvat's estimates of technological change. In his production function estimates, the flow of labor services was measured by the number of persons employed (with adjustments for underutilization). Apart from possible difficulties with this measure arising from changes in hours worked per person,[36] there is little doubt that the quality of labor services improved during the period of his study. The level of education generally rose, and although comparable data subject to precise interpretation are not readily available (if at all), the qualifications of industrial workers appear to have risen steadily.[37] These changes were not taken into account in Horvat's estimates, and the changes appear to have been positively correlated with the labor variable actually used in the estimates (the number of persons employed) as well as with the capital stock variable and with time.

Less can be said about the importance of changes in the quality of the flow of capital. In Horvat's estimates, as in many others, that flow was taken to be proportional to the value of the capital stock (in constant prices). Horvat used Vinski's estimates of capital stock, which were made by splicing a deflated investment series, in which the deflator was a price index for investment goods, onto an initial capital stock value.[38] Under certain weak assumptions, it can be shown that if the rate of growth of the price index is understated relative to the rate of growth of nominal investment, downward bias in the calculated rate of growth of the real capital stock results.[39] That bias could behave like an omitted variable in the regressions; if so, it would produce the same result as a qualitative change in an included variable. If the bias were correlated with the included variable (viz., the estimated real capital stock), the result would be a biased estimate of the coefficients of the regression. However, there is little evidence that suggests the existence of downward relative bias in the investment goods price index. Nor is there much other evidence that indicates whether there were qualitative changes in the capital stock that were positively correlated with its growth. It seems unlikely that there occurred any deterioriation in quality during this period, however, and any bias that might be present is probably positive.

These considerations suggest that, to the extent that there were unmeasured qualitative changes in the inputs, they probably were improvements and probably were positively correlated with the movements of the measured inputs. In turn, at least for the period for which Horvat estimated his equations, this implies that the estimates of the labor and capital coefficients (in equation 3 of table 40) are biased downward.[40]

Implications of Bias in the Estimates

This downward bias has some important implications. First, it raises questions about the validity of Horvat's conclusion that there were constant returns to scale during the period he studied. His conclusion rests on the observation that the sum of the estimated coefficients is very close to 1.0 (see equation 3 in table 40). This procedure, however, does not consider possible biases in the coefficients. Since both coefficients are likely to be biased downward, the sum of the true coefficients is probably greater than 1.0, indicating increasing, not constant, returns to scale. It follows that scale economies reaped during industrialization were one of the sources of growth in the industrial sector. In view of the sweeping transformation from handicraft to industrialized system described in chapter 2, this should come as no surprise.

Second, a downward bias in the parameter estimates implies that the weights assigned to the factors in calculating technical change were too small. Recall that Horvat estimated the rate of technical change by subtracting the weighted sum of the factor growth rates from the rate of growth of output. The use of downward-biased factor weights would, for any set of factor growth rates, lead to an upward bias in the estimates of technical change. Furthermore, to the extent that factor growth rates were underestimated (which may have been the case for the capital stock growth rate) or that output growth rates were overstated (as by the social product measure), additional upward bias would be produced in the estimates of technical change. It is unlikely that these biases are in a direction opposite to the true biases. Therefore, it is reasonable to conclude that the estimates shown in table 40 overstate the importance of technical change or total factor productivity increases in the growth of industrial output during the period studied by Horvat. Unfortunately, quantitative estimates of the overstatement could be only speculative.

Estimating the production function presumes an underlying stability in the relationship being studied. Horvat argued that a fundamental change in the aggregate production function occurred around 1956.[41] For that reason, he excluded the data for earlier years. But there also appears to have been a substantial shift after 1965, near the end of the period he studied, as shown by the data depicted in figure 8. This graph plots the average capital-output ratio as a function of the average ratio of capital per worker. Both ratios are expressed as index numbers. Through 1960, the average capital-output ratio moved downward with relatively little increase in the average capital per worker. The high rate of increase in capital stock was roughly matched by the rate of increase in the

FIGURE 8

AVERAGE CAPITAL-OUTPUT AND CAPITAL-LABOR RATIOS (1952 = 100), 1952–71

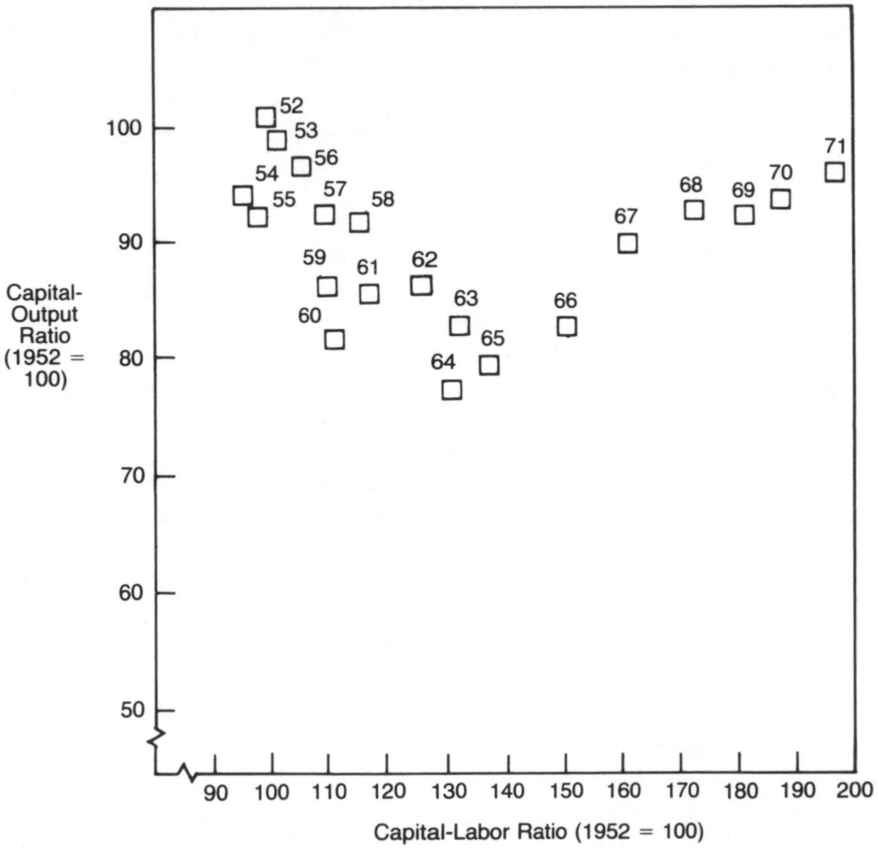

SOURCES: Capital data: see table 38. Labor data: see table 36. Output data: 1961 direct weights index.

number of workers employed during that period. After 1960, average capital productivity continued to rise for a few years, but the rate of growth of capital stock increased relative to that of the number of persons employed, causing the capital-labor ratio to rise more rapidly. Sometime in the mid-sixties, the direction of change of the capital-output ratio reversed. After 1964 or 1965, the rapid growth of capital stock (again, more rapid than the growth of labor input) led to a decrease rather than an increase in average capital productivity. From these movements, it appears that the initial successes of the industrialization policy, which were based on high rates of investment, were succeeded by difficulties in assimilating new capital stock, a view held by some Yugoslav economists.[42] But whatever the reason, there was a marked shift in the directions of change in factor productivity beginning around 1964–65, a shift that necessarily would be reflected in statistical estimates of an aggregate production function.

Such changes could be taken to represent shifts in the underlying production technology, as opposed to shifts in the disembodied technological change normally estimated by aggregate production function techniques.[43] In the normal application (regardless of the form chosen for the aggregate production function), a key maintained hypothesis is that the parameters of the function are constants; the estimation procedure is based on that assumption and no attempt to identify changes in the parameters is made. When shifts such as that represented in figure 8 occur, however, it is clear either that parameter values have changed or that some variable has not been measured properly. If appropriate data were available, the question of measurement could be addressed or application could be made of the techniques described by Brown for identifying technological "epochs."[44] But the data that are available do not enable the measurement question to be resolved and scarcely justify the use of more sophisticated techniques.

As a result, quantitative estimates of total factor productivity or technological change appear to rest on shaky foundations. Horvat's estimates of technical change from 1955 to 1967 are probably biased upward, but his work nevertheless indicates that improvements in total factor productivity were one source of the growth in output during that period. The abrupt reversal in the direction of movement of the capital-output ratio after 1965, however, leaves unanswered the question of subsequent changes in total factor productivity.

CHAPTER TEN

Impact of Regional Development Policy

Regional policy, like the national program for economic development, was based on industrialization.[1] Improved training and education and better social services were to be provided, and out-migration from the less developed areas was anticipated and encouraged. The most important and most controversial aspect of the policy, however, was the program for transferring investment funds, both directly and indirectly, from the more developed regions to the backward parts of the country. Along with accelerated capital formation, the policymakers evidently believed that rapid rates of investment in the less developed regions would induce rapid rates of increase in industrial employment by drawing on the large reserves of labor believed to exist there.[2]

From the national perspective, transferring investment resources from the more advanced to the backward regions entailed the risk that overall growth would be adversely affected by movement of funds into less efficient managerial hands. In retrospect, the scanty and rather speculative evidence that pertains to this issue remains equivocal; the evidence does not clearly indicate that industrial growth for the country as a whole was adversely affected by the transfers, but neither does it support the conclusion that growth would have been faster if a more single-minded investment policy had been followed.

Naturally, taxing one part of the country in order to subsidize investment in another part created resentment in the areas being taxed. The repercussions of this resentment must be included when the overall success of the program is judged; consequently, its success cannot be assessed on economic grounds alone, and final judgment cannot be reached in this study. It can be said, however, that the regional program—in all its aspects—generally failed to meet its economic objectives. Whether it satisfied its political purposes—i.e., whether political benefits gained in the less developed areas offset the costs suffered in the advanced regions—is a question answerable only by the Yugoslavs themselves. If the program was a wash politically and its impact on overall growth was nil, then the benefits of the program accrued largely to its administrators, a result familiar to observers of bureaucratic behavior in the West.

INVESTMENT TRANSFERS, CAPITAL GROWTH, AND PRODUCTIVITY

The size of the investment fund transfers cannot be calculated precisely,[3] but an estimate based on a strong assumption about enterprise behavior under an alternative central investment policy is presented below. The importance of the transfers to industrial investment in the less developed areas can be deduced from data about sources of investment finance (see table 42). The most striking and most easily interpreted difference among regions is the share of enterprise funds (including amortization and investments made from the enterprise business fund) of the less developed regions compared with the shares of other regions. With few exceptions, that share is substantially smaller in the less developed regions; it would be smaller still if the ambivalent case of Bosnia-Hercegovina were eliminated.

The evolution of the system of investment finance is clearly reflected in the data. The share of banks was zero in 1958 and 1961, when investments were financed through the GIF and other social funds and through enterprise funds. By 1966, the banks had assumed the role formerly played by the social funds; the sum of the bank share and the remaining government share in 1966 approximated the government share in 1961. In 1971, the government share was once again important in the less developed regions, reflecting the importance of the FAD for investment finance. There is no doubt about the importance of the transfer program for investment in the less developed areas; investment rates there clearly were higher than they would have been otherwise.

In real terms, the investment transfer program apparently resulted in higher rates of capital formation in the less developed regions (see table 43), but the interregional differential between growth rates of capital stock narrowed steadily between 1957 and 1971, the time covered by the five-year plans of the period studied. In part, this reflects the growing size of capital stock in the less developed regions. It should be noted, however, that the growth rate of capital stock in the more developed areas exhibited no tendency to slacken, which indicates that the retardation in the rate of industrial capital formation noted above (see table 32) was due entirely to reductions in the capital formation rate in the less developed regions. Declines in the growth rates of fixed capital in the last subperiod were especially marked in Montenegro, Kosovo, and Macedonia; there was no noticeable trend, either upward or downward, in the growth rate of capital stock in Bosnia-Hercegovina during the fourteen years for which comparable data are available. These declines in growth rates occurred simultaneously with increases in the share of nonenterprise funds in the financing of

TABLE 42

DISTRIBUTION OF SOURCES OF INVESTMENT FUNDS IN INDUSTRY AND MINING, BY REGION: SELECTED YEARS (Percentage)[a]

	Less Developed Regions					Other Regions				
Year and Source	Total	Macedonia	Montenegro	Kosovo	Bosnia-Hercegovina	Total	Serbia[b]	Vojvodina	Croatia	Slovenia
1958										
Government funds[c]	75.4	82.9	92.3	nsa	68.2	60.7	69.9	nsa	55.4	40.8
Banks	0	0	0	0	0	0	0	0	0	0
Enterprise funds[d]	24.6	17.1	7.8	nsa	31.8	39.3	30.1	nsa	44.6	59.2
1961										
Government funds[c]	75.9	87.0	91.8	nsa	65.4	56.6	65.3	nsa	55.1	27.9
Banks	0	0	0	0	0	0	0	0	0	0
Enterprise funds[d]	24.1	13.0	8.2	nsa	34.6	43.4	34.7	nsa	44.9	72.1
1966										
Government funds[c]	4.5	10.2	1.0	nsa	0	0.9	1.3	nsa	0.1	0.5
Banks	64.9	77.9	59.0	nsa	54.7	50.7	58.3	nsa	32.2	50.3
Enterprise funds[d]	30.6	11.9	40.0	nsa	45.4	48.4	40.5	nsa	67.7	49.2
1971										
Government funds[c]	43.4	40.1	67.2	74.1	24.1	0.3	0.3	0	0.4	0.1
Banks	39.4	50.2	28.2	17.6	45.1	60.7	70.3	64.4	59.2	45.1
Enterprise funds[d]	17.2	9.8	4.6	8.3	30.8	39.1	29.5	35.6	40.3	54.7

SOURCES: SZS, *Statistički godišnjak FNRJ 1960* (Belgrade: SZS, 1960), pp. 423–26; idem, *Statistički godišnjak SFRJ 1963* (Belgrade: SZS, 1963), pp. 456–58; idem, *Statistički godišnjak SFRJ 1966* (Belgrade: SZS, 1966), pp. 458–60; and idem, *Statistički godišnjak SFRJ 1972* (Belgrade: SZS, 1972), pp. 474–76.

[a]Details may not add to 100 because of rounding.

[b]Serbia total in 1958, 1961, and 1966; Serbia proper in 1971.

[c]Includes GIF, budget, and FAD, as well as other minor sources.

[d]Includes amortization and enterprise business fund.

TABLE 43

AVERAGE ANNUAL GROWTH RATES OF INDUSTRIAL EMPLOYMENT AND FIXED CAPITAL: REGIONS OF YUGOSLAVIA, SELECTED PERIODS[a]
(Percentage)

Period and Region	Industrial Employment[b]	*Industrial Fixed Capital* Total[c]	Equipment[d]
1957–71			
Less Developed Regions	3.7	9.6	9.5
Other Regions	3.5	8.5	8.6
1957–61			
Less Developed Regions	3.3	11.4	10.3
Other Regions	5.1	8.2	8.1
1961–65			
Less Developed Regions	6.0	10.1	10.6
Other Regions	4.6	9.0	9.3
1966–71			
Less Developed Regions	2.8	8.2	9.0
Other Regions	2.6	8.3	8.8

SOURCES: Employment data: SZS, *Statistički godišnjak FNRJ 1958* (Belgrade: SZS, 1958), p. 315; idem, *Statistički godišnjak FNRJ 1962* (Belgrade: SZS, 1962), p. 337; idem, *Statistički godišnjak SFRJ 1966* (Belgrade: SZS, 1966), p. 356; idem, *Statistički godišnjak SFRJ 1967* (Belgrade: SZS, 1967), p. 338; and idem, *Statistički godišnjak SFRJ 1972* (Belgrade: SZS, 1972), p. 354. Capital stock data: SZS, *Osnovna sredstva društvene privrede SFRJ, SR i SAP 1952–1971* (Belgrade: SZS, 1973), pp. 108–57.

[a]Calculated between terminal years by the compound interest formula.

[b]Based on the number of employed personnel in industry and mining as of September 30 of each year. These data are not fully comparable to the annual average employment data used in preceding chapters.

[c]Includes structures, equipment, and "other" fixed capital; does not include inventories.

[d]Includes machinery and other types of productive equipment, but not hand tools.

investment (see table 42) and the growing importance of the FAD in investment finance in the less developed regions. After the expansion of base capital stocks, the government was evidently unwilling to undertake the larger absolute transfers necessary to maintain the earlier high rates of capital formation.[4]

Employment Growth in Less Developed Regions

The other side of the regional strategy—the expected stimulation of industrial employment in the less developed regions—was a disappointment, as the figures for industrial employment growth rate in table 43 show. During the first subperiod, industrial employment actually grew more slowly in the less developed areas. Employment growth might lag behind investment, and the 1961–65 results are consistent with this view. But in 1966–71 employment in the less developed areas grew only marginally faster than it did elsewhere. The results for the period as a whole lend little support to the idea that the investment program had the intended result of stimulating industrial employment. In a broader perspective, the results were even less satisfactory. Due to higher population growth rates in the less developed areas, the growth of industrial employment per thousand persons was substantially lower in these areas than elsewhere throughout the period.[5]

Should this result have come as a surprise? The basis for expecting investment to induce employment expansion is questionable. According to Yugoslav economists, in the less developed areas the proportion of economically active persons was low, the proportion engaged in nonagricultural activities was relatively low, and the proportion in primary activities within the industrial sector was relatively high.[6] These are all characteristic of low levels of economic development, but their existence does not necessarily imply that the opportunity cost of labor is zero from the standpoint of industrial growth. Market values may be low, especially where market relations are not extensive (as was certainly true in Kosovo,[7] and probably in the other less developed areas as well), but individuals may nevertheless place relatively high values on the alternatives open to them.

Furthermore, investment in industry may not lead to an important increase in labor's value if effective demand for industrial products is low. In this respect, the complaints of Yugoslav economists that the lack of infrastructure caused the failure of the industrial policy make some sense.[8] Besides the problems emphasized by the Yugoslavs of maintaining adequate supplies of materials to plants where large investments were made, the absence of adequate marketing channels, including transportation from the plants in the less developed areas to markets, would lead to production of goods with low effective value at the plant. For these reasons, industrial investment might not have raised the value of labor to industrial enterprises above the opportunity costs perceived by the potential industrial workers.

The more rapid growth of capital stock in the backward areas together with employment growth rates nearly equal to those elsewhere caused higher rates of growth of industrial fixed capital per worker in the less developed areas (see table 44). The fluctuations in the growth rate of employment in the three subperiods were reflected in the growth rates of the capital-labor ratio in the less developed regions. In contrast to these fluctuations, in the more developed areas steadily declining industrial employment growth rates and roughly constant capital stock growth rates produced steadily rising rates of growth of capital per person employed there. Steady or not, the rates of capital formation and employment growth and the initial levels of fixed capital throughout the country were such that ranking regions in 1971 by simple capital-labor ratios produces, for industry, a ranking almost opposite to the ranking in terms of level of industrial development.[9]

Thus, the investment policy and its resulting high rates of capital formation in the less developed areas left workers there in an advantageous position. If simple capital-to-labor ratios are used as a measure of capital endowment, by 1971 employees in the less developed regions were endowed with at least as much

TABLE 44

AVERAGE ANNUAL GROWTH RATES[a] OF FIXED CAPITAL PER PERSON EMPLOYED:[b] INDUSTRY AND MINING, SELECTED PERIODS
(Percentage)

Region	All Fixed Capital[c]				Equipment Only[d]			
	1957–71	1957–61	1961–65	1966–71	1957–71	1957–61	1961–65	1966–71
Less Developed Regions								
Total	5.6	7.9	3.9	5.2	5.6	6.8	4.3	6.0
Macedonia	6.3	11.2	5.0	3.7	6.9	12.1	4.8	4.8
Montenegro	10.0	30.9	1.2	2.5	10.1	26.4	2.0	5.3
Kosovo	7.5	0.9	13.6	8.5	8.9	0.4	16.2	10.8
Bosnia-Hercegovina	5.2	6.8	2.6	5.8	5.0	6.2	2.8	5.8
Other Regions								
Total	4.8	2.9	4.5	5.6	4.9	2.8	4.8	6.0
Serbia proper	5.0	3.7	4.9	5.8	4.8	4.0	4.9	5.1
Vojvodina	6.7	2.7	10.3	5.3	6.5	1.9	9.7	6.0
Croatia	5.3	4.2	3.8	6.3	5.6	3.4	4.5	7.8
Slovenia	3.2	1.0	2.9	4.5	3.5	1.6	3.3	4.8

SOURCES: See table 43.

[a]Calculated as growth rate of capital-labor ratio between terminal years by the compound interest formula.

[b]Data availability restrictions require the use of employment figures as of September 30 of each year, thus interjecting an element of seasonal variation into the absolute value of the capital-labor ratios. Growth rates of the ratios should be relatively unaffected by the seasonality, but it is possible that an unknown error due to year-to-year fluctuations in seasonal movements may remain in them.

[c]Includes structures, equipment, and "other" capital.

[d]Includes machinery and other forms of productive equipment, but not hand tools.

fixed capital as employees in the more advanced parts of the country. Furthermore, the structure of industrial capital does not appear to have been grossly different in the less developed regions. Differences between capital-labor ratios calculated on the basis of total capital including structures and on the basis of equipment alone appear to be unimportant.

Concentration of Investment in Less Developed Regions

The aggregate growth rates in table 44 conceal significant details about capital formation in the less developed regions. For example, the huge rate of growth in Montenegro between 1957 and 1961 was due almost entirely to investment in two branches of industry: electric power production (35.1 percent of the total increase in fixed capital) and ferrous metallurgy (54.3 percent). The high rate of increase in Kosovo after 1961 was due largely to investment in electric power, chemicals, coal, and food products.[10] These observations raise the question of whether investment in the less developed regions was more highly concentrated in a few branches or on a few projects than was the case elsewhere.

Evidence that provides at least a partial answer to this question is available. If investment is highly concentrated, a relatively large share of capital stock growth takes place in relatively few branches of industry. Thus, relative concentration could be measured by the share of the top few branches in capital stock growth or by the extent of variation in capital stock growth rates among branches. Measurement in these terms (see table 45) shows only a weak tendency for investment to be more concentrated in the less developed regions. Although not

TABLE 45

CONCENTRATION OF INDUSTRIAL CAPITAL STOCK GROWTH: REGIONS OF YUGOSLAVIA, 1957–71

Region	Percentage of Capital Stock Growth Accounted for by Five Leading Branches	Coefficient of Variation, Branch Shares of Capital Stock Growth
Less Developed Regions		
Macedonia	68.9	1.22
Montenegro	85.1	1.73
Kosovo	83.9	1.58
Bosnia-Hercegovina	71.4	1.39
Other Regions		
Serbia Proper	71.4	1.43
Vojvodina	73.2	1.25
Croatia	65.2	1.32
Slovenia	60.8	1.16

SOURCES: For capital stock data, see table 43.

shown in the table, the branches with the highest rates of investment were much the same in all regions. This suggests that the concentration data reflect the general policy of industrialization and the relative capital intensities of different branches of industry, rather than a particular aspect of the regional development policy.[11] Certain large projects may at times have had relatively important impacts on the capital stock and investment allocations in the less developed regions, but over longer periods concentration does not seem to have been a factor of great importance in the pattern of investment. From this evidence, it is hard to conclude that the less developed areas were handicapped by excessive attention on a few branches of industry.

Interregional Differences in Productivity Change

Faster rates of growth of capital per person employed in the less developed regions should have led to faster increases in labor productivity there. The simple arithmetic of the faster output growth rates in those regions (see chapter 6) coupled with their more or less equal rates of employment growth implies higher rates of growth in output per person employed. As the figures in table 46 show, this expectation is borne out, although the differences in growth rates per person

TABLE 46

OUTPUT PER PERSON ENGAGED, INDUSTRY AND MINING, REGIONS OF YUGOSLAVIA: AVERAGE ANNUAL GROWTH RATES, SELECTED PERIODS[a]
(Percentage)

	Period			
Region	1957–71	1957–61	1961–65	1966–71
Less Developed Regions				
Total	5.0	8.4	5.8	2.3
Macedonia	4.3	4.8	6.1	2.5
Montenegro	8.5	20.6	4.5	2.7
Kosovo	-0.5	-9.1	6.6	0.9
Bosnia-Hercegovina	6.4	12.2	6.1	3.3
Other Regions				
Total	4.5	6.0	6.2	2.0
Serbia proper	4.4	4.9	8.2	1.6
Vojvodina	4.9	5.6	9.7	-0.3
Croatia	5.1	7.2	5.7	2.4
Slovenia	3.6	6.0	2.8	2.8

SOURCES: Calculated from the 1961 direct weights index (table 20) and employment data given in the sources to table 43.

[a]Calculated as the average annual rate of change of the output-employment ratio between terminal years according to the compound interest formula.

employed appear small, perhaps surprisingly so.[12]

There are some apparent anomalies in the data. For 1957–61, there was a wide disparity in the growth rates of the less developed regions and a very rapid decline in average labor productivity in Kosovo. Montenegro's rapid growth reflected the extremely high output growth during that first plan period, a rate of increase largely due to the very small industrial base that existed in 1957. The opposite was true for Kosovo; a rapid rate of increase in industrial employment accompanied virtual stagnation in output during the 1957–61 plan. This was also a period of very slow capital formation in Kosovo (see table 44), suggesting that low investment rates were partially responsible for the slow output growth rates. This may be so, but the explanation surely goes deeper because there is little reason to expect a correlation between contemporaneous rates of growth of capital stock per person employed and output per person employed.[13]

Apart from these apparent exceptions, on the average the difference in the growth rates of output per person employed was only about 0.5 percentage point per year over the whole period. After 1961, there was no essential difference between the less developed areas and the rest of the country.

Yugoslav economists have commented on the relatively slow improvement of labor productivity in the less developed regions. Nikolić investigated a number of possible explanations for the relatively low productivity in the backward areas.[14] Interregional differences in the branch structure of industry could have contributed to differences in measured labor productivity since there might have been a bias toward larger shares of total output in more productive branches in some regions. Nikolić found that differences in the branch structure of the industrial sector made only a small difference in the rankings of regions according to labor productivity in 1967. Even when productivities were adjusted to account for structural differences (by weighting regional branch productivities with branch weights derived from the branch structure for the country as a whole), only minor changes resulted. Macedonia and Montenegro still ranked at the bottom, along with Serbia (which includes Kosovo and Vojvodina in the study by Nikolić); Slovenia, Bosnia-Hercegovina, and Croatia still ranked at the top.[15]

Going one step further, Nikolić noted that there were interregional differences in the structure of industry within branches. For example, Montenegro's electricity output was mostly in the generation of hydroelectric power; distribution accounted for little of the value of production in the branch. Similarly, productivity in the Serbian petroleum branch was attributable mainly to extraction; refining had little importance. But even disaggregating at the level of industry groups in an effort to adjust for these differences led to little change in interregional productivity variations. For 1967, the adjustments increased estimated labor productivity in Slovenia and Macedonia and, in the case of disaggregating to the branch level, in Montenegro. (The improvement in

Montenegro was largely wiped out by further disaggregation to the group level.) Estimated labor productivity declined in Croatia as a result of the adjustments and remained about the same in Serbia and Bosnia-Hercegovina.[16] None of these changes, themselves not very well correlated with levels of development, led to a realignment of the regions more consistent with expectations based on the rates of investment and capital formation. Thus, although structural differences affected estimated labor productivity, interregional differences in rankings according to the unadjusted data were not affected significantly by those structural differences.

Nikolić considered several other factors that might have systematically affected interregional differences in labor productivity. One was the provision of capital goods and power to workers. Nikolić studied the value of fixed capital per worker, of equipment per worker, and of power machinery per worker. None of these gave a ranking of branches consistent with rankings according to levels of labor productivity; in all of them, the two republics with the highest rankings according to capital goods criteria were Montenegro and Bosnia-Hercegovina.[17] Testing the hypothesis that scale economies could account for observed differences in average labor productivity, Nikolić ranked the republics according to the share of industrial output produced in 1967 in large enterprises; size was measured by social product (over 50 million dinars), fixed capital (over 50 million dinars), and number of employees (over 2,000). Once more, the rankings by these measures were not consistent with the rankings by level of labor productivity.[18]

Unfortunately, all tests carried out by Nikolić were single-variable tests, and the data he reported are not adequate for performing independent multivariate experiments. The combined effect of the variables mentioned might be more important than the effects taken singly, and a weighting of the several variables might produce a ranking more consistent with the rankings according to average labor productivity. However, the single-variable results cast doubt on these possibilities. In too many cases, republics with low productivity rank at the top according to factors that should be positively correlated with productivity.

Nikolić found one set of variables that did have a reasonable connection with differences in productivity. These were variables measuring the level of development of the republic. He measured that level in two ways: by the proportion of industrial workers in the population and by the value of social product per inhabitant. Rankings according to either of these variables were much closer to rankings according to industrial labor productivity, although unexplained differences in the rankings remained.[19] Nikolić interpreted these measures of the level of development as substitutes for intangible influences on labor productivity—e.g., the interest of potential and actual workers in industrial occupations, the quality of management, work habits, and labor discipline, the skills of workers, and industrial tradition. Whether the variables chosen by Nikolić provide adequate substitutes for these factors is questionable.

A more interesting aspect of the matter is its implication for development in the less developed areas. According to the results of Nikolić's investigation, a low proportion of industrial workers in the population is an indication of a low level of development and is linked with low labor productivity. As a matter of arithmetic, industrial development—i.e., increasing the rate of industrial production—is the result of raising industrial employment or labor productivity or both. The capital transfer program had, as we have seen, only a small relative effect on labor productivity, and the anticipated stimulation of industrial employment failed to materialize. If that program had been the only aspect of economic policy impinging upon regional development, it would have to be judged an utter failure. In fact, certain other parts of economic policy, discussed below, tended to offset the impact of the capital transfer program and negated its effects. To judge the potential impact of the transfer program, the impacts of these other lines of policy must be considered.

THE TRANSFER PROGRAM AND NATIONAL INDUSTRIAL GROWTH

The investment transfer program, although not as successful as expected, undoubtedly was an important factor in the rapid rates of growth of industrial output in the less developed regions described in chapter 6. In this respect, the program achieved its purpose. But it is reasonable to raise the question of the cost of this acceleration. The answer depends in part on how cost is measured. No single definition is fully satisfactory. For example, although the policy may have mollified critics of the regime in the less developed regions and thereby contributed to national stability, it had the opposite effect in the regions that were taxed to provide the investment funds, especially in Croatia.[20] The net effect of such an intangible factor cannot be evaluated, however important it might be. Many other ways to measure the cost of the program could be devised and discussed, but, in view of the central subject of this study, one measure seems most appropriate: the impact it had on the growth of industrial production in the country as a whole. In other words, what would the national growth rate have been in the absence of the investment fund transfer program?

Any answer to this question is necessarily hypothetical, and the reader must judge its usefulness in view of the methods used to reach it. The approach used here is to apply estimates of capital productivity in the different regions to hypothetical capital stock increases estimated by assuming that the investment transfer program was replaced by a policy intended to raise overall levels of investment, but not to shift capital from one region to another. The procedure, described in more detail below, requires estimates of the transfers of investment funds; hence, those estimates are a by-product of the calculations.

Estimates of the Transfers

How can the transfers be estimated? As noted earlier, interregional flows cannot be measured directly on the basis of available data. A glance at table 42, however, shows that after 1966 essentially only the less developed areas received investment support from government funds, a category which, for that period, includes all sources other than the banks and the funds of the enterprises themselves. These government funds appear to have been predominantly supplied by the FAD, although relatively small amounts of funds from other sources are included. The available data are not sufficient for calculating the exact share of FAD funds in this category; so it was assumed that the category included only FAD funds, and this category was taken as the basis for subsequent estimates of the transfers.

By itself, this would overstate the transfers. However, although the FAD was the main source of investment subsidies in the less developed regions, it is clear that it was not the only one. Preferential loan treatment and other forms of direct and indirect subsidies that would be reflected (in unknown amounts) in bank credits also played a role. The value of these subsidies cannot be estimated, but they would tend to offset the overstatement arising from considering all government funding in the less developed areas to be FAD funds. Thus, for the years 1967 through 1971, the total value of the transfers was assumed to equal the value of the funds for investment originating in government sources.

Before the FAD went into full operation in 1967, investment transfers to the less developed regions were included in other categories of investment finance and cannot be separated from those overall amounts except on the basis of some assumption about the level of the subsidies. The approach used here is to estimate the subsidy levels for earlier years[21] by assuming that the average proportion of government-supplied investment funds to total nonenterprise funding during 1967–71 holds true for earlier years. Using the post-1966 proportion may lead to underestimating transfers in earlier years because political pressures from the "donor" regions in the latter years led to a cutback in the volume of transfers.[22] No viable alternative basis for estimation is available, however. Furthermore, the procedure may lead to an overestimate for Bosnia-Hercegovina because of its ambivalent position in the regional program in earlier years, but the alternative—assuming transfers to Bosnia-Hercegovina in those years to be zero—is less tenable.

The results of this rough estimating procedure are presented in table 47. From the beginning of the program in 1958, the volume of funds transferred appeared

TABLE 47

ESTIMATES OF INVESTMENT FUND TRANSFERS IN REGIONAL DEVELOPMENT PROGRAM

Year	Total Funds Transferred[a] (millions of new dinars, current prices)	*Percentage of Total Investment Expenditures*	
		Yugoslavia	Donor Regions[b]
1958	160	8.9	10.8
1959	180	8.3	9.9
1960	270	8.8	10.7
1961	380	9.4	11.5
1962	470	10.7	13.3
1963	580	11.0	13.8
1964	770	11.8	15.0
1965	–	–	–
1966	689	8.5	10.9
1967	1,039	13.4	17.3
1968	1,124	11.5	14.8
1969	1,328	13.5	16.2
1970	1,702	14.0	16.8
1971	1,699	13.2	16.0

SOURCES: See table 35.

[a]For 1967–71, the total amount of government funds (assumed to be FAD funds) used in investment finance in the less developed areas. For 1958–66, estimated from nonenterprise investment finance in the less developed areas by multiplying that sum by the average proportion which FAD funds bore to total nonenterprise funds during 1967–71. See text for further discussion.

[b]For 1958–66, Croatia, Slovenia, and Serbia. For 1967–71, Croatia, Slovenia, Serbia proper, and Vojvodina.

to rise steadily in nominal terms, but inflation during the period must have caused a lower real rate of increase. As a share of total investment expenditures (including funds from the government, the banks, and the enterprises), transfers attributable to the regional industrialization program also rose more or less steadily throughout the period. The possibility of understatement of transfers in the earlier period means that the upward trend may be exaggerated. This bias would be partially offset if transfers to Bosnia-Hercegovina were overestimated in the period before 1966. In any event, there is no doubt that very substantial amounts were transferred to the less developed areas.

The Impact on Overall Growth

Assessing the impact of the transfers on the overall rate of industrial growth requires estimating what growth would have been in the absence of the transfer program. Rough estimates of marginal capital productivities[23] for the republics and autonomous provinces of the country can be calculated from the measurements of output growth reported in chapter 6 and from capital stock data. These estimated capital productivities can then be applied to estimates of changes in capital stocks that would have occurred without the transfer program to produce estimates of regional growth rates. Finally, these growth rates can be combined by means of appropriate weights to give estimates of overall growth rates.

Changes in capital stock were estimated by assuming that the transfer program was financed by taxes levied on enterprises in the more developed regions and that the tax was proportional to national income produced in the industrial sector in each region.[24] On this assumption, the investment transfers, shown in table 47, were allocated to the more developed regions in proportion to their shares of national income produced in industry.[25] Along with the adjusted investment figures in the less developed regions, this provided a set of hypothetical levels of investment that, by hypothesis, would have existed in the absence of the transfer program. Then, hypothetical annual changes in capital stock were obtained by multiplying the actual change by the ratio of the hypothetical to the actual investments in each region.

From beginning to end, the process of estimating the impact of the transfer program on the overall growth rate is fraught with points of potential weakness. Despite efforts to make it rest on plausible assumptions and to remain reasonably faithful to the actual procedures for transferring funds, arbitrary choices are necessary. The assumption about fund transfer rates before 1967 is only the most glaring of these. Other technical shortcomings are readily apparent. For example, there can be no doubt that investment behavior by enterprises, both recipients and "donors," would have been different without the transfer program. Again, the computations assume that the estimated marginal capital productivities would remain constant over inframarginal changes.[26] For all these reasons, the results of the calculations can be regarded only as very rough estimates.

There is considerable variation between the annual growth rates for the industrial sector calculated by this procedure and those calculated for the same years from the sample index reported in table 5 (the direct weights index). In six of the twelve years for which estimates are made, the estimated annual growth rate is higher than the rate calculated from the sample index; in the other six years, it is lower. The average difference between estimated and calculated growth rates is positive (about 0.5 percentage point per year), but the variance is so great that the difference is not statistically significantly different from zero.[27]

On the basis of this limited evidence, then, it cannot be concluded with confidence that the regional investment transfer program caused a reduction in the overall rate of growth of industrial production, although the direction of the average difference in growth rates is consistent with that effect. From that narrow point of view, there is only weak evidence of conflict between the objectives of accelerated growth in the backward regions and the growth of the industrial sector of the country as a whole.

INCONSISTENCIES OF THE REGIONAL POLICY

This result is surprising in view of the well-publicized examples of wastefulness in investments made as part of the regional program. It means that the waste seen in the more glaring examples—the Nikšić steel mill and the rest of the political factories—was offset by higher productivity elsewhere. In other words, marginal capital productivities, on average, did not vary appreciably from one region to another. This might encourage advocates of the program since they could argue that capital transfers would not reduce overall growth rates. But at the same time, it means that the rapid investment rates stimulated by the transfer program failed to produce above-average capital productivities in the recipient areas. In that sense, this finding is a symptom of failure in the regional development program.

There is, in fact, broad agreement among Yugoslav economists that the program was a failure. Many have noted that gaps in per capita national income among regions widened during the period,[28] a result blamed mostly on the rapid population growth rates in the less developed regions. They usually fail to see, however, that even if population growth rates had not been different, reducing the absolute size of the gaps in per capita national income would have required very large differentials in growth rates of output. For example, in 1952 national income per capita in Slovenia was more than four times as great as in Kosovo and about three times as large as in Macedonia.[29] Suppose that the populations of Slovenia and Kosovo did not grow at all over the following twenty years, and, for the sake of simplicity, that the 1952 ratio of per capita national incomes in the two regions was exactly 4.0. If national income in Slovenia had grown at an annual rate of 5 percent over the subsequent twenty years, merely maintaining the same absolute gap in per capita national income would have required an average annual growth rate in Kosovo over the entire period of 10.7 percent. The higher rates of population growth in the less developed regions contributed to widening gaps in per capita incomes, but the growth rates of output were too low to achieve an actual narrowing even without population growth.

Other symptoms of the disappointing outcome of the policy echo criticisms made by Yugoslav economists. The less developed regions lagged behind the other areas more in per capita income than in capital assets per worker or per capita, implying relatively low levels of efficiency. The policy failed to stimulate rapid increases in industrial employment.[30] Performance was poor despite the fact that investment as a share of national income was higher in the less developed regions than elsewhere.[31] The list of symptoms could be extended and documented further.[32]

Why the Policy Failed

This widespread agreement among Yugoslav economists about the failure of the policy is not matched by full agreement about its causes, although there are common themes, ranging from charges of inadequate planning to allegations of poor investment decisions, in their discussions.

Many writers complain about the poor infrastructure of less developed areas.[33] They contend that the lack of adequate transportation services created difficulties in moving workers to and from plants and in maintaining a smooth flow of raw materials and semifabricates to plants and of finished products from plants to markets. Moreover, the lack of auxiliary services—trade, catering, health care, and even water—prevented the effective use of new production facilities. New installations, they charge, were located where these services did not exist, and the location of supplies of raw materials and of potential purchasers was ignored. They further observe that the technologies employed in the new plants exceeded the skills of the available labor force, with the result that investments in advanced technology were wasted and output was less than it would have been had an appropriate technology been chosen.[34] They cite the shortage of trained personnel to man new installations as still another cause of the disappointing results of the policy.[35] The implication of these charges is that better planning would have resolved or avoided these problems.

Social factors also receive part of the blame for the failure of the regional policy. Most notably, the rapid population growth rates in the less developed areas are the object of much criticism. Other charges include the failure to stimulate the movement of ablebodied persons into industrial work as well as the failure to modify other social characteristics that acted as hindrances to economic development.[36] Other Yugoslav writers stress the importance of traditional methods in processing industries in the backward areas.[37]

Poor agricultural conditions in the less developed areas are also cited.[38] In most cases, agricultural problems persisted because of natural, not social, factors although the limits on landholdings must be considered a social factor inhibiting agricultural development throughout Yugoslavia. But in the poorest province, Kosovo, at least one writer argues that the opposite is true.[39] There, natural conditions are favorable for agriculture. The problem is not poor soil, a bad terrain, or a deficient climate, but rather the high population density in the agricultural areas and the adherence to traditional forms of social organization and methods of cultivation.

Another set of diagnoses of the problems with regional policy concerns investment shortcomings. One line of this argument holds that the structure of investment in the less developed regions was unfavorable to industrial development and concentrated too heavily on establishing facilities for raw materials production, energy, the extractive industries in general, and transportation.[40]

(The last-mentioned criticism obviously contradicts the complaints that lack of adequate transportation services was one of the reasons for the failure of the program.) There is, however, little evidence, as we have seen, that investment was concentrated in raw materials, energy, and the extractive industries.

Another line of argument concerning investment pertains to its level, rather than to its structure. Although the rate of growth of industrial fixed capital per employed person was higher in the less developed regions, the high rates of population growth in the backward areas resulted in relatively low rates of growth of investment per capita. This, in turn, was reflected in relatively low levels of investment per capita, a fact taken to be a cause of the policy's failure.[41] In view of the outcome, given the relatively high rates of investment that existed in these regions, it is doubtful that still higher levels would have made much difference. Nevertheless, the possibilities for independent accumulation of investment funds are a subject of comment by Yugoslav economists.

One writer cites several reasons for relatively poor capital accumulation possibilities in the less developed regions. During the last part of the period, there was a trend in the distribution of enterprise income that favored personal income payments at the expense of retaining income for enterprise business funds. This had the effect of squeezing the residual available for investment more in the less developed areas than elsewhere because enterprises in less developed areas, whose per employee incomes were smaller than in other enterprises, nevertheless tried to pay similar wages.[42] This argument, it might be noted, rests on the assumption that an essentially national labor market exists. This is not consistent with well-known evidence about internal labor migration, which suggests that cultural differences restricted migration in large measure to intraregional movements. If it is true that enterprises felt pressured to pay equal wages, it must have been for some other reason, possibly political.

It is also argued that the federal government's price and foreign trade policies were systematically biased against enterprises in the less developed regions.[43] The goal of these policies was to promote general industrialization, and the conflict between them and the objectives of regional development policy seems to reflect a fundamental ambivalence in economic policy. Price policy was intended to stimulate the production of manufactured goods; broadly speaking, it maintained relatively high prices for highly fabricated finished products and relatively low prices for raw materials, semifabricates, and agricultural products. According to Yugoslav economists, this led to the creation of unfavorable terms of trade for the less developed regions, which tended to specialize in the low-priced goods, compared with the rest of the country. In turn, the poor terms of trade constrained income-generating possibilities—and hence capital accumulation possibilities—of enterprises in the less developed areas. A similar situation prevailed in foreign trade policy, which tended to favor producers of manufactured goods and to penalize enterprises producing raw materials. Import duties were low on raw materials and semifabricates but high on final products; exports of finished products often were encouraged by subsidies. These policies limited capital accumulation possibilities for enterprises specializing in products with low levels of fabrication—enterprises which, according to Yugoslav observers, were concentrated in the relatively less developed regions.

Interpreted in this way, there was an internal contradiction in Yugoslav economic policy, an ambivalence that implies either a mistake or a failure to perceive the consequences of the two aspects of policy. But this interpretation views the motivation behind regional policy as primarily economic. This view is too narrow. The motivation for the regional program was undoubtedly more political than economic, as—among other things—the epithet "political factories," associated with the regional program, suggests. The investment fund transfer program, in this perspective, was a means of pacifying the political leadership in the backward areas while devoting the main force of economic policy to the main objective of overall industrialization.

CHAPTER ELEVEN

Industrialization and Yugoslav Workers' Self-Management

In the quarter century following the adoption of workers' self-management, Yugoslavia rose from the ranks of the world's economic backwaters to a position just short of the development levels of the less developed West European states. Unquestionably a great transformation occurred in a relatively short period, and the importance of industrialization in this transformation is obvious. The course of Yugoslav industrial development is especially interesting because it provides an insight into the operation of a unique economic system from a point of view different from the more usual theoretical analyses of the properties of the system. Inevitably, the analysis must turn to the role of the government in the system. Various government interventions had important modifying effects on the performance of the self-management system. The economic and political characteristics of Yugoslav self-management observable in the course of industrialization are important in understanding and interpreting the past performance of self-management and therefore in forecasting future developments in Yugoslavia.

ECONOMY AND STATE IN INDUSTRIALIZATION

At the first level of analysis, industrialization in Yugoslavia resembles industrialization in a number of other countries. For a country at Yugoslavia's initial level of development, the pace of growth was about what might be expected—perhaps not quite as rapid as Japan's or Israel's, but in the same range—when due allowance is made for measurement errors and methodological differences that inevitably blur international comparisons. The official Yugoslav index appears to overstate annual growth rates by a percentage point or so, at least in comparison with the indexes commonly used to measure growth in noncommunist countries, and comparisons based on the official index could mislead the observer about the relative pace of Yugoslav industrialization. The sample indexes developed for this study eliminate much of the methodological difference that causes incomparability, and with their use the Yugoslav industrialization record fits international patterns very well.

The pace of output growth, measured by standard index numbers, is only one dimension of industrialization. In the course of a transformation like the one that occurred in Yugoslavia, growth in output is necessarily accompanied by changes in the composition of output. There was, as has been shown, substantial change in the structure of output, but, for the level of development at which the economy began, the change in structure was again unremarkable. International comparisons of change in output composition are statistically difficult, but the limited comparisons that can be made show that although output structure in Yugoslavia changed more than in such mature economies as West Germany and the United States, it shifted more or less to the same degree as Japan's. Again, following a pattern commonly observed, Yugoslavia's industrial growth rate declined from early, higher levels.

Sources of Growth

Published Yugoslav data do not allow sophisticated analyses of the sources of industrial growth.[1] Much the same sources of growth as in other countries appear to have been responsible for the expansion of industrial output, although their relative importance cannot be determined with available data.

For example, capital formation was clearly central to the government's industrialization policy and was certainly a major factor in growth. If conceptual problems of measuring capital in a socialist economy and statistical shortcomings in the capital stock data available for Yugoslavia are disregarded, the rate of growth of reproducible capital in Yugoslav industry and mining averaged 9.3 percent per year during the period 1952–71. To put this in perspective, during this same period Japanese capital stock—for the whole economy—rose at an average annual rate of 9.9 percent.[2] Moreover, it is known that capital stock growth was slightly faster in the Yugoslav economy as a whole than in the industrial sector alone. Denison and Chung attribute about a quarter of Japanese economic growth from 1953 to 1971 to capital growth,[3] and Denison's estimates for the United States and Western Europe for 1950 to 1962 are, in most cases, in the same general range.[4] It would be surprising, in view of Yugoslavia's high relative rate of growth to find the contribution of capital stock growth much outside this range.[5]

Second, from 1952 to 1971, labor employment in industry rose at the rapid average annual rate of 5.4 percent. This is largely a reflection of the shift from the handicraft and agricultural sectors to the industrial sector that was an outstanding characteristic of the transformation to a modernized economy. Because of shortcomings in the Yugoslav data, employment data cannot be adjusted for changes in hours worked, education and training of the industrial labor force, and age-sex composition.

Partly because of these difficulties in refining measurements of capital and labor and partly because the determination of weights for them is fundamentally arbitrary in the Yugoslav system, reliable and comparable quantitative estimates of elements contributing to improved factor productivity cannot be made. Discussion of technological change, economies of scale, and improved management and organization therefore must be carried out in qualitative terms. Horvat's study attributes about 40 percent of industrial growth between 1955 and 1967 to technological change,[6] but his estimates are clearly overstatements and include economies of scale as well as improved technology. His estimates probably also subsume the impact of improved management practices and organization in industry. The importance of scale economies for industrial growth cannot be evaluated quantitatively, but analysis of likely bias in Horvat's estimating procedures leaves little doubt that they were important. For Japan, advances in knowledge and economies of scale accounted for about 44 percent of growth in the economy as a whole from 1953 to 1961, and about 47 percent from 1961 to 1971, according to Denison and Chung;[7] a figure in that general range would not be surprising for the Yugoslav industrial sector.

The Unique System

Both the industrial growth rate and the sources of that growth thus appear not greatly different from those observed in other countries, after due allowance is made for the focus in Yugoslavia on the industrial sector alone, the initial level of development, and the extent of change in the composition of output. What sets Yugoslav experience apart is the nature of the institutional framework, the only important system of workers' self-management in the world.

The system formally features decentralization of authority and responsibility. Through the system of workers' councils, the workers, as members of an enterprise, in principle control its operations—indeed, are legally responsible for maintaining the value of its capital. Through the political process, the workers, again in principle, exercise ultimate control over economic policy, including the formation of economic plans. The plans, although not legally binding on any enterprise or individual, define—in principle—development policy and crucial investment priorities. During the period covered by this study, reforms that formally advanced decentralization occurred. It is perhaps not an exaggeration to say that the decentralization of decision making and its locus in the worker-members of an enterprise have been the major causes of interest in the Yugoslav economic system.[8]

Yet it is easy to exaggerate the degree of actual decentralization in the Yugoslav economy. Despite de jure decentralization, the central government and the communist party have retained control of the economy, not merely through aggregate economic policy, but also through a variety of channels reaching to the enterprises. As in any one-party communist state, the Yugoslav League of Communists is an elite party that maintains full control of the political process;[9] the political turmoil of the late sixties was largely (but not entirely) an internecine affair. Given this setting, the political influence of nonparty workers could not have been strong.

Control of developments in the economy has been exercised in a variety of ways and can be illustrated by a few examples. The government has controlled industrialization policy—which it could not renounce in view of the tenuous position of Yugoslavia between East and West—largely by controlling investment volume and allocation. Before the reforms of the mid-sixties, allocative control was exercised through centralized investment funds; after that time, it appears that the banks took over the role previously played by the funds. Nominally independent, the banks were subject to central influence and control through the presence of government representatives on the banks' governing bodies, through the control of the National Bank over the policies of the commercial banks, and doubtlessly through the government's informal power to influence the selection and dismissal of bank directors. The level of investment was effectively determined by taxation of enterprise income, which set the level of savings. Taxation also served as a means of limiting enterprise autonomy because the actual tax rates were so high that enterprises had little discretionary income remaining after payment of taxes, obligatory contributions, and mandated payments to various funds.

The depth to which workers' earnings were cut to finance the investment rates recorded in Yugoslavia can be appreciated by a comparison with corresponding U.S. data, although differences in national income accounting methods make precise comparisons impossible and peculiarities in Yugoslav procedures preclude comparisons based on industry alone. In 1965, disposable personal incomes in the United States were 69.1 percent of GNP.[10] For Yugoslavia, something approximating the U.S. concept of gross national product may be obtained by adding gross investment to total consumption funds (including both personal and "social" consumption). In 1966, total consumption was 60.8 percent and personal consumption 52.2 percent of this sum.[11] Direct wage payments (personal incomes, in Yugoslav parlance) in industry amounted to just 36.2 percent of national income produced in this sector.[12] Tax constraints on enterprise decisions regarding wages were effective; when constraints were temporarily relaxed after the 1965 reform, wage payments increased sharply.[13] Even in Japan, with its high rate of capital formation, it is doubtful that net labor incomes occupied such a small share of national product. Although labor earnings in Japan were at the low end of the scale established in the United States and Western Europe, they were not dramatically different from those in other countries.[14] The main difference in financing investment between Japan and Yugoslavia was that investment in Japan was financed nearly equally by corporate retained earnings and voluntary private savings;[15] about three-fourths of Yugoslavia's came from taxation of enterprise income.

Yugoslavia's central government also exercised control over the economy and its enterprises less directly, through its intervention in the domestic and foreign trade markets. Price and foreign exchange controls played important roles in the execution of industrialization policy. Ostensibly intended to foster development by encouraging production of highly fabricated goods in favored industrial branches, these controls necessarily functioned by conditioning the incentive structures that enterprise management faced. In that respect, they constituted a form of indirect control over the enterprises.

Besides these central controls resulting from conscious government policy, it is important to take note of a characteristic of the system of self-management that gives the central government a natural means of controlling enterprise actions. Yugoslav industrial enterprises typically are large—not the giants found in American industry, but large enough to exhibit scale economies.[16] In organizations of such size, the extent of actual influence over enterprise policies and decisions exercised by individual workers is inevitably limited by a host of factors familiar from analysis of bureaucratic behavior, including the cost of information, the probability of affecting decisions in a large group, the costs of monitoring managerial behavior, and free rider problems. The costs of obtaining information about external business conditions and about the operations of all parts of the enterprise and of making positions on enterprise policy credible are much smaller for an enterprise director than for anyone else in the organization (especially rank-and-file workers). For these reasons, the director is in a position to dominate enterprise decisions, especially those concerning business policy—investment, pricing, and product lines. Possibly as a result of this and possibly because of the more immediate impact on workers, rank-and-file workers apparently exert relatively more influence over decisions regarding working conditions and, to a lesser extent, wage payments than they do over broader business policy decisions.[17] Normally, then, the director of any reasonably good sized enterprise, aided by his staff, is the dominant figure in key facets of enterprise decision making.

The director's dominance in these aspects of enterprise policy gives the central authorities an obvious opportunity for control. Private alternatives to employment in the socialized sector of the one-party state are open to managerial personnel only at substantial opportunity cost. This places the political authorities in an excellent position to influence and control the behavior of enterprise directors and, thereby, the activities of the enterprises. The authorities, seeking high investment rates, can control the aggregate real wage level to produce the desired level of savings by manipulating tax rates. These rates are so high that the director's ability to decide on the allocation of net income is closely constrained. In such a situation, there is no need for the central authorities to attempt to interfere with relative wages or microeconomic wage policy in general. The very aspects of enterprise decision making in which directors would tend to have most independence are those which the central authorities have the strongest interest in controlling. It would be most surprising if the government failed to avail itself of these opportunities for control; indeed, it would be surprising if this aspect of workers' self-management, of all the unknowns facing the party in 1950, did not receive careful consideration before the decision to adopt this revolutionary economic system.

The Yugoslav economic system is, in fact, thoroughly politicized, a natural occurrence in a communist state with an elite party. The adoption of self-management was motivated in large measure by political considerations, especially the ideological claims that could be made for the system. It is reasonable to argue that economic policy has been more strongly influenced by political factors than in other countries. Certainly regional policy existed largely because of political considerations. Enterprises are far more likely to be the creations of government units, which inevitably retain interest in them, than they are to be formed by groups of private individuals because enterprise founders renounce their rights to the initial capital of the enterprise when it is formed. A final example of the politicization of the Yugoslav economy is found in the importance of banks in economic policy execution and the important role played by government officials in the execution of bank policy. More examples could be given, but it should be clear that economic policy from the very outset of the self-management period—and even before, when one objective of Yugoslav economic policy was to demonstrate loyalty to Stalin—was dictated to an important degree by political considerations.

Industrialization and the State

The retention of centralized control and the general politicization of the economy strengthen the view that in Yugoslavia, as in other communist states, industrialization was primarily a creation of the state, not the result of individual choice. It seems clear that investment rates were higher than they would have been if freely chosen by Yugoslav citizens, both from the very low share that wages were of national product and from behavior when controls were briefly relaxed.[18] The pattern of development was probably different than it would have been in the absence of central control of investment fund allocation, price controls, and foreign exchange intervention.[19] Industrial development was also stimulated, perhaps inadvertently, by the state's policy of limiting opportunities in agriculture. Specifically, opportunities in private agriculture were restricted for reasons that originated in ideological and political considerations, with the result that rural dwellers found industrial employment relatively more attractive than it would have otherwise been.

These factors support the view that the industrialization policy amounted to a Yugoslav version of forced-draft industrialization. The coercive nature of investment finance is perhaps the dominant feature of Yugoslav industrialization, a feature that clearly distinguishes Yugoslav from Japanese development. In Japan, the savings rate was controlled by individual choices; the very high rates of capital formation were made possible by a combination of factors: a high growth rate of output with which to finance savings, falling relative prices of capital goods, and a high and rising rate of private savings, both individual and corporate.[20] Indeed, in contrast to the heavy taxation in Yugoslavia that was the prime source of investment finance, in Japan tax rates were kept low.[21] Yugoslav policy did not entail the Draconian measures concerning labor familiar in Stalinist forced-draft industrialization, but rapid mobilization of resources that were believed to be potential contributors to industrial growth was certainly at its center.

There were, naturally, some distinctly Yugoslav characteristics in this version of industrialization. It was implemented under the banner of workers' self-management in the aftermath of the war, and the authorities were able to utilize the pioneering nature of the new system as well as Yugoslavia's precarious international position and postwar patriotic feelings to justify the sacrifices imposed on the population. Local decision making, even on matters of lesser import than those of real interest to economic policy, provided a safety valve for the pressures generated by forced-draft industrialization. Furthermore, to a certain extent the tax system masked the real burden of taxation. Personal income taxes were kept low; just as the withholding tax makes tax burdens appear lighter than they actually are, taxation of enterprise income before the wage determination process begins conceals the real tax burden, at least for a while. But none of these factors that contributed to the acceptance of forced-draft industrialization could be expected to last over long periods. Emotions cool, and people learn to penetrate the tax structure and see the real costs imposed on them. By the end of the first twenty years of self-management, strains that presaged difficulties for the future of industrialization in Yugoslavia began to appear.

FUTURE INDUSTRIAL GROWTH

As early as 1962, signs of slackening in the pace of industrial growth can be perceived in the indexes of industrial production. Through the middle part of the sixties, with the economic reforms and the political developments of that period, growth was erratic, and retardation more marked. This was a time of some genuine decentralization of authority to the enterprises, of greater discretion for decisions about disposal of net income and other aspects of enterprise operations. By the beginning of the seventies, central authority had been reasserted, and earlier investment levels more or less reattained. Through the middle of the decade, growth was steadier than during the unsettled reform period, but at a lower pace. But the regional program had been a serious disappointment, and the experience with genuine decentralization indicated that the rate of investment desired by the people was lower than that enforced by the growth-minded government. More serious than this, perhaps, were the signs of political unrest manifested in recrudescent Croatian nationalism, the revelation of the existence of splinter communist groups, and the growing independence of republic governments. The immediate problem was resolved in the usual communist way, by a purge of dissidents and independently inclined politicians. These political difficulties underline the fact that communism per se has been no more able to unite the peoples of Yugoslavia than any other government. The charisma of Tito and the chauvinism inspired by the war have been responsible for preventing the country's disintegration for thirty years, by Yugoslav standards a long time. Neither is eternal, and political uncertainties cloud any forecast of Yugoslavia's future. In the discussion that follows, political matters are largely disregarded, although they cannot be ignored altogether.

Economic Factors and Future Industrial Growth

Industrial Employment: The growth rate of industrial employment began to slow in the sixties. Continuation of the downward trend must be expected for demographic and other reasons. The pace of qualitative change in the labor force—the growth rate of human capital—must be expected to slow, on average, in the future. The implications of these facts transcend the obvious point that the growth rate of labor input to industry will be lower than during the period studied here. They further affect the efficacy of continued capital stock growth as a source of maintaining industrial expansion.

The most reliable estimates of Yugoslav population growth rates to the end of the century predict substantially slower growth than was experienced in the quarter century beginning in 1950. During that earlier period, the average annual increase in population was 1.08 percent; the U.S. Department of Commerce estimates that the average annual rate of population growth from 1975 to 2000 will fall between a minimum of 0.58 and a maximum of 1.03 percent. The Commerce Department's so-called medium projection gives an average annual rate of 0.81 percent, and their estimate based on assuming a constant fertility rate equal to that of 1974 is 0.80 percent.[22] The pool from which industrial labor will be drawn in the future seems almost certain to widen at a slower pace than that experienced to date.

Yugoslav successes in the postwar period in raising schooling levels have diminished the likelihood of increasing the human capital embodied in the slower growing population. According to official Yugoslav data, illiteracy, widespread before the war, was dramatically reduced by the end of the 1970s.[23] Years of schooling had risen with similar rapidity.[24] Opportunities for improved education (especially in the broad sense of the term) still exist in Yugoslavia, and human capital should continue to grow in the future. Whether improvement on a mass scale can continue at the same rate as in the postwar quarter century is conjectural, however. It may be that the rapid gains are now largely exhausted; if so, one of the sources of above-average growth in output is also exhausted.

Industrial sector employment grew faster than the population as a whole during the thirty years after the war, and it could do so in the future. There are systemic and circumstantial factors, however, that suggest that the slower growth of the population will be reflected in lower industrial employment growth rates.

Theoretically, there are disincentives to expansion of membership in a self-managed enterprise even when demand for its product grows.[25] If so, expansion of employment in the industrial sector must in large measure come through the creation of new enterprises. But it has already been emphasized that private incentives to form new enterprises are blunted by the rules governing their formation, in particular the fact that founders do not retain individual rights to the capital that they invest in the enterprise. It can be expected, then, that government units will play a disproportionately important role in forming new enterprises. Creating employment within their jurisdictions might be a factor motivating local and regional governments to create enterprises, but it is not the only one. This means that the enterprises created will not be the same in either line of business or size of operation as privately financed, for-profit firms formed in a capitalist system confronting the same demand conditions. In short, the relative importance of the government in establishing new enterprises will cause inefficiencies in the number, size, and mix of enterprises. This means that even if government units formed enterprises at a rate that maintained earlier growth rates of industrial employment, the labor involved would be inefficiently employed. Yugoslav history is replete with examples of this problem. To the extent that government intervention offsets private disincentives to employment expansion, the resulting employment growth will be partly illusory because of these inefficiencies.

There is a further problem. The agricultural sector is commonly an important source of growth in the labor force in the course of development. In Japan, for example, the agricultural labor force fell by nearly one-half between 1953 and 1971; it constituted 35.6 percent of total employment in 1953, but only 14.6 percent in 1971.[26] Even so, Denison and Chung argue that in Japan the contribution to growth resulting from the reallocation of labor from inefficiently scaled agricultural operations to other, more efficient, employment was limited by remaining overallocations to the agricultural sector.[27]

As noted in chapter 2, industrialization in Yugoslavia coincided with a substantial decline in agricultural employment, but the decline was much less dramatic than in Japan. At the beginning of the self-management period, agricultural employment (including fishing and forestry) was relatively more important than it was in Japan at the same time, and constituted nearly two-thirds of all economically active persons in 1953.[28] In the following eighteen years, there was a net reduction of about 1.3 million in the number of economically active persons employed in agriculture, leaving agriculture with about 45 percent of the economically active population. Between 1953 and 1971 Japanese agricultural employment fell at an average annual rate of about 3.3 percent; for that period the corresponding rate for Yugoslavia was 1.2 percent.[29]

The slower decline in the Yugoslav agricultural sector may partly reflect slow-dying peasant resistance to change. From an economic point of view, however, the most significant characteristic of the Yugoslav agricultural sector is its structure of property rights. The near catastrophic attempt at collectivizing agriculture during the late forties left the government little choice but to sanction private enterprise in agriculture. Despite the fact that the social sector of agriculture was the beneficiary of the vast bulk of centralized agricultural investment,[30] in 1970 more than two-thirds of total farmland was in the private sector.[31] But ideology and inheritance customs in the countryside have caused the private holdings to be uneconomically small; private landholdings are limited by law (in the case of farmland) to ten hectares, and the average size in 1970 of private farms was 3.9 hectares, a fact attributed by the authors of the World Bank study of Yugoslavia to the tendency of farms to be divided in intergenerational transfers.[32]

Agricultural productivity is surely lower than it would be with larger-scale operations, and it can hardly be doubted that total output could be higher if there were less employment in agriculture and more in other sectors of the economy. For industry, however, the pertinent fact is that employment growth is restricted by, among other things, the slow and decelerating movement of labor out of agriculture.

The policy options available to the government for ameliorating this situation are not conducive to optimism. The earlier experience with collectivization and current internal political problems probably rule out any attempt to achieve scale economies and acceleration in the decline of agricultural employment by authoritarian fiat. The state can establish more labor-managed agricultural enterprises, but then the problem becomes one of attracting peasants from their private holdings to the collectives. That kind of option has been open in industry for many years, and the peasants have not responded to it with enthusiasm. Nor have they moved to existing labor-managed agricultural enterprises. The latter may be more appealing than industrial enterprises to farm-bred peasants, but the fundamental difference in ownership rights evidently discourages membership in either. It is easy to say that the solution lies in removing or relaxing the restriction on the size of private landholdings, but that is probably incorrect. The peasants have continued to subdivide existing land in private ownership, and it is doubtful that allowing larger plots would result in important changes in tenure.

The path to improvement may well lie in an entirely different direction: relaxing restrictions on private enterprise outside the agricultural sector. At present, private enterprise too is closely constrained by rules limiting the number of hired workers that a private enterprise may employ. Among other things, by restricting private opportunities in this way, the government has lowered the (opportunity) cost to peasants of remaining on their tiny landholdings. The peasants have demonstrated that the value of their alternatives open in agricultural, industrial, and other self-managed enterprises is to them lower than the value they place on returns open in private agriculture. The solution is to raise the value of the alternatives, and one way to do this is to make the nonagricultural private sector more attractive. That this will happen is, of course, highly unlikely; by permitting individuals to hire any workers at all, the Yugoslavs are already skating on thin ideological ice.

Capital Growth: As the rate of industrial employment declines, continuation of the same growth rate of capital implies an eventual reduction in productivity if no technological change occurs and human capital grows no faster than employment.[33] In a free market economy, this would cause a reduction in the rate of investment and a decline in the rate of growth of output as the growth rate of the capital stock slowed.[34] In a socialist system, there is no automatic mechanism that would cause a slowing in the investment rate since the central authorities can, within broad limits, determine the rate. By demonstrating reduced capital productivity political groups dissatisfied with the high level of forced savings could possibly create pressure to reduce investment rates. But whether they would do so or would be successful is beyond the scope of economic analysis.

More importantly, in a wide variety of circumstances continuing capital stock growth at a rate in excess of the labor growth rate—assuming, still, that technological change and other factors potentially contributing to increased factor productivity are inactive—will result in a reduction in the output growth rate.[35] This point was discussed in chapter 9, and its quantitative importance was considered less important than the same phenomenon in the Soviet Union largely because the growth rates of labor and capital were closer to each other during the period studied than they were in the Soviet Union. It is not known whether the technical conditions that cause this slowing of output growth, given unequal factor growth rates, exist in the Yugoslav industrial sector;[36] hence, no firm conclusion can be reached about the slackening pace of growth. The anticipated slowing in the growth rate of industrial labor, however, will have a greater impact quantitatively. The retardation of output growth during the late sixties, when capital was growing substantially more rapidly than labor, is at least superficially consistent with this interpretation.

Other Factors: The analysis to this point suggests that continuation of earlier performance in creating sheer physical output rests largely on improving factor productivity through technological change, exploitation of scale economies, and raising the growth rate of human capital. These are even more speculative matters than those discussed so far, but consideration of them leads to the conclusion that they are unlikely to be the source of unusually rapid growth.

Countries with backward economies can for a time reap gains from technological advances made earlier by industrialized countries. By adopting production processes, by purchasing or copying capital goods that embody modern technology, and by utilizing management and organizational principles proved efficient elsewhere, countries embarking on industrialization can take advantage of knowledge developed elsewhere to achieve unusually large increments in output growth. Along with the rapid growth of productive factors, the adoption of modern technology (in this broad sense) can be a source of extraordinary growth.

But this source of growth is necessarily temporary. It is part of a catching-up process. Once a country has caught up, the opportunities for unusual growth stemming from this source no longer exist. Thereafter, technological advance is limited by the general pace of the progress of knowledge worldwide and by the capacities and behavior of the country itself. Yugoslavs are no less intelligent or inventive than any other group, and, with the appropriate incentives, a normal rate of technological progress can be expected. Certainly there have been innovation and invention in the Yugoslav economy, and the importance placed on them by the government is reflected in the fact that individuals may, with restrictions, retain property rights in inventions. But the state retains the right of first purchase, which attenuates incentives to innovate, and, as has been emphasized, the incentives to form new enterprises to exploit inventions are weak. The definition of property rights under workers' self-management seems likely to dampen future indigenous technological development.

The economic system may also retard advances due to adoption of business practices and management methods found effective elsewhere. This source of growth has apparently been important in other places, notably Japan.[37] It is not unavailable to the Yugoslavs, of course, nor has it been unavailed of; systems analysis, computerization, and the rest of the apparatus of modern business management are much in evidence, even to the casual observer. Yet the application of all of this must take place within the framework of workers' self-management, and the system creates obstacles to the most effective use of modern techniques.

Moreover, the efficiency of the capitalist free market system rests in large measure on its particular incentive system—most importantly, in this context, on the incentives facing an owner who has a claim on the residual income of a firm.[38] Even in the theory of the self-managed system, these incentives are weakened by the system of property rights; in the actual politicized system of Yugoslavia, they must be weaker still.

Scale economies are another source of unusually rapid growth in output. They were, as noted above, evidently important in early industrial growth under workers' self-management. Like technological change, however, this source will probably not result in further extraordinary gains in output. Future exploitation of scale economies will rest not on the large investments in energy production and metallurgical and other heavy industries that have already been made, but on new opportunities that arise from the development of new industries and technological advances. In this respect, scale economies as a source of rapid growth are intimately linked to and limited by the pace of technological advance.

Here the self-management system, particularly in Yugoslavia, creates special problems. The incentive structure tends to restrict the size of enterprises because of the disincentive to accept new members. This implication of property rights is compounded by the role of government in forming new enterprises; it was shown earlier that the system in Yugoslavia tends to proliferate smaller enterprises, partly because of the importance of political considerations in decisions to found enterprises.[39] This problem is intensified in Yugoslavia by regional rivalries that seem an ineradicable feature of the polity. The potential for a one-time surge in output may exist in remedying the uneconomical scale of industrial operations, but to do so would require truly revolutionary change in Yugoslavia.

Finally, one might note two external factors that have been important in Yugoslav industrialization. For many years, Yugoslavia ran a large and persistent deficit in the balance on current account. This deficit and the problem of dealing with it were sources of great concern to many Yugoslav economists. But few noticed that the deficit represented an important source of finance for economic development. In effect, Yugoslavia was able to borrow abroad in large volume through the importation of capital and other goods and thus partially relieved the burden placed on its own citizens to finance development. The deficit itself should not have been an object of concern. Reliance on it over long periods of time, however, would be. If foreigners become less willing to underwrite Yugoslav imports, the burden of financing development inevitably will rise.

Much more attention has been focused on the second external factor: the phenomenon of the *gastarbeiter*, or foreign workers. Before the reforms of the 1960s, Yugoslavs were effectively prohibited from seeking or accepting employment outside the country. The reforms brought with them a relaxation of the barriers against foreign employment, and a movement began that reached massive proportions by the mid-seventies. Attracted by higher wages, workers left by the hundreds of thousands. By 1971, almost 600,000 Yugoslavs were working abroad; they represented almost 6 percent of the economically active population enumerated in the 1971 census. According to that census, there were some 4.4 million employees and supervisory personnel in 1971; hence, the *gastarbeiter* represented well over 10 percent of Yugoslavs falling in this general category.[40]

The phenomenon of foreign employment had numerous ramifications for Yugoslavia. There can be no doubt that the experience of living in Western Europe profoundly affected the social and political attitudes of hundreds of thousands of Yugoslavs. The implications of those changes may be the most important effect of *gastarbeiter* emigration.[41] Economically, there were important consequences. First, the emigration eased domestic unemployment problems.[42] Second, remittances from workers abroad were an important factor in the Yugoslav balance of payments and contributed to more favorable terms of trade, thereby augmenting the effect of the balance of payments deficit on financing of industrialization.

But the economic benefits of foreign employment are even more dubious than those of the balance of payments deficit. Employment security for most of the workers is practically nil; any serious economic setbacks in Western Europe almost surely would affect the employment of foreigners first. It is impossible to predict with confidence the numbers of Yugoslavs who would lose their foreign jobs in the event of a West European recession or to know what proportion of them would return home. But any substantial return movement would simultaneously worsen currency problems and exacerbate the persistent unemployment in the economy. The future of industry and the economy as a whole is haunted by the specter of the hundreds of thousands of workers now abroad.

CONCLUSION

Despite the reservations always appropriate in forecasting, it seems likely that Yugoslav industrial output in the future will grow at progressively declining rates. Some of the causes for the retardation—notably demographic factors—are not amenable to substantial change by government policy actions. Others seemingly leave the leadership with only a Hobson's choice as far as industrial growth is concerned. One alternative is to liberalize the economic system in important, perhaps fundamental ways. The reforms necessary to this course involve strengthening the private sector and private initiatives in general. Liberalizing the laws governing ownership of land, the size of private firms, the rights of enterprise founders to capital, and the rights of enterprise members to the capital of the enterprise all fall under this rubric. Unfortunately, this amounts to abandoning some of the central tenets of workers' self-management as it has been practiced in Yugoslavia, a truly revolutionary step and certainly not one to be expected.

A Draconian repression in the system might produce a temporary respite from growth retardation. This would include eliminating the private sector in agriculture, substituting some form of state-run agricultural organization, and channeling more labor to the industrial sector. The history of the collectivization attempt and growing internal political problems indicate that this is an unlikely course, at least without the active support of an outside power. It would constitute a revolution from above, one that would almost certainly provoke a counterrevolution that would have to be extinguished.

If neither of these drastic courses of policy is elected, the future for industrialization seems likely to contain more deceleration of output growth and continued tinkering with the system. But even this unsurprising conclusion must be qualified with cautionary notes about political developments. The jealousies, antagonisms, ethnic differences, and other sources of discord in Yugoslavia will likely continue. No durable stabilization of the country has taken place. Prewar Yugoslavia lasted for twenty years and might have gone on longer except for the intervention of the war. Tito's Yugoslavia has lasted a decade longer than that; how long it will survive him is a question that his surprising longevity has made banal, even though it defines the central political issues in Yugoslavia's future. When the government changes, internal and external forces will be thrown into a struggle whose outcome could dramatically change the face of the country.

Appendixes

APPENDIX A

Value-Added Weights in the Sample Indexes

All weight sets were constructed using the same methods but drawing on different primary sources and base years. The imputed weights were based on producer prices reported in CENE, a series of SZS publications devoted to prices. The direct weights were based on unit values calculated from output and realized sales values reported in *Industrijski proizvodi*, an SZS series that was available only after 1968. For that reason, the only Laspeyres index that could be calculated with a 1952 base was the imputed weights index. (Full citations for the price and unit value data as well as for other data used in calculating the weights are given in the sources for table A-1.)

The price or unit-value datum for each product included in the weight set was first adjusted by eliminating the turnover tax. Data for turnover tax rates were compiled from *Službeni list*, the official gazette of the Yugoslav parliament. The tax rates given for 1952 were updated with data from *Službeni list* for subsequent years. In 1961, there was a flat 0.5 percent tax levied on all goods for which separate rates were not specified. This flat tax was ignored in adjusting 1961 prices and unit values.

Finally, the data net of turnover tax were adjusted by the following procedure to give estimates of value added. SZS published a series of bulletins entitled *Industrijska preduzeća* that contained financial data on industrial enterprises, including costs of materials and data enabling the calculation of gross revenues. The ratio of gross revenues less materials costs to gross revenues (all values net of turnover tax) gives an estimate of the ratio of value added to sales. This ratio can be used to adjust product prices or unit values (net of turnover tax) to provide estimates of value-added weights for the products. Ideally, of course, each price or unit value would be adjusted by its own unique ratio of value added to gross value. *Industrijska preduzeća* did not, however, provide the necessary information at this level of detail. Instead, the financial data were reported by groups of products. Each individual product for which net price or unit value data was available was, therefore, assigned to one of these groups and adjusted by the ratio pertaining to that group. In all branches of industry except rubber and rubber products, data for two or more subgroups were available from *Industrijska preduzeća*.

The nature of the sources for value and output data and the varying extent of reporting at different times (generally more extensive in later periods) combined to produce differing sample sizes in the indexes. The producer prices upon which the imputed weights were based pertained to specific, individual products. They were imputed to products whose outputs were reported in the basic SZS production data series, *Industrija*. In fact, the *Industrija* data frequently referred not to individual products but to collections of items that were grouped together under one generic name. In some of these cases, the bounds of the collection were narrow enough that producer prices for single products could reasonably be imputed to them. In many others, however, this could not be done, with the result that sample size was constricted in the imputed weight indexes. Moreover, the sample sizes for the indexes that begin in 1952 were limited, to a lesser degree, by the availability of output data in that year.

The unit-value weights could be assigned to many more product groups. Unit values could be calculated for a much larger number of individual products, and groups of those products often could be associated with collections of items that corresponded to product listings in the output data. In all those cases, the weight finally assigned to an individual product listing was calculated as a weighted average of the unit values of the products in the grouping corresponding to the product listing for which data were available, the weights being the base year outputs. This procedure made it reasonable to include output of "products" like fodder, hand agricultural implements, dairy products, and "other" pharmaceutical products, in at least some of the direct weights indexes. In other cases, the output data corresponded directly to individual products whose unit values could be calculated from the value data.

There was considerable variation in the sample sizes of the indexes reported in table 5. The 1952 imputed weights index contained 159 and the 1961 imputed weights index 208 product series. The 1961 direct weights index was calculated from 401 series for the 1952–75 period. The moving weights index was constructed by linking the 1952 imputed weights index to the 1961 direct weights index at 1961, and, in turn, linking that to a 1971 direct weights index at 1971. The latter index included 442 series. Some of the other indexes reported elsewhere in the text had different sample sizes, but all were of the same orders of magnitude.

The sample indexes were constructed by directly summing the weighted outputs of the products included in their samples. The calculation was done in a single stage; no separate branch weights were employed. As shown in chapter 5, this is equivalent to weighting each branch by its base year share of value added, where that share is determined by the value added represented by the products included in the base year sample.

Table A-1 contains all weights used in forming the sample indexes of industrial production. The weights for 1952 and 1961 are based on value data reported in old dinars. The 1971 weights are derived from data in new dinars.

TABLE A-1

WEIGHTS USED IN SAMPLE INDEXES, BY PRODUCT

Code	Description	1952 Imputed Weights	1961 Imputed Weights	1961 Direct Weights	1971 Direct Weights
11–0101	Hydroelectric power	6,753	5,646	2,866	49.96
11–0102	Thermoelectric power	8,120	6,788	3,466	62.88
12–0101	Anthracite	4,082	5,097	4,960	116.20
12–0102	Brown coal	2,644	3,092	3,024	66.29
12–0103	Lignite	1,629	1,741	1,639	32.72
12–0200	Artificially dried lignite	na	na	2,888	59.04
12–0400	Large metallurgical coke	9,674	7,380	7,548	248.8
12–0500	Small metallurgical coke	na	na	6.960	0.3318
12–0600	Gasworks gas	na	na	8.760	0.1445
12–0800	Gasworks coke	na	na	7.565	na
13–0100	Crude petroleum	9,502	13,670	12,950	103.2
13–0200	Natural gas	na	na	3,574	79.20
13–0300	Propane-butane	na	16.31	11.01	0.1119
13–0400	Gasoline and pentane	na	9.182	8.535	0.1127
13–0500	Petrol (aviation, motor, and special)	4,237	16,900	12,140	255.1
13–0600	White spirit	na	na	11.54	0.2293
13–0700	Kerosene for lighting	na	19.98	20.09	0.2385
13–0800	Kerosene for motors	na	8.986	9.650	0.2482
13–0900	Gas oil	7,335	9,216	9,347	222.9
13–1000	Fuel oil	2,001	2,600	3,002	136.7
13–1100	Motor oil	6.997	43.58	35.96	1.582
13–1200	Bearing and other lubricating oils	32.32	na	19.01	1.120
13–1300	Mineral lubricating greases	na	na	19.53	1.649
13–1400	Paraffin wax	na	na	34.57	0.7775
13–1500	Bitumen	na	9,591	8,511	237.3
13–1600	Carbon black	na	na	97.70	1.065

14–0100	Iron ore, over 42% Fe	927.9	2,802	2,715	53.41
14–0200	Iron ore, less than 42% Fe	779.7	2,452	1,960	47.21
14–0300	Pig iron, white	9,250	15,020	15,990	324.7
14–0400	Pig iron, gray	na	17,230	18,840	487.3
14–0500	Ingots	13,320	16,920	na	na
14–0701	Steel rails	26.67	23.95	10.57	0.8850
14–0800	Steel sheets	na	32.57	49.63	na
14–0900	Other heavy sections	na	na	7.005	0.8274
14–1000	Strip steel	na	na	29.93	0.7535
14–1101	Rolled wire	23.73	27.54	26.11	0.7410
14–1102	Extruded wire	23.50	37.72	28.35	1.058
14–1200	Profiles	24.50	25.74	31.34	0.8324
14–1301	Thick and medium plates	25.14	29.26	32.66	0.9551
14–1302	Hot-rolled dynamo and transformer plates	na	61.07	62.62	0.9779
14–1305	Other thin and fine plates	na	38.91	42.27	0.9962
14–1400	Galvanized sheets	30.23	46.10	44.75	na
14–1600	Strips	35.02	41.61	49.18	1.233
14–1700	Rolled rims	na	na	69.15	1.949
14–1801	Seamless tubes	29.65	59.57	61.19	1.587
14–1802	Welded tubes	25.73	40.41	60,92	1.195
15–0200	Copper ore	na	na	na	60.58
15–0300	Bauxite	1,459	2,328	2,777	98.40
15–0400	Lead-zinc ore	na	4,097	3,715	140.7
15–0500	Chromium ore	9.069	na	na	na
15–0502	Chromium ore II	na	na	na	0.4395
15–0503	Chromium ore III	na	na	na	0.03270
15–0700	Manganese ore	5.238	5.283	73.44	0.1419
15–1700	Pyrites concentrate	1.806	na	na	na
15–1800	Chromium concentrate	8.366	na	na	na
15–2200	Crude copper	115.4	na	na	na
15–2300	Zinc (crude and powder)	76.63	67.61	76.63	2.024
15–2400	Crude lead	na	na	70.18	1.332
15–2500	Aluminum ingots	103.7	175.8	187.7	2.907
15–2600	Antimony regulus	212.8	270.5	260.6	7.453
15–2700	Electrolytic copper	128.4	235.3	233.6	6.404
15–2800	Refined zinc	79.77	74.38	80.73	1.737
15–2900	Refined lead	59.50	71.22	71.04	1.546
15–3000	Anodic silver	4.625	9.682	9.822	0.2948

TABLE A-1 (Cont.)

Code	Description	1952 Imputed Weights	1961 Imputed Weights	1961 Direct Weights	1971 Direct Weights
15–3100	Gold	152.4	367.4	320.8	6.557
15–3200	Mercury	939.8	2,164	1,837	51.87
15–3300	Bismuth	1,154	1,397	1,452	69.64
15–3400	Selen	na	na	na	0.9038
15–3500	Aluminum alloys	na	na	na	3.224
15–3600	Silicomanganese	na	na	85.20	1.036
15–3700	Ferromanganese	63.11	93.31	87.81	1.091
15–3800	Ferrochrome	188.9	200.1	200.5	2.226
15–3900	Silicochrome	na	na	101.3	1.540
15–4000	Ferrosilicon	144.2	166.8	123.0	1.689
15–4100	Silicocalcium	na	na	190.3	0.7983
15–4300	Rolled products of copper and its alloys	111.1	196.2	201.0	na
15–4301	Rolled copper wire	nsa	nsa	nsa	4.090
15–4302	Rolled sheets of copper and copper alloys	nsa	nsa	nsa	4.200
15–4303	Rolled strips of copper and copper alloys	nsa	nsa	nsa	4.249
15–4304	Rolled rondels of copper and copper alloys	nsa	nsa	nsa	0.4417
15–4500	Extruded copper products	129.5	246.8	245.0	4.609
15–4700	Uninsulated copper ropes	138.3	248.1	220.3	6.378
15–5000	Extruded products of aluminum and aluminum alloys	na	193.9	145.6	2.325
15–5100	Rolled zinc products	74.04	64.00	71.95	1.266
15–5200	Rolled lead products	54.78	69.42	70.46	1.176
16–0100	Quartz sand, stone, and flour for glass	na	3,679	1,101	34.09
16–0200	Crude fireclay	1.949	3.065	3.660	0.05810
16–0300	Crude magnesite	na	2.514	4.905	0.1123
16–0500	Crude feldspar	na	na	8.534	0.1823
16–0600	Mica	na	na	na	0.002600

16–0800	Crude barites	na	na	7.320	0.1440
16–0900	Asbestos fiber (except meal and padding)	68.97	41.69	135.2	1.130
16–1000	Caustic magnesite, calcined	na	na	19.35	0.3976
16–1100	Sea salt	na	12.39	12.30	0.4408
16–1200	Salt from brine	12.28	11.63	12.12	0.3717
16–1300	Flat glass	143.0	197.1	207.5	4.098
16–1400	Blown glass	na	na	48.15	0.9466
16–1500	Cut glass	na	na	1,951	23.72
16–1600	Glass wool	na	na	77.16	2.694
16–1700	Calcined clay	na	na	81.86	0.1453
16–1800	Sinter magnesite	na	10.52	15.25	0.4110
16–1900	Fireclay	8.234	na	16.63	0.4853
16–2000	Basic bricks (thermal process)	na	na	29.78	0.9124
16–2100	Chrome-magnesite refractory material	26.76	26.96	36.75	0.8537
16–2200	Acid refractory fire-baked bricks	na	na	21.01	0.3778
16–2300	Silico-dinas material	na	na	33.92	0.5918
16–2400	Other refractories	na	na	62.92	0.9068
16–2500	Ceramic ware for households	na	na	217.8	8.797
16–2600	Ceramic ware for construction	20.05	56.79	58.17	1.107
16–2700	Sanitary ceramics	na	na	178.8	3.962
16–2800	Insulators, etc., of electroporcelain	151.4	265.9	269.9	5.274
16–2900	Insulators, etc., of steatite	na	na	na	9.065
16–3000	Asbestos products	na	na	725.9	11.97
16–3200	Artificial abrasives	na	na	495.7	9.098
16–3500	Electrodes, amorphous	na	na	83.70	4.075
16–3600	Amorphous matter	na	na	39.43	0.9298
17–0100	Castings, steel	165.5	146.6	171.8	3.637
17–0200	Castings, tempered and gray steel	129.0	98.01	57.20	1.849
17–0300	Castings, nonferrous metals	na	na	410.9	12.91
17–0400	Forgings	na	na	110.5	3.407
17–0500	Cast-iron pipes and fashioned parts	53.56	46.73	77.09	1.656
17–0600	Boilers for central heating	na	na	117.4	3.903
17–0700	Equipment for steam heating	na	na	106.4	2.020
17–0800	Sanitary equipment	na	na	na	4.732
17–0900	Armatures	na	na	483.6	10.13
17–1000	Rivets	na	na	196.8	5.100

TABLE A-1 (Cont.)

Code	Description	1952 Imputed Weights	1961 Imputed Weights	1961 Direct Weights	1971 Direct Weights
17–1100	Fittings and accessories	na	na	na	5.190
17–1200	Screws	na	na	222.4	4.814
17–1300	Nails	61.90	80.41	86.06	1.560
17–1400	Steel ropes	na	na	326.1	4.083
17–1500	Barbed wire, wire netting, and wire cloth	262.4	na	151.4	2.245
17–1600	Chains	146.3	na	305.6	5.014
17–1700	Chain sets, complete	na	na	302.5	8.795
17–1800	Metal utensils	na	na	965.4	9.077
17–1900	Metal packing containers	na	na	226.7	3.879
17–2000	Bends and springs	na	na	184.0	2.854
17–2100	Metal electrodes for welding	89.87	156.1	173.6	2.014
17–2200	Agricultural tools, forged and pressed	na	na	168.8	5.319
17–2300	Cutting tools	na	na	18.16	36.76
17–2500	Roller bearings	na	176.0	661.1	22.23
17–2600	Pumps	na	na	425.4	12.08
17–2700	Steam boilers (not central heating)	na	na	282.8	8.707
17–2800	Water turbines	na	na	329.7	7.789
17–2900	Steam turbines	na	na	166.2	47.81
17–3100	Construction machinery and equipment	na	na	399.9	9.698
17–3200	Metal- and woodworking machines, total	na	na	716.0	na
17–3201	Metalworking machines	nsa	nsa	nsa	15.02
17–3202	Woodworking machines	nsa	nsa	nsa	12.92
17–3300	Agricultural machinery, equipment and tools	199.5	na	418.3	8.278
17–3600	Ventilating and air conditioning equipment	na	na	311.4	11.32
17–3700	Refrigeration equipment	na	na	431.7	11.50
17–3900	Balances	na	na	283.7	8.962

17–4000	Sewing machines	na	na	40.15	0.6419
17–4100	Typewriters and accounting machines	na	na	80.89	0.2722
17–4200	Clocks	na	0.8923	1.157	0.0298
17–4300	Products for medical and veterinary purposes	na	na	2,299	145.2
17–4400	Motor and electrolocomotives	na	na	735.6	12.97
17–4500	Steam locomotives	na	na	374.0	na
17–4600	Freight and other special coaches	na	na	164.9	3.255
17–4700	Other railway coaches and mail vans	na	na	414.7	9.632
17–4800	Tramcars, rail motor coaches, etc.	na	na	930.4	16.15
17–4900	Tubs, mine-cars, and hand trolleys	27.05	83.19	298.2	5.174
17–5100	Internal combustion engines	na	na	795.9	13.54
17–5200	Spare parts for internal combustion engines	na	na	na	23.79
17–5300	Bodies: trucks, buses, and other vehicles	na	na	193.8	9.525
17–5400	Trucks and light trucks	253.1	283.2	591.7	4.837
17–5500	Buses	na	na	607.9	11.15
17–5600	Passenger automobiles	na	na	482.4	11.09
17–5800	Tractors	433.8	na	469.5	9.280
17–5900	Trailers for trucks and tractors	na	na	248.0	5.082
17–6000	Camping trailers for automobiles	na	na	na	16.56
17–6100	Motorcycles	280.8	na	834.7	13.00
17–6200	Spare parts for motor vehicles	na	na	858.8	10.38
17–6300	Bicycles	6,155	9,257	17,160	115.9
17–6400	Spare parts for bicycles	na	na	437.1	1.384
17–6500	Metal kitchenware	na	na	214.9	5.710
17–6600	Aluminum kitchenware	na	na	556.4	18.00
17–6700	Tableware	na	na	549.0	27.59
17–6800	Metal furniture	na	na	165.9	7.148
17–6900	Stoves, ranges, etc.	na	na	100.5	4.464
17–7100	Fire extinguishers and accessories	na	na	693.1	12.20
19–0100	Large rotating machines (more than 70 kw)	na	na	3,929	31.23
19–0200	Medium rotating machines (1.6–70 kw)	5.835	5.680	5.696	0.4349

TABLE A-1 (Cont.)

Code	Description	1952 Imputed Weights	1961 Imputed Weights	1961 Direct Weights	1971 Direct Weights
19–0300	Small rotating machines (less than 1.6 kw)	11,040	2,233	4,496	80.39
19–0400	Accessories for rotating machines	na	na	712.4	16.34
19–0500	Power transformers	na	na	187.9	2.607
19–0600	Transformers for electric motors	na	na	515.0	29.80
19–0700	Power rectification condensers	na	na	2,412	10.57
19–0800	Switchgear	34.63	na	931.4	27.58
19–0900	Distribution equipment	na	na	725.9	17.83
19–1000	Industrial electric furnaces	na	na	516.6	10.86
19–1200	Electric irons	na	na	529.5	16.59
19–1400	Kitchen ranges	na	na	14,600	183.1
19–1600	Heaters	na	na	1.909	0.01200
19–1700	Boilers	na	na	8,770	94.91
19–1800	Refrigeration equipment	na	na	na	7.577
19–1900	Household refrigerators	19,250	28,310	29,660	227.8
19–2100	Vacuum cleaners	na	na	8,664	92.63
19–2200	Cables and similar conductors	295.9	na	278.1	3.709
19–2300	Insulated conductors	na	na	149.2	5.666
19–2400	Radio receivers	15.64	15.05	12.09	0.2686
19–2500	Television receivers	na	63.95	59.20	0.8772
19–2900	Electric phonographs	na	na	5,432	171.1
19–3000	Cinema projectors (except capacitors)	na	na	1,859	109.7
19–3100	Capacitors for cinema projectors	na	na	1,503	na
19–3200	Telephones	na	6.741	7.324	0.1319
19–3300	Telephone exchanges	na	na	3,268	47.92
19–3400	X-ray apparatus	na	na	772.9	22.90
19–3500	Installation materials	na	na	598.7	15.97
19–3600	Installation pipes and accessories	3.206	na	93.53	4.548
19–3700	Electric bulbs, high voltage	71.76	39.75	46.54	1.057
19–3800	Electric bulbs, low voltage	na	na	36.39	0.8803
19–3900	Fluorescent tubes	na	na	316.5	3.648

19–4000	Lamps	na	na	909.0	19.00
19–4100	Accumulators	604.6	228.1	221.9	4.717
19–4200	Primary cells	na	na	372.3	16.37
19–4400	Electrical measuring instruments	na	na	na	107.5
19–4500	Electric meters	2,851	3,001	na	38.21
19–4600	Machines for washing and drying clothes	na	na	116.6	6.456
20–0100	Sulfuric acid, 66° Be	5,936	6,181	6,385	97.89
20–0200	Hydrochloric acid	12.39	16.36	22.31	0.1816
20–0300	Nitric acid (100%)	na	24,140	24,600	503.0
20–0400	Phosphoric acid	na	na	na	1.381
20–0600	Ammonium nitrate (100%)	na	27.86	25.40	1.053
20–0700	Sodium hydroxide	25.76	22.33	21.50	0.5081
20–0800	Chlorine	45.69	36.40	36.12	0.4136
20–0900	Sodium bichromate	na	na	113.9	1.556
20–1000	Sodium carbonate (calcined soda)	10.14	10.03	8.369	0.2581
20–1100	Sodium sulfide	na	na	27.37	0.5219
20–1300	Sodium tripolyphosphate	na	na	na	1.205
20–1400	Sodium sulfate	na	na	na	0.2929
20–1500	Sodium hypochlorite	na	na	6.114	0.1460
20–1700	Sodium silicate 100%	na	na	na	0.2111
20–1800	Calcium carbide	10,450	26,410	25,410	547.7
20–1900	Magnesium chloride	na	na	na	0.4599
20–2000	Barium sulfide	na	na	22.79	na
20–2100	Silver nitrate	na	na	5.341	0.2128
20–2200	Aluminum sulfate	na	na	12.07	0.2440
20–2300	Copper sulfate	44.57	78.52	72.77	2.108
20–2400	Borates and perborates	na	na	114.3	1.282
20–2500	Hydrogen peroxide (100%)	na	na	128.3	5.186
20–2600	Compressed technical gases, n.e.c.	na	na	105.5	1.437
20–2800	Acetone	na	na	na	0.4898
20–2900	Phenols	na	na	na	0.9168
20–3000	Dodecyl benzol	na	na	na	1.028
20–3100	Dodecyl benzene sulfonate	na	na	64.15	1.405
20–3200	Styrol	na	na	na	1.051
20–3300	Trichlorethylene	96.95	99.92	109.2	1.286
20–3400	Phthalic acid anhydride	na	na	130.3	1.454
20–3500	Methanol	na	na	na	0.4286
20–3600	Formaldehyde	na	na	31.65	0.2873
20–3800	Pepein insecticide	117.6	625.9	392.1	na

TABLE A-1 (Cont.)

Code	Description	1952 Imputed Weights	1961 Imputed Weights	1961 Direct Weights	1971 Direct Weights
20–3900	Flotation agents	na	na	na	2.602
20–4000	Superphosphate	10,050	15,250	13,470	118.0
20–4100	Ammonium sulfate	na	na	29.50	na
20–4200	Calcium cyanamide	na	na	na	0.4746
20–4300	Mixed fertilizers	na	na	20,660	270.9
20–4400	Plant protection preparations	na	na	204.0	2.916
20–4500	Gunpowder	na	na	214.8	4.857
20–4600	Mining explosives	na	na	75.58	1.529
20–4800	Industrial nitrocellulose	na	na	305.5	2.656
20–4900	Carboxymethyl cellulose	na	na	212.3	1.788
20–5000	Cellophane	na	na	577.6	4.655
20–5100	Other artificial material based on cellulose	na	na	806.4	2.996
20–5200	Phenoplasts	na	na	na	3.907
20–5300	Aminoplasts	na	na	125.3	2.254
20–5400	Polyesters	na	na	na	2.660
20–5500	PVC powder	203.3	170.1	149.0	1.471
20–5600	Polyvinyl acetate (100%)	na	na	na	1.588
20–5700	Polystyrol	na	na	na	2.340
20–5800	Polyethylene	na	na	na	2.046
20–5900	Primary preparations of PVC	331.8	389.6	288.7	3.762
20–6000	Cellulose fiber, cotton type	na	na	181.3	2.660
20–6100	Cellulose fiber, wool type	na	na	187.6	2.896
20–6200	Rayon	na	na	478.1	6.851
20–6300	Cord	na	na	375.7	6.699
20–6400	Polyacrylonitrile fibers	na	na	na	7.013
20–6500	Penicillin	na	na	93.27	0.3462
20–6700	Vitamin C	na	na	6,644	34.17
20–6800	Other pharmaceutical materials	na	na	na	32.12
20–6900	Cleaning and washing agents	na	na	na	1.649
20–7000	Cosmetic preparations	na	na	584.1	20.33
20–7100	Ethereal oils	na	na	5.991	0.00860
20–7300	Lead minium	77.32	69.93	69.75	2.050

20–7400	Lithopone	na	36.33	36.36	0.8164
20–7500	Mineral pigments	na	na	532.6	12.83
20–7600	Organic dyes	na	na	136.1	0.7686
20–7700	Mastics	na	na	101.9	1.915
20–7800	Oil paints	64.66	56.54	86.41	1.815
20–7900	Lacquers and enamels	146.9	91.67	169.2	3.247
20–8000	Printer's ink	na	na	233.6	4.218
20–8100	Mineral lubricating oils	24.06	na	67.55	1.874
20–8200	Shoe and floor polish	na	na	126.0	2.941
20–8400	Auxiliary agents for textiles	na	na	na	1.861
20–8500	Auxiliary agents for leather and rubber	na	na	na	1.118
20–8600	Glue and gelatin	na	na	97.00	2.026
20–8700	Pastes	91.85	87.52	na	na
20–8800	Photographic chemicals	na	na	na	4.391
20–8900	Diazotype paper	na	na	262.8	5.737
20–9000	Films	na	na	1,173	9.399
20–9100	Photographic paper	na	281.2	238.3	4.345
20–9200	Percussion caps and fuses	na	na	9.925	0.3009
20–9300	Candles	na	na	137.7	3.222
20–9500	Oxygen	na	na	na	0.6986
21–0100	Stone blocks for building and cutting	na	na	19.81	na
21–0101	Stone and marble blocks for cutting	na	na	na	1.043
21–0102	Stone blocks for building purposes	na	na	na	0.6865
21–0200	Pulverized stone, marble, sand, and gravel	na	837.0	733.8	na
21–0201	Broken stone and marble	na	na	na	32.14
21–0202	Crushed stone and marble	na	na	na	27.33
21–0204	Gravel and sand	na	na	na	22.38
21–0300	Ground stone	na	na	1,702	40.49
21–0400	Ground marble	na	na	4.884	0.1118
21–0500	Stone and marble slabs	na	na	na	0.2374
21–0600	Sections	na	na	8.495	0.3160
21–0700	Crude gypsum	na	na	3.919	0.02510
21–0800	Calcined gypsum	3.276	6.100	4.468	0.1897
21–0900	Unslaked lime	4,380	5,927	5,787	143.8
21–1000	Hydrated lime	na	6,923	7,458	166.5

TABLE A-1 (Cont.)

Code	Description	1952 Imputed Weights	1961 Imputed Weights	1961 Direct Weights	1971 Direct Weights
21–1100	Bricks, total	2,794	9,854	na	na
21–1101	Hollow bricks, standard pattern	na	na	8,362	301.3
21–1102	Hollow and porous wallbricks of other patterns	na	na	9,781	327.4
21–1104	Solid bricks	na	na	9,028	346.3
21–1200	Hollow clay blocks, roof and ceiling	na	na	8.975	0.2991
21–1300	Tiles, total	7.750	24.11	20.50	na
21–1301	Plain and gutter tiles	na	na	na	0.6703
21–1302	Roofing tiles	na	na	na	0.6305
21–1400	Portland cement	4,138	4,778	3,189	117.1
21–1500	Other types of cement	5.239	5.327	7.342	0.2408
21–1600	Asbestos-cement products	na	na	34.02	0.5678
21–1700	Light building panels	na	na	209.1	8.324
21–1900	Blocks for walls and partitions	na	na	11.35	0.2180
21–2000	Wall panels	na	na	17.67	0.4487
21–2100	Blocks for roof construction	na	na	na	0.2886
21–2200	Roofing felt	16.06	31.59	28.38	0.6462
22–0100	Sawn conifers	3,889	10,780	8,750	359.0
22–0200	Sawn oak	8,220	20,760	17,050	789.1
22–0300	Sawn beech	7,102	15,860	13,290	399.1
22–0400	Other sawn timber	na	na	11,900	443.7
22–0500	Sawn sleepers	na	na	11.06	0.3658
22–0600	Veneer	115.7	79.86	71.21	1.685
22–0700	Reconstituted wood panels: plywood	31.28	38.10	39.81	1.182
22–0800	Panel boards	15.20	35.35	na	0.7993
22–1000	Reconstituted particle boards	na	na	na	0.4812
22–1100	Containers and boxes	9.314	16.03	20.52	0.5515
22–1200	Barrels	na	na	0.6670	0.006100
22–1300	Household furniture, total	33.45	23.80	19.57	na
22–1301	Bedroom furniture	na	na	na	1.107

22–1302	Bed- and sitting room furniture	na	na	na	2.038
22–1303	Other nonkitchen furniture	na	na	na	1.695
22–1304	Kitchen furniture	na	na	na	0.5777
22–1400	Office and school furniture	na	na	7.353	0.1618
22–1500	Incomplete household and bentwood furniture	na	na	7,086	194.8
22–1700	Builder's joinery	na	na	na	1.338
22–1800	Parquet flooring, solid	na	30.05	24.32	0.8787
22–1900	Parquet flooring, laminated	na	na	823.2	13.11
22–2000	Cork manufactures	na	na	256.8	5.915
22–2100	Tanning materials	84.78	104.4	99.86	2.470
22–2200	Impregnated wood	na	na	8.504	0.5603
22–2300	Colophony and turpentine	78.54	129.9	117.5	3.189
22–2400	Charcoal distillates	na	na	14.63	0.7765
22–2500	Acetic acid (100%)	na	na	222.2	5.635
22–2600	Acetone (100%)	na	na	205.1	na
22–2700	Matches	3.747	11.33	9.454	0.2947
23–0100	Sulfite cellulose, total	na	38.39	na	na
23–0105	Bleached sulfite cellulose	na	na	49.37	0.4204
23–0106	Unbleached sulfite cellulose	na	na	35.17	0.6403
23–0500	Wood pulp, white and brown	na	na	22.36	0.4997
23–0600	Newsprint	na	36.60	37.20	0.6846
23–0700	Writing and printing paper	na	na	59.45	1.210
23–0800	Kraft paper	61.25	45.48	47.35	1.048
23–0900	Wrapping and other packing paper	32.25	36.99	38.32	0.7429
23–1000	Cigarette paper	197.7	366.9	257.3	4.764
23–1100	Other paper	na	na	89.63	1.680
23–1200	Cardboard	47.64	47.35	44.83	0.9475
23–1300	Roofing felt	26.63	42.02	44.21	0.7015
23–1400	Corrugated roofing felt	na	na	60.45	0.9890
23–1500	Kraft paper bags	74.57	67.47	77.74	1.721
24–0100	Fibers, hemp	88.84	163.6	173.4	3.394
24–0200	Fibers, flax	na	247.8	na	3.197
24–0300	Yarn, cotton type	894.5	448.4	435.8	9.045
24–0400	Sewing thread	na	na	1,318	24.40
24–0500	Cotton fabrics	na	110.3	112.1	2.870
24–0600	Fabrics of synthetic fiber, 100%, cotton type	na	na	na	3.994
24–0700	Woolen yarn, total	1,532	1,156	1,411	na

TABLE A-1 (Cont.)

Code	Description	1952 Imputed Weights	1961 Imputed Weights	1961 Direct Weights	1971 Direct Weights
24–0701	Woolen yarn, carded	na	na	na	11.41
24–0702	Woolen yarn, combed	na	na	na	25.56
24–0900	Woolen fabrics, total	624.3	662.7	542.1	na
24–0901	Fabrics of carded wool	na	na	na	12.97
24–0902	Fabrics of worsted wool	na	na	na	20.78
24–1000	Fabrics of synthetic fiber, 100%, woolen type	na	na	417.6	5.113
24–1100	Grege, raw silk	na	na	4,017	na
24–1200	Yarn, natural silk	na	na	7,668	32.49
24–1300	Fabrics of natural silk	na	na	401.1	37.51
24–1400	Fabrics of synthetic silk (rayon)	348.1	199.8	230.5	3.834
24–1500	Fabrics of synthetic filaments	na	na	na	7.062
24–1600	Yarn, flax	na	na	564.4	23.21
24–1700	Yarn, hemp	178.1	na	346.7	5.280
24–1800	Yarn, jute	na	na	238.1	3.138
24–1900	Fabrics, flax	na	na	178.8	3.552
24–2000	Fabrics, hemp	na	na	146.3	2.064
24–2100	Fabrics, jute	na	na	116.8	0.9681
24–2200	Hemp cordage, strips, and ropes	na	na	297.9	5.949
24–2400	Hose	88.60	143.1	82.71	2.763
24–2500	Knitwear	na	na	2,213	64.69
24–2600	Fabrics, net	na	na	na	4.712
24–2700	Fishing nets	na	na	na	53.17
24–2800	Ready-made underwear	na	195.3	176.7	6.361
24–2900	Ready-made clothing	na	501.2	668.1	27.74
24–3000	Woolen carpets, woven	na	na	1,243	35.29
24–3100	Mattresses and quilting products	na	na	416.1	9.551
24–3200	Tarpaulins, tents, and kindred products	na	na	482.6	5.936
24–3300	Hats	na	na	na	8.877
24–3400	Hat bodies	na	na	na	6.396
24–3500	Felt	na	na	na	8.112
25–0100	Sole leather	197.8	251.6	212.4	7.567

25–0200	Leather for technical purposes	239.1	na	na	na
25–0300	Whole hides	897.5	1,115	833.7	24.55
25–0400	Split upper leather	na	na	na	11.17
25–0500	Technical ready-made goods	na	na	727.4	22.41
25–0600	Pigskin, upper leather	na	na	389.7	22.09
25–0700	Pigskin for fancy goods manufacture	295.1	502.6	468.3	15.76
25–0800	Lining leather, sheep and goat	327.4	444.2	411.9	14.91
25–0900	Furs	na	na	740.3	23.76
25–1000	Clothes, leather and fur	na	na	2,565	56.87
25–1100	Artificial leather	na	na	106.0	6.067
25–1200	Heavy leather footwear	801.3	929.2	1,182	44.44
25–1300	Civilian leather footwear	796.0	873.4	948.1	31.33
25–1400	Other leather footwear	na	na	490.3	19.92
26–0100	Tires, bicycle	270.7	276.7	288.8	9.928
26–0200	Tubes, bicycle	99.51	97.69	95.54	2.052
26–0300	Tires, auto, motocycle, and aircraft	10,160	17,110	6,403	44.52
26–0400	Tubes, auto, motorcycle, and aircraft	882.1	1,104	635.8	8.452
26–0500	Rubber pipes, all types	na	na	342.2	8.143
26–0700	Rubber sanitary ware	na	na	1,615	na
26–0800	Rubberized canvas	na	na	732.7	11.97
26–0900	Rubber footwear products	na	na	na	3.567
26–1100	Reclaimed rubber (except ground)	na	na	51.19	0.9685
26–1200	Peasants' rubber sandals	226.0	203.0	170.5	4.661
26–1300	Rubber boots	654.2	646.2	413.5	10.26
26–1400	Other rubber footwear	219.5	191.2	186.9	7.459
26–1500	Rubber adhesives	na	na	125.2	4.047
26–1600	Rubberized fibers of animal origin	na	na	na	4.803
27–0100	Flour, white cereals	na	12,090	12,060	577.5
27–0200	Corn flour	na	na	6.209	0.4631
27–0300	Husked rice	na	na	17.91	1.231
27–0400	Bread and pastry	na	na	na	0.7812
27–0500	Pasta products	23.30	36.30	29.58	1.523
27–0600	Sugarless semiprocessed fruit	na	na	26.19	0.7487
27–0700	Fruit products, total	na	na	34.91	na
27–0701	Fruit products, sugarless	na	na	na	1.096
27–0702	Fruit products, with sugar	na	na	na	1.090
27–0800	Dried fruit	na	na	na	1.571

TABLE A-1 (Cont.)

Code	Description	1952 Imputed Weights	1961 Imputed Weights	1961 Direct Weights	1971 Direct Weights
27–0900	Canned vegetables	na	35.21	33.87	1.204
27–1000	Dried vegetables	na	na	na	2.926
27–1100	Other vegetable products	na	na	7.149	0.9740
27–1300	Fresh meat	na	67.72	59.66	3.225
27–1400	Salted and cured meat	na	na	68.59	3.758
27–1500	Cured bacon and sausage	40.60	86.00	67.01	3.832
27–1600	Canned meat	na	137.1	103.7	3.300
27–1700	Concentrated soup	na	na	160.8	4.813
27–1800	Edible animal fats	20.46	55.13	63.08	1.205
27–1900	Salted, smoked, and cured fish	na	na	39.81	1.983
27–2000	Canned fish	na	109.7	93.08	2.428
27–2100	Powdered eggs	na	na	na	4.760
27–2200	Powdered milk	na	67.42	68.90	2.604
27–2300	Canned milk	na	na	10.34	0.4098
27–2400	Butter	na	na	113.2	5.268
27–2500	Cheese	37.76	65.92	64.23	3.285
27–2600	Other dairy products	na	na	na	2.528
27–2700	Sugar	29.20	36.83	37.72	1.237
27–2800	Confectionery, flour	68.81	95.89	91.70	3.244
27–2900	Candy and chocolate products, total	92.42	na	119.2	na
27–2901	Candies	na	na	na	2.953
27–2902	Chocolate products	na	na	na	5.749
27–3000	Edible oil	35.07	na	na	1.097
27–3100	Oil for technical uses	na	na	na	0.9052
27–3200	Margarine	na	70.91	71.25	1.281
27–3300	Refined spirits	37.22	64.49	59.33	1.421
27–3400	Denatured spirits	39.80	75.18	77.68	1.357
27–3600	Beer	995.0	1,990	2,484	67.66
27–3700	Artificial nonalcoholic beverages	na	na	2,987	114.8
27–3800	Starches, total	19.91	20.91	43.63	0.5659
27–3900	Starch preparations	na	na	27.50	0.5883
27–4000	Yeast	25.14	48.53	48.13	0.7411
27–4100	Coffee extract	na	na	na	30.32

27–4300	Coffee substitutes	20.16	32.68	44.97	7.804
27–4400	Ground pepper	78.65	151.8	118.4	4.019
27–4500	Fodder, total	na	na	na	350.7
28–0100	Newspapers, magazines, and periodicals	na	na	158.9	3.239
28–0200	Books and brochures	na	na	335.6	5.990
28–0300	Printed matter and blank forms	na	na	253.9	8.115
28–0400	School exercise books	na	na	222.0	2.916
29–0100	Cured tobacco	465.8	264.0	291.9	5.910
29–0200	Cigarettes	386.8	345.8	270.1	9.228
29–0300	Other tobacco products	na	na	248.3	18.17

Legend: na: not available or unable to calculate from available data. nsa: not separately available.

SOURCES: 1952 prices from SZS, *CENE, Januar-Mart 1957* (Belgrade: SZS, 1957), pp. 14–18. 1961 prices from SZS, *CENE, April-Jun 1962* (Belgrade: SZS, 1962), pp. 27–38. 1961 unit values from SZS, *Industrijski proizvodi 1970* (Belgrade: SZS, 1972), pp. 5–48. 1971 unit values from SZS, *Industrijski proizvodi 1971* (Belgrade: SZS, 1973), pp. 5–45. Value-added adjustment data from SZS, *Industrijska preduzeća 1962* (Belgrade: SZS, 1963), pp. 7–10; and *Industrijska preduzeća 1971* (Belgrade: SZS, 1973), pp. 10–13. Turnover tax data from *Službeni list* 1952, no. 9: 126–28; 1952, no. 34: 1–5; 1952, no. 58: 905–6; 1952, no. 63: 983–84; 1961, no. 19: 485–95; 1961, no. 27: 737; 1961, no. 31: 798–800; 1965, no. 33: 1,251–85; 1965, no. 57: 1,893–95; 1966, no. 4: 70; 1966, no. 28: 545; 1966, no. 52: 1,098–1,103; 1967, no. 5: 117–18; 1967, no. 18: 488, 1967, no. 31: 31; 1968, no. 24: 445–46; 1968, no. 30: 609–10; 1968, no. 45: 913; 1968, no. 55: 1,298–300; 1969, no. 50: 1,223–24; 1970, no. 18: 581–82; 1970, no. 52: 1,253; 1971, no. 24: 413–14; 1971, no. 32: 620–21.

APPENDIX B

Basic Production Data

Table B-1 contains the physical production data on which the sample indexes are based. In most cases, the data were taken directly from the sources shown at the end of the table. In others, data missing from the sources were estimated by methods described in the notes to the table. Additional details about output of some products are presented in tables B-2 to B-17. These data were used to make some of the tests mentioned in chapter 5.

The letters at the foot of each column signify the sample or samples in which the product is included. The letter "A" denotes the 1952 imputed weights sample; "B," the 1961 imputed weights sample; "C," the 1961 direct weights sample; and "D," the 1971 direct weights sample.

TABLE B-1

OUTPUT SERIES, YUGOSLAVIA: 1952–75

	11–0101 Hydroelectric Power (mill. kwh)	11–0102 Thermoelectric Power (mill. kwh)	12–0101 Anthracite (th. MT)	12–0102 Brown Coal (th. MT)	12–0103 Lignite (th. MT)	12–0200 Artificially Dried Lignite (th. MT)	12–0400 Large Metallurgical Coke (th. MT)	12–0500 Small Metallurgical Coke (MT)
1952	1,423	1,277	1,011	6,842	4,245	na	13.1	1,916
1953	1,500	1,482	925	6,362	3,959	na	234.5	61,209
1954	1,810	1,630	988	7,100	5,575	na	297.8	106,372
1955	2,610	1,730	1,134	7,682	6,388	na	665.4	66,003
1956	2,870	2,178	1,232	8,442	7,427	na	868.3	55,110
1957	3,522	2,730	1,227	8,525	8,255	na	972.7	64,571
1958	4,300	3,056	1,208	8,378	9,401	240	968.1	61,701
1959	4,708	3,398	1,298	9,122	10,687	417	1,003	66,885
1960	5,984	2,944	1,283	9,628	11,801	486	1,013	70,207
1961	5,658	4,266	1,313	9,494	13,266	496	1,028	70,757
1962	6,851	4,424	1,188	9,319	14,186	512	1,030	77,240
1963	8,028	5,507	1,286	9,945	16,191	613	1,009	81,863
1964	7,575	6,614	1,262	10,715	17,532	668	1,089	70,408
1965	8,985	6,538	1,169	10,509	18,279	788	1,153	99,743
1966	9,880	7,294	1,133	10,080	18,080	882	1,165	61,458
1967	10,655	8,047	909	9,023	16,535	782	1,157	61,893
1968	11,768	8,874	835	9,508	16,389	690	1,173	60,619
1969	14,732	8,643	681	9,442	16,373	587	1,165	61,096
1970	14,741	11,283	643	8,989	18,790	628	1,226	82,515
1971	15,644	13,685	707	9,333	20,862	793	1,229	68,125
1972	17,982	15,249	599	9,184	21,157	755	1,226	72,499
1973	16,394	18,668	576	9,145	22,729	660	1,249	69,376
1974	20,659	18,797	601	9,380	23,601	811	1,245	78,076
1975	19,317	20,722	598	9,429	25,509	858	1,263	80,190
Index	A,B,C,D	A,B,C,D	A,B,C,D	A,B,C,D	A,B,C,D	C,D	A,B,C,D	C,D

TABLE B-1 (Cont.)

	12–0600 Gasworks Gas (th. m.^{3})	12–0800 Gasworks Coke (MT)	13–0100 Crude Petroleum (th. MT)	13–0200 Natural Gas (mill. m.^{3})	13–0300 Propane-Butane (MT)	13–0400 Gasoline and Pentane (MT)	13–0500 Petrol (Aviation, Motor, and Special) (th. MT)	13–0600 White Spirit (MT)
1952	24,362	25,606	151.5	13.8	315	2,055	99.67	4,700
1953	24,969	25,058	171.7	73.1	491	2,347	111.3	5,437
1954	25,294	23,722	216.3	90.1	1,041	2,548	119.5	5,398
1955	25,936	23,797	257.2	55.1	1,600	2,650	133.8	7,983
1956	26,626	23,052	293.7	68.6	3,565	2,614	171.7	6,427
1957	26,046	24,629	395.6	41.5	7,907	4,079	220.7	8,617
1958	25,856	25,801	462.2	46.1	8,035	4,324	252.1	6,937
1959	25,947	20,833	592.5	50.0	11,202	5,079	249.3	8,051
1960	40,266	19,839	943.6	52.9	13,133	5,771	277.2	8,846
1961	37,290	16,979	1,340.7	68.8	15,156	4,693	293.6	8,430
1962	45,543	17,557	1,525.5	95.3	15,345	5,322	321.6	10,594
1963	52,620	16,730	1,610	191	16,707	6,339	344	12,301
1964	61,276	17,247	1,798	274	23,489	9,788	385	16,084
1965	64,666	14,386	2,063	330	35,727	14,882	546	15,619
1966	62,750	10,787	2,222	402	48,621	17,042	788	16,288
1967	68,334	7,243	2,374	461	54,154	18,020	886	16,870
1968	74,799	2,030	2,494	584	68,639	22,578	935	17,871
1969	86,210	0	2,699	730	77,825	22,836	1,003	18,764
1970	97,880	0	2,854	977	95,020	24,560	1,232	20,540
1971	168,791	0	2,961	1,151	104,860	27,959	1,472	21,043
1972	143,402	0	3,200	1,242	196,402	27,890	1,394	21,345
1973	155,117	0	3,332	1,329	45,192	23,974	1,528	24,166
1974	151,488	0	3,458	1,447	49,730	13,535	1,626	27,205
1975	144,635	0	3,692	1,553	53,660	14,073	1,745	25,566
Index	C,D	C	A,B,C,D	C,D	B,C,D	B,C,D	A,B,C,D	C,D

	13–0700 Kerosene for Lighting (MT)	13–0800 Kerosene for Motors (MT)	13–0900 Gas Oil (th. MT)	13–1000 Fuel Oil (th. MT)	13–1100 Motor Oil (MT)	13–1200 Bearing and Other Lubricating Oils (MT)	13–1300 Mineral Lubricating Greases (MT)	13–1400 Paraffin Wax (MT)
1952	15,881	17,306	122.5	185.3	6,396	15,227	838	854
1953	13,507	28,175	134.1	195.7	11,522	18,124	1,281	1,016
1954	19,309	41,486	161.0	233.0	14,838	14,646	1,655	1,224
1955	23,863	51,586	173.9	275.0	15,046	20,018	1,915	1,433
1956	22,996	59,444	202.3	311.2	13,343	18,214	1,844	1,641
1957	26,837	46,416	251.5	356.5	20,021	21,448	1,897	2,296
1958	19,131	42,507	298.0	332.3	19,713	23,081	2,096	1,992
1959	19,031	44,270	331.5	357.8	25,612	25,653	2,151	1,991
1960	15,003	59,013	353.7	396.2	32,578	28,599	2,649	2,102
1961	10,680	48,186	404.5	409.4	43,448	28,788	2,606	1,557
1962	14,520	66,465	532.3	492.2	68,857	30,214	2,499	1,096
1963	14,142	74,719	618	480	78,656	33,598	2,258	1,195
1964	13,343	84,536	701	683	88,804	37,512	2,101	1,062
1965	15,613	66,083	890	1,148	94,456	39,694	2,323	1,138
1966	14,428	79,236	1,142	1,764	117,973	39,827	1,907	1,005
1967	12,592	81,473	1,389	1,816	102,616	35,668	1,033	830
1968	15,689	103,762	1,380	1,847	68,773	34,052	1,062	667
1969	12,479	133,603	1,722	1,967	54,249	34,247	1,770	509
1970	11,854	151,356	2,091	2,509	58,411	44,297	1,652	547
1971	10,511	204,205	2,665	2,930	71,387	42,794	1,361	3,704
1972	9,404	202,091	2,495	2,989	73,291	48,948	1,226	6,031
1973	12,048	239,109	2,558	3,480	74,184	49,318	1,276	8,944
1974	12,715	302,233	2,725	4,317	96,034	55,607	5,791	8,428
1975	10,824	319,709	2,816	4,276	101,862	61,175	6,849	7,705
Index	B,C,D	B,C,D	A,B,C,D	A,B,C,D	A,B,C,D	A,C,D	C,D	C,D

TABLE B-1 (Cont.)

	13–1500 Bitumen (th. MT)	13–1600 Carbon Black (MT)	14–0100 Iron Ore, over 42% Fe (th. MT)	14–0200 Iron Ore, less than 42% Fe (th. MT)	14–0300 Pig Iron, white (th. MT)	14–0400 Pig Iron, Gray (th. MT)	14–0500 Ingots (th. MT)	14–0701 Steel Rails (MT)
1952	22.1	658	518.1	157.9	251.6	21.3	428.1	36,441
1953	45.2	999	670.8	124.1	232.6	36.9	498.3	31,721
1954	40.9	888	660.3	450.5	330.7	25.3	600.3	38,591
1955	35.5	1,287	663.7	734.6	465.3	48.5	781.3	48,588
1956	38.8	1,634	684.0	1,041	570.6	59.9	864.4	35,076
1957	44.8	1,924	710.1	1,166	650.2	64.1	1,027	35,430
1958	67.9	2,238	768.5	1,229	665.3	83.0	1,097	53,614
1959	82.4	2,921	719.7	1,376	778.9	84.4	1,272	56,401
1960	71.9	3,862	731.6	1,468	848.0	123.8	1,411	64,007
1961	80.0	4,398	779.7	1,404	871.8	125.1	1,495	81,718
1962	113.8	3,375	875.2	1,315	913.9	135.8	1,556	77,650
1963	120	4,281	1,329	968	851	145.4	1,542	84,722
1964	151	4,907	1,172	1,135	869	157	1,625	77,169
1965	112	5,099	1,574	930	940	175	1,718	69,364
1966	140	6,560	1,605	887	986	157	1,823	88,637
1967	171	12,423	1,693	886	1,066	111	1,797	93,584
1968	245	8,936	1,762	958	1,115	86	1,960	63,448
1969	314	15,531	1,642	1,079	1,119	79	2,176	68,228
1970	358	13,469	1,783	1,911	1,175	99	2,180	51,525
1971	376	15,685	1,897	1,827	1,341	173	2,402	86,361
1972	368	13,035	1,985	1,975	1,649	170	2,538	66,941
1973	326	15,366	1,987	2,684	1,763	192	2,630	78,824
1974	349	18,576	2,116	2,918	1,932	194	2,786	97,696
1975	386	19,240	2,264	2,975	1,787	213	2,865	97,325
Index	B,C,D	C,D	A,B,C,D	A,B,C,D	A,B,C,D	B,C,D	A,B	A,B,C,D

	14–0800 Steel Sheets (MT)	14–0900 Other Heavy Sections (MT)	14–1000 Strip Steel (MT)	14–1101 Rolled Wire (MT)	14–1102 Extruded Wire (MT)	14–1200 Profiles (MT)	14–1301 Thick and Medium Plates (MT)	14–1302 Hot-Rolled Dynamo and Transformer Plates (MT)
1952	0	15,757	15,175	21,860	20,578	125,203	47,760	774
1953	0	20,928	43,107	27,637	23,423	111,405	56,351	761
1954	0	29,118	44,479	41,390	31,280	117,578	66,056	723
1955	0	32,516	21,300	56,119	42,035	190,494	70,083	530
1956	946	26,187	24,927	45,795	42,594	210,803	68,939	562
1957	1,310	22,840	27,317	55,100	48,469	289,980	83,050	945
1958	583	13,992	36,848	64,282	55,540	338,710	99,392	1,341
1959	798	30,157	41,941	80,081	62,336	384,372	99,850	2,842
1960	910	31,611	36,749	87,593	69,148	481,297	113,422	2,916
1961	816	17,623	36,447	117,370	76,597	495,394	111,081	2,779
1962	611	34,586	48,387	139,874	74,267	479,081	102,226	3,910
1963	566	48,762	38,003	119,502	78,510	515,001	125,863	3,718
1964	247	57,355	61,154	122,208	88,265	558,841	130,679	4,429
1965	205	54,623	94,372	137,842	100,317	570,647	146,525	6,749
1966	385	49,390	95,032	155,353	118,000	603,019	144,328	8,595
1967	358	44,324	88,302	112,610	101,348	667,725	137,635	8,453
1968	554	73,402	226,502	130,891	109,292	671,657	211,216	5,974
1969	595	87,405	326,940	181,388	127,928	665,673	275,791	6,674
1970	32	112,427	275,360	181,473	148,260	703,857	435,005	7,158
1971	0	87,598	287,578	216,835	177,325	693,347	419,658	0
1972	0	15,555	364,921	255,232	190,839	794,277	393,727	0
1973	0	6,330	373,681	262,317	212,170	780,386	365,224	0
1974	0	8,226	485,869	298,877	226,644	833,025	451,271	0
1975	0	17,105	453,039	335,221	230,331	829,917	515,497	0
Index	B,C	C,D	C,D	A,B,C,D	A,B,C,D	A,B,C,D	A,B,C,D	B,C,D

TABLE B-1 (Cont.)

	14–1305 Other Thin and Fine Plates (MT)	14–1400 Galvanized Sheets (MT)	14–1600 Strips (MT)	14–1700 Rolled Rims (MT)	14–1801 Seamless Tubes (MT)	14–1802 Welded Tubes (MT)	15–0200 Copper Ore (th. MT)	15–0300 Bauxite (th. MT)
1952	25,747	7,182	7,214	0	0	6,697	1,173	613.4
1953	34,549	7,511	6,746	0	4,017	10,828	1,344	477.6
1954	31,933	6,776	9,777	0	16,001	7,104	1,299	686,7
1955	40,881	7,136	9,626	0	26,740	7,976	1,477	791.0
1956	54,499	11,688	11,186	0	27,576	10,688	1,741	881.4
1957	55,250	15,257	17,890	1,866	54,350	12,690	1,953	888.2
1958	59,574	16,406	22,850	3,854	56,242	13,778	2,268	732.6
1959	77,191	19,731	25,714	3,997	64,102	16,376	2,228	815.5
1960	81,284	23,133	30,782	6,156	68,232	18,863	2,370	1,025
1961	82,987	22,563	28,736	9,045	73,205	21,285	3,236	1,232
1962	90,243	22,460	29,658	6,649	68,588	22,292	5,070	1,331
1963	90,738	25,342	31,190	5,359	72,934	30,774	5,629	1,285
1964	98,947	25,029	41,278	10,487	77,800	61,849	5,928	1,293
1965	81,659	14,840	47,474	14,772	70,332	89,649	6,003	1,574
1966	77,088	18,823	49,386	14,397	77,257	88,274	5,624	1,887
1967	67,901	18,712	38,559	10,904	77,379	88,495	5,873	2,131
1968	83,810	22,097	44,963	8,085	74,889	134,757	7,002	2,072
1969	71,913	18,912	52,705	10,453	76,204	147,708	8,715	2,128
1970	75,157	17,116	49,708	8,952	74,310	149,918	9,421	2,098
1971	48,570	18,071	48,114	11,099	77,961	209,735	10,314	1,958
1972	22,685	4,628	48,255	13,133	83,387	223,605	11,918	2,197
1973	35,538	3,521	46,548	14,386	88,291	239,659	14,206	2,167
1974	16,727	3,443	48,961	12,328	119,080	241,198	14,930	2,370
1975	15,126	1,898	49,755	16,060	132,851	295,341	14,576	2,306
Index	B,C,D	A,B,C	A,B,C,D	C,D	A,B,C,D	A,B,C,D	D	A,B,C,D

	15–0400 Lead-Zinc Ore (th. MT)	15–0500 Chromium Ore (MT)	15–0700 Manganese Ore (MT)	15–1700 Pyrites Concentrate (MT)	15–1800 Chromium Concentrate (MT)	15–2200 Crude Copper (MT)	15–2300 Zinc (Crude and Powder) (MT)	15–2400 Crude Lead (MT)
1952	1,204	107,645	12,687	167,397	25,872	32,819	14,463	72,179
1953	1,432	127,927	10,017	165,833	23,777	31,190	14,549	79,150
1954	1,485	129,848	9,206	160,109	23,486	30,295	13,644	76,138
1955	1,650	126,207	10,955	226,682	29,079	28,260	13,768	80,938
1956	1,726	118,762	11,573	255,947	29,718	29,384	14,003	86,248
1957	1,764	120,266	10,234	312,600	34,704	33,735	16,741	92,194
1958	1,796	113,569	10,036	331,084	37,434	33,672	17,959	85,007
1959	1,831	107,016	8,084	290,470	42,620	35,251	18,302	97,934
1960	1,920	100,582	13,314	417,394	41,641	35,729	19,748	99,738
1961	2,063	108,126	14,148	364,313	43,481	30,869	20,401	101,698
1962	2,239	97,045	14,839	414,202	44,088	45,741	20,232	113,018
1963	2,288	93,770	8,132	356,459	56,176	50,779	22,022	117,481
1964	2,364	88,358	7,784	427,802	52,591	51,716	25,290	117,224
1965	2,358	79,851	8,097	406,773	46,990	56,919	24,729	116,166
1966	2,439	54,211	8,616	378,134	38,982	71,341	28,159	111,923
1967	2,612	47,162	9,821	424,648	38,888	76,707	26,572	101,890
1968	2,693	45,261	14,136	273,663	44,304	83,821	28,147	108,715
1969	2,928	39,434	12,331	272,422	23,666	95,923	29,580	123,512
1970	3,113	40,565	14,785	354,900	60,906	107,803	16,472	112,232
1971	3,155	34,319	16,113	276,084	57,803	113,241	3,377	118,748
1972	3,111	28,137	15,340	230,806	47,390	150,511	6,722	102,164
1973	3,196	9,594	9,718	216,732	31,056	160,025	7,105	112,632
1974	3,379	596	13,282	254,741	49,213	176,958	6,990	118,428
1975	3,606	1,694	16,925	398,988	38,482	162,012	8,543	140,018
Index	B,C,D	A	A,B,C,D	A	A	A	A,B,C,D	C,D

TABLE B-1 (Cont.)

	15–2500 Aluminum Ingots (MT)	15–2600 Antimony Regulus (MT)	15–2700 Electrolytic Copper (MT)	15–2800 Refined Zinc (MT)	15–2900 Refined Lead (MT)	15–3000 Anodic Silver (kg.)	15–3100 Gold (kg.)	15–3200 Mercury (MT)
1952	2,563	1,329	21,390	8,911	67,180	80,155	707	504
1953	2,792	1,410	27,764	8,506	70,796	94,804	1,204	492
1954	3,496	1,552	26,946	7,192	66,729	88,004	1,453	498
1955	11,499	1,605	24,837	4,675	75,612	92,800	1,588	503
1956	14,662	1,663	25,088	11,005	75,759	85,846	1,397	456
1957	18,134	1,769	30,128	18,284	78,504	80,550	1,647	425
1958	21,681	1,660	29,905	19,387	84,281	116,691	1,690	423
1959	19,245	2,281	31,567	19,690	85,395	87,940	1,855	460
1960	25,070	2,410	35,063	22,877	89,143	94,083	1,990	485
1961	27,407	2,463	30,108	25,971	90,401	107,434	2,090	550
1962	27,980	2,691	45,520	30,135	97,926	116,667	2,193	561
1963	35,895	2,661	49,032	36,864	104,174	117,942	2,602	546
1964	34,314	2,729	51,941	34,969	101,085	125,561	3,321	597
1965	38,772	2,768	56,354	34,690	101,576	115,641	3,232	566
1966	42,022	2,645	62,920	39,037	97,476	101,593	2,642	548
1967	44,574	2,297	66,189	45,787	105,596	95,658	2,117	545
1968	48,080	1,755	70,054	72,428	105,982	79,415	2,187	510
1969	48,248	2,037	82,003	67,189	106,956	107,510	2,615	494
1970	47,738	1,967	89,287	59,011	97,399	98,050	3,029	533
1971	46,584	1,381	92,576	49,897	99,139	96,240	3,850	572
1972	72,716	1,744	129,974	41,988	87,496	102,805	4,258	566
1973	90,845	1,999	137,500	63,121	98,033	123,442	5,485	538
1974	147,089	2,349	150,006	79,390	113,876	134,927	5,297	546
1975	168,270	2,159	137,902	89,062	126,099	155,307	5,534	584
Index	A,B,C,D	A,B,C,D	A,B,C,D	A,B,C,D	A,B,C,D	A,B,C,D	A,B,C,D	A,B,C,D

	15–3300 Bismuth (MT)	15–3400 Selen (kg.)	15–3500 Aluminum Alloys (MT)	15–3600 Silico-manganese (MT)	15–3700 Ferro-manganese (MT)	15–3800 Ferrochrome (MT)	15–3900 Silicochrome (MT)	15–4000 Ferrosilicon (MT)
1952	99	na	577	1,019	5,871	3,304	na	4,336
1953	98	na	647	1,327	3,456	1,929	na	3,858
1954	110	na	997	679	4,615	2,612	na	3,603
1955	104	na	1,306	1,707	6,615	4,096	na	4,207
1956	111	na	1,311	1,968	5,929	3,557	na	3,959
1957	100	na	1,619	1,538	6,969	5,268	2,157	6,906
1958	77	na	2,121	1,532	9,526	8,146	1,230	11,184
1959	91	na	2,773	2,631	12,255	8,632	3,500	12,915
1960	105	na	3,913	2,965	15,509	9,974	2,633	15,093
1961	98	849	6,382	5,401	15,991	10,174	9,636	14,127
1962	91	1,808	5,379	5,241	12,713	8,455	7,557	18,825
1963	88	1,869	9,675	7,259	16,500	11,410	5,810	22,486
1964	84	3,828	14,166	5,030	12,181	8,881	5,559	15,430
1965	88	7,911	21,515	6,322	11,589	11,966	7,965	21,514
1966	104	9,325	20,260	15,217	10,538	11,730	10,702	25,748
1967	107	4,644	14,861	21,295	9,649	11,562	10,921	24,932
1968	86	9,637	14,566	17,298	8,619	11,949	8,662	35,652
1969	102	8,866	14,690	19,570	13,085	9,013	5,970	38,908
1970	75	16,000	19,368	17,219	12,472	15,856	7,867	47,146
1971	92	24,320	14,011	16,915	15,143	18,502	8,748	56,133
1972	89	40,880	21,608	14,949	18,539	27,145	6,489	62,960
1973	55	42,880	17,736	11,750	18,653	35,044	8,912	78,418
1974	100	40,201	15,428	17,059	22,626	38,875	5,120	104,102
1975	55	43,320	23,164	14,409	30,674	53,902	10,053	83,168
Index	A,B,C,D	D	D	C,D	A,B,C,D	A,B,C,D	C,D	A,B,C,D

TABLE B-1 (Cont.)

	15–4100 Silicocalcium (MT)	15–4300 Rolled Products of Copper and Its Alloys (MT)	15–4301 Rolled Copper Wire (MT)	15–4302 Rolled Sheets of Copper and Copper Alloys (MT)	15–4303 Rolled Strips of Copper and Copper Alloys (MT)	15–4304 Rolled Rondels of Copper and Copper Alloys (MT)	15–4500 Extruded Copper Products (MT)	15–4700 Uninsulated Copper Ropes (MT)
1952	0	6,487	na	na	na	na	7,161	3,397
1953	0	7,154	na	na	na	na	5,469	2,654
1954	0	8,085	na	na	na	na	5,367	2,155
1955	0	12,606	na	na	na	na	10,141	2,408
1956	266	18,757	na	na	na	na	12,229	4,759
1957	214	25,155	na	na	na	na	18,654	7,973
1958	204	31,355	na	na	na	na	25,290	12,476
1959	87	26,888	na	na	na	na	23,100	11,200
1960	577	33,001	na	na	na	na	26,900	11,700
1961	270	32,625	23,900	5,620	10,200	894	31,300	12,300
1962	538	37,230	23,510	5,554	6,508	1,658	41,069	12,337
1963	212	45,972	27,047	6,364	12,103	458	50,043	15,196
1964	351	48,519	30,058	6,830	10,981	650	55,208	16,400
1965	485	48,954	30,421	7,495	10,171	867	56,949	16,560
1966	134	48,711	29,773	7,845	9,747	1,346	60,403	14,535
1967	306	52,958	32,383	8,294	10,955	1,326	61,712	15,419
1968	905	54,965	31,760	9,525	11,705	1,975	56,058	14,739
1969	0	60,793	36,637	9,626	12,756	1,774	66,758	18,016
1970	468	63,211	36,744	11,293	13,425	1,749	73,073	18,221
1971	46	66,538	41,176	8,714	14,460	2,188	72,688	20,781
1972	623	60,921	35,700	8,147	14,870	2,204	68,031	20,358
1973	0	63,704	37,179	7,504	15,974	3,047	67,504	20,200
1974	0	79,662	50,789	8,308	18,186	2,379	75,995	21,379
1975	0	82,441	52,736	9,160	17,925	2,620	69,845	19,112
Index	C,D	A,B,C	D	D	D	D	A,B,C,D	A,B,C,D

	15–5000 Extruded Products of Aluminum and Aluminum Alloys (MT)	15–5100 Rolled Zinc Products (MT)	15–5200 Rolled Lead Products (MT)	16–0100 Quartz Sand, Stone, and Flour for Glass (th. MT)	16–0200 Crude Fireclay (MT)	16–0300 Crude Magnesite (MT)	16–0500 Crude Feldspar (MT)	16–0600 Mica (kg.)
1952	617	1,328	3,000	52.10	56,193	37,782	1,214	0
1953	1,158	1,872	4,700	60.71	66,561	152,517	1,624	3,479
1954	2,038	2,078	4,800	83.22	76,394	139,318	2,459	4,465
1955	3,033	1,961	6,900	101.1	118,938	117,130	4,824	5,923
1956	4,070	2,721	2,500	123.0	101,472	194,372	5,564	8,361
1957	5,604	3,410	2,700	152.5	92,718	212,266	9,762	16,957
1958	7,075	3,669	4,477	176.7	106,324	223,197	12,666	1,760
1959	8,500	4,065	4,876	220.6	120,618	244,805	19,619	2,054
1960	10,500	5,255	6,963	215.7	132,777	251,847	14,001	2,354
1961	12,900	5,957	12,817	279.7	152,264	273,065	20,539	1,686
1962	25,502	6,948	16,295	342.6	144,707	373,262	32,085	2,433
1963	23,948	10,063	18,256	468.8	210,346	411,959	29,885	35,330
1964	23,042	12,233	19,445	558.7	232,354	497,420	33,794	11,660
1965	26,702	14,015	16,258	533.3	245,080	525,941	55,935	53,890
1966	30,375	15,632	13,420	604.9	247,244	526,685	41,570	54,630
1967	38,046	16,288	14,497	629.2	168,004	424,762	36,996	118,659
1968	28,200	15,002	12,407	660.4	178,192	400,316	44,078	143,501
1969	30,683	19,817	11,395	812	259,529	477,417	44,982	135,565
1970	33,683	14,464	13,037	982	292,070	511,853	49,504	227,467
1971	26,361	11,728	12,528	1,065	282,503	492,716	53,617	554,026
1972	26,579	11,419	12,986	1,114	335,604	421,674	48,335	126,000
1973	31,856	11,848	12,400	1,424	300,236	383,709	50,807	28,000
1974	45,111	12,939	14,092	1,520	317,658	463,510	56,094	87,000
1975	49,907	8,442	11,116	1,605	349,747	485,301	54,548	86,000
Index	B,C,D	A,B,C,D	A,B,C,D	B,C,D	A,B,C,D	B,C,D	C,D	D

TABLE B-1 (Cont.)

	16–0800 Crude Barites (MT)	16–0900 Asbestos Fiber (Except Meal and Padding) (MT)	16–1000 Caustic Magnesite, Calcined (MT)	16–1100 Sea Salt (MT)	16–1200 Salt from Brine (MT)	16–1300 Flat Glass (th. M.^{2})	16–1400 Blown Glass (MT)	16–1500 Cut Glass (MT)
1952	34,819	2,506	10,643	100,754	82,801	3,415	20,333	0
1953	81,154	3,748	18,077	38,853	98,415	3,267	20,441	0
1954	95,794	3,264	18,411	41,853	96,135	5,025	21,029	0
1955	88,123	3,906	19,727	36,458	99,505	4,583	28,690	0
1956	93,322	3,778	21,932	41,586	103,143	4,728	32,310	0
1957	120,780	5,559	20,883	40,020	108,022	5,526	34,377	0
1958	94,167	5,407	18,740	60,949	111,295	5,719	41,201	102
1959	107,290	4,307	21,958	21,662	114,745	5,713	54,296	169
1960	109,489	5,416	21,805	35,687	115,745	6,806	61,529	250
1961	104,210	6,086	25,591	45,193	115,754	8,702	66,921	331
1962	103,763	6,714	24,019	86,522	128,331	8,307	70,737	327
1963	104,486	8,232	26,466	32,618	133,934	9,650	74,590	479
1964	101,670	8,419	32,068	52,748	131,230	7,744	93,959	550
1965	97,110	9,603	28,163	39,238	133,241	6,873	106,728	405
1966	80,189	7,630	25,631	34,283	130,221	13,906	138,504	524
1967	84,478	9,021	17,807	40,776	127,656	16,377	144,292	593
1968	70,436	10,393	17,074	10,574	127,000	13,414	174,110	548
1969	81,511	11,461	14,410	17,696	127,887	14,852	187,609	633
1970	79,729	12,104	10,135	23,510	101,668	18,499	227,155	557
1971	64,690	15,432	9,685	53,715	63,239	19,933	260,652	2,336
1972	70,528	11,040	5,145	8,654	27,122	16,148	278,749	2,824
1973	62,053	9,391	5,961	50,940	17,114	16,594	287,428	2,172
1974	50,157	12,247	15,301	23,375	15,273	16,618	316,918	2,551
1975	60,645	12,203	5,128	37,444	5,530	21,223	306,256	3,049
Index	C,D	A,B,C,D	C,D	B,C,D	A,B,C,D	A,B,C,D	C,D	C,D

	16–1600 Glass Wool (MT)	16–1700 Calcined Clay (MT)	16–1800 Sinter Magnesite (MT)	16–1900 Fireclay (MT)	16–2000 Basic Bricks (Thermal Process) (MT)	16–2100 Chrome-Magnesite Refractory Material (MT)	16–2200 Acid Refractory Fire-Baked Bricks (MT)	16–2300 Silico-dinas Material (MT)
1952	0	11,977	3,237	52,147	0	0	1,220	na
1953	0	17,072	32,985	61,503	3,493	1,216	1,436	na
1954	0	18,027	43,589	63,817	5,215	7,503	977	na
1955	305	29,672	44,703	86,376	3,143	8,807	896	na
1956	280	27,722	62,218	95,517	4,981	8,980	418	na
1957	488	27,147	74,748	90,263	11,233	15,351	565	na
1958	540	27,507	81,187	96,925	16,139	18,835	392	na
1959	584	27,060	86,788	106,893	18,033	20,070	96	na
1960	820	30,070	90,891	120,678	20,526	21,546	135	na
1961	1,317	34,282	97,885	120,579	20,726	22,746	354	4,590
1962	1,294	35,937	131,626	134,834	29,549	26,776	543	2,778
1963	2,020	39,393	155,016	136,021	31,025	31,932	801	5,656
1964	2,789	43,520	177,933	166,470	34,897	32,858	1,132	6,460
1965	3,623	46,590	195,880	171,740	42,371	49,684	1,186	4,743
1966	3,264	46,314	188,807	165,892	43,988	49,329	4,950	4,713
1967	3,181	34,677	149,516	149,702	30,439	41,190	7,804	5,197
1968	4,791	38,410	156,301	138,067	44,646	28,088	3,874	3,403
1969	4,827	71,671	193,160	145,317	64,268	34,947	3,522	4,136
1970	4,032	88,370	210,310	144,553	81,591	17,094	4,282	10,001
1971	4,134	69,726	202,231	150,921	106,342	23,666	4,342	10,144
1972	3,710	95,750	149,335	149,820	119,736	24,659	2,471	14,896
1973	3,147	86,247	169,709	150,680	93,840	25,607	4,473	12,828
1974	3,181	82,867	269,029	170,795	116,408	27,969	3,566	9,487
1975	4,098	99,198	256,588	184,619	115,013	33,608	2,012	12,427
Index	C,D	C,D	B,C,D	A,C,D	C,D	A,B,C,D	C,D	B,C,D

TABLE B-1 (Cont.)

	16–2400 Other Refractories (MT)	16–2500 Ceramic Ware for Households (MT)	16–2600 Ceramic Ware for Construction (MT)	16–2700 Sanitary Ceramics (MT)	16–2800 Insulators, etc., of Electroporcelain (MT)	16–2900 Insulators, etc., of Steatite (MT)	16–3000 Asbestos Products (MT)	16–3200 Artificial Abrasives (MT)
1952	2,114	1,534	6,244	21	1,047	0	250	418
1953	2,115	1,316	6,896	14	1,059	0	236	455
1954	2,319	1,800	9,225	231	1,332	0	327	645
1955	3,114	3,070	13,349	510	2,664	0	339	960
1956	1,113	3,353	10,933	1,061	2,223	0	329	712
1957	3,743	3,942	22,582	1,267	3,047	0	428	753
1958	6,305	4,966	23,646	1,556	4,332	0	526	787
1959	6,181	5,689	23,505	2,146	4,904	0	687	1,007
1960	10,404	6,094	27,924	2,723	5,998	0	1,170	1,331
1961	7,487	5,474	32,617	3,385	6,378	0	955	1,857
1962	5,128	6,241	39,830	3,408	5,403	7	1,874	1,640
1963	15,866	7,000	42,591	3,755	6,375	5	2,670	3,009
1964	11,286	8,359	51,380	4,415	9,796	33	4,358	3,543
1965	11,437	8,735	58,899	4,387	10,214	80	4,678	4,511
1966	15,663	8,985	57,541	5,146	9,818	259	4,560	5,297
1967	13,877	9,030	56,369	4,295	9,361	443	4,018	4,955
1968	15,665	8,590	62,181	5,017	11,260	392	5,100	3,756
1969	16,962	8,609	79,843	5,507	12,462	525	7,101	4,482
1970	19,574	8,490	94,545	5,815	12,029	609	9,013	5,005
1971	20,888	8,657	99,821	6,014	11,318	835	9,498	4,879
1972	20,102	9,830	116,310	6,259	11,461	913	10,221	5,259
1973	25,637	9,992	114,595	5,944	11,447	1,199	11,066	6,173
1974	27,690	10,710	132,530	6,446	12,941	3,115	12,746	7,163
1975	29,476	11,456	162,720	7,727	14,825	3,488	15,303	7,595
Index	C,D	C,D	A,B,C,D	C,D	A,B,C,D	D	C,D	C,D

	16–3500 Electrodes, Amorphous (MT)	16–3600 Amorphous Matter (MT)	17–0100 Castings, Steel (MT)	17–0200 Castings, Tempered and Gray Steel (MT)	17–0300 Castings, Nonferrous Metals (MT)	17–0400 Forgings (MT)	17–0500 Cast-Iron Pipes and Fashioned Parts (MT)	17–0600 Boilers for Central Heating (MT)
1952	2,512	3,224	10,460	54,621	4,274	6,080	10,292	1,071
1953	2,182	3,179	10,666	66,854	4,600	6,852	13,027	1,974
1954	1,907	3,091	12,343	81,667	5,161	7,773	12,847	2,289
1955	2,675	4,154	14,151	98,174	6,335	5,971	19,555	3,152
1956	2,812	3,020	13,717	106,320	7,566	11,900	17,926	3,234
1957	4,013	3,677	15,024	122,903	10,124	12,322	29,948	3,161
1958	4,322	4,152	17,170	140,768	10,314	12,858	36,672	3,114
1959	4,688	13,995	20,433	159,263	13,313	16,004	41,220	3,665
1960	3,522	17,602	23,320	192,318	15,915	16,649	46,972	6,163
1961	4,006	19,615	27,094	205,638	16,102	24,152	49,530	7,495
1962	2,529	21,145	29,480	203,287	15,750	24,870	48,322	5,592
1963	2,105	29,393	34,804	227,950	17,740	30,690	56,001	7,898
1964	2,355	25,101	39,281	278,740	19,952	44,683	61,417	6,453
1965	4,431	28,893	41,958	310,042	21,196	51,542	68,431	8,694
1966	5,728	34,309	36,048	288,987	20,657	43,044	65,554	7,410
1967	3,824	33,871	30,102	253,153	20,756	35,921	59,500	6,676
1968	2,726	36,051	32,121	259,430	21,323	43,602	64,897	6,788
1969	3,240	37,707	39,300	306,157	23,234	52,011	65,676	6,881
1970	3,756	38,004	43,847	344,901	25,139	56,624	73,673	5,014
1971	2,874	41,516	50,102	360,722	28,560	60,737	71,392	6,872
1972	3,217	54,806	51,959	372,906	28,422	59,712	67,258	6,294
1973	3,106	62,313	53,059	382,125	25,806	63,301	67,182	7,802
1974	2,686	101,346	57,190	413,876	30,499	67,411	75,650	9,414
1975	2,614	127,119	63,490	449,887	30,325	75,762	82,350	9,026
Index	C,D	C,D	A,B,C,D	A,B,C,D	C,D	C,D	A,B,C,D	C,D

TABLE B-1 (Cont.)

	17–0700 Equipment for Steam Heating (MT)	17–0800 Sanitary Equipment (MT)	17–0900 Armatures (MT)	17–1000 Rivets (MT)	17–1100 Fittings and Accessories (MT)	17–1200 Screws (MT)	17–1300 Nails (MT)	17–1400 Steel Ropes (MT)
1952	1,666	1,229	815	1,572	338	7,357	15,438	161
1953	2,605	1,911	1,465	2,376	318	9,227	16,967	564
1954	3,028	2,039	1,605	2,029	386	9,906	18,460	1,173
1955	3,072	2,316	2,127	2,389	584	10,849	21,051	1,323
1956	3,642	1,973	1,744	2,427	609	10,511	21,296	1,450
1957	4,967	2,972	2,881	2,531	1,152	11,943	26,303	1,627
1958	5,175	3,489	3,719	3,239	1,420	12,868	30,381	1,635
1959	7,369	4,647	5,016	2,631	1,987	16,793	37,941	2,887
1960	11,881	6,689	5,852	2,382	3,747	19,346	41,422	3,116
1961	10,815	4,856	6,407	2,123	4,145	18,678	39,679	2,907
1962	10,197	5,147	6,998	1,862	4,488	16,861	40,928	3,120
1963	14,790	6,596	7,086	2,393	4,362	17,502	41,661	4,651
1964	20,123	11,967	9,379	2,852	5,825	25,556	49,416	6,462
1965	20,036	12,921	11,125	2,197	6,457	26,942	46,045	4,805
1966	14,833	13,331	10,123	2,000	6,193	24,930	37,257	5,659
1967	18,670	14,302	12,694	1,372	7,481	24,058	35,545	4,961
1968	19,286	14,955	15,285	2,060	8,066	24,425	35,522	4,582
1969	25,662	18,270	17,358	2,398	10,502	31,832	35,425	5,274
1970	30,889	19,673	18,817	2,386	10,629	37,524	38,506	4,960
1971	32,669	19,047	24,223	1,732	11,653	41,041	39,463	3,924
1972	32,178	15,442	26,792	2,230	12,134	41,882	40,898	4,623
1973	32,805	16,029	27,823	2,103	11,568	41,089	45,031	5,770
1974	35,061	17,244	29,053	1,999	13,174	49,210	44,798	5,836
1975	41,165	15,300	40,800	1,611	15,707	57,652	42,749	5,436
Index	C,D	D	C,D	C,D	D	C,D	A,B,C,D	C,D

	17–1500 Barbed Wire, Wire Netting, and Wire Cloth (MT)	17–1600 Chains (MT)	17–1700 Chain Sets, Complete (MT)	17–1800 Metal Utensils (MT)	17–1900 Metal Packing Containers (MT)	17–2000 Bends and Springs (MT)	17–2100 Metal Electrodes for Welding (MT)	17–2200 Agricultural Tools, Forged and Pressed (MT)
1952	3,738	1,084	2,865	123	5,820	na	1,816	2,993
1953	5,241	1,063	4,063	133	9,300	na	2,902	2,842
1954	4,745	1,406	4,315	172	12,879	na	3,539	3,539
1955	4,404	1,968	5,007	239	14,049	2,852	4,954	4,515
1956	3,817	2,289	4,336	228	12,531	3,429	3,875	4,221
1957	4,122	2,504	4,753	235	18,856	5,452	4,877	4,022
1958	4,465	2,402	5,345	221	20,761	6,682	6,214	4,137
1959	5,535	2,543	5,373	519	29,261	9,543	9,652	4,741
1960	7,091	3,113	5,458	1,049	38,108	10,885	11,559	5,524
1961	8,004	4,136	6,497	1,120	41,772	11,294	12,744	5,246
1962	9,805	4,462	7,757	1,282	50,168	12,420	10,210	4,628
1963	12,015	5,463	8,715	1,307	57,750	15,084	12,260	4,192
1964	19,867	6,713	12,905	1,766	72,677	20,877	14,804	4,480
1965	18,618	7,359	11,306	2,253	70,224	21,999	14,371	4,657
1966	23,704	8,743	11,163	3,065	70,723	22,479	16,589	5,040
1967	19,267	8,509	9,058	1,259	78,352	19,046	15,722	4,782
1968	23,227	9,051	11,906	1,094	80,010	21,796	16,677	4,195
1969	29,177	10,798	15,244	1,628	85,689	25,487	17,832	3,900
1970	23,520	11,168	14,812	1,806	90,280	23,788	18,496	4,251
1971	27,363	12,813	14,738	2,084	87,487	23,437	21,053	4,638
1972	34,396	13,181	15,286	2,371	84,362	23,702	21,584	4,611
1973	39,855	14,166	15,516	2,288	84,841	27,767	23,565	3,889
1974	53,639	16,197	18,211	2,061	99,186	31,595	24,936	5,192
1975	80,951	17,471	19,715	2,565	105,435	33,173	32,074	5,794
Index	A,C,D	A,C,D	C,D	C,D	C,D	C,D	A,B,C,D	C,D

TABLE B-1 (Cont.)

	17–2300 Cutting Tools (MT)	17–2500 Roller Bearings (MT)	17–2600 Pumps (MT)	17–2700 Steam Boilers (not Cental Heating) (MT)	17–2800 Water Turbines (MT)	17–2900 Steam Turbines (MT)	17–3100 Construction Machinery and Equipment (MT)	17–3200 Metal- and Woodworking Machines, Total (MT)
1952	876	87	1,124	1,300	1,949	0	1,054	1,963
1953	1,128	117	1,213	1,281	1,491	0	1,534	2,394
1954	854	139	1,044	2,135	1,392	0	4,614	3,681
1955	914	154	1,353	4,322	1,806	0	8,360	3,119
1956	1,439	150	1,361	2,198	2,591	267	5,121	2,738
1957	1,629	207	2,115	2,659	1,916	126	8,440	3,890
1958	1,193	256	2,099	3,672	1,215	206	14,037	3,444
1959	1,658	691	2,672	6,651	2,988	320	11,623	3,528
1960	1,986	767	3,021	6,731	2,493	268	6,919	4,545
1961	1,906	1,446	4,124	8,725	1,021	228	8,323	5,780
1962	2,060	1,522	4,414	9,641	923	469	7,195	5,881
1963	2,975	1,596	3,511	9,158	1,523	93	7,305	6,240
1964	2,842	2,438	4,491	12,000	1,203	267	13,355	9,027
1965	3,858	2,790	5,259	9,297	1,371	1,171	12,977	11,044
1966	3,692	2,228	5,090	8,165	1,752	714	16,949	10,299
1967	3,021	1,399	6,210	11,787	2,414	217	13,061	9,574
1968	2,508	1,508	6,630	12,670	2,367	249	15,429	8,014
1969	3,886	1,347	6,856	9,523	1,161	607	23,359	9,885
1970	4,614	1,866	7,033	9,724	980	337	26,772	10,906
1971	5,485	2,211	7,205	7,778	1,297	285	28,364	12,589
1972	5,656	2,517	7,446	7,250	1,328	529	28,030	15,947
1973	5,278	2,986	4,927	7,315	1,469	997	34,351	12,545
1974	5,930	2,767	5,552	6,879	1,764	1,141	34,626	15,487
1975	6,480	3,455	7,257	12,548	1,097	799	34,639	17,116
Index	C,D	B,C,D	C,D	C,D	C,D	C,D	C,D	C

	17–3201 Metal-working Machines (MT)	17–3202 Wood-working Machines (MT)	17–3300 Agricultural Machinery, Equipment and Tools (MT)	17–3600 Ventilation and Air Conditioning Equipment (MT)	17–3700 Refrigeration Equipment (MT)	17–3900 Balances (MT)	17–4000 Sewing Machines (units)	17–4100 Typewriters and Accounting Machines (units)
1952	nsa	nsa	6,761	1,387	85	264	0	na
1953	nsa	nsa	8,339	1,489	85	504	0	na
1954	nsa	nsa	8,744	1,362	148	923	0	na
1955	2,488	631	13,244	1,294	343	1,031	0	1,885
1956	2,214	524	14,722	1,146	470	1,142	0	3,513
1957	3,334	556	17,930	1,471	1,086	1,185	1,924	7,240
1958	2,760	684	17,627	1,847	1,280	1,141	18,905	7,840
1959	2,812	716	21,401	2,268	1,699	1,684	22,234	9,162
1960	3,920	625	24,923	3,069	2,185	2,504	35,508	19,064
1961	4,600	1,180	18,073	4,181	2,377	2,376	38,687	24,563
1962	4,433	1,448	16,823	4,249	780	1,981	44,579	27,720
1963	4,900	1,340	22,207	4,188	860	2,563	55,987	31,362
1964	7,686	1,341	26,582	3,757	1,428	2,674	82,966	28,768
1965	9,195	1,849	31,936	3,125	1,606	2,676	97,745	40,600
1966	8,902	1,397	30,312	4,302	1,700	2,863	107,743	46,836
1967	8,086	1,488	25,590	5,636	1,668	2,735	93,722	31,789
1968	6,607	1,407	23,659	7,472	2,174	2,937	113,164	38,268
1969	8,357	1,528	25,439	7,205	2,158	3,110	107,922	42,307
1970	9,162	1,744	27,387	7,457	3,027	2,695	116,801	44,346
1971	10,713	1,876	38,323	7,668	2,951	3,218	115,555	32,356
1972	14,183	1,764	45,267	9,239	3,081	3,344	112,508	189,521
1973	10,992	1,553	56,633	9,649	2,792	3,468	107,733	220,290
1974	12,527	2,960	72,272	11,647	3,575	2,786	111,466	241,302
1975	14,485	2,631	69,249	11,316	3,664	3,484	112,207	242,905
Index	B,D	D	A,C,D	C,D	C,D	C,D	C,D	B,C,D

TABLE B-1 (Cont.)

	17–4200 Clocks (pcs.)	17–4300 Products for Medical and Veterinary Purposes (MT)	17–4400 Motor and Electro-Locomotives (MT)	17–4500 Steam Locomotives (MT)	17–4600 Freight and Other Special Coaches (MT)	17–4700 Other Railway Coaches and Mail Vans (MT)	17–4800 Tramcars, Rail Motor Coaches, etc. (MT)	17–4900 Tubs, Mine Cars, and Hand Trolleys (MT)
1952	40,738	247	0	206	2,951	1,252	0	4,448
1953	66,307	286	0	1,135	12,199	16	13	2,719
1954	78,016	299	0	1,662	13,772	0	13	3,346
1955	125,392	343	0	1,475	6,932	14	0	2,788
1956	168,207	282	28	500	2,162	1,000	66	2,509
1957	190,057	257	211	840	10,950	1,109	343	2,197
1958	240,867	249	305	557	29,488	704	128	2,181
1959	284,499	284	212	626	38,965	708	101	3,105
1960	354,562	372	1,032	242	53,566	1,090	158	3,385
1961	421,537	419	1,321	0	42,214	4,707	196	2,868
1962	456,473	458	1,558	0	43,168	5,503	187	2,127
1963	556,900	302	1,931	103	45,510	2,769	1,283	2,170
1964	621,200	391	2,234	58	54,298	4,982	508	2,262
1965	596,700	489	2,124	108	80,764	6,915	671	2,116
1966	440,200	409	1,354	72	70,049	6,688	919	1,784
1967	183,800	336	1,163	0	47,164	3,932	1,220	1,059
1968	231,700	340	1,139	0	49,383	5,070	1,228	1,133
1969	350,000	392	2,143	0	67,473	3,712	629	800
1970	494,500	537	4,205	0	50,679	4,387	255	735
1971	556,400	699	4,465	0	77,951	3,320	840	1,150
1972	625,457	656	3,557	0	64,659	1,944	199	1,360
1973	564,131	605	3,028	0	59,422	600	478	1,042
1974	638,469	596	3,535	0	44,389	3,447	1,801	878
1975	659,428	732	3,456	0	57,823	570	1,056	858
Index	B,C,D	C,D	C,D	C	C,D	C,D	C,D	A,B,C,D

	17–5100 Internal Combustion Engines (MT)	17–5200 Spare Parts for Internal Combustion Engines (MT)	17–5300 Bodies: Trucks, Buses, and Other Vehicles (MT)	17–5400 Trucks and Light Trucks (MT)	17–5500 Buses (MT)	17–5600 Passenger Automobiles (MT)	17–5800 Tractors (MT)	17–5900 Trailers for Trucks and Tractors (MT)	17–6000 Camping Trailers for Automobiles (MT)
1952	na	na	562	1,875	164	na	2,706	240	0
1953	na	na	513	3,654	300	na	5,865	3,501	0
1954	na	na	647	4,785	498	na	2,904	1,275	0
1955	1,629	na	1,254	6,313	1,098	760	2,750	3,436	0
1956	3,026	na	2,344	7,457	2,261	1,119	6,179	5,892	0
1957	3,981	na	3,135	9,085	3,662	3,530	9,427	6,911	0
1958	5,969	na	2,350	12,378	4,099	2,598	11,115	8,870	0
1959	8,430	na	3,114	12,106	3,467	3,747	13,305	12,363	0
1960	12,711	na	4,243	15,834	5,645	8,168	15,897	10,819	0
1961	13,366	na	3,865	18,302	5,839	11,040	12,216	10,999	0
1962	13,638	na	5,153	21,753	9,373	7,872	12,414	5,531	0
1963	16,474	2,257	8,379	27,986	7,219	11,935	20,140	4,718	0
1964	23,579	3,193	10,610	30,440	11,011	17,410	23,763	9,660	0
1965	23,396	5,394	10,533	29,625	11,688	22,634	16,543	14,605	0
1966	23,863	4,599	10,912	29,017	11,937	23,849	15,159	18,322	0
1967	25,264	4,413	12,050	32,997	11,496	30,870	14,615	15,762	0
1968	25,054	4,675	11,739	36,456	11,617	39,989	16,288	12,266	1,267
1969	28,230	5,885	12,581	39,906	13,110	55,576	18,335	16,471	3,594
1970	32,390	6,241	14,462	44,316	19,229	79,191	20,357	15,213	4,433
1971	31,751	7,254	15,064	46,508	19,748	81,541	24,178	18,470	5,053
1972	35,881	9,202	15,822	46,141	22,025	81,948	29,495	22,308	6,582
1973	38,562	11,046	17,336	43,498	23,102	93,074	32,724	32,983	9,022
1974	41,801	10,960	18,072	43,750	21,025	125,215	36,248	37,261	9,240
1975	50,105	18,713	20,688	51,620	22,828	140,267	42,417	44,075	10,276
Index	B,C,D	D	C,D	A,B,C,D	C,D	D	A,C,D	C,D	D

TABLE B-1 (Cont.)

	17–6100 Motor-cycles (MT)	17–6200 Spare Parts for Motor vehicles (MT)	17–6300 Bicycles (th. pcs.)	17–6400 Spare Parts for Bicycles (MT)	17–6500 Metal Kitchenware (MT)	17–6600 Aluminum Kitchenware (MT)	17–6700 Tableware (MT)	17–6800 Metal Furniture (MT)
1952	0	1,299	9.33	na	5,005	538	197	3,910
1953	0	879	20.7	na	3,952	205	241	5,890
1954	0	938	32.9	na	4,864	28	274	6,433
1955	0	1,233	48.0	na	5,367	115	307	7,364
1956	242	2,004	66.0	na	6,182	112	286	6,658
1957	856	3,046	86.4	na	7,625	301	291	8,796
1958	621	5,017	107	593	8,126	322	440	10,195
1959	1,750	10,495	135	711	9,429	296	510	10,806
1960	2,741	14,812	191	921	10,394	433	653	13,431
1961	2,806	12,755	241	1,257	10,768	608	551	14,168
1962	2,041	16,561	265	1,178	12,490	466	668	14,102
1963	3,039	23,424	290	988	13,390	686	710	15,142
1964	3,516	28,511	337	1,224	13,730	718	1,044	19,561
1965	3,251	32,331	272	1,254	14,748	819	827	17,180
1966	3,112	33,375	345	1,498	15,329	444	724	15,007
1967	3,090	34,208	289	1,376	18,231	325	615	13,583
1968	3,501	36,505	263	1,560	19,286	337	642	18,748
1969	3,828	42,132	315	1,457	18,132	239	634	21,994
1970	4,634	49,515	350	1,648	19,015	244	707	21,995
1971	4,073	56,908	312	2,104	19,836	333	836	26,663
1972	4,029	62,536	426	2,596	18,561	276	1,059	23,304
1973	3,981	75,874	442	3,319	19,383	280	1,176	23,697
1974	3,802	86,525	483	3,540	20,717	373	1,036	24,911
1975	4,160	97,728	373	2,631	16,947	367	1,206	30,124
Index	A,C,D	C,D	A,B,C,D	C,D	C,D	C,D	C,D	C,D

	17–6900 Stoves, Ranges, etc. (MT)	17–7100 Fire Extinguishers and Accessories (MT)	19–0100 Large Rotating Machines (More than 70 kw) (pcs.)	19–0200 Medium Rotating Machines (1.6–70 kw) (pcs.)	19–0300 Small Rotating Machines (Less than 1.6 kw) (th. pcs.)	19–0400 Accessories for Rotating Machines (MT)	19–0500 Power Transformers (units)	19–0600 Transformers for Electric Motors (MT)
1952	6,557	76	138	20,838	26.71	188	na	76
1953	9,913	117	92	23,191	19.33	163	na	102
1954	12,498	84	72	21,053	21.09	147	na	88
1955	15,872	504	106	23,419	34.26	138	6,633	128
1956	16,836	615	128	20,943	33.0	116	6,852	116
1957	23,168	899	163	27,993	50.0	173	5,879	123
1958	22,478	1,116	282	29,848	83.1	143	8,725	204
1959	26,033	1,096	265	28,771	128	189	12,234	301
1960	31,785	1,381	301	37,478	232	281	17,669	310
1961	41,991	1,161	463	50,139	311	188	22,139	302
1962	38,558	1,328	667	47,680	381	157	16,901	351
1963	39,922	1,333	740	40,923	581	223	21,633	329
1964	53,251	1,530	841	39,725	901	172	29,361	413
1965	49,309	1,486	613	50,807	1,317	165	29,351	446
1966	49,743	1,534	803	90,781	1,243	451	26,350	440
1967	54,833	1,741	993	83,665	976	724	36,047	595
1968	40,442	2,251	600	62,101	1,431	389	54,467	823
1969	62,413	2,228	505	62,962	2,003	399	53,430	841
1970	66,723	2,273	963	116,683	2,277	158	56,379	744
1971	69,189	2,713	1,060	157,487	943	204	48,366	726
1972	74,452	2,564	960	108,851	1,874	163	60,691	2,089
1973	63,541	2,046	1,516	126,523	2,062	129	87,331	1,129
1974	67,077	2,873	1,738	137,740	2,035	148	79,321	1,005
1975	56,557	3,128	2,874	225,007	2,296	246	83,393	1,544
Index	C,D	C,D	C,D	A,B,C,D	A,B,C,D	C,D	B,C,D	C,D

TABLE B-1 (Cont.)

	19–0700 Power Rectification Condensers (MT)	19–0800 Switchgear (MT)	19–0900 Distribution Equipment (MT)	19–1000 Industrial Electric Furnaces (MT)	19–1200 Electric Irons (th. units)	19–1400 Kitchen Ranges (th. units)	19–1600 Heaters (units)	19–1700 Boilers (th. units)
1952	na	343	551	0	na	na	na	na
1953	na	606	576	479	na	na	na	na
1954	na	546	693	301	na	na	na	na
1955	na	809	805	446	na	na	na	na
1956	na	914	618	360	na	na	na	na
1957	40	1,050	615	405	na	na	na	na
1958	32	1,638	1,017	494	na	na	na	na
1959	52	2,318	1,321	443	195	42.9	73,810	26.7
1960	78	2,419	1,931	491	260	54.2	20,194	39.4
1961	83	2,165	2,275	597	223	62.6	18,290	60.0
1962	139	2,631	2,336	634	269	152	66,606	75.3
1963	218	2,129	2,372	1,900	334	220	94,056	119.9
1964	178	2,863	3,989	1,368	431	234	143,854	145.7
1965	125	2,638	4,157	1,685	281	203	65,237	133.3
1966	162	3,792	5,072	1,591	248	309	70,504	163.1
1967	77	3,720	8,209	790	325	328	72,754	179
1968	148	4,925	8,756	714	414	360	79,364	228
1969	239	6,150	10,767	797	562	386	131,327	311
1970	539	5,436	8,649	1,367	620	420	145,139	366
1971	587	5,399	7,643	931	640	506	178,262	426
1972	165	5,568	10,944	708	797	542	203,000	474
1973	505	5,062	4,443	689	787	499	213,000	493
1974	527	6,662	5,918	386	803	509	248,000	532
1975	647	8,386	7,834	618	627	436	238,000	455
Index	C,D	A,C,D	C,D	C,D	B,C,D	B,C,D	C,D	B,C,D

	19–1800 Refrigeration Equipment (MT)	19–1900 Household Refrigerators (th. units)	19–2100 Vacuum Cleaners (th. units)	19–2200 Cables and Similar Conductors (MT)	19–2300 Insulated Conductors (MT)	19–2400 Radio Receivers (units)	19–2500 Television Receivers (units)	19–2900 Electric Phono-graphs (th. units)
1952	na	0	na	995	1,959	27,298	0	na
1953	na	0	na	1,238	2,410	37,613	0	na
1954	na	0	na	1,134	2,895	59,286	0	na
1955	na	0.04	na	1,672	3,609	81,995	0	na
1956	na	5.01	na	8,154	5,083	125,449	0	na
1957	na	6.32	na	20,728	6,778	209,275	1	na
1958	na	7.41	na	25,502	7,928	258,830	222	na
1959	na	17.9	20.26	35,360	10,601	250,153	5,423	5.54
1960	na	35.6	34.11	42,015	14,522	244,108	13,775	37.8
1961	1,280	64.6	33.63	41,542	14,684	274,677	38,272	35.7
1962	1,719	74.9	40.26	45,162	16,712	289,071	68,645	59.4
1963	2,789	122.2	52.59	53,722	18,735	377,254	117,052	183
1964	3,752	177.2	79.5	58,486	21,986	527,611	262,545	255
1965	4,591	172.8	96.1	56,786	23,602	504,439	253,516	274
1966	4,301	206.2	95.9	54,801	27,350	369,069	286,371	224
1967	4,374	187.8	61.8	59,444	31,715	239,862	252,400	137
1968	3,347	270	101	49,649	31,554	226,516	285,876	125
1969	4,381	382	143	62,610	26,938	281,722	333,579	204
1970	3,285	425	154	71,217	33,046	276,758	320,471	204
1971	4,947	427	210	73,290	38,763	236,129	317,421	191
1972	6,304	536	244	73,692	29,615	146,556	350,280	154
1973	3,242	663	278	82,435	28,326	103,818	353,547	118
1974	2,900	871	270	92,096	32,958	154,927	417,868	121
1975	2,838	806	228	98,444	36,188	140,251	425,282	120
Index	D	A,B,C,D	C,D	A,C,D	C,D	A,B,C,D	B,C,D	C,D

TABLE B-1 (Cont.)

	19–3000 Cinema Projectors (Except Capacitors) (MT)	19–3100 Capacitors for Cinema Projectors (MT)	19–3200 Telephones (Units)	19–3300 Telephone Exchanges (MT)	19–3400 X-ray Apparatus (units)	19–3500 Installation Materials (MT)	19–3600 Installation Pipes and Accessories (MT)	19–3700 Electric Bulbs, High Voltage (th. units)
1952	74	15	19,741	53	0	366	771	4,787
1953	82	26	33,156	45	45	390	1,085	4,235
1954	78	11	47,190	148	206	501	1,382	5,867
1955	100	18	50,242	316	214	732	1,527	6,435
1956	83	29	32,107	207	158	809	2,015	8,058
1957	95	56	19,715	268	171	1,029	2,556	12,187
1958	53	52	30,601	431	224	1,236	2,996	11,363
1959	68	44	44,851	418	268	1,603	2,966	7,810
1960	73	48	39,822	541	325	1,409	3,399	9,867
1961	120	77	60,132	569	420	1,609	2,516	12,252
1962	132	50	77,180	685	269	2,031	2,533	16,945
1963	137	61	87,635	750	291	3,023	2,664	21,199
1964	67	29	98,004	1,051	198	3,808	2,906	28,229
1965	63	15	94,207	1,145	318	4,051	2,293	29,430
1966	42	13	102,342	1,252	184	3,452	1,681	29,146
1967	71	9	76,191	1,620	68	3,299	1,898	28,606
1968	93	14	79,360	1,863	109	4,215	1,286	37,909
1969	54	20	130,315	2,331	168	5,801	923	37,831
1970	22	7	192,961	2,596	358	6,787	393	30,336
1971	9	4	259,846	3,563	308	9,066	332	41,294
1972	0	2	116,000	3,065	143	10,288	488	50,334
1973	2	0	107,000	3,344	255	11,796	288	60,201
1974	0	0	286,000	4,010	301	12,797	183	66,841
1975	0	0	243,000	4,883	751	13,595	169	58,846
Index	C,D	C	B,C,D	C,D	C,D	C,D	A,C,D	A,B,C,D

	19–3800 Electric Bulbs, Low Voltage (th. units)	19–3900 Fluorescent Tubes (th. units)	19–4000 Lamps (MT)	19–4100 Accumulators (MT)	19–4200 Primary Cells (MT)	19–4400 Electrical Measuring Instruments (MT)	19–4500 Electric Meters (th. units)	19–4600 Machines for Washing and Drying Clothes (MT)	20–0100 Sulfuric Acid 66° Be (th. MT)
1952	na	na	332	1,309	846	19	85.4	na	36.41
1953	na	na	654	1,637	1,098	15	139.7	na	40.28
1954	na	na	846	1,678	1,745	27	91.5	na	59.95
1955	na	40.12	1,083	1,881	1,313	37	103	na	73.01
1956	na	111.9	983	1,601	1,317	32	111	na	106.7
1957	5,810	381.6	1,080	2,145	1,720	66	188	132	123.9
1958	4,877	470.4	1,450	2,666	1,267	50	238	318	124.8
1959	5,463	531.2	1,705	2,919	1,358	60	240	590	127.7
1960	5,786	705.6	2,150	3,929	1,658	57	353	712	130.1
1961	6,025	836	2,129	4,091	1,718	90	416	896	234.0
1962	7,244	1,022	2,177	5,361	1,680	89	422	937	286.5
1963	8,796	1,406	2,356	5,937	2,015	80	464	1,147	391
1964	12,390	1,867	2,989	9,187	1,975	119	534	1,303	472
1965	9,758	1,536	3,043	11,908	2,194	112	623	3,270	435
1966	10,045	1,495	2,701	13,671	1,971	148	717	4,218	542
1967	9,953	1,172	2,472	11,131	2,405	133	842	4,422	592
1968	8,641	1,520	3,216	14,684	2,381	154	757	9,235	589
1969	11,768	1,857	4,390	19,688	2,517	202	671	15,505	696
1970	11,608	2,463	5,583	20,490	3,080	222	610	19,668	747
1971	13,090	3,398	6,040	28,223	3,230	297	855	29,546	807
1972	16,974	3,180	6,019	35,516	3,749	301	1,086	34,942	849
1973	19,080	3,707	6,495	40,262	5,289	293	1,283	32,690	947
1974	25,077	4,222	9,104	44,077	5,741	404	1,302	39,663	926
1975	28,975	4,455	10,066	48,712	4,996	625	1,370	35,499	935
Index	B,C,D	B,C,D	C,D	A,B,C,D	C,D	D	A,B,D	C,D	A,B,C,D

TABLE B-1 (Cont.)

	20–0200 Hydrochloric Acid (MT)	20–0300 Nitric Acid (100%) (th. MT)	20–0400 Phosphoric Acid (MT)	20–0600 Ammonium Nitrate (100%) (MT)	20–0700 Sodium Hydroxide (MT)	20–0800 Chlorine (MT)	20–0900 Sodium Bichromate (MT)	20–1000 Sodium Carbonate (Calcined Soda) (MT)	20–1100 Sodium Sulfide (MT)
1952	3,970	0	na	0	20,428	3,493	0	33,004	965
1953	3,668	0	na	0	22,545	3,400	0	34,358	639
1954	4,661	2.52	na	680	23,392	3,873	0	32,360	896
1955	5,187	8.21	na	3,345	30,675	4,252	0	39,231	1,205
1956	5,182	9.39	na	3,357	41,962	5,234	0	68,453	933
1957	5,642	8.97	na	4,058	43,498	5,881	13	72,184	997
1958	5,662	7.36	na	4,637	42,373	6,485	28	77,380	720
1959	6,831	7.78	na	4,800	47,907	7,408	0	91,846	724
1960	6,527	9.32	na	5,074	48,440	9,775	701	89,017	727
1961	7,123	8.38	na	4,929	48,523	10,305	716	90,302	345
1962	9,834	41.7	na	4,154	52,948	17,426	280	96,311	984
1963	12,859	165	4,599	5,332	70,206	27,019	0	90,887	1,112
1964	14,526	228	5,887	6,486	76,072	30,244	0	92,473	846
1965	16,831	247	6,461	6,581	87,696	38,093	0	92,627	1,556
1966	20,807	266	7,381	7,112	90,908	35,961	1,214	94,324	1,580
1967	15,281	269	8,674	7,484	87,301	36,326	448	97,802	681
1968	18,371	340	17,619	8,694	87,364	37,880	2,516	99,868	2,073
1969	21,253	488	91,918	8,620	83,736	40,654	3,223	108,827	1,528
1970	24,551	579	132,300	6,406	92,648	43,564	4,041	113,361	2,423
1971	25,219	644	133,295	7,717	92,081	41,781	3,355	105,075	2,595
1972	29,503	670	135,357	23,652	95,073	44,998	3,729	117,037	3,486
1973	34,856	634	149,685	20,675	93,166	44,317	3,783	128,589	2,613
1974	36,848	666	142,900	18,548	100,311	47,730	4,018	142,467	2,325
1975	41,926	634	164,497	19,563	97,477	43,244	3,247	146,777	2,676
Index	A,B,C,D	B,C,D		B,C,D	A,B,C,D	A,B,C,D	C,D	A,B,C,D	C,D

	20–1300 Sodium Tripolyphosphate (MT)	20–1400 Sodium Sulfate (MT)	20–1500 Sodium Hypochlorite (MT)	20–1700 Sodium Silicate (100%) (MT)	20–1800 Calcium Carbide (th. MT)	20–1900 Magnesium Chloride (MT)	20–2000 Barium Sulfide (MT)	20–2100 Silver Nitrate (kg.)
1952	na	na	2,377	na	39.7	653	2,510	na
1953	na	na	2,378	na	41.3	1,347	2,616	na
1954	na	na	3,475	na	39.7	1,684	1,840	na
1955	na	na	3,041	na	44.1	2,454	2,988	na
1956	na	na	3,370	na	45.0	2,425	2,810	na
1957	na	na	4,169	na	61.0	2,520	3,002	18,640
1958	na	na	4,613	na	54.5	3,258	2,255	42,542
1959	na	na	4,795	na	56.7	3,600	2,816	35,472
1960	na	na	8,926	na	72.9	3,513	3,048	21,112
1961	na	na	9,928	na	81.5	4,245	3,058	22,642
1962	na	na	15,342	na	84.4	4,737	3,939	26,029
1963	4,471	14,364	16,515	11,061	107	4,666	4,327	31,880
1964	5,679	13,298	17,244	11,481	91	5,407	6,732	28,417
1965	6,052	13,954	23,282	9,184	105	6,984	8,339	22,700
1966	6,232	13,627	27,608	9,891	112	6,561	10,431	23,348
1967	8,251	9,425	25,663	11,032	121	4,192	9,772	8,677
1968	9,326	14,440	26,924	8,406	133	6,661	5,828	6,502
1969	23,962	15,761	28,999	14,951	132	5,646	5,604	8,330
1970	28,341	18,341	28,515	13,051	113	5,625	5,016	9,431
1971	29,224	22,721	27,918	12,837	66	4,772	5,425	14,008
1972	31,286	32,084	29,437	14,273	77	na	3,725	8,862
1973	35,178	33,805	31,384	12,354	53	na	3,940	10,318
1974	44,308	29,935	41,338	9,865	65	na	4,773	9,048
1975	44,475	29,726	38,761	13,794	48	na	2,160	6,552
Index			C,D		A,B,C,D		C	C,D

TABLE B-1 (Cont.)

	20–2200 Aluminum Sulfate (MT)	20–2300 Copper Sulfate (MT)	20–2400 Borates and Perborates (MT)	20–2500 Hydrogen Peroxide (100%) (MT)	20–2600 Compressed Technical Gases, n.e.c. (MT)	20–2800 Acetone (MT)	20–2900 Phenol (MT)	20–3000 Dodecyl Benzol (MT)
1952	na	14,358	na	na	na	na	na	na
1953	na	15,133	na	na	na	na	na	na
1954	na	13,080	na	na	na	na	na	na
1955	na	13,965	na	na	na	na	na	na
1956	na	17,290	na	na	na	na	na	na
1957	na	23,039	na	na	na	na	na	na
1958	na	13,489	254	392	na	na	na	na
1959	na	15,987	594	463	na	na	na	na
1960	na	14,140	776	600	na	na	na	na
1961	9,640	14,371	1,088	631	15,914	na	na	na
1962	9,586	14,891	1,132	623	17,946	na	na	na
1963	10,202	18,498	1,342	657	21,762	na	980	na
1964	14,384	18,626	1,437	818	37,043	na	2,937	na
1965	21,127	14,931	1,493	909	51,544	1,642	5,571	1,093
1966	22,840	11,905	1,517	886	40,526	4,236	9,490	3,622
1967	31,450	14,697	1,503	874	43,624	4,396	7,854	633
1968	31,869	11,518	4,221	901	46,616	3,546	6,588	3,736
1969	32,298	18,077	8,012	834	51,328	4,036	6,840	6,425
1970	26,819	14,914	9,809	915	56,231	4,164	7,564	3,663
1971	34,853	18,875	12,785	588	63,151	4,447	7,021	5,412
1972	38,574	15,390	18,739	225	66,528	4,908	9,505	4,899
1973	47,687	11,621	21,731	1,140	68,922	5,497	9,237	4,002
1974	53,942	14,684	18,461	1,171	72,832	5,694	9,309	2,915
1975	56,023	16,372	22,580	1,534	80,779	4,434	7,969	3,666
Index	C,D	A,B,C,D	C,D	C,D	B,C,D			

	20–3100 Dodecyl Benzene Sulfonate (MT)	20–3200 Styrol (MT)	20–3300 Trichlorethylene (MT)	20–3400 Phthalic Acid Anhydride (MT)	20–3500 Methanol (MT)	20–3600 Formaldehyde (MT)	20–3800 Pepein Insecticide (MT)	20–3900 Flotation Agents (MT)
1952	na	na	335	na	na	na	204	na
1953	na	na	327	na	na	na	187	na
1954	na	na	450	na	na	na	224	na
1955	na	na	291	na	na	na	238	na
1956	na	na	520	na	na	na	233	na
1957	na	na	572	na	na	na	292	na
1958	na	na	800	na	na	na	246	na
1959	na	na	609	na	na	na	285	na
1960	na	na	947	na	na	na	253	na
1961	6,113	na	944	1,240	na	4,900	265	na
1962	4,401	na	1,590	589	1,192	5,133	408	na
1963	5,108	na	2,393	1,118	3,842	9,386	455	1,128
1964	8,207	1,777	3,068	987	6,753	9,431	568	857
1965	13,940	6,006	3,432	1,295	7,900	12,037	517	622
1966	10,202	8,053	3,710	1,885	7,263	14,471	799	832
1967	6,444	7,818	3,639	1,650	6,551	18,676	1,193	975
1968	6,933	7,808	3,565	1,750	5,191	22,358	556	1,354
1969	8,996	9,686	5,348	1,790	13	20,596	200	3,671
1970	8,272	8,394	5,601	1,211	4,970	33,377	11	4,514
1971	11,068	9,619	6,070	1,301	1,153	51,600	0	3,411
1972	9,937	10,602	6,359	844	na	55,376	0	3,763
1973	11,432	7,791	6,480	986	na	63,122	0	2,134
1974	11,513	9,304	5,381	1,300	na	71,561	0	4,122
1975	13,155	10,317	6,741	975	na	72,585	0	3,572
Index	C,D		A,B,C,D	C,D		C,D	A,B,C	

TABLE B-1 (Cont.)

	20–4000 Superphosphate (th. MT)	20–4100 Ammonium Sulfate (MT)	20–4200 Calcium Cyanamide (MT)	20–4300 Mixed Fertilizers (th. MT)	20–4400 Plant Protection Preparations (MT)	20–4500 Gunpowder (MT)	20–4600 Mining Explosives (MT)	20–4800 Industrial Nitrocellulose (MT)
1952	48.71	1,996	18,919	na	268	na	na	na
1953	42.91	2,086	23,303	na	2,263	na	na	na
1954	79.40	2,353	15,371	na	2,466	na	na	na
1955	128.1	3,513	15,472	na	3,768	na	na	na
1956	165.2	5,890	15,698	na	5,380	na	na	na
1957	215.8	7,179	17,722	132.0	7,094	na	na	na
1958	264.9	8,793	21,710	142.7	11,099	na	na	na
1959	277.2	10.798	12,272	174.6	13,299	274	15,629	na
1960	247.7	12,292	7,383	155.9	10,144	365	17,489	na
1961	412.5	12,476	10,742	227.2	10,765	384	17,276	1,053
1962	520.6	11,130	29,744	367.8	14,450	487	18,703	1,267
1963	732	11,450	29,696	586	45,369	442	21,453	1,903
1964	967	12,416	888	600	72,331	647	23,345	1,984
1965	801	12,173	1,884	587	81,249	549	25,501	2,265
1966	1,012	12,448	5,097	710	46,664	392	23,813	1,208
1967	1,075	12,800	7,407	698	28,864	463	23,501	2,402
1968	924	12,178	4,873	817	31,909	504	28,515	2,042
1969	837	10,922	na	828	39,787	641	34,442	2,295
1970	422	11,266	na	349	34,739	348	36,230	3,167
1971	491	11,588	na	311	37,662	340	39,509	3,645
1972	497	11,039	na	265	41,346	479	39,722	4,766
1973	880	12,260	na	236	56,335	544	39,744	5,173
1974	831	10,268	na	199	60,794	554	41,968	5,166
1975	632	12,666	na	184	56,260	508	43,706	3,145
Index	A,B,C,D	C		C,D	C,D	C,D	B,C,D	C,D

	20–4900 Carboxymethyl Cellulose (MT)	20–5000 Cellophane (MT)	20–5100 Other Artificial Material Based on Cellulose (MT)	20–5200 Phenoplasts (MT)	20–5300 Aminoplasts (MT)	20–5400 Polyesters (MT)	20–5500 PVC Powder (MT)	20–5600 Polyvinyl Acetate (100%) (MT)
1952	na	na	na	na	na	na	1,976	na
1953	na	na	na	na	na	na	2,400	na
1954	na	na	na	na	na	na	3,045	na
1955	na	na	na	na	na	na	3,365	na
1956	na	na	na	na	na	na	3,684	na
1957	na	na	na	na	na	na	4,253	na
1958	na	251	na	na	na	na	4,734	na
1959	na	526	na	na	na	na	6,329	na
1960	na	634	na	na	na	na	7,462	na
1961	1,087	753	75	na	2,110	na	8,117	na
1962	1,122	762	149	2,623	7,119	404	8,193	na
1963	1,340	780	396	2,644	6,499	567	8,444	363
1964	1,690	965	562	3,294	6,565	1,549	8,275	736
1965	2,133	1,051	324	3,693	7,715	1,566	8,501	1,703
1966	2,161	99	1,094	2,897	4,758	2,075	14,999	1,968
1967	2,541	0	504	2,692	3,137	2,755	15,704	2,892
1968	3,334	0	454	5,360	3,145	3,491	17,437	3,730
1969	3,711	2,775	428	5,562	3,303	4,436	18,766	6,686
1970	3,935	4,740	131	6,449	3,032	6,122	23,116	8,255
1971	3,981	6,121	385	8,590	3,869	7,639	18,395	9,143
1972	3,801	9,009	856	10,627	3,979	7,699	19,239	12,111
1973	4,409	8,909	1,026	10,423	5,220	10,992	19,218	12,964
1974	3,771	9,572	1,193	20,301	4,392	9,838	43,008	11,891
1975	4,138	9,308	1,024	22,815	4,014	12,065	40,333	11,661
Index	C,D	B,C,D	C,D	D	C,D	D	A,B,C,D	

TABLE B-1 (Cont.)

	20–5700 Polystyrol (MT)	20–5800 Polyethylene (MT)	20–5900 Primary Preparations of PVC (MT)	20–6000 Cellulose Fiber, Cotton Type (MT)	20–6100 Cellulose Fiber, Wool Type (MT)	20–6200 Rayon (MT)	20–6300 Cord (MT)	20–6400 Polyacrylonitrile Fibers (MT)
1952	na	na	824	na	na	na	na	na
1953	na	na	1,168	na	na	na	na	na
1954	na	na	2,158	na	na	na	na	na
1955	na	na	2,984	na	na	na	na	na
1956	na	na	3,264	na	na	na	na	na
1957	na	na	3,726	na	na	na	na	na
1958	na	na	4,817	5,134	3,419	1,504	210	na
1959	na	na	7,912	10,273	6,501	2,703	176	na
1960	na	na	10,471	12,170	5,810	3,117	223	na
1961	na	na	11,282	11,131	4,835	3,091	714	na
1962	na	na	11,883	7,152	9,878	3,239	747	na
1963	258	na	15,197	5,235	11,533	3,492	786	na
1964	2,153	1,953	18,108	2,287	15,376	3,471	853	na
1965	6,153	14,915	18,502	1,684	15,929	3,811	811	1,047
1966	6,757	18,282	25,034	634	18,745	4,238	939	3,761
1967	6,549	15,315	25,574	4,710	14,936	4,125	749	3,921
1968	6,441	18,569	27,807	5,965	19,301	6,375	612	3,739
1969	6,895	20,767	33,293	6,576	15,711	7,441	699	5,633
1970	7,674	20,364	35,643	9,766	13,593	7,432	1,232	6,145
1971	8,655	19,820	39,722	16,476	16,505	7,477	3,069	8,417
1972	13,135	20,267	40,251	27,302	24,927	7,762	3,874	9,715
1973	13,076	23,398	40,705	34,627	20,170	7,855	4,704	13,261
1974	14,882	26,124	47,518	33,496	21,506	8,094	7,459	13,736
1975	13,868	20,304	42,554	26,760	21,503	7,831	7,781	14,421
Index			A,B,C,D	B,C,D	B,C,D	B,C,D	B,C,D	

	20–6500 Penicillin (billion int. units)	20–6700 Vitamin C (MT)	20–6800 Other Pharmaceutical Materials (MT)	20–6900 Cleaning and Washing Agents (MT)	20–7000 Cosmetic Preparations (MT)	20–7100 Ethereal Oils (kg.)	20–7300 Lead Minium (MT)	20–7400 Lithopone (MT)
1952	na	na	466	na	763	na	1,229	1,597
1953	na	na	415	na	829	na	1,128	2,157
1954	na	na	599	na	891	na	1,407	1,945
1955	741	na	801	na	1,027	na	1,667	2,923
1956	1,667	na	852	na	957	na	1,820	2,743
1957	965	na	923	38,812	1,207	16,900	1,929	2,995
1958	79	na	964	42,233	1,363	23,370	1,962	2,954
1959	2,668	na	895	51,948	1,628	33,758	2,000	3,047
1960	3,354	na	837	54,192	1,894	50,807	2,083	2,680
1961	5,982	26.1	671	56,805	2,198	44,080	2,174	2,699
1962	5,091	19.4	763	67,243	2,312	49,546	2,998	2,916
1963	10,228	59.2	777	71,876	2,488	54,901	2,449	2,962
1964	18,226	87	963	82,415	2,610	70,438	3,453	6,320
1965	30,669	76	1,087	87,838	2,815	55,707	3,224	7,349
1966	30,609	122	1,521	101,702	3,406	93,627	3,172	9,653
1967	25,026	131	1,433	105,806	3,474	79,582	2,757	7,819
1968	37,469	147	1,530	111,151	4,790	53,023	3,161	6,030
1969	28,208	229	1,644	126,890	4,912	62,732	4,809	6,196
1970	32,987	312	1,835	137,545	5,393	72,614	3,156	5,570
1971	52,576	366	1,963	157,318	7,025	179,017	3,185	6,133
1972	46,549	394	2,410	156,279	7,955	131,576	2,119	3,997
1973	57,623	380	2,105	198,597	8,066	152,769	2,362	4,475
1974	36,292	427	2,695	186,751	11,030	170,471	2,249	4,889
1975	35.846	489	2,433	203,690	11,106	153,561	1,890	3,907
Index	B,C,D	C,D	D	B,D	C,D	C,D	A,B,C,D	B,C,D

TABLE B-1 (Cont.)

	20–7500 Mineral Pigments (MT)	20–7600 Organic Dyes (MT)	20–7700 Mastics (MT)	20–7800 Oil Paints (MT)	20–7900 Lacquers and Enamels (MT)	20–8000 Printer's Ink (MT)	20–8100 Mineral Lubricating Oils (MT)	20–8200 Shoe and Floor Polish (MT)
1952	4,354	na	2,768	4,302	4,153	472	2,506	1,090
1953	6,175	na	3,204	5,503	5,140	647	2,812	1,150
1954	8,092	na	4,024	6,115	5,495	719	2,663	1,364
1955	7,446	na	3,705	6,372	6,598	706	3,002	1,682
1956	7,311	na	3,479	6,268	8,741	759	3,313	1,741
1957	8,236	592	4,821	7,806	11,842	896	3,468	1,879
1958	7,546	700	3,699	7,719	12,902	1,181	4,077	2,082
1959	8,726	970	4,317	7,874	14,848	1,367	4,625	2,255
1960	9,102	790	4,409	9,411	16,264	1,679	4,678	2,584
1961	9,611	745	4,496	10,736	17,028	1,551	5,121	2,783
1962	9,640	843	4,605	10,118	19,753	2,056	4,778	3,639
1963	10,342	1,509	6,418	12,267	23,927	2,349	5,640	3,908
1964	10,130	1,552	6,921	12,187	32,052	2,755	9,153	4,962
1965	9,866	1,882	6,658	15,348	31,128	3,306	6,026	5,655
1966	10,878	1,888	7,632	14,208	34,166	3,558	4,207	6,122
1967	10,388	1,509	7,469	16,437	40,197	3,578	4,044	6,432
1968	9,650	1,331	6,580	15,624	38,822	3,946	4,345	6,982
1969	9,997	1,435	7,733	16,725	45,472	4,116	4,212	6,666
1970	10,235	1,419	6,715	16,640	53,805	4,788	4,712	7,128
1971	10,302	1,367	6,629	12,224	69,012	6,222	6,542	6,462
1972	9,989	1,315	6,618	10,367	74,748	6,408	6,199	5,407
1973	9,168	1,025	3,573	6,994	76,449	6,694	7,087	5,320
1974	10,929	1,202	4,376	7,347	82,948	7,218	1,063	5,598
1975	9,689	1,310	2,843	6,259	86,415	6,754	833	4,876
Index	C,D	C,D	C,D	A,B,C,D	A,B,C,D	C,D	A,C,D	C,D

	20–8400 Auxiliary Agents for Textiles (MT)	20–8500 Auxiliary Agents for Leather and Rubber (MT)	20–8600 Glue and Gelatin (MT)	20–8700 Pastes (MT)	20–8800 Photographic Chemicals (MT)	20–8900 Diazotype Paper (MT)	20–9000 Films (th. m.^{2})	20–9100 Photographic paper (th. m.^{2})
1952	1,293	na	1,659	352	na	218	15	292
1953	1,218	1,182	1,849	815	na	217	9	400
1954	1,894	1,358	1,837	864	na	332	20	704
1955	2,130	1,851	2,254	1,130	na	369	21	657
1956	2,388	2,283	2,466	1,589	na	341	59	761
1957	3,504	2,740	2,607	1,938	64.3	436	75	914
1958	4,300	2,859	2,958	2,434	84.8	476	171	1,024
1959	3,645	3,236	3,352	3,871	124	602	357	1,074
1960	4,024	4,128	3,516	6,411	147	735	249	1,277
1961	4,217	5,009	3,879	7,335	141	819	522	1,306
1962	4,575	6,230	4,260	11,429	155	786	677	1,225
1963	5,201	7,993	4,383	16,425	187	1,048	724	1,749
1964	5,141	8,908	4,204	20,609	258	1,214	914	2,765
1965	5,484	8,475	4,508	25,337	187	1,387	680	2,315
1966	6,362	7,259	3,909	23,551	207	1,185	748	1,705
1967	5,311	7,215	4,359	23,314	191	1,234	803	1,036
1968	5,475	7,003	3,805	26,777	173	1,472	617	1,143
1969	5,675	8,036	3,293	34,096	237	1,551	812	1,458
1970	5,854	9,622	3,479	42,810	254	1,769	888	1,618
1971	6,599	11,063	3,067	55,586	269	1,750	868	1,450
1972	6,311	12,476	3,277	68,207	181	1,899	924	1,790
1973	10,238	13,646	2,538	78,263	141	2,660	926	1,864
1974	10,894	15,731	3,762	83,397	175	2,908	1,085	2,455
1975	12,100	17,079	3,459	86,446	482	2,706	1,017	2,540
Index	D	D	C,D	A,B	C,D	C,D	C,D	B,C,D

TABLE B-1 (Cont.)

	20–9200 Percussion Caps and Fuses (th. units)	20–9300 Candles (MT)	20–9500 Oxygen (MT)	21–0100 Stone Blocks for Building and Cutting (m.^{3})	21–0101 Stone and Marble Blocks for Cutting (m.^{3})	21–0102 Stone Blocks for Building Purposes (m.^{3})	21–0200 Pulverized Stone, Marble, Sand, and Gravel (th. m.^{3})	21–0201 Broken Stone and Marble (th. m.^{3})
1952	na	261	10,640	11,073	nsa	nsa	1,526	nsa
1953	na	231	8,210	11,301	nsa	nsa	1,592	nsa
1954	na	244	13,395	11,732	nsa	nsa	1,813	nsa
1955	na	483	24,170	14,825	nsa	nsa	2,124	nsa
1956	na	300	26,559	11,798	nsa	nsa	2,397	nsa
1957	na	297	32,891	11,484	nsa	nsa	2,822	nsa
1958	na	354	35,304	12,900	nsa	nsa	3,187	nsa
1959	27,929	377	37,530	19,035	nsa	nsa	3,763	nsa
1960	39,235	317	42,778	23,926	17,929	5,997	4,434	1,795
1961	40,807	308	46,961	32,474	22,736	9,938	4,895	1,770
1962	40,010	487	51,239	52,166	24,375	27,791	6,759	1,710
1963	39,884	593	na	50,199	27,088	23,111	7,874	1,945
1964	43,208	695	na	40,950	28,055	12,895	9,091	1,958
1965	40,206	755	na	44,617	28,964	15,653	9,587	2,235
1966	31,942	786	na	41,295	26,453	14,842	10,272	2,214
1967	37,507	902	na	37,953	23,154	14,799	10,810	2,171
1968	38,835	1,018	na	45,043	27,639	17,404	11,630	2,128
1969	37,527	1,161	na	54,726	35,579	19,147	12,727	2,253
1970	13,424	1,145	na	45,972	39,228	6,744	13,780	2,414
1971	20,603	1,464	na	48,932	41,630	7,302	15,239	2,709
1972	51,838	1,702	na	54,562	42,095	12,467	16,129	2,761
1973	49,868	2,193	na	52,029	43,039	8,990	15,984	2,775
1974	53,015	2,534	na	56,284	48,849	7,435	19,456	3,293
1975	52,895	2,125	na	47,289	46,162	1,127	22,399	3,923
Index	C,D	C,D		C	D	D	B,C	D

	21–0202 Crushed Stone and Marble (th. $m.^3$)	21–0204 Gravel and Sand (th. $m.^3$)	21–0300 Ground Stone (th. $m.^3$)	21–0400 Ground Marble ($m.^3$)	21–0500 Stone and Marble Slabs ($m.^2$)	21–0600 Sections ($m.^3$)	21–0700 Crude Gypsum (MT)	21–0800 Calcined Gypsum (MT)
1952	nsa	nsa	na	na	45,658	70,513	45,420	8,278
1953	nsa	nsa	na	na	60,919	105,913	44,487	14,943
1954	nsa	nsa	na	na	82,088	101,501	89,618	13,987
1955	nsa	504.9	na	24,848	104,901	82,482	67,079	17,142
1956	nsa	556.4	na	20,275	96,375	48,084	99,035	21,040
1957	nsa	618,7	na	28,833	117,475	74,199	84,695	22,921
1958	nsa	796.3	25.05	31,860	157,073	72,452	75,927	21,486
1959	nsa	924.8	66.98	25,395	167,457	65,881	92,368	24,760
1960	1,388	1,251	99.83	57,512	213,416	66,091	124,363	26,934
1961	1,519	1,606	227.1	72,252	256,791	55,402	97,005	32,133
1962	1,923	3,126	347.5	53,940	253,298	79,261	118,046	30,553
1963	1,973	3,956	468	78,009	280,280	95,605	138,046	39,330
1964	2,136	4,997	691	87,468	317,705	91,027	154,739	44,314
1965	2,289	5,063	582	93,848	301,938	77,944	167,204	40,260
1966	2,605	5,453	633	95,590	335,496	73,834	168,694	40,968
1967	2,547	6,092	774	99,369	305,527	78,489	170,925	43,747
1968	2,858	6,644	989	103,271	369,631	71,130	196,630	52,213
1969	3,311	7,163	1,305	105,342	427,426	64,092	231,829	63,069
1970	3,653	7,713	1,763	99,413	484,746	51,109	250,619	66,010
1971	4,073	8,457	2,507	100,826	528,633	54,654	250,241	76,564
1972	3,875	9,493	2,485	111,029	628,685	45,570	270,532	82,064
1973	3,517	9,692	2,820	118,390	549,379	36,631	256,290	72,911
1974	4,366	11,797	3,443	108,318	591,954	24,259	283,458	89,591
1975	4,354	14,122	3,864	125,903	749,226	34,652	449,568	96,159
Index	D	D	C,D	C,D	D	C,D	C,D	A,B,C,D

TABLE B-1 (Cont.)

	21–0900 Unslaked Lime (th. MT)	21–1000 Hydrated Lime (th. MT)	21–1100 Bricks, Total (mill. units)	21–1101 Hollow Bricks, standard pattern (mill. units)	21–1102 Hollow and Porous Wall Bricks of other patterns (mill. units)	21–1104 Solid Bricks (mill. units)	21–1200 Hollow Clay Blocks, Roof and Ceiling Construction (th. units)	21–1300 Tiles, Total (th. units)
1952	291	0	551	nsa	nsa	nsa	na	191,000
1953	327	0	664	nsa	nsa	nsa	na	190,000
1954	328	0	751	nsa	nsa	nsa	na	186,000
1955	400	0	798.8	nsa	nsa	nsa	na	176,616
1956	449	0	813.0	nsa	nsa	nsa	na	185,675
1957	545	0	896.5	nsa	nsa	nsa	na	191,048
1958	567	2.67	1,015	nsa	nsa	948	na	197,456
1959	618	6.64	1,082	nsa	nsa	985	na	219,817
1960	697	6.88	1,201	80.8	68.0	1,052	120,224	228,850
1961	725	25.1	1,280	91.5	65.2	1,123	108,118	247,610
1962	768	48.1	1,044	82.9	98.7	862	120,942	218,600
1963	860	90.0	1,164	81.5	149.4	933	144,878	243,900
1964	906	129.2	1,444	165.0	221.0	1,058	194,753	253,100
1965	946	166.0	1,523	162.3	269.6	1,091	194,442	281,000
1966	949	189.6	1,332	118.0	255.1	959	175,991	344,500
1967	941	257.9	1,396	140.0	300.9	955	233,969	342,000
1968	983	322.6	1,551	178.8	395.1	977	304,246	302,800
1969	1,030	366	1,634	196.5	522.0	915	419,384	285,900
1970	1,078	429	1,822	239.2	702.1	881	364,135	290,100
1971	1,070	521	2,019	279.9	832.1	907	476,177	297,600
1972	1,128	585	2,069	330.3	871.9	867	600,914	308,422
1973	1,211	659	2,360	389.7	1,119.0	851	620,934	302,869
1974	1,333	706	2,573	448.3	1,298.0	827	668,338	344,617
1975	1,335	748	2,752	492.7	1,427.1	833	578,302	356,165
Index	A,B,C,D	B,C,D	A,B	C,D	C,D	C,D	C,D	A,B,C

	21–1301 Plain and Gutter Tiles (th. units)	21–1302 Roofing Tiles (th. units)	21–1400 Portland Cement (th. MT)	21–1500 Other Types of Cement (MT)	21–1600 Asbestos-Cement Products (MT)	21–1700 Light Building Panels (th. m.^{2})	21–1900 Blocks for Walls and Partitions (th. units)	21–2000 Wall Panels (th. units)
1952	nsa	nsa	1,291	22,062	na	553	na	na
1953	nsa	nsa	1,241	40,079	na	871	na	na
1954	nsa	nsa	1,340	53,054	na	920	na	na
1955	nsa	nsa	1,542	30,001	na	979.5	na	na
1956	nsa	nsa	1,538	16,785	na	709.4	na	na
1957	nsa	nsa	1,966	16,355	na	1,011	na	na
1958	nsa	nsa	1,939	27,927	na	1,357	na	na
1959	nsa	nsa	2,185	35,742	na	1,767	na	na
1960	34,750	194,100	2,363	34,612	87,193	1,740	35,580	5,759
1961	38,007	209,600	2,307	29,168	90,118	2,228	56,500	22,521
1962	34,089	184,500	2,445	73,633	92,439	1,457	49,533	7,291
1963	27,933	216,000	2,825	22,014	118,411	1,569	85,024	24,662
1964	28,052	225,000	3,018	21,621	143,685	3,117	126,093	22,314
1965	28,039	253,000	3,078	24,367	153,327	3,186	143,420	34,407
1966	32,543	312,000	3,211	21,014	169,974	2,921	145,463	25,866
1967	33,991	308,000	3,178	136,123	204,841	2,418	184,572	33,782
1968	25,758	277,000	3,616	149,146	190,692	3,244	220,949	29,767
1969	18,857	267,000	3,887	76,848	252,457	3,415	240,584	30,653
1970	17,136	273,000	4,330	68,762	275,025	3,815	292,899	41,238
1971	17,616	280,000	4,928	25,872	301,418	4,178	395,455	41,800
1972	14,422	294,000	5,693	58,165	340,769	3,134	405,605	76,545
1973	10,869	292,000	6,315	60,684	343,604	3,295	422,003	57,877
1974	12,617	332,000	6,507	140,116	388,145	3,853	507,201	79,023
1975	21,165	335,000	6,933	132,205	382,339	4,173	496,823	71,884
Index	D	D	A,B,C,D	A,B,C,D	C,D	C,D	B,C,D	C,D

TABLE B-1 (Cont.)

	21–2100 Blocks for Roof Construction (th. units)	21–2200 Roofing Felt (MT)	22–0100 Sawn Conifers (th. m.^{3})	22–0200 Sawn Oak (th. m.^{3})	22–0300 Sawn Beech (th. m.^{3})	22–0400 Other Sawn Timber (th. m.^{3})	22–0500 Sawn Sleepers (m.^{3})	22–0600 Veneer (m.^{3})
1952	na	15,649	1,609	113.3	260	62.5	66,686	6,164
1953	na	15,006	1,631	94.7	275	77.5	29,469	6,681
1954	na	15,894	1,343	104.0	345	77.7	11,375	8,616
1955	na	17,434	1,259	120.3	395	81.2	23,032	12,053
1956	na	13,971	1,207	112.5	414	83.4	15,782	15,556
1957	na	17,134	1,210	116.6	420.5	89.62	23,254	19,538
1958	na	17,876	1,189	114.2	470.1	89.27	31,053	25,589
1959	na	24,426	1,360	122.9	514.1	112.9	29,674	36,397
1960	4,243	28,800	1,448	140.3	570.6	136.1	25,758	45,901
1961	15,772	27,657	1,425	150.6	637.2	139.3	20,884	100,622
1962	20,648	27,100	1,796	144.6	579.2	143.3	27,188	141,545
1963	43,878	33,884	1,722	152.2	681.4	138.8	27,207	143,148
1964	53,229	46,007	1,614	178.6	728.4	168.8	30,345	182,929
1965	45,158	45,027	1,494	195.3	762.4	198.2	26,812	206,860
1966	47,078	42,083	1,539	207.4	904.1	206.0	31,151	198,838
1967	44,933	46,790	1,576	197.1	930.8	174.9	24,686	181,704
1968	57,677	49,847	1,742	206.2	863.1	158.6	18,830	170,129
1969	72,592	60,984	1,780	180.7	887.6	172.9	21,832	191,547
1970	96,518	62,467	1,741	192.3	939.4	174.4	18,559	200,308
1971	57,894	64,704	1,847	205.3	994.4	202.7	29,032	215,155
1972	88,377	70,196	1,822	208.3	983.4	182.9	18,933	191,829
1973	78,118	72,814	1,939	208.6	1,074.5	197.3	9,628	179,711
1974	84,730	79,762	2,079	225.5	1,122.8	226.9	16,740	210,039
1975	89,774	78,736	2,164	224.1	882.8	212.7	33,621	207,249
Index	D	A,B,C,D	A,B,C,D	A,B,C,D	A,B,C,D	C,D	C,D	A,B,C,D

	22–0700 Reconstituted Wood Panels: Plywood (m.^{3})	22–0800 Panel Boards (m.^{3})	22–1000 Reconstituted Particle Boards (m.^{3})	22–1100 Containers and Boxes (m.^{3})	22–1200 Barrels (hl.)	22–1300 Household Furniture, Total (suites)	22–1301 Bedroom Furniture (suites)	22–1302 Bed- and Sitting Room Furniture (suites)
1952	13,966	7,657	na	98,867	na	49,911	nsa	nsa
1953	15,431	8,770	na	118,152	na	61,867	nsa	nsa
1954	24,453	11,990	na	136,225	na	52,156	nsa	nsa
1955	25,268	14,167	na	153,435	na	76,846	nsa	nsa
1956	24,688	14,076	na	149,687	na	81,841	nsa	nsa
1957	28,441	16,961	na	153,990	na	108,790	nsa	nsa
1958	32,685	22,813	na	161,859	340,239	99,966	49,110	9,775
1959	46,172	37,495	3,621	181,832	402,414	142,722	73,598	5,327
1960	60,955	41,153	8,216	185,989	419,769	152,088	82,731	8,054
1961	65,568	49,684	13,573	161,679	341,370	176,582	98,920	11,393
1962	68,876	51,272	38,156	147,515	373,274	247,367	111,168	15,264
1963	74,991	43,113	78,185	167,597	351,816	299,951	124,697	22,092
1964	96,947	48,288	127,047	176,860	409,005	376,324	157,938	34,946
1965	110,810	44,535	149,670	177,828	528,138	407,073	157,632	58,125
1966	107,477	41,081	155,564	178,982	427,737	401,395	136,271	54,178
1967	90,205	41,397	146,646	178,099	395,138	343,751	109,571	71,476
1968	86,560	48,249	134,776	183,729	322,769	348,099	110,810	75,805
1969	97,264	58,196	166,239	198,840	324,362	340,361	107,177	85,156
1970	103,058	58,918	189,564	200,860	285,093	342,147	105,854	94,784
1971	100,021	64,657	215,048	193,704	290,054	385,662	98,762	116,359
1972	101,097	70,863	263,914	199,531	243,015	443,162	100,333	141,188
1973	95,003	65,509	320,997	188,437	194,749	459,871	116,917	132,809
1974	126,674	67,293	374,212	190,105	278,133	485,317	119,191	163,840
1975	125,977	49,380	412,683	207,683	233,425	412,895	123,201	138,015
Index	A,B,C,D	A,B,D	D	A,B,C,D	C,D	A,B,C	D	D

TABLE B-1 (Cont.)

	22–1303 Other Nonkitchen Furniture (suites)	22–1304 Kitchen Furniture (suites)	22–1400 Office and School Furniture (suites)	22–1500 Incomplete Household and Bentwood Furniture (th. units)	22–1700 Builder's Joinery (m.^{3})	22–1800 Parquet Flooring, Solid (m.^{3})	22–1900 Parquet Flooring, Laminated (th. m.^{2})	22–2000 Cork Manufactures (MT)
1952	nsa	nsa	41,903	932.6	17,480	14,915	na	579
1953	nsa	nsa	46,566	1,259	16,936	21,507	na	761
1954	nsa	nsa	101,960	1,514	29,636	30,461	na	858
1955	nsa	nsa	154,571	1,714	34,484	34,543	na	746
1956	nsa	nsa	100,652	2,172	25,989	37,262	na	1,760
1957	nsa	nsa	111,898	2,743	38,894	41,708	na	2,737
1958	1,281	39,800	108,822	3,465	40,300	46,897	45.70	1,885
1959	814	62,984	133,030	4,689	53,399	52,008	88.31	1,792
1960	1,311	59,992	202,184	5,357	62,551	67,755	270.7	2,388
1961	3,261	63,008	221,537	6,152	78,628	68,533	453.0	2,544
1962	2,516	118,419	280,638	6,638	78,647	71,225	912.4	2,779
1963	2,323	150,839	412,213	6,803	112,189	73,431	1,136	3,993
1964	3,605	179,835	504,566	8,192	134,303	78,394	1,145	4,251
1965	674	190,642	418,506	8,704	151,580	78,219	1,429	4,721
1966	902	210,044	322,646	8,408	150,010	89,618	1,180	3,922
1967	4,088	158,616	338,935	8,052	152,426	77,800	908	4,289
1968	6,417	155,067	325,224	8,915	176,371	74,361	1,312	4,877
1969	7,123	140,905	343,890	9,463	214,298	72,353	1,454	4,986
1970	18,720	122,789	481,898	9,536	na	82,733	1,466	5,856
1971	28,368	142,173	594,899	10,527	na	99,155	1,650	5,514
1972	28,514	173,127	614,807	11,723	na	106,939	1,567	6,129
1973	32,099	178,046	654,943	11,967	na	87,347	1,455	2,257
1974	39,891	162,395	765,000	12,879	na	81,807	1,574	2,509
1975	43,954	107,725	814,000	12,555	na	92,592	1,705	2,189
Index	D	D	C,D	C,D		B,C,D	C,D	C,D

	22–2100 Tanning Materials (MT)	22–2200 Impregnated Wood (m.^{3})	22–2300 Colophony and Turpentine (MT)	22–2400 Charcoal Distillates (MT)	22–2500 Acetic Acid (100%) (MT)	22–2600 Acetone (100%) (th. MT)	22–2700 Matches (cases of 5,000 boxes)	23–0100 Sulfite Cellulose, Total (MT)
1952	9,689	97,695	1,548	na	na	na	56,459	34,162
1953	9,823	107,782	1,870	na	na	na	68,073	36,053
1954	9,820	81,462	1,896	na	na	na	82,224	43,546
1955	9,368	138,648	2,042	21,378	527	209	81,735	53,211
1956	10,014	148,514	2,048	21,932	987	249	81,372	66,770
1957	11,122	150,590	2,478	23,567	1,160	273	79,975	70,446
1958	10,732	160,352	1,742	24,338	1,178	293	73,194	74,175
1959	11,688	188,912	2,330	24,695	1,109	395	92,690	80,826
1960	11,877	170,202	2,781	26,048	1,107	334	85,107	12,597
1961	10,493	171,669	2,819	27,111	1,120	286	80,591	140,352
1962	9,493	188,064	3,350	24,394	1,086	220	78,852	153,336
1963	8,577	185,751	3,334	26,636	1,262	104	88,039	167,723
1964	8,164	178,531	4,345	27,007	1,457	0	93,003	168,619
1965	7,217	154,684	5,456	26,703	1,633	27	100,356	173,648
1966	5,698	210,960	7,384	26,621	1,502	15	102,533	190,939
1967	5,362	188,878	4,060	28,168	1,904	12	107,355	181,474
1968	4,101	147,325	3,634	25,815	2,159	0	116,884	178,614
1969	3,122	174,693	3,798	27,214	2,093	4	111,640	185,307
1970	2,089	174,861	3,528	23,141	1,669	0	122,091	185,220
1971	2,066	200,388	3,622	25,949	1,893	0	121,022	216,987
1972	2,172	206,009	3,592	27,697	2,346	0	121,020	225,907
1973	1,911	99,959	2,464	26,842	2,328	0	131,828	233,614
1974	2,559	157,610	4,868	27,002	2,435	0	143,405	249,660
1975	1,970	200,028	4,662	30,426	2,302	0	136,297	231,847
Index	A,B,C,D	C,D	A,B,C,D	B,C,D	C,D	C	A,B,C,D	B

TABLE B-1 (Cont.)

	23–0105 Bleached Sulfite Cellulose (MT)	23–0106 Unbleached Sulfite Cellulose (MT)	23–0500 Wood Pulp, White and Brown (MT)	23–0600 Newsprint (MT)	23–0700 Writing and Printing Paper (MT)	23–0800 Kraft Paper (MT)	23–0900 Wrapping and Other Packing Paper (MT)	23–1000 Cigarette Paper (MT)
1952	nsa	nsa	na	3,280	na	3,803	13,823	1,242
1953	nsa	nsa	na	3,236	na	4,049	14,796	1,102
1954	nsa	nsa	na	1,501	na	3,054	14,707	1,075
1955	nsa	nsa	27,187	5,102	28,688	4,416	18,172	1,744
1956	18,721	48,049	38,731	19,548	33,450	15,837	19,037	1,602
1957	20,056	50,390	44,733	23,969	38,686	22,498	20,656	1,946
1958	22,174	52,001	49,244	28,335	38,542	23,197	21,542	1,808
1959	29,996	50,830	52,132	28,946	39,385	27,392	21,748	1,879
1960	61,368	64,607	56,665	28,454	46,920	30,550	28,536	2,144
1961	79,157	61,195	60,499	25,816	68,453	33,719	38,530	2,348
1962	91,165	62,171	60,248	25,216	77,029	39,454	51,238	2,400
1963	105,284	62,439	66,339	31,931	82,225	43,886	68,871	2,352
1964	113,425	55,194	84,800	45,794	110,743	47,305	85,635	2,487
1965	127,126	46,522	84,479	45,937	127,754	74,796	97,121	2,582
1966	148,293	42,646	89,906	52,875	137,941	77,597	103,420	2,734
1967	143,252	38,222	95,756	62,251	139,654	107,195	107,093	2,746
1968	136,233	42,381	110,191	72,732	156,964	101,484	109,009	2,935
1969	139,480	45,827	104,620	68,968	157,763	106,880	133,495	2,965
1970	141,076	44,144	93,858	74,989	139,890	105,975	129,976	3,093
1971	171,977	45,010	95,148	79,633	137,147	107,762	141,764	3,478
1972	184,127	41,780	95,195	75,919	144,986	122,031	167,513	3,930
1973	193,457	40,157	89,514	75,861	156,741	128,831	169,927	4,088
1974	201,805	47,855	94,877	79,280	179,596	146,345	157,601	4,053
1975	191,317	40,530	87,862	85,335	157,282	143,706	197,304	4,515
Index	C,D	C,D	B,C,D	B,C,D	B,C,D	A,B,C,D	A,B,C,D	A,B,C,D

	23–1100 Other Paper (MT)	23–1200 Cardboard (MT)	23–1300 Roofing Felt (MT)	23–1400 Corrugated Roofing Felt (MT)	23–1500 Kraft Paper Bags (MT)	24–0100 Fibers, Hemp (MT)	24–0200 Fibers, Flax (MT)	24–0300 Yarn, Cotton Type (eff. MT)
1952	2,650	7,599	5,262	na	8,353	16,071	720	25,909
1953	2,521	7,892	7,180	na	8,238	10,978	345	27,720
1954	3,160	8,964	8,067	na	10,404	15,262	437	34,102
1955	3,907	9,960	10,857	na	10,756	20,564	310	38,167
1956	6,921	9,156	11,238	na	14,222	21,671	318	38,853
1957	3,926	10,271	12,734	na	16,404	19,926	541	42,563
1958	6,400	11,083	14,448	na	19,655	20,948	444	45,196
1959	6,996	12,009	19,226	na	22,626	21,394	543	46,963
1960	5,675	13,511	23,648	na	22,401	22,779	280	50,558
1961	8,390	21,950	27,360	29,700	21,075	23,726	527	55,295
1962	9,920	25,717	25,069	25,478	25,557	25,337	539	68,595
1963	11,748	26,480	36,588	38,105	31,417	25,784	412	74,853
1964	16,828	28,161	44,126	48,854	37,077	25,622	356	82,031
1965	16,752	28,901	52,615	53,807	40,412	27,633	233	85,976
1966	20,280	30,176	53,870	62,872	42,097	28,685	373	88,004
1967	22,707	35,344	52,951	76,832	48,323	26,495	357	85,595
1968	23,793	44,021	53,620	96,797	45,214	21,532	290	87,274
1969	23,505	46,972	55,507	116,090	48,781	17,119	315	88,334
1970	24,332	49,624	56,785	140,660	54,231	11,901	402	93,920
1971	31,246	50,539	55,511	154,204	60,911	10,822	328	91,512
1972	29,667	55,285	51,209	169,852	58,440	8,660	295	92,886
1973	32,110	57,342	50,216	169,643	55,599	6,422	156	94,834
1974	34,329	66,157	56,288	201,605	67,844	6,546	191	100,044
1975	31,936	64,643	55,412	200,241	65,779	7,257	132	100,894
Index	C,D	A,B,C,D	A,B,C,D	A,B,C,D	C,D	A,B,C,D	B,D	A,B,C,D

TABLE B-1 (Cont.)

	24–0400 Sewing Thread (eff. MT)	24–0500 Cotton Fabrics (th. m.^{2})	24–0600 Fabrics of Synthetic Fiber, 100%, Cotton Type (th. m.^{2})	24–0700 Woolen Yarn, Total (eff. MT)	24–0701 Woolen Yarn, Carded (eff. MT)	24–0702 Woolen Yarn, Combed (eff. MT)	24–0900 Woolen Fabrics, Total (th. m.^{2})	24–0901 Fabrics of Carded Wool (th. m.^{2})
1952	704	111,910	na	10,290	nsa	nsa	19,983	nsa
1953	525	131,712	na	7,671	nsa	nsa	17,291	nsa
1954	659	165,585	993	8,717	nsa	nsa	19,771	nsa
1955	874	173,663	4,336	10,743	nsa	nsa	25,849	nsa
1956	815	182,911	11,731	12,178	nsa	nsa	23,700	nsa
1957	906	195,863	17,535	14,763	nsa	nsa	26,616	nsa
1958	1,184	209,559	14,520	16,665	14,436	2,229	26,779	24,323
1959	1,492	211,142	17,729	17,343	14,146	3,197	27,978	23,847
1960	1,771	235,841	20,882	20,615	16,535	4,080	32,739	27,763
1961	2,036	254,266	14,946	19,801	15,621	4,180	29,828	23,545
1962	2,265	300,824	11,363	19,341	13,925	5,416	28,640	20,637
1963	1,459	331,973	15,811	20,933	14,272	6,661	32,816	23,741
1964	1,830	361,104	17,749	24,408	16,587	7,821	37,562	25,914
1965	2,128	379,319	15,901	25,958	17,224	8,734	39,268	26,187
1966	2,300	380,472	17,635	27,456	17,285	10,171	38,359	25,845
1967	2,107	342,920	15,982	24,306	14,286	10,020	33,166	19,304
1968	2,039	362,713	17,466	23,669	13,395	10,274	33,226	15,417
1969	2,261	372,658	20,769	26,848	14,865	11,983	34,238	15,359
1970	2,528	345,814	17,678	28,543	15,859	12,684	32,579	14,986
1971	2,789	336,873	23,419	29,007	15,920	13,087	34,859	15,432
1972	3,021	308,093	24,320	30,642	16,463	14,179	36,006	15,265
1973	3,316	294,423	25,345	28,302	15,302	13,000	37,231	17,211
1974	3,620	292,066	21,619	26,532	15,205	11,327	40,211	18,978
1975	3,507	285,356	23,818	25,241	14,423	10,818	39,562	21,342
Index	C,D	B,C,D	D	A,B,C	D	D	A,B,C	D

	24–0902 Fabrics of Worsted Wool (th. m.^{2})	24–1000 Fabrics of Synthetic Fiber, 100%, Woolen Type (th. m.^{2})	24–1100 Grege, Raw Silk (MT)	24–1200 Yarn, Natural Silk (eff. MT)	24–1300 Fabrics of Natural Silk (th. m.^{2})	24–1400 Fabrics of Synthetic Silk (Rayon) (th. m.^{2})	24–1500 Fabrics of Synthetic Filaments (th. m.^{2})	24–1600 Yarn, Flax (eff. MT)
1952	nsa	na	40	32	385	6,795	na	491
1953	nsa	na	43	24	263	7,554	na	400
1954	nsa	na	46	15	263	8,522	na	429
1955	nsa	na	50	28	230	12,334	na	566
1956	nsa	na	50	22	207	12,275	na	515
1957	nsa	6,982	59	71	299	14,492	na	542
1958	2,456	5,865	61	54	376	15,867	na	527
1959	4,131	10,025	71	25	332	16,528	na	540
1960	4,976	12,471	69	39	558	19,420	na	400
1961	6,283	12,546	50	52	654	21,723	na	554
1962	8,003	13,783	56	55	768	21,807	1,565	794
1963	9,075	14,972	58	47	604	20,648	6,199	821
1964	11,648	14,952	54	52	673	22,710	8,576	933
1965	13,081	15,278	50	45	434	24,298	8,886	582
1966	12,514	16,726	43	13	224	29,873	9,338	462
1967	13,862	14,028	19	16	133	27,374	8,980	493
1968	17,809	12,582	13	10	60	31,335	7,993	236
1969	18,879	10,804	16	13	70	29,870	10,807	275
1970	17,593	14,813	18	9	33	28,929	14,012	59
1971	19,427	12,879	17	9	20	33,949	13,928	202
1972	20,741	12,144	15	11	28	36,059	18,725	162
1973	20,020	10,847	7	10	52	35,899	18,439	113
1974	21,233	12,179	2	8	69	35,085	24,856	138
1975	18,220	12,721	3	6	160	39,465	30,820	46
Index	D	C,D	C	C,D	C,D	A,B,C,D	D	C,D

TABLE B-1 (Cont.)

	24–1700 Yarn, Hemp (eff. MT)	24–1800 Yarn, Jute (eff. MT)	24–1900 Fabrics, Flax (th. m.^{2})	24–2000 Fabrics, Hemp (th. m.^{2})	24–2100 Fabrics, Jute (th. m.^{2})	24–2200 Hemp Cordage, Strips, and Ropes (MT)	24–2400 Hose (th. prs.)	24–2500 Knitwear (MT)
1952	3,937	2,882	1,549	5,337	4,884	1,713	22,635	na
1953	3,456	2,867	2,313	2,973	7,938	2,250	18,972	na
1954	5,084	2,273	2,670	6,743	5,353	2,493	25,685	na
1955	5,277	3,747	2,417	5,243	8,526	3,204	30,230	4,049
1956	5,398	3,935	2,255	5,921	9,706	3,325	30,206	3,857
1957	6,376	4,000	2,549	6,503	10,283	4,109	32,343	4,837
1958	8,313	5,589	3,113	8,421	12,282	4,615	33,277	5,726
1959	8,258	6,930	3,082	8,646	15,969	4,871	36,369	6,664
1960	10,787	7,573	3,650	9,056	16,229	5,582	41,755	7,853
1961	12,167	6,743	3,535	8,750	14,935	5,657	40,292	8,378
1962	11,105	10,769	4,032	7,181	25,630	5,930	41,754	8,482
1963	13,671	14,252	5,092	11,132	36,333	7,114	47,302	9,865
1964	11,949	15,070	4,864	12,178	39,403	8,208	57,565	11,849
1965	12,556	14,573	4,990	12,239	42,715	8,522	61,322	12,568
1966	13,671	15,034	3,561	15,387	50,334	8,328	67,421	12,373
1967	13,497	14,459	3,375	14,370	44,943	7,114	73,789	12,309
1968	12,550	13,982	2,449	11,688	45,170	7,101	83,766	12,454
1969	10,623	12,939	2,528	9,995	43,420	7,064	82,807	12,819
1970	10,210	12,965	1,707	7,991	39,302	6,554	89,523	13,938
1971	10,550	12,143	2,264	6,355	35,919	6,827	101,541	15,777
1972	10,176	11,275	1,711	7,369	28,315	7,098	117,226	18,562
1973	9,469	12,833	984	7,834	28,531	6,462	125,654	18,775
1974	8,851	14,593	1,207	6,334	40,624	6,710	154,741	20,119
1975	7,308	13,972	730	4,445	38,671	6,166	179,326	20,596
Index	A,C,D	C,D	C,D	C,D	C,D	C,D	A,B,C,D	C,D

	24–2600 Fabrics, Net (th. m.^{2})	24–2700 Fishing Nets (MT)	24–2800 Ready-Made Underwear (th. m.^{2})	24–2900 Ready-Made Clothing (th. m.^{2})	24–3000 Woolen Carpets, Woven (th. m.^{2})	24–3100 Mattresses and Quilting Products (th. m.^{2})	24–3200 Tarpaulins, Tents, and Kindred Products (th. units)	24–3300 Hats (th. units)
1952	na	na	15,741	9,027	na	na	579	na
1953	na	na	16,138	8,102	na	na	356	na
1954	na	na	18,687	8,385	na	na	974	na
1955	na	na	19,527	9,855	na	968	939	na
1956	na	na	16,282	9,399	na	923	1,190	na
1957	na	na	19,920	11,247	na	1,088	933	na
1958	na	na	24,771	12,052	419	1,101	1,093	1,257
1959	na	na	26,184	13,779	525	1,201	919	583
1960	na	na	26,743	17,483	620	1,407	1,413	574
1961	na	na	28,448	18,286	820	1,459	1,050	489
1962	na	na	34,886	24,208	960	1,819	1,708	572
1963	3,272	47	38,152	29,458	1,639	2,164	1,197	805
1964	3,757	52	48,307	33,710	1,959	3,482	2,780	874
1965	2,683	66	57,235	38,871	2,287	3,607	2,776	774
1966	3,398	65	62,951	41,009	2,749	3,327	3,287	633
1967	2,606	49	68,284	39,983	2,955	3,174	2,959	454
1968	4,098	34	71,706	45,047	3,181	4,314	3,056	409
1969	4,876	36	78,656	49,409	3,544	5,195	2,609	469
1970	7,071	25	73,542	51,812	4,112	3,693	2,130	482
1971	9,491	39	81,640	59,784	4,141	4,729	1,899	744
1972	10,730	35	75,355	74,991	4,262	4,910	2,494	880
1973	11,677	41	77,714	81,424	4,826	4,675	2,923	1,142
1974	13,681	46	73,420	84,271	5,310	5,366	3,109	978
1975	15,359	47	74,560	92,117	6,518	5,452	5,007	719
Index			B,C,D	B,C,D	B,C,D	C,D	C,D	D

TABLE B-1 (Cont.)

	24–3400 Hat Bodies (th. units)	24–3500 Felt (MT)	25–0100 Sole Leather (MT)	25–0200 Leather for Technical Purposes (MT)	25–0300 Whole Hides (th. $m.^2$)	25–0400 Split Upper Leather (th. $m.^2$)	25–0500 Technical Ready-Made Goods (MT)	25–0600 Pigskin, Upper Leather (th. $m.^2$)
1952	na	na	8,150	1,267	2,411	na	275	na
1953	na	na	7,668	1,035	2,440	na	366	na
1954	na	na	8,578	1,332	2,508	na	392	na
1955	na	na	9,691	1,539	3,070	na	520	na
1956	na	na	10,911	1,371	3,402	na	555	na
1957	na	na	12,735	996	3,612	na	548	na
1958	1,308	364	10,806	1,255	3,985	109	522	na
1959	1,545	362	10,670	1,287	4,413	283	595	165
1960	1,126	463	11,574	2,220	4,949	319	817	158
1961	1,111	504	10,729	1,083	5,760	353	730	256
1962	1,119	463	9,798	1,008	6,214	326	645	366
1963	1,330	559	11,313	1,300	8,490	356	905	421
1964	1,342	816	11,591	1,550	10,406	448	1,086	444
1965	1,382	986	7,751	1,175	11,042	632	1,031	593
1966	1,356	1,330	8,916	1,396	11,205	948	1,227	849
1967	836	1,556	9,426	1,295	11,133	812	887	814
1968	790	1,171	6,110	738	11,072	743	875	1,121
1969	736	2,285	4,111	802	12,540	949	961	1,271
1970	711	2,065	2,530	964	12,430	1,123	984	1,561
1971	1,056	2,664	2,794	989	12,751	1,310	1,190	2,049
1972	885	2,950	3,150	582	13,799	1,319	1,315	3,059
1973	920	3,258	2,562	569	11,967	1,509	1,150	3,552
1974	940	3,425	2,902	664	12,491	1,600	1,172	3,544
1975	748	5,930	3,238	606	15,042	1,771	1,401	4,097
Index	D	D	A,B,C,D	A	A,B,C,D	D	C,D	C,D

	25–0700 Pigskin for Fancy Goods Manufacture (th. $m.^2$)	25–0800 Lining Leather, Sheep and Goat (th. $m.^2$)	25–0900 Furs (th. $m.^2$)	25–1000 Clothes, Leather and Fur (th. $m.^2$)	25–1100 Artificial Leather (MT)	25–1200 Heavy Leather Footwear (th. prs.)	25–1300 Civilian Leather Footwear (th. prs.)	25–1400 Other Leather Footwear (th. prs.)
1952	432	1,120	123	187	na	926	3,049	1,781
1953	425	802	105	267	na	1,015	2,297	1,937
1954	468	1,173	144	230	na	929	3,351	1,641
1955	549	1,601	291	284	na	793	3,866	2,055
1956	582	809	297	291	na	623	4,805	1,908
1957	634	592	366	355	na	556	6,082	2,254
1958	627	510	383	417	516	548	6,894	2,840
1959	605	525	483	476	749	393	8,614	3,190
1960	712	653	517	616	938	478	10,842	3,620
1961	577	665	543	506	1,024	676	12,302	4,080
1962	526	614	616	591	1,990	977	13,406	4,232
1963	499	732	695	854	2,084	1,025	15,665	4,988
1964	551	728	1,061	1,170	2,477	929	20,839	5,108
1065	328	647	1,163	1,412	2,335	1,041	23,692	5,163
1966	369	590	976	1,285	2,543	1,195	23,028	5,942
1967	279	504	871	1,225	2,516	1,178	22,739	5,315
1968	200	690	1,094	1,294	2,529	1,136	22,637	6,097
1969	197	681	1,527	1,884	2,538	770	24,433	6,234
1970	100	573	1,624	1,903	2,160	868	24,394	5,812
1971	39	811	1,893	2,028	2,120	909	27,188	8,542
1972	54	695	1,912	2,441	2,279	1,024	29,697	10,074
1973	118	482	2,137	2,986	5,484	1,065	30,094	9,403
1974	62	475	1,821	3,596	5,967	1,035	31,250	9,644
1975	76	698	2,327	4,991	6,094	957	33,760	11,273
Index	A,B,C,D	A,B,C,D	C,D	C,D	C,D	A,B,C,D	A,B,C,D	C,D

TABLE B-1 (Cont.)

	26–0100 Tires, Bicycle (th. units)	26–0200 Tubes, Bicycle (th. units)	26–0300 Tires, Auto, Motorcycle, and Aircraft (th. units)	26–0400 Tubes, Auto, Motorcycle, and Aircraft (th. units)	26–0500 Rubber Pipes, All Types (MT)	26–0700 Rubber Sanitary Ware (MT)	26–0800 Rubberized Canvas (MT)	26–0900 Rubber Footwear Products (MT)
1952	106	171	55.2	85.4	493	51.7	404	1,198
1953	289	298	59.6	78.4	632	57.6	527	1,289
1954	490	383	75.3	68.3	649	59.1	347	1,387
1955	548	414	87.1	95.0	607	64.0	333	1,231
1956	621	499	103.4	110.9	645	115	429	1,877
1957	685	508	135.1	151.5	772	117	523	2,145
1958	673	626	144.5	142.8	932	124	605	2,549
1959	702	653	190.9	184.9	1,141	132	627	3,185
1960	903	938	390.8	314.4	1,092	182	942	4,238
1961	1,335	886	423.9	454.6	1,191	159	1,148	4,595
1962	1,428	1,179	517.4	618.4	1,457	170	831	4,601
1963	1,504	1,058	732.6	806.7	1,682	229	907	6,772
1964	1,438	1,160	932.3	941.2	1,917	276	1,596	8,684
1965	1,456	1,219	955	878	2,010	388	2,441	9,123
1966	1,671	1,623	1,613	1,224	2,269	390	1,351	11,574
1967	1,578	2,264	1,578	1,335	2,136	186	914	11,089
1968	1,899	2,705	1,779	1,688	2,222	250	775	9,879
1969	1,944	2,740	2,294	2,149	2,531	419	1,049	10,519
1970	1,790	2,490	2,763	2,614	3,037	530	1,301	10,325
1971	1,946	2,692	3,195	2,805	3,941	498	1,175	10,321
1972	2,345	3,450	3,756	3,854	3,821	588	934	12,900
1973	2,778	3,856	4,589	4,436	3,506	528	1,040	11,873
1974	3,128	4,273	4,669	4,927	4,161	632	1,028	12,289
1975	3,028	3,718	5,110	5,612	4,684	629	1,485	11,378
Index	A,B,C,D	A,B,C,D	A,B,C,D	A,B,C,D	C,D	C	C,D	D

	26–1100 Reclaimed Rubber (Except Ground) (MT)	26–1200 Peasants' Rubber Sandals (th. prs.)	26–1300 Rubber Boots (th. prs.)	26–1400 Other Rubber Footwear (th. prs.)	26–1500 Rubber Adhesives (MT)	26–1600 Rubberized Fibers of Animal Origin (MT)	27–0100 Flour, White Cereals (th. MT)	27–0200 Corn Flour (MT)
1952	1,190	3,513	1,238	3,124	457	na	1,312	na
1953	766	2,381	1,360	2,723	640	na	1,474	na
1954	678	3,934	1,405	2,915	662	na	1,370	na
1955	1,081	3,788	1,528	3,238	705	na	1,397	34,739
1956	1,481	4,414	1,887	3,105	875	na	1,469	36,593
1957	1,925	5,785	2,388	3,538	1,151	na	1,527	27,535
1958	1,779	6,193	2,412	4,041	1,311	na	1,409	50,259
1959	1,685	6,461	3,121	3,752	1,511	na	1,587	40,186
1960	2,199	7,414	3,189	4,335	1,825	na	1,597	52,656
1961	2,040	6,228	4,027	3,936	1,975	na	1,746	51,963
1962	2,000	5,185	3,557	5,750	1,864	654	1,902	58,258
1963	2,005	5,531	4,052	7,218	2,183	684	1,994	71,255
1964	3,293	6,261	4,749	7,529	2,309	888	2,021	60,535
1965	6,190	7,035	4,880	5,003	2,418	782	2,110	67,342
1966	6,058	6,389	4,875	5,805	2,897	646	2,120	58,237
1967	6,169	9,335	4,710	7,949	2,776	761	1,986	60,633
1968	3,973	9,837	5,288	5,939	3,305	998	2,021	50,769
1969	6,593	6,338	5,354	4,411	3,877	1,227	2,076	48,422
1970	6,219	5,732	5,245	5,173	4,608	1,448	2,172	51,163
1971	6,046	3,828	5,636	5,364	5,117	3,125	2,285	47,105
1972	5,143	3,367	5,073	7,571	8,972	3,849	2,265	50,414
1973	7,233	3,549	4,823	8,153	9,074	4,413	2,260	48,282
1974	7,088	2,393	4,579	10,282	9,599	4,742	2,386	41,781
1975	6,424	2,297	4,849	9,665	12,643	4,128	2,314	38,794
Index	C,D	A,B,C,D	A,B,C,D	A,B,C,D	C,D	D	B,C,D	C,D

TABLE B-1 (Cont.)

	27–0300 Husked Rice (MT)	27–0400 Bread and Pastry (MT)	27–0500 Pasta Products (MT)	27–0600 Sugarless Semiprocessed Fruit (MT)	27–0700 Fruit Products, Total (MT)	27–0701 Fruit Products, Sugarless (MT)	27–0702 Fruit Products, with Sugar (MT)	27–0800 Dried Fruit (MT)
1952	na	na	23,857	na	14,946	nsa	nsa	na
1953	na	na	28,443	na	14,373	nsa	nsa	na
1954	na	na	31,477	na	19,295	nsa	nsa	na
1955	na	na	32,916	27,227	21,904	467	21,437	na
1956	na	na	28,351	14,084	14,641	715	13,926	na
1957	na	na	32,486	15,452	18,324	1,454	16,870	na
1958	12,013	na	33,722	18,959	21,267	1,850	19,417	na
1959	10,242	na	38,626	9,734	25,533	2,710	22,823	na
1960	8,358	na	41,133	12,431	31,608	4,531	27,077	na
1961	11,168	na	43,579	18,021	37,381	6,708	30,673	na
1962	15,728	na	52,078	10,360	41,260	6,942	34,318	na
1963	12,469	na	52,220	16,342	46,007	9,284	36,723	831
1964	7,271	437,777	48,761	18,372	55,462	7,251	48,211	1,895
1965	17,606	454,383	52,597	19,720	55,958	7,919	48,039	1,246
1966	14,326	409,746	45,564	16,460	48,378	5,208	43,170	1,680
1967	16,118	485,522	43,207	14,594	54,563	7,573	46,990	1,342
1968	15,594	480,104	46,332	16,238	66,264	14,468	51,796	1,018
1969	9,961	494,473	47,601	17,796	94,336	23,937	70,399	1,620
1970	10,626	550,328	52,166	14,560	45,397	5,835	39,562	1,608
1971	24,638	578,585	50,054	22,750	43,792	6,160	37,632	565
1972	23,920	617,201	52,152	23,628	54,382	10,196	44,186	4,176
1973	23,470	723,247	54,448	42,218	69,344	9,786	59,558	1,076
1974	20,512	782,003	62,588	32,228	79,117	11,311	67,806	2,405
1975	22,347	849,244	53,980	31,056	75,707	9,287	66,420	5,237
Index	C,D	D	A,B,C,D	C,D	C	D	B,D	

	27–0900 Canned Vegetables (MT)	27–1000 Dried Vegetables (MT)	27–1100 Other Vegetable Products (MT)	27–1300 Fresh Meat (MT)	27–1400 Salted and Cured Meat (MT)	27–1500 Cured Bacon and Sausage (MT)	27–1600 Canned Meat (MT)	27–1700 Concentrated Soup (MT)
1952	2,148	na	na	22,894	na	7,817	1,845	na
1953	5,083	na	na	48,578	na	9,692	2,141	na
1954	5,271	na	na	62,316	na	9,823	3,736	na
1955	5,054	na	na	67,818	10,704	11,313	5,303	na
1956	8,749	na	na	90,617	8,202	10,910	8,627	na
1957	10,643	na	na	114,508	7,968	12,524	14,548	na
1958	9,477	na	1,613	130,800	7,718	12,528	16,244	311
1959	12,503	na	3,643	178,655	14,830	16,864	23,827	1,183
1960	20,246	na	5,188	200,538	16,209	21,755	32,685	2,166
1961	18,090	na	5,651	225,959	22,556	26,925	34,808	2,589
1962	23,797	na	10,012	299,552	26,224	37,986	35,688	3,389
1963	30,637	619	7,765	310,984	21,419	41,072	39,248	3,561
1964	29,978	1,545	4,847	371,826	24,941	37,902	53,228	5,428
1965	29,915	645	4,497	409,830	28,927	40,854	58,767	5,876
1966	52,063	804	10,624	354,512	24,423	44,860	44,539	5,236
1967	45,702	586	6,136	361,827	24,236	46,784	52,685	6,248
1968	47,684	518	7,446	384,147	26,292	51,256	50,011	6,130
1969	58,534	1,091	8,608	358,398	26,120	62,500	48,220	7,989
1970	78,575	670	9,212	407,604	26,488	72,512	56,741	5,392
1971	97,187	661	10,253	478,891	28,592	78,852	59,487	4,897
1972	101,481	306	8,790	445,763	30,988	93,077	57,593	6,815
1973	103,231	966	7,048	425,702	32,027	98,677	61,713	6,835
1974	122,447	855	10,015	547,354	36,554	99,598	70,060	7,206
1975	110,759	678	13,257	556,144	42,583	113,077	73,277	6,378
Index	B,C,D		C,D	B,C,D	B,C,D	A,B,C,D	B,C,D	C,D

TABLE B-1 (Cont.)

	27–1800 Edible Animal Fats (MT)	27–1900 Salted, Smoked, and Cured Fish (MT)	27–2000 Canned Fish, Total (MT)	27–2100 Powdered Eggs (MT)	27–2200 Powdered Milk (MT)	27–2300 Canned Milk (MT)	27–2400 Butter (MT)	27–2500 Cheese (MT)
1952	11,245	1,133	3,873	na	277	na	395	1,392
1953	6,773	2,026	4,541	na	443	na	513	1,574
1954	12,163	1,302	5,016	na	749	na	862	1,706
1955	9,768	1,577	4,298	na	902	na	1,033	1,683
1956	13,165	2,238	7,530	na	912	na	1,252	1,833
1957	14,608	2,259	10,542	na	1,515	na	1,645	2,839
1958	17,142	1,815	12,041	na	1,314	na	1,550	2,785
1959	30,022	989	12,497	na	1,791	na	1,440	2,787
1960	39,514	1,077	16,545	na	2,311	na	1,720	3,462
1961	32,576	1,753	19,997	na	2,606	79	2,355	5,137
1962	30,522	1,369	23,599	na	2,235	70	3,457	7,285
1963	30,728	1,215	27,452	na	2,736	76	3,425	9,331
1964	42,188	1,672	30,414	658	3,034	335	4,422	12,947
1965	51,373	1,886	26,429	444	4,251	438	4,519	14,864
1966	31,626	2,810	19,871	933	6,230	384	5,576	18,537
1967	35,482	4,779	17,524	1,211	6,608	445	5,942	18,938
1968	37,919	2,703	19,530	652	4,892	669	5,924	19,153
1969	28,317	2,381	19,343	1,052	5,868	754	4,566	21,478
1970	35,401	2,430	22,149	1,128	5,460	837	4,071	21,504
1971	41,744	2,200	24,270	863	5,684	1,205	4,365	19,901
1972	41,045	2,062	26,699	699	6,968	1,152	4,640	23,713
1973	18,611	2,285	27,518	499	6,798	1,183	4,395	24,564
1974	40,491	1,295	31,958	874	8,201	1,368	5,543	27,794
1975	45,832	1,296	30,504	754	9,020	1,401	6,039	30,031
Index	A,B,C,D	C,D	B,C,D		B,C,D	C,D	C,D	A,B,C,D

	27–2600 Other Dairy Products (MT)	27–2700 Sugar (MT)	27–2800 Confectionery, Flour (MT)	27–2900 Candy and Chocolate Products, Total (MT)	27–2901 Candies (MT)	27–2902 Chocolate Products (MT)	27–3000 Edible Oil (MT)	27–3100 Oil for Technical Uses (MT)
1952	na	57,560	6,151	8,637	nsa	nsa	19,148	3,521
1953	na	172,200	6,594	7,124	nsa	nsa	26,390	2,248
1954	na	132,099	6,088	11,176	nsa	nsa	35,300	4,100
1955	na	116,765	7,705	14,798	12,793	2,005	36,817	6,297
1956	na	148,748	7,437	15,041	11,785	3,256	32,010	5,523
1957	na	235,260	9,726	18,837	14,264	4,573	33,283	6,584
1958	na	168,576	11,915	23,010	17,526	5,484	40,639	8,654
1959	na	247,224	15,318	25,590	18,846	6,744	45,565	12,729
1960	na	265,714	18,895	31,031	22,871	8,160	51,542	11,041
1961	11,074	230,352	22,854	34,994	24,708	10,286	62,342	13,806
1962	15,893	226,899	28,155	37,544	25,639	11,905	73,343	12,634
1963	20,115	313,227	35,639	45,125	29,626	15,499	93,279	13,050
1964	23,774	331,113	38,548	49,962	29,860	20,102	105,635	14,947
1965	25,601	333,566	47,839	56,583	31,449	25,134	98,140	16,195
1966	36,475	529,553	45,203	62,393	33,305	29,088	104,161	12,970
1967	44,934	450,649	47,451	63,552	34,326	29,226	114,978	10,255
1968	52,771	360,041	48,892	59,903	34,167	25,736	120,013	5,740
1969	73,190	511,846	53,321	56,296	32,243	24,053	121,396	6,147
1970	81,214	354,109	62,681	58,580	33,144	25,436	151,450	5,521
1971	86,771	393,756	69,982	69,137	38,301	30,836	178,195	6,760
1972	90,058	345,558	78,645	78,291	43,276	35,015	165,319	4,463
1973	126,255	406,420	86,291	77,487	42,332	35,155	168,322	2,695
1974	144,063	478,938	90,901	83,272	42,623	40,649	179,339	3,775
1975	173,414	524,968	73,199	79,267	40,335	38,932	175,232	2,572
Index	D	A,B,C,D	A,B,C,D	A,C	B,D	B,D	A,D	D

TABLE B-1 (Cont.)

	27–3200 Margarine (MT)	27–3300 Refined Spirits (th. hl.°)	27–3400 Denatured Spirits (th. hl.°)	27–3600 Beer (th. hl.)	27–3700 Artificial Nonalcoholic Beverages (th. hl.)	27–3800 Starches, Total (MT)	27–3900 Starch Preparations (MT)	27–4000 Yeast (MT)
1952	0	13,851	1,717	922	na	9,410	4,459	6,986
1953	0	7,530	1,656	567	na	4,994	4,010	6,800
1954	0	12,668	2,815	801	na	6,123	6,563	7,168
1955	0	9,949	1,838	804.5	na	15,184	6,988	7,195
1956	231	12,235	2,502	770.1	na	11,094	6,916	7,611
1957	3,212	19,735	2,903	1,043	na	24,973	6,653	8,171
1958	6,284	23,017	3,292	1,230	32.55	29,863	7,667	8,985
1959	8,999	18,604	3,846	1,262	65.19	25,108	20,180	9,518
1960	9,496	20,832	4,491	1,630	80.70	39,817	21,247	9,468
1961	11,373	19,400	4,029	1,860	96.19	41,590	18,969	9,299
1962	15,206	19,917	3,490	1,788	135.1	40,625	21,204	9,998
1963	17,944	25,136	3,455	2,241	175.5	38,825	25,282	10,862
1964	21,078	26,229	3,493	2,669	225.4	37,288	26,214	11,261
1965	22,801	25,839	3,525	2,995	275.5	36,286	25,515	12,044
1966	24,392	28,002	2,626	4,051	315.6	34,133	24,045	13,222
1967	24,330	27,135	2,317	4,367	425.4	24,918	24,769	14,003
1968	22,625	31,422	1,738	4,752	467.3	26,388	22,074	15,386
1969	27,479	31,088	1,657	5,344	647	36,853	24,272	15,901
1970	33,769	35,096	2,068	6,665	857	27,161	25,728	18,470
1971	33,587	36,679	1,972	8,327	1,246	30,794	26,960	21,140
1972	38,500	41,505	2,393	9,345	1,630	22,161	28,578	23,030
1973	41,953	32,039	1,354	9,704	1,915	23,572	26,885	24,049
1974	45,093	46,850	1,455	9,429	2,416	27,786	28,779	26,342
1975	40,304	25,249	1,326	8,454	2,695	30,309	31,852	27,512
Index	B,C,D	A,B,C,D	A,B,C,D	A,B,C,D	C,D	A,B,C,D	C,D	A,B,C,D

	27–4100 Coffee Extract (MT)	27–4300 Coffee Substitutes (MT)	27–4400 Ground Pepper (MT)	27–4500 Fodder, Total (th. MT)	28–0100 Newspapers, Magazines, and Periodicals (MT)	28–0200 Books and Brochures (MT)
1952	na	8,316	949	na	10,480	4,890
1953	na	8,484	679	na	8,852	4,324
1954	na	8,997	941	na	16,604	5,106
1955	na	8,558	1,699	12.85	19,391	4,700
1956	na	8,143	2,165	24.78	22,930	6,160
1957	na	8,578	2,292	21.76	26,504	5,900
1958	na	8,069	1,881	24.07	32,221	6,983
1959	na	7,330	2,344	58.13	37,456	8,301
1960	na	7,787	2,079	100.4	45,911	9,142
1961	na	7,896	2,287	93.46	45,603	11,707
1962	na	7,681	2,680	216.0	49,517	13,904
1963	45	7,566	4,126	334.5	54,599	14,029
1964	62	7,013	4,938	522.3	66,479	15,786
1965	75	6,886	5,282	571.9	66,616	18,398
1966	51	6,531	5,338	778.8	69,478	19,834
1967	93	5,976	4,833	991.2	79,163	20,951
1968	78	5,534	5,054	1,063	90,340	20,394
1969	88	4,962	4,918	1,129	98,285	22,654
1970	61	4,755	3,932	1,566	110,596	23,313
1971	84	4,488	3,489	1,617	117,115	26,403
1972	66	4,608	3,990	1,788	120,526	31,270
1973	104	4,507	4,300	1,659	125,391	33,579
1974	119	4,184	4,027	1,989	126,525	37,094
1975	80	3,975	3,405	1,708	123,305	38,693
Index		A,B,C,D	A,B,C,D		C,D	C,D

TABLE B-1 (Cont.)

	28–0300 Printed Matter and Blank Forms (MT)	28–0400 School Exercise Books (MT)	29–0100 Cured Tobacco (MT)	29–0200 Cigarettes (MT)	29–0300 Other Tobacco Products (MT)
1952	6,140	na	24,369	12,243	328
1953	6,880	na	16,771	13,599	186
1954	7,735	na	30,475	15,419	180
1955	9,444	na	32,109	15,996	205
1956	9,655	3,708	40,998	16,191	219
1957	12,579	4,384	31,154	17,526	342
1958	14,249	4,877	53,089	17,800	232
1959	14,452	4,843	37,260	18,506	261
1960	17,661	5,333	34,837	20,123	220
1961	18,945	7,275	21,587	22,804	110
1962	22,434	9,092	15,094	22,455	113
1963	24,202	9,940	33,448	23,215	105
1964	27,317	11,133	56,279	23,880	72
1965	27,805	11,747	59,188	26,011	91
1966	26,855	10,777	48,781	28,493	86
1967	27,081	10,765	50,082	27,411	87
1968	27,369	13,686	48,936	29,329	107
1969	30,788	15,823	40,356	31,162	110
1970	33,777	16,932	41,387	32,072	107
1971	38,212	17,082	42,987	33,862	108
1972	40,364	14,242	46,958	34,365	106
1973	42,265	14,061	57,383	37,254	96
1974	48,328	16,996	59,042	39,960	130
1975	48,153	12,737	59,114	40,887	160
Index	C,D	C,D	A,B,C,D	A,B,C,D	C,D

Legend: na: not available
nsa: not separately available.

SOURCES: SZS, *Industrija 1939 i 1946–1956* (Belgrade: SZS, 1957), pp. 15–69; idem, *Industrija 1957* (Belgrade: SZS, 1958), pp. 15–38; idem, *Industrija 1958* (Belgrade: SZS, 1959), pp. 17–40; idem, *Industrija 1959* (Belgrade: SZS, 1960), pp. 17–43; idem, *Industrija 1960* (Belgrade: SZS, 1961), pp. 18–45; idem, *Industrija 1961* (Belgrade:

SZS, 1962), pp. 18–45; idem, *Industrija 1962* (Belgrade: SZS, 1963), pp. 18–45; idem, *Industrija 1963* (Belgrade: SZS, 1964), pp. 19–47; *Industrija 1966* (Belgrade: SZS, 1967), pp. 21–57; idem, *Industrija 1967* (Belgrade: SZS, 1968), pp. 19–56; idem, *Industrija 1968* (Belgrade: SZS, 1969), pp. 19–56; idem, *Industrija 1969* (Belgrade: SZS, 1970), pp. 19–56; idem, *Industrija 1970* (Belgrade: SZS, 1971), pp. 19–57; idem, *Industrija 1971* (Belgrade: SZS, 1972), pp. 19–57; idem, *Industrija 1972* (Belgrade: SZS, 1973), pp. 19–61; idem, *Industrija 1973* (Belgrade: SZS, 1974), pp. 19–62; idem, *Industrija 1974* (Belgrade: SZS, 1975), pp. 21–65; and idem, *Industrija 1975* (Belgrade: SZS, 1976), pp. 21–65.

NOTES:

Series 14–0500, 1952–71: The sum of open hearth, LD, electric furnace, and Bessemer converter ingots.

Series 14–0701, 1952–62: Calculated from the series for rails plus accessories by assuming that the output of rails was the same fraction (0.8108) of the output of rails plus accessories in 1952–62 as it was in 1963–67.

Series 14–0800, 1967: In *Industrija 1968*, output of steel sheets in 1967 was given as 585 tons; in *Industrija 1969*, it was given as 358. The more recent figure was used.

Series 14=0900, 1952–75: Disaggregated data available for 1970 and 1971 indicate that this includes girders and heavy molded sections.

Series 14–1000, 1952–75: The sum of strip steel for tubing and cold-rolled and finished strip steel.

Series 14–1200, 1952–75: Includes steel-reinforced concrete profiles.

Series 15–2200, 1952–75: Includes primary and secondary crude copper.

Series 15–2700, 1952–75: Includes primary and secondary electrolytic copper.

Series 15–3000, 1963–71: Until 1963, a simple series entitled "silver" (*srebro*) was given by the basic source. Beginning in 1963, two series were given: one, entitled "anodic silver" (*anodno srebro*) linked with the previous series; the other, called "refined silver" (*rafinirano srebro*) evidently corresponded to a narrower coverage. After 1969, only the narrower coverage was given; output of the broader series was estimated for 1970–75 by assuming that the ratio of the two series was the same in those years as it had been in the preceding five years, on average.

Series 15–4301, 15–4302, 15–4303, 15–4304, 1961: Estimated by logarithmic interpolation from following ten years.

Series 15–4500, 1952–56: Taken from SZS, *Industrija 1939 i 1946–1956*, Statistički bilten, no. 81 (Belgrade: SZS, 1957), p. 26, as the figure for extruded copper products. For 1957 and 1958, the sum of extruded copper wire, extruded copper tubing, extruded copper shapes and profiles, and other extruded copper products. For 1962–75, the sum of extruded copper wire and other extruded products of copper and copper alloys. For 1959–61, estimated by logarithmic interpolation using data for the preceding and following five-year periods.

Series 15–4700, 1959–61: Estimated by logarithmic interpolation using data for the preceding and following five-year periods.

Series 15–5000, 1952–58: Taken as the sum of base aluminum and aluminum alloy ropes and other extruded products of aluminum and aluminum alloys. For 1962–75, the sum of those items plus extruded aluminum and aluminum alloy wire. For 1959–61, estimated by logarithmic interpolation using data for the preceding and following five-year periods.

Series 16–0600, 1952: Assumed to be zero.

Series 16–1400, 1952–75: Includes glass packaging materials and other blown-glass products.

Series 16–1900, 1952–75: Includes firebricks and mortar and sand of fireclay.

Series 16–2200, 1952: Estimated by logarithmic interpolation from data for following ten years.

Series 17–0400, 1952–55: The data for 1952–54 do not link precisely with the data for 1955 and afterwards. According to *Industrija 1939 i 1946–1956*, 1955 output was 4,851 MT instead of the 5,971 MT shown here, which was taken from *Industrija 1957*.

Series 17–0600, 1952–75: Includes cast and plate boilers.

TABLE B-1 (Cont.)

Series 17–0700, 1952–71: After 1963, output in $m.^2$ of heating surface was also published. See table B-3 for this data.

Series 17–1900, 1955–71: For more detailed data, see table B-4.

Series 17–2500, 1963–71: For data about the number of bearings, see table B-5.

Series 17–2600, 1959–71: For data about the number of pumps, see table B-6.

Series 17–2800, 17–2900, 1959–71: See table B-7 for additional information about these series.

Series 17–3900, 1952–55: Weighbridges and other balances are given separately after 1955, but not before. The figures given in the source for ''other balances'' (*ostale vage*) are taken to include weighbridges for the early period.

Series 17–4200, 1952–71: The sum of wall, street, table, and similar clocks and, through 1962, pocket watches and wristwatches.

Series 17–4400, 17–4500, 17–4600, 17–4700, and 17–4800, 1952–71: Additional details are given in table B-8.

Series 17–5100, 1952–71: Includes marine and other internal combustion engines.

Series 17–5400, 1952–71: See table B-9 for production in number of trucks.

Series 17–5500, 1952–71: See table B-9 for production in number of buses. The sources disagree about production for 1962 and 1963. In both cases, the most recent figures were used.

Series 17–5600, 1955–71: See table B-9 for production in number of automobiles. The sources disagree about production for 1962 and 1963. In both cases, the most recent figures were used.

Series 17–5800, 1952–71: See table B-9 for production in number of tractors.

Series 17–6100, 1956–71: See table B-9 for production in number of motorcycles.

Series 17–6500, 1952–75: Includes enameled and other metal kitchenware.

Series 19–0100, 19–0200, 19–0300, 1952–71: See table B-10 for additional details about production of electrical rotating machinery.

Series 19–0500, 1952–71: See table B-11 for additional details about the production of power transformers.

Series 19–1000, 1952–75: Data measuring output in units other than weight are available only after 1962.

Series 19–1900, 1955–56: Estimated by assuming that the number of refrigerators per ton was the same in those years as the average (16.00) of the succeeding ten years.

Series 19–2400, 1952–71: Data are not available to provide further information about types of radios produced.

Series 19–3300, 1955–71: Data are also reported for production in thousands of connections. See table B-12.

Series 20–0600, 1954–60: Converted to 100 percent basis by multiplying basic data by 0.20.

Series 20–6900, 1952–75: Includes soaps and powders for washing, detergents for washing and laundering, and other washing preparations. See table B-13.

Series 20–8200, 1952: Estimated by logarithmic interpolation based on data for succeeding five years.

Series 20–8900, 1952: Estimated by logarithmic interpolation based on data for succeeding five years.

Series 21–0200, 1955–75: Gravel and sand plus broken stone and marble and crushed stone and marble.

Series 21–1100, 1952–57: Taken to be the sum of hollow and solid bricks.

Series 21–1700, 1966–75: Taken to be the sum of light building panels for interior walls, exterior walls, ceilings, and roofs.

Series 21−1900, 21−2000, and 21−2100, 1963−71: Data relating production in units to production in $m.^2$ are given in table B-14.

Series 22−0600, 1962−63: This is the sum of several items, including blind veneer. In 1962−63, output of blind veneer in Bosnia-Hercegovina was underreported. Estimates for that part of total production were obtained by logarithmic interpolation on the basis of the output of the succeeding eight years.

Series 23−0700, 1952−75: Includes non−wood-based writing and printing paper, illustration and copying paper, and other writing and printing paper.

Series 24−0300, 1952−75: Includes carded and combed cotton yarn, carded and combed cotton-type yarn with 55 percent and higher synthetic yarn, and vigogne.

Series 24−0900, 1957: The sources disagree on production for 1957. The most recent figure was taken.

Series 24−2500, 1955−75: The sum of cotton, wool, silk, and other knitwear. See table B-15 for detailed data for 1963−71.

Series 25−0200, 1952: Estimated by logarithmic interpolation on the basis of data for the succeeding six years.

Series 25−0300, 1963−75: The sum of cattle, swine, sheep, goat, and horse hides for footwear, linings, and other purposes.

Series 26−0100, 26−0200, 26−0300, and 26−0400, 1955−71: For production in tons, see table B-16.

Series 27−0100, 1952: Estimated by logarithmic interpolation based on data for succeeding ten years.

Series 27−2000, 1952−75: Includes both sterilized and unsterilized canned fish.

Series 27−3200, 1952−55: Not given in source; assumed to be zero.

Series 29−0200, 1956−71: For production in millions of units, see table B-17.

Series 15−4801, 15−4802, and 15−4900, included in the 1971 direct weights index, are not shown in table B-1.

TABLE B-2

PRODUCTION OF TEMPERED AND GRAY STEEL CASTINGS, 1964–69

	Tempered Steel				Gray Steel			
	Less than 5 kg. (MT)	6–50 kg. (MT)	More than 50 kg. (MT)	Total (MT)	Less than 5 kg. (MT)	6–50 kg. (MT)	More than 50 kg. (MT)	Total (MT)
1964	8,109	1,068	1,305	10,482	43,828	70,581	151,849	266,258
1965	8,004	1,217	1,201	10,422	52,708	75,356	171,736	299,800
1966	8,765	1,471	960	11,196	45,559	78,786	153,446	277,791
1967	8.520	1,140	1,037	10,697	44,100	71,780	126,576	242,456
1968	9,589	1,052	1,264	11,905	43,070	76,512	127,943	247,525
1969	11,082	1,047	1,206	13,335	56,696	79,245	156,881	292,822

SOURCES: See table B-1.

TABLE B-3

STEAM HEATING EQUIPMENT, 1963–71

	Cast Steam Heating Equipment			Boilerplate Steam Heating Equipment		
	(MT)	(Th. m.^{2})	$\frac{m.^2}{MT}$	(MT)	(Th. m^2)	$\frac{m.^2}{MT}$
1963	10,078	326	32.4	4,712	498	105.7
1964	13,144	404	30.7	6,979	672	96.3
1965	12,839	404	31.5	7,197	715	99.4
1966	9,798	325	33.2	5,035	496	98.5
1967	12,221	402	32.9	6,449	627	97.2
1968	12,256	429	35.0	7,030	698	99.3
1969	17,437	602	34.5	8,225	814	99.0
1970	20,808	717	34.5	10,081	856	84.9
1971	22,228	766	34.5	10,441	1,048	100.4

SOURCES: See table B-1.

TABLE B-4

PRODUCTION OF METAL PACKING CONTAINERS, 1955–71

	Tinplate (MT)	Aluminum (MT)	Lead (MT)	Others (MT)
1955	4,688	43	285	9,033
1956	4,778	145	138	7,470
1957	8,084	160	324	10,288
1958	8,403	100	349	11,909
1959	12,322	241	334	16,364
1960	16,596	571	383	20,558
1961	19,237	496	239	21,800
1962	23,384	568	325	25,891
1963	27,949	727	398	28,676
1964	33,693	779	457	37,748
1965	34,317	1,066	434	34,407
1966	33,540	1,266	497	35,420
1967	36,613	1,460	416	39,863
1968	37,542	1,857	427	40,184
1969	41,821	1,876	390	41,602
1970	45,953	1,787	320	42,220
1971	48,441	2,340	270	36,436

SOURCES: See table B-1.

TABLE B-5

PRODUCTION OF ROLLER BEARINGS, 1963–71

	Output (MT)	Output (th. units)	Bearings per ton
1963	1,596	1,367	856.5
1964	2,438	1,583	649.3
1965	2,790	1,914	686.0
1966	2,228	2,393	1,074.1
1967	1,399	1,976	1,412.4
1968	1,508	2,481	1,645.2
1969	1,347	3,148	2,337.1
1970	1,866	3,968	2,126.5
1971	2,211	4,201	1,900.1

SOURCES: See table B-1.

TABLE B-6

PRODUCTION OF PUMPS, 1959–71

	Output (MT)	Output (th. units)	Pumps per ton
1959	2,672	39.9	14.9
1960	3,021	53.2	17.6
1961	4,124	56.6	13.7
1962	4,414	77.0	17.4
1963	3,511	79.8	22.7
1964	4,491	135	30.1
1965	5,259	198	37.7
1966	5,090	238	46.8
1967	6,210	136	21.9
1968	6,630	144	21.7
1969	6,856	213	31.1
1970	7,033	188	26.7
1971	7,205	204	28.3

SOURCES: See table B-1.

TABLE B-7

PRODUCTION OF TURBINES, 1959–71

	Water Turbines					Steam Turbines				
	tons	units	th. kw	tons/unit	kw/ton	tons	units	th. kw	tons/unit	kw/ton
1959	2,988	13	199.4	229.8	66.7	320	392	94	0.82	293.8
1960	2,493	2	155.1	1,246.5	62.2	268	310	104	0.86	388.1
1961	1,021	10	142.9	102.1	140.0	228	308	22	0.74	96.5
1962	923	8	28.4	115.4	30.8	469	139	63	3.37	134.3
1963	1,523	3	20.3	507.7	13.3	93	55	17	1.69	182.8
1964	1,203	7	158	171.9	131.3	267	72	35	3.71	131.1
1965	1,371	10	285	137.1	207.9	1,171	72	150	16.3	128.1
1966	1,752	6	367	292.0	209.5	714	15	89	47.6	124.7
1967	2,414	10	54	241.4	22.4	217	110	16	1.97	73.7
1968	2,367	na	na	na	na	249	6	128	41.5	514.1
1969	1,161	11	559	105.5	481.5	607	33	78	18.4	128.5
1970	980	4	26	245.0	26.5	337	7	37	48.1	109.8
1971	1,297	2	57	648.5	44.0	285	10	68	28.5	238.6

SOURCES: See table B-1.

TABLE B-8

PRODUCTION OF RAILWAY ROLLING STOCK, 1952–71

	Diesel and Electric Locomotives		Steam Locomotives		Freight and Other Special Coaches		Other Railway Coaches and Mail Vans		Tramcars, Rail Motor Coaches, etc.	
	tons	units	tons	units	tons	units	tons	units	tons	units
1952	na	na	206	17	2,951	210	1,252	35	na	na
1953	na	na	1,135	44	12,199	1,015	16	1	13	1
1954	na	na	1,662	109	13,772	1,283	na	na	13	1
1955	na	na	1,475	188	6,932	477	14	1	na	na
1956	28	7	500	21	2,162	206	1,000	53	66	3
1957	211	21	840	20	10,950	981	1,109	32	343	21
1958	305	29	557	11	29,488	2,292	704	46	128	10
1959	212	17	626	17	38,965	2,923	708	21	101	11
1960	1,032	64	242	6	53,566	3,422	1,090	46	158	16
1961	1,321	55	na	na	42,214	2,348	4,707	136	196	7
1962	1,558	45	na	na	43,168	2,850	5,503	188	187	18
1963	1,931	77	103	2	45,510	2,762	2,769	100	1,283	106
1964	2,234	85	58	1	54,298	3,486	4,982	194	508	58
1965	2,124	127	108	3	80,764	4,848	6,915	238	671	56
1966	1,354	84	72	2	70,049	4,242	6,688	226	919	70
1967	1,163	45	na	na	47,164	2,372	3,932	116	1,220	78
1968	1,139	55	na	na	49,383	2,684	5,070	131	1,228	67
1969	2,143	60	na	na	67,473	4,228	3,712	94	629	57
1970	4,205	118	na	na	50,674	2,609	4,387	110	255	31
1971	4,465	121	na	na	77,951	3,790	3,320	83	840	61

SOURCES: See table B-1.

TABLE B-9

PRODUCTION OF MOTOR VEHICLES, TRACTORS, AND MOTORCYCLES, 1952–71

	Trucks		*Buses*		*Passenger Automobiles*		*Tractors*		*Motorcycles*	
	tons	units	tons	units	tons	units	tons	units	tons	units
1952	1,875	654	164	41		na	2,706	789		na
1953		1,329		75		na		1,360		na
1954		1,651		114		na		1,059		na
1955		2,450		239	760	760		1,100		na
1956		2,765		426		990		2,961	242	3,421
1957		3,459		666		3,088		4,032		13,060
1958		4,089		671		2,935		5,189		8,202
1959		3,716		511		4,431		5,919		24,530
1960		4,564		896		10,461		7,309		41,414
1961	18,302	5,426	5,859	829	11,040	14,999	12,216	4,865	2,806	37,751
1962		6,454		2,144[a]		11,435[a]		5,410		31,968
1963		7,975		1,823[a]		17,892[a]		8,092		43,113
1964		9,081		2,588		26,387		9,423		48,142
1965		9,572		2,568		34,445		7,430		48,774
1966		8,870		2,899		36,098		8,668		48,773
1967		9,654		2,421		46,178		8,793		49,959
1968		10,465		2,857		58,295		10,929		61,154
1969		11,097		3,162		78,934		10,818		67,066
1970		12,901		3,830		111,819		12,047		84,039
1971	46,508	13,294	19,748	3,856	81,541	109,902	24,178	15,045	4,073	73,978

SOURCES: See table B-1.

[a]The sources disagree about these production quantities. In all cases, the most recently published figures were used.

TABLE B-10

PRODUCTION OF ELECTRICAL ROTATING MACHINERY, 1952–71

	Large Rotating Machinery (over 70 kw)			Medium Rotating Machinery (1.6 to 70 kw)			Small Rotating Machinery (less than 1.6 kw)		
	tons	units	kw per unit	tons	units	kw per unit	tons	th. units	kw per unit
1952	697	138	368	2,317	20,838	7.44	191	26.71	2.01
1953	1,598	92	1,283	1,827	23,191	4.96	276	19.33	3.03
1954	1,392	72	1,597	1,738	21,053	5.13	283	21.09	0.459
1955	973	106	733	1,983	23,419	4.70	441	34.26	0.400
1956	2,104	128	1,516	1,904	20,943	4.87	486	33.0	0.547
1957	2,375	163	1,613	2,703	27,993	5.11	507	50.0	0.389
1958	1,410	282	610	2,627	29,848	4.82	863	83.1	0.420
1959	1,278	265	475	3,237	28,771	6.78	1,239	128	0.493
1960	2,848	301	1,030	3,693	37,478	6.32	1,622	232	0.269
1961	2,572	463	702	4,866	50,139	6.24	1,545	311	0.211
1962	1,758	667	268	5,208	47,680	7.13	1,741	381	0.184
1963	2,802	740	339	4,394	40,923	7.23	2,101	581	0.169
1964	2,317	841	288	4,055	39,725	6.72	2,857	901	0.153
1965	2,642	613	927	4,964	50,807	6.67	3,441	1,317	0.120
1966	4,334	803	917	5,795	90,781	4.47	3,801	1,243	0.129
1967	3,281	993	286	5,964	83,665	5.21	3,853	976	0.137
1968	4,152	600	1,293	5,914	62,101	5.99	4,515	1,431	0.103
1969	2,100	505	541	6,015	62,962	7.15	7,206	2,003	0.127
1970	2,553	963	388	9,211	116,683	6.89	9,688	2,277	0.157
1971	5,504	1,060	883	9,893	157,487	5.47	9,079	943	0.370

SOURCES: See table B-1.

TABLE B-11

PRODUCTION OF POWER TRANSFORMERS, 1955–71

	Units	Th. kVA	kVA per unit
1955	6,633	614.8	92.7
1956	6,852	705.3	102.9
1957	5,879	794.2	135.1
1958	8,725	1,335	153.1
1959	12,234	1,624	132.7
1960	17,669	2,082	117.8
1961	22,139	2,236	101.0
1962	16,901	1,905	112.7
1963	21,633	2,301	106.4
1964	29,361	2,706	92.2
1965	29,351	3,355	114.3
1966	26,350	2,759	104.7
1967	36,047	4,671	129.6
1968	54,467	5,068	93.1
1969	53,430	5,045	94.4
1970	56,379	5,760	102.2
1971	48,366	5,359	110.8

SOURCES: See table B-1.

TABLE B-12

PRODUCTION OF TELEPHONE EXCHANGES, 1955–71

	Tons	Th. of Connections	Connections Per Ton
1955	316	54.0	171
1956	207	40.6	197
1957	268	38.5	144
1958	431	58.6	136
1959	418	67.0	160
1960	541	79.5	147
1961	569	95.2	167
1962	685	101	147
1963	750	119	159
1964	1,051	160	152
1965	1,145	183	160
1966	1,252	206	165
1967	1,620	263	162
1968	1,863	331	178
1969	2,331	369	158
1970	2,596	406	156
1971	3,563	553	155

SOURCES: See table B-1.

TABLE B-13

PRODUCTION OF CLEANING AGENTS, 1952–71
(metric tons)

	Soaps and Washing Powders (60% fatty acid basis)	Detergents (15% alkyl sulfate basis)	Other Cleaning and Washing Agents
1952	23,322	na	nsa
1953	22,321	na	1,652
1954	26,947	na	3,172
1955	26,845	na	2,979
1956	27,402	na	4,895
1957	30,269	3,590	4,953
1958	29,567	10,563	2,103
1959	32,743	16,580	2,625
1960	32,465	18,493	3,234
1961	32,273	21,260	3,272
1962	32,622	26,086	8,535
1963	34,856	30,320	6,700
1964	35,557	38,122	8,736
1965	32,549	46,983	8,306
1966	38,935	53,532	9,235
1967	36,253	58,813	10,740
1968	35,024	63,860	12,267
1969	26,260	88,739	11,891
1970	26,445	98,536	12,564
1971	25,465	118,083	13,770

SOURCES: See table B-1.

TABLE B-14

PRODUCTION OF MISCELLANEOUS BLOCKS AND PANELS, 1963–71

	Blocks for Walls and Partitions		*Walls Elements (Panels)*		*Blocks for Roof Construction*	
	Th. m.^{2}	m.^{2} per unit	Th. m.^{2}	m.^{2} per unit	Th. m.^{2}	m.^{2} per unit
1963	na	na	531	21.5	587	13.4
1964	na	na	475	21.3	729	13.7
1965	1,876	13.1	526	15.3	720	15.9
1966	1,871	12.9	459	17.8	754	16.0
1967	2,404	13.0	590	17.5	759	16.9
1968	2,813	12.7	646	21.7	875	15.2
1969	3,359	14.0	667	21.8	1,116	15.4
1970	3,524	12.0	810	19.6	1,292	13.4
1971	4,495	11.4	759	18.2	1,109	19.2

SOURCES: See table B-1.

TABLE B-15

PRODUCTION OF KNITWEAR, 1963–71

	Cotton		*Wool*		*Other*[a]	
	tons	Percent of total	tons	Percent of total	tons	Percent of total
1963	5,178	52.5	3,099	31.4	1,588	16.1
1964	5,924	50.0	3,783	31.9	2,142	18.1
1965	5,948	47.3	4,310	34.3	2,310	18.4
1966	5,310	42.9	4,105	33.2	2,958	23.9
1967	4,698	38.2	3,751	30.5	3,860	31.4
1968	4,388	35.2	3,654	29.3	4,412	35.4
1969	4,026	31.4	3,674	28.7	5,119	39.9
1970	4,585	32.9	3,549	25.5	5,804	41.5
1971	5,149	32.7	4,157	26.4	6,451	40.9

SOURCES: See table B-1.
[a]Silk and synthetic knitwear.

TABLE B-16

PRODUCTION OF RUBBER TIRES AND TUBES, 1955–71

	Bicycle Tires		*Bicycle Tubes*		*Automobile, Motorcycle, and Airplane Tires*		*Automobile, Motorcycle, and Airplane Tubes*	
	tons	tons per th. units	tons	tons per th. units	tons	tons per th. units	tons	tons per th. units
1955	510	0.931	103	0.249	1,535	17.6	192	2.02
1956	572	0.921	127	0.255	2,249	21.8	255	2.30
1957	627	0.915	129	0.254	2,712	20.1	306	2.02
1958	620	0.921	160	0.256	2,891	20.0	291	2.04
1959	657	0.936	163	0.250	3,391	17.8	345	1.87
1960	848	0.939	232	0.247	7,328	18.8	598	1.90
1961	1,259	0.943	227	0.256	8,989	21.2	991	2.18
1962	1,300	0.910	317	0.269	10,516	20.3	1,343	2.17
1963	1,374	0.914	259	0.245	14,081	19.2	1,759	2.18
1964	1,320	0.918	300	0.259	16,624	17.8	1,873	1.99
1965	1,326	0.911	311	0.255	17,802	18.6	1,733	1.97
1966	1,493	0.894	398	0.245	22,337	13.8	2,387	1.95
1967	1,807	1.145	530	0.234	23,681	15.0	2,763	2.07
1968	1,702	0.896	628	0.232	24,409	13.7	2,941	1.74
1969	1,632	0.840	594	0.217	33,868	14.8	3,370	1.57
1970	1,419	0.793	551	0.221	36,250	13.1	4,002	1.53
1971	1,596	0.820	557	0.207	40,881	12.8	4,308	1.54

SOURCES: See table B-1.

TABLE B-17

PRODUCTION OF CIGARETTES, 1955–71

	Tons	Mill. Units	Mill. Units Per Ton
1955	15,996	17,120	1.07
1956	16,191	17,291	1.07
1957	17,526	18,665	1.06
1958	17,800	18,937	1.06
1959	18,506	19,718	1.07
1960	20,123	21,564	1.07
1961	22,804	24,405	1.07
1962	22,455	24,073	1.07
1963	23,215	24,831	1.07
1964	23,880	25,442	1.07
1965	26,011	27,915	1.07
1966	28,493	30,511	1.07
1967	27,411	29,391	1.07
1968	29,329	31,369	1.07
1969	31,162	33,385	1.07
1970	32,072	33,772	1.05
1971	33,862	35,413	1.05

SOURCES: See table B-1.

APPENDIX C

Yugoslav and U.S. Industry Classifications

The official Yugoslav classification of products and enterprises into industry groups or branches differs in important respects from that used in the United States. One major difference is that the Yugoslav industrial sector includes some activities that are not classified within the U.S. manufacturing sector, notably mining and electric power generation. Mining activities in Yugoslavia are distributed among the branches of industry that process ores and other raw materials produced in mining. Electric power production is reported as a separate branch of industry, not as a nonindustrial sector; electric power output reported in Yugoslav industrial statistics includes power produced both by electric power enterprises and (to the extent that reporting is complete) by other enterprises that generate power for their own use.

The other differences between the Yugoslav and American classifications result from the grouping together in Yugoslav branches of products that are in different groups in the American system. The most important example is found in the Yugoslav branch designated in this book as metal products, which contains a wide variety of products. It includes rough steel castings and precision balances, nails and diesel locomotives, barbed wire and household refrigerators, passenger automobiles and a host of other fabricated metal products. Of all Yugoslav industrial branches (except shipbuilding), it presents the most serious measurement problems.

To tabulate the correspondences and differences between the two classifications precisely would be an uneconomic task. Table C-1 presents a rough comparison of the two systems. The English versions of the Serbo-Croat branch names are not intended to be literal translations.

TABLE C-1

CORRESPONDENCE OF YUGOSLAV INDUSTRIAL BRANCHES TO U.S. INDUSTRY OR MINING GROUPS

Yugoslav branch	U.S. groups in which products in the Yugoslav branch are included	SIC Code
Electric power production *(Proizvodnja električne energija)*	Electric energy	–
Coal and coal products *(Proizvodnja i prerada uglja)*	Mining: Coal and coal products	29
Petroleum and petroleum products *(Proizvodnja i prerada nafta)*	Mining: Petroleum products	29
Ferrous metallurgy *(Crna metalurgija)*	Mining: Primary metals	33
Nonferrous metallurgy *(Obojena metalurgija)*	Mining: Primary metals	33
Stone, clay and glass *(Proizvodnja i prerada nemetala)*	Mining: Stone, clay, and glass products	32
Metal products *(Metalna industrija)*	Fabricated metal products	34
	Machinery, except electrical	35
	Transportation equipment	37
	Instruments and related products	38
Electrical products *(Elektroindustrija)*	Electrical and electronic equipment	36
	Instruments and related products	38
Chemicals *(Hemijska industrija)*	Chemicals and allied products	28
Building materials *(Industrija gradjevinskog materijala)*	Stone, clay, and glass products	32
	Lumber and wood products	24
Lumber and wood products *(Drvna industrija)*	Lumber and wood products	24
	Furniture and fixtures	25
	Chemicals and allied products	28
Paper and paper products *(Industrija papira)*	Paper and allied products	26
Textiles and textile products *(Tekstilna industrija)*	Textile mill products	22
	Apparel and related products	23
Hides and leather products *(Industrija kože i obuće)*	Leather and tanning	31
	Apparel and related products	23
Rubber products *(Industrija gume)*	Rubber and miscellaneous plastic products	30
Food products *(Prehrambena industrija)*	Food and kindred products	20
Printing and publishing *(Grafička industrija)*	Printing and publishing	27
Tobacco products *(Industrija duvana)*	Tobacco manufactures	21

SOURCES: SZS, *Industrija 1971* (Belgrade: SZS, 1972); and U.S., Bureau of the Census, *Statistical Abstract of the United States, 1974* (Washington, D.C.: Government Printing Office, 1974).

APPENDIX D

The Crude Materials Index Sample

In the analysis of the reasons for the failure of the regional development program, a special index of crude materials output was developed to test the hypothesis that production of these materials rose more rapidly in the less developed regions than elsewhere. This index was based on the output of certain products deemed to represent production of nonfabricated or semiprocessed goods. The list of products used in the index is given in table D-1.

TABLE D-1

PRODUCTS INCLUDED IN CRUDE MATERIALS INDEX

Code	Name	Code	Name
11–0101	Hydroelectric power	21–0100	Stone blocks for building and cutting
11–0102	Thermoelectric power		
12–0101	Anthracite	21–0200	Pulverized stone, marble, sand, and gravel
12–0102	Brown coal		
12–0103	Lignite	21–0700	Crude gypsum
		21–0800	Calcined gypsum
13–0100	Crude petroleum	21–0900	Unslaked lime
13–0200	Natural gas	22–0100	Sawn conifers
14–0100	Iron ore, over 42% Fe	22–0200	Sawn oak
14–0200	Iron ore, less than 42% Fe	22–0300	Sawn beech
		22–0400	Other sawn timber
15–0300	Bauxite	22–0500	Sawn sleepers
15–0400	Lead-zinc ore		
15–0502	Chromium ore II	24–0100	Fibers, hemp
15–0700	Manganese ore	24–0300	Yarn, cotton type
15–2300	Zinc (crude and powder)	24–0400	Sewing thread
15–2400	Crude lead	24–0700	Woolen yarn
15–2600	Antimony regulus	24–1200	Yarn, natural silk
15–3100	Gold	24–1600	Yarn, flax
15–3200	Mercury	24–1700	Yarn, hemp
15–3300	Bismuth	24–1800	Yarn, jute
16–0100	Quartz sand, stone, and flour for glass	25–0100	Sole leather
		25–0300	Whole hides
16–0200	Crude fireclay	25–0900	Furs
16–0300	Crude magnesite		
16–0500	Crude feldspar	27–0100	Flour, white cereals
16–0800	Crude barites	27–2700	Sugar
16–0900	Asbestos fibers except meal and padding	29–0100	Cured tobacco
16–1000	Caustic magnesite, calcined		
16–1100	Sea salt		
16–1200	Salt from brine		

APPENDIX E

Measuring Structural Change in Output

The index of structural change derives from consideration of the classic index number problem.[1] That problem arises because the outputs of all commodities do not grow at equal rates; that is, growth in output is generally accompanied by structural change. Laspeyres and Paasche output index numbers like those used in this study estimate growth in productive capacity by effectively treating the commodity bundles of the base and given years as if their compositions were the same, a procedure which gives rise to well-known measurement biases.[2] These biases depend, among other things, on the extent of structural change in output that occurs over the period in question. It is desirable to have a measure of structural change based on the same theoretical foundations as the index numbers commonly used to measure the rate of growth of output. The measure also should abstract from the overall growth rate measured by those index numbers. The measure used in chapter 7 is developed in this appendix.

Several approaches to measuring structural change have been suggested. One approach is based on the observation that structural change can occur only if there are differences in growth rates among the various elements of the output bundles. In 1969, Zoltan Roman proposed using the (weighted) average of the ratios of individual branch growth rates to the average growth rate for the economy as a whole.[3] Similarly, several Yugoslav economists have measured structural change by the standard deviation of the (unweighted) growth rates of the individual components of the output vector.[4] Although there might be a case for measuring structural change in terms of divergence in growth rates, there is no analytic relation between such a measure and a production index or the process of growth itself. Furthermore, as is readily seen by appropriate substitution in the formulas, neither of the measures mentioned here is invariant to homogeneous growth in the output bundle, and hence neither is independent of changes in the overall growth rate unaccompanied by structural change. Consequently, both are analytically weak.

A second approach enlists information theory concepts. Industrial output for any period can be characterized as a vector whose coordinates are the quantities of the goods produced. Changes in the coordinates of an output vector—i.e., changes in the relative quantities of goods—may be taken to indicate "surprise" in the information theory conception of the term. As this approach has been practiced, the basic data are shares of aggregated output values (industry branches and sectors of the economy) rather than physical outputs; hence, the elements necessarily are expressed in value terms. These shares are then used in the calculation of entropy in a way similar to that in which the information content of bits of information enters the entropy measure familiar in information theory.[5] Its novelty notwithstanding, this approach seems weak. Not only is there little link to the theory of growth or the index numbers measuring it, but the basic concept seems odd: it is the absence of structural change that would be surprising, not its presence.

Finally, brief mention may be made of another measure based on output value shares. This is the simplest of all approaches: for each of two output vectors, rank the elements by their shares; correlate the ranks; and measure the degree of structural change by the inverse of the rank correlation coefficient.[6] Although this measure is distantly related to the new measure proposed below, there is little theoretical justification for it, and it is subject to the weaknesses of rank correlation methods.

THE MEASURE EMPLOYED IN CHAPTER SEVEN

This measure is based on the fact that the structure of output in any period can be described by a vector whose coordinates are the quantities of outputs that form the basis for calculating the index numbers. In measuring economic growth with Laspeyres or Paasche index numbers, the commodity bundles described by these vectors are assumed to lie on the production possibility surfaces. Economic growth corresponds to an outward shift of those surfaces, and the extent of that growth is estimated by index numbers calculated by weighting the elements of the output vectors. If growth in output is measured this way, structural change can be measured by the angle between the two vectors and calculated by the linear algebra formula for the cosine of the angle between vectors.

This measurement may be illustrated by the two-commodity case (the extension to any number of commodities is simple). In figure E-1, the original or base-period output bundle is represented by vector *OP* (which corresponds to

FIGURE E-1

CHANGE IN THE STRUCTURE OF OUTPUT

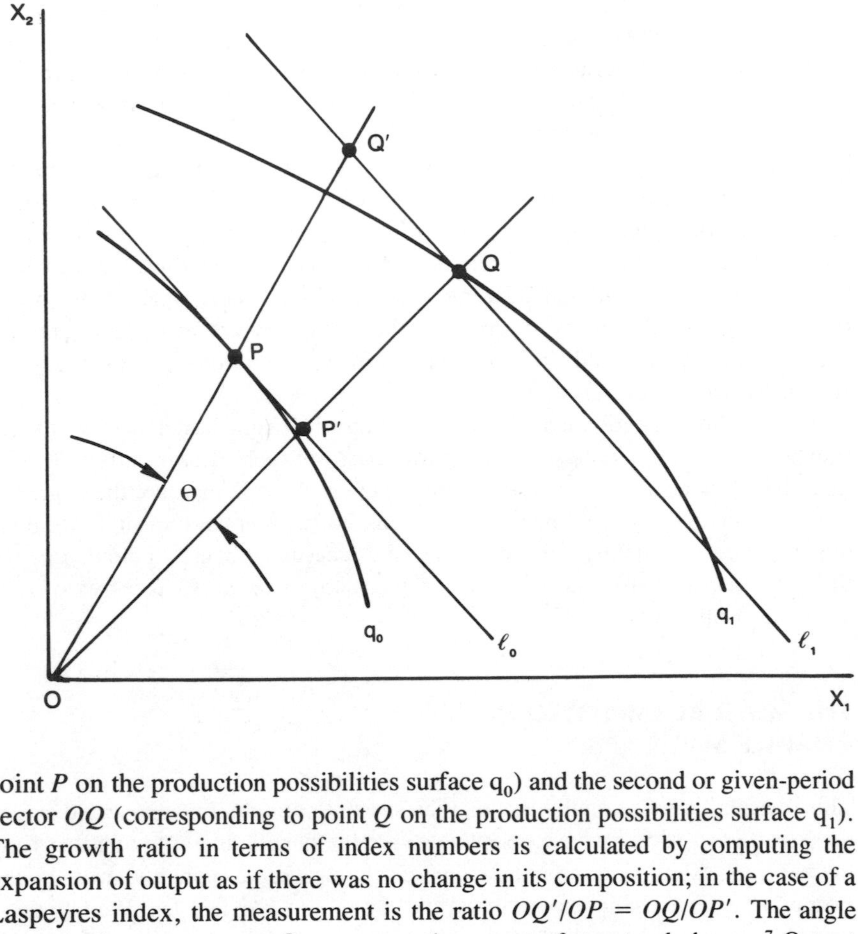

point P on the production possibilities surface q_0) and the second or given-period vector OQ (corresponding to point Q on the production possibilities surface q_1). The growth ratio in terms of index numbers is calculated by computing the expansion of output as if there was no change in its composition; in the case of a Laspeyres index, the measurement is the ratio $OQ'/OP = OQ/OP'$. The angle between the two vectors, Θ, measures the extent of structural change.[7] Output bundles lying on the same ray from the origin have the same relative composition. Thus, for any two output bundle compositions, the angle between vectors is the same; this means that it is invariant to equiproportional changes in the growth rates of the individual commodities and hence to the overall growth rate if the commodity composition of output in the two bundles remains the same.[8] On the other hand, it is clear that the same measured growth rate could, depending on the actual movement of the production possibilities surface, correspond to different degrees of measured structural change, since any given-period output along the "index frontier" ℓ_1 (which would result from different movements of the production possibilities surface) would give the same measured growth rate but different measured structural change.

The growth process can therefore be characterized by two parameters computed from the same physical output data: a production index measuring growth, and a structural change index, the angle between successive output vectors. These parameters yield derivative measures. For example, the structural component of total change in output can be calculated by the ratio of the vector distance *PQ* (readily computed by use of the law of cosines) to the vector distance *PQ'*. This measure is reported in chapter 7 as ρ. If there is no structural change (so that expansion takes place along the ray *OP*), the value of this measure is unity. Otherwise, it is greater than 1.0, and the larger its magnitude, the greater is structural change relative to the change in measured output alone. In addition, an index of total change in output, denoted by γ, can be calculated as the sum of the vector lengths *OP* and *PQ* divided by the base year vector length *OP*. For any given growth ratio measured between two years, the measure γ will be larger than that ratio if there is structural change, and the greater the structural change, the greater will be the difference between γ and the growth ratio. If there is no structural change between two years, the ordinary growth ratio and γ will be equal.

The structural change index is intended for use with conventional Paasche and Laspeyres output indexes. Thus, the structural change index, like those output indexes, has a fixed sample; once the sample is chosen for the base period, the same sample is used for the given period. Therefore, in order to make the interpretations suggested below, the same level of detail, to the extent that ordinary measurement problems allow, must be used in both base and given period samples. However, the properties of the index and its relationship to Laspeyres and Paasche indexes defined for the same sample remain the same regardless of the level of detail used. Changes in level of detail between base and given periods or differences in level of detail between the structural change index and the corresponding Laspeyres or Paasche index cause unpredictable changes in those relationships. The interpretation of the structural change index in such cases becomes obscure.

The vector angle index has several other important properties. First, for many purposes it is convenient and useful to express outputs in value, rather than physical, terms. The vector angle can still be used as an index of structural change if this is done, but its relation to the production indexes then becomes indirect. Second, the calculated vector angle is the same whether physical quantities or output values, on the one hand, or their respective shares on the other, are used in the computation.[9] Third, the angle between two output vectors is inversely related to the covariance of the elements of the two vectors—a relationship that is clearly desirable—and directly related to the variance of the elements of the base-period vector.[10] The last property is desirable for measuring structural change in a single country because it implies that measured change for different initial output bundle compositions is different even with the same set of individual growth rates (a property not shared by the standard deviation measure).

Vector angles measuring structural change over a series of years or subperiods are not additive in the sense that the sum of angles for a sequence of years or subperiods generally equals the angle measured between the vectors defining the first and last years of the period. Structural changes in intermediate years define vectors whose movements in the output space are complex since the directions of change, in the sense of the relative growth rates of different components of the output vector, are not likely to be the same in each subperiod. The output vector conceivably could return to its original composition at the end of a series of structural changes; if so, the vector angle between base and final year outputs would be zero. Since the values of the angles for intermediate years cannot, by the definition of their measurement, be negative, their sum could not be zero unless each was identically zero.

The relation of the measure of structural change to the bias in growth rates measured by conventional index numbers can be described qualitatively. It is not true that there is a uniform positive relationship between the index of structural change and the degree to which a Laspeyres index overstates growth in capacity to produce the base-year output mix. A uniform relationship would hold only over a range of the value of the structural change index, and that range cannot be specified on a priori grounds because the degree of overstatement of the Laspeyres eventually declines as the mix changes.[11] However, it is possible to delineate the range over which there is a positive relationship: as long as the value of the Laspeyres index exceeds that of the Paasche for the same period, there is a positive relation between the value of the index of structural change and the bias in the Laspeyres index.[12] Mutatis mutandis, the same statements hold for the bias in the Paasche index.

Finally, international comparisons of structural change based on vector angles observed in different countries must be treated with caution. It is highly unlikely that the structure of output is the same, even in value terms or shares of output, in two countries at a particular time or at two different times chosen as base periods for the two countries, and simple comparison of the vector angles for the two is thus likely to be misleading. Provided that the number of elements in the output vector for the base year is the same in the two countries, the extent of incomparability between structural change as measured by the two vector angles may be determined by comparing the coefficients of variation in the base year output vectors used in the computation. The smaller the difference in coefficients of variation, the smaller the degree of incomparability.[13] Given the vector angle for the country and if the number of elements is the same, the vector angle for the second country will be over- or understated as its coefficient of variation is greater or smaller than that for the first country.[14]

Notes

CHAPTER ONE

1. Milovan Djilas, *The Unperfect Society: Beyond the New Class* (New York: Harcourt, Brace & World, 1969), pp. 220–23. In his account of how he arrived at the idea of workers' self-management, Djilas does not document Marx's discussion of this idea. Numerous allusions, however, to the idea of worker control of the workplace can be found in Marx, and the idea has clear connections with overcoming the alienation of the worker in the capitalist system. There are repeated references in Marx to control of the workplace by society, meaning the workers. The famous Marxian utopian vision of a man being a hunter in the morning, a fisherman in the afternoon, a shepherd in the evening, and a critic after dinner is prefaced by the condition that society regulates production (*The German Ideology*, as reprinted in *The Marx-Engels Reader*, ed. Robert C. Tucker [New York: W. W. Norton, 1972], p. 124). Supervision by cooperative labor is also advocated in Marx's "Inaugural Address of the Working Men's International Association" (ibid., p. 380), and the general idea—along with specification of income distribution that could well have formed the pattern for the actual Yugoslav system—can be found in *Critique of the Gotha Programme* (ibid., pp. 385–86). The general idea of cooperative effort by the proletariat is advanced as part of the program in the *Manifesto of the Communist Party* (ibid., p. 353). As a longtime Marxist, Djilas's thinking undoubtedly was conditioned by Marx's vision of the end of the capitalist order and its replacement in industry by an organization more political than economic. The precise idea of workers' self-management was not, of course, delineated by Marx.

2. Branko Horvat, "Business Cycles in Yugoslavia," *Eastern European Economics* 9 (1971): 171.

3. See Ivan Paj, "The Development of the System of Distribution of the Social Product and Net Income," *Yugoslav Survey* new series 11 (1970): 65–88, for a concise description of changes in the system of distribution of enterprise net income.

4. Dennison Rusinow, *The Yugoslav Experiment, 1948–1974* (Berkeley and Los Angeles: University of California Press, 1977), pp. 103–4.

5. Ibid., p. 110. See also Svetozar A. Pejovich, *The Market-Planned Economy of Yugoslavia* (Minneapolis: University of Minnesota Press, 1966), pp. 97–98.

6. Rusinow, *The Yugoslav Experiment*, pp. 110, 121.

7. Ibid., p. 125.

8. For discussion, see ibid., pp. 145–48.

9. Laid down at the Eighth Congress of the League of Yugoslav Communists, December 1964. See ibid., pp. 165–66.

10. Ibid., p. 329.

11. Calculated from Savezni zavod za statistiku (hereafter SZS), *Statistički godišnjak SFRJ 1965* (Belgrade: SZS, 1965), p. 124.

12. Calculated from the source given in note 11; SZS, *Statistički godišnjak SFRJ 1968* (Belgrade: SZS, 1968), p. 111; idem, *Statistički godišnjak SFRJ 1971* (Belgrade: SZS, 1971), p. 105; and idem, *Statistički godišnjak SFRJ 1963* (Belgrade: SZS, 1963), p. 122.

13. The reform also transferred the turnover tax from producers of intermediate goods to sellers of final consumption goods. The government's role in the economy was further reduced by eliminating its direct influence on investment (ratifying, in effect, the separation of the government from investment that had been initiated by the abolition of the General Investment Fund in 1963) and by terminating or reducing a number of subsidies and rebates for exports and in support of weak industries. For the law defining the new terms of organization and operation of enterprises, see "Osnovni zakon o poduzećima," *Službeni list* 1965, no. 17: 813–39. For a succinct discussion of the reforms, see Rusinow, *The Yugoslav Experiment*, pp. 176ff.

14. The ratio of the average fraction of national income paid in personal incomes for the years 1966–71 to that for 1961–64 (omitting the transition year of 1965) was 1.54. The corresponding ratio for payments to the funds was 1.31. There was also considerably greater variation in the fraction paid to the funds over the whole period, suggesting that payments to the funds, especially the business fund, were, in effect, residuals remaining after all other payments.

15. See Eirik G. Furubotn and Svetozar A. Pejovich, "Property Rights and the Behavior of the Firm in a Socialist State: The Example of Yugoslavia," *Zeitschrift für Nationalökonomie* 30 (1970): 431–54; and Pejovich, "A Note on Bank Credit and the Investment Behavior of the Firm in Socialism," *Jahrbuch der Wirtschaft Osteuropas* 5 (1974): 155–70.

16. See Pejovich, "A Note on Bank Credit," pp. 167–68.

17. See Rusinow, *The Yugoslav Experiment*, pp. 173–75, 208–9; see also chap. 8 above for further discussion of these reforms.

18. Joseph T. Bombelles, *Economic Development of Communist Yugoslavia, 1947–1964* (Stanford: Hoover Institution Press, 1968), p. 67.

19. Dušan Dragosavac et al., eds., *Aktuelni problemi privrednih kretanja i ekonomske politike Jugoslavije* (Zagreb: Informator, 1968), p. 88.

20. The account in Dragosavac contains a biting criticism of this approach to price reform. Besides the economic irrationality of making all prices, including those of nontraded goods, conform to world market prices, Dragosavac criticizes the use of the artificial Yugoslav exchange rate as a means for establishing dinar prices. He also points out that only a small fraction of Yugoslav commodities (corresponding to about 5 percent of the value of gross product) entered into foreign trade; thus, only for that small fraction would there be direct evidence

on prices relative to other commodities traded on world markets. He observes that the process of recalculating the prices took over 2½ years, by which time the calculated prices were already obsolete. (See ibid., pp. 88-90.)

21. Ibid., pp. 92-93.

22. Bombelles, *Economic Development*, pp. 65, 205; Dragosavac, *Aktuelni problemi*, p. 90. This general policy was intended to stimulate industrial growth by making the production of highly fabricated goods profitable. It also had the effect of exacerbating regional antagonisms, ironically enough in both developed and less developed areas. In Croatia, strong interest in processing industries motivated leaders to urge the freeing of prices; in the less developed areas, the importance of raw materials industries created resentment of the price policy.

23. For example, the prices were sufficiently distorted that in some cases costs of materials were greater than the price allowed for the final product. Some enterprises demanded price increases because they were producing a product identical to that of another enterprise, but were allowed only a lower price. Enterprises evaded the controls by introducing "new" products, presumably differing from existing ones only in minor detail. Arguments were made that the price of some products should be raised because world market prices had changed. For discussion, see Dragosavac, *Aktuelni problemi*, p. 92.

24. For discussion, see Branko Horvat, *Privredni sistem i ekonomska politika Jugoslavije* (Belgrade: Institut ekonomskih nauka, 1970), pp. 68-76; Nikola Čobeljić, *Privreda Jugoslavije: Rast, struktura i funkcionisanje* (Belgrade: Savremena administracija, 1974), pp. 172-221; Velimir Vasić, *Ekonomska politika Jugoslavije* (Belgrade: Savremena administracija, 1970), pp. 372-92.

25. Čobeljić, *Privreda Jugoslavije*, p. 221.

26. Horvat, *Privredni sistem*, p. 73.

27. Uroš Dujšin, "Sistem ekonomskih odnosa s inozenstvom," in *Aktuelni problemi privrednog razvoja i privrednog sistema Jugoslavije*, ed. Dragomir Vojnić (Zagreb: Informator, 1971), p. 97.

28. See Čobeljić, *Privreda Jugoslavije*, p. 223.

29. Rusinow, *The Yugoslav Experiment*, p. 130.

30. Total employment (all sectors) in Kosovo, Montenegro, and Macedonia accounted for 10.8 percent of the Yugoslav total in 1961, but the number of persons seeking work in those areas accounted for 26.8 percent of the total seeking work in the whole country. If Bosnia-Hercegovina is included with Kosovo, Montenegro, and Macedonia, the figures are 24.3 and 37.3 percent, respectively. In 1971, for Kosovo, Montenegro, and Macedonia alone, these figures were 11.7 and 30.3 percent; including Bosnia-Hercegovina, they were 25.2 and 40.8 percent. (Calculated from data in SZS, *Statistički godišnjak SFRJ 1962* [Belgrade: SZS, 1962], p. 337; idem, *Statistički godišnjak SFRJ 1967* [Belgrade: SZS, 1967], pp. 338, 352; idem, *Statistički godišnjak SFRJ 1972* [Belgrade: SZS, 1972], pp. 354, 366.) The data for employment are as of September 30 of each year, while those for persons seeking work are as of December 30; so the comparisons are not precise.

31. Čobeljić, *Privreda Jugoslavije*, pp. 222-23.

32. Ibid.

33. For example, Bombelles notes that in 1964, two enterprises in Slovenia together produced a total of 361 cars, and the total number of buses produced

by three Serbian enterprises was 388 (Bombelles, *Economic Development*, pp. 139–41). Examples of this kind can be found even in 1972: a Macedonian factory producing 461 auto and truck bodies, five Croation producers making a total of 414 marine engines, a Montenegrin enterprise with a total yearly output of 45,000 clothes washers. (Data from SZS, *Industrija 1974* [Belgrade: SZS, 1975], pp. 33, 40.) For a discussion of excess capacity in industry, see Miloš Bogdanović, *Ekonomika industrije SFRJ* (Belgrade: Privredno finansijski zavod, 1971), pp. 90–91.

34. As a practical matter, the authority of the director and his staff overwhelms that of the workers' council. The director is usually better trained and more highly educated than the workers on the council. He also has the great advantage of superior knowledge of the operations of the enterprise, both day-to-day and long-term, and within the enterprise and in its external relations with other organizations—banks, suppliers, customers. For a discussion of the relations among different groups in the management of Yugoslav enterprises, see Josip Obradović, *Workers' Participation in Yugoslavia: Theory and Research*, University of South Carolina, Institute of International Studies, Occasional Paper (Columbia: Institute of International Studies, n.d.).

35. Reforms late in the period of this study introduced the so-called organizations of united workers (OOUR) in all types of institutions, including educational, medical, governmental, and others. With these reforms, the concept of "worker" was effectively broadened to include intellectuals, clerks, nurses, and the like. Even in the industrial enterprise, the term embraced all enterprise members, including clerical workers, designers, engineers, and other white-collar workers along with the production, maintenance, and other blue-collar workers.

CHAPTER TWO

1. On occasion, specific enterprises were directed to supply fixed quantities of certain items to other industrial branches. Some, but not all, of this was in connection with the supply of metals for defense-related purposes. This practice persisted at least until 1965. (See "Naredbu o obaveznoj isporuci bakra, aluminija, olova, cinka, srebra, bizmuta i žive određenim kategorijama potrošača u 1963. godinu," *Službeni list* 1963, no. 4: 71–72; "Naredbu o obaveznoj isporuci bakra, aluminija, olova, cinku, srebra, bizmuta i žive određenim kategorijama potrošača u 1964. godinu," *Službeni list* 1964, no. 9: 221–22; and "Naredbu o obaveznoj isporuci elektrolitnog bakra, elektrolitnog cinku u bloku, kadmija, cink-lima, rafiniranog olova u bloku, srebra, aluminija u bloku i metalne žive za potrebe Jugoslavenske narodne armije u 1965. godinu," *Službeni list* 1965, No. 24: 1,060.)

2. For discussion and evidence on this point, see Eugene Zaleski, *Planning for Economic Growth in the Soviet Union, 1918–1932* (Chapel Hill: University of North Carolina Press, 1971); and idem, *Stalinist Planning for Economic Growth, 1933–1952* (Chapel Hill: University of North Carolina Press, forthcoming).

3. Nicholas Mirkovich, ed., *Jugoslav Postwar Reconstruction Papers*, 4 vols., mimeographed (New York: Yugoslavia, Office of Reconstruction and Economic Affairs, 1942–43).

4. See "Društveni plan privrednog razvoja Jugoslavije od 1957. do 1961. godine" (hereafter Plan 2), *Službeni list* 1957, no. 53: 1,030; "Društveni plan privrednog razvitka Jugoslavije od 1961. do 1965. godine" (hereafter Plan 3), *Službeni list* 1960, no. 53: 975; and "Društveni plan razvoja Jugoslavije od 1966. do 1970. godine" (hereafter Plan 4), *Službeni list* 1966, No. 28: 479.

5. The 1957-61 Five-Year Plan called for the industrial sector to have 41.2 percent of total social sector investment funds in 1961; the 1961-65 plan specified 48.0 percent for industry in 1965; and the 1966-70 plan set the share for the whole period at 50.7 percent. (See Plan 2, p. 1,032; Plan 3, p. 978; and Plan 4, p. 499.)

6. See Plan 4, pp. 473, 491-93.

7. Plan 2, pp. 1032-33.

8. See, e.g., Plan 3, pp. 979-80; Plan 4, pp. 477-78.

9. For the data underlying these statements, see Mirkovich, *Postwar Reconstruction*, vol. 4.

10. Because "firm" might not be equal to "plant," the data in the table may exaggerate the scale of plant operations. On this score, the average size in leather and leather products seem especially suspect.

11. For example, annual superphosphate production capacity was about 200,000 tons, but actual output in 1939 was only 23,800 tons (Mirkovich, *Postwar Reconstruction*, vol. 4, part 5, pp. 1-3). Only six of eight glass works were in operation; the annual production capacity of five of these was 2.0 million $m.^2$ of flat glass, but only 1.0 million $m.^2$ were produced in 1933, and 1.4 million $m.^2$ in 1936 (ibid., vol. 4, part 8, p. 5). Wheat and sugar mills were operating below capacity, as were breweries (ibid., vol. 4, part 3, pp. 2-5). It might be noted that measurements of the growth of production based on 1939 output—as are some Yugoslav indexes—measure from an evident cyclical trough and may therefore be misleading.

12. In the immediate prewar period, Yugoslavia was first among European countries in the production of lead and antimony ore, second in copper ore and chromite, third in crude copper production, silver, and magnesite, fourth in bauxite and lignite, and fifth in gold. It also was an important producer of manganese, pyrites, iron ore, and zinc and aluminum. (Ibid., vol. 3, part 1, p. 1.)

13. Yugoslavia in 1939 and Russia in 1913 share a number of similarities. In both, industrial development had begun, but was not well advanced; both could be termed preindustrial economies. In both, there was extensive state intervention and direct participation in industrial development. In both, there existed an industrial base and the nucleus, at least, of a trained labor force when the new regime came to power. In both, the level of industrial development that had been reached was financed with the help of large amounts of foreign capital.

14. For estimates of damage, see UNRRA, *Agriculture and Food in Yugoslavia*, Operational Analysis Papers, No. 23 (London: UNRRA, European Regional Office, 1947), pp. 1-7. The statement about transportation losses is from Jozo Tomasevich, "Postwar Foreign Economic Relations," in *Yugoslavia*, ed. Robert J. Kerner (Berkeley and Los Angeles: University of California Press, 1949), p. 392.

15. Estimates of the value of reparations and other aid received, not to mention the damages suffered, are extremely difficult to make. Data on reparations payments expressed in so-called 1938 reichsmarks can be found in Inter-

Allied Reparation Agency, *Report of the Secretary General for the Year 1949* (Brussels: IARA, 1950), annex 4, p. 86. Conversion of these values to an appropriate dinar figure would be extremely difficult, and, in any event, the data were probably incomplete. The total given is RM 87.9 million. Besides reparations, Yugoslavia received economic aid, notably from UNRRA. Tomasevich estimates that aid amounted to the equivalent of about 23 percent of 1938 Yugoslav national income ("Postwar Foreign Economic Relations," p. 393). The Yugoslav economist Vladimir Stipetić puts total postwar foreign assistance at U.S. $4 billion, including UNRRA, P.L. 480, technical aid, and other forms of assistance ("Ekonomska odnosi s inovenstvom," in *Aktuelni problemi privrednog razvoja i privrednog sistema Jugoslavie*, ed. Dragomir Vojnić [Zagreb: Informator, 1971], p. 250.)

16. 1931 census data from United Nations, *Demographic Yearbook, 1948* (Lake Success, N.Y.: U.N., 1949), pp. 180–81. 1948 census data from SZS, *Konačni rezultati popisa stanovništva od 15 Marta 1948. godine* (Belgrade: SZS, 1954), pp. 2–5.

17. The outlines of industrialization policy are drawn from the five-year plans on the assumption that the 1957–61 plan reflected an endorsement of previous policy rather than a basic change in it. The implications of this assumption are consistent with observed growth patterns.

18. The discussion that follows in the text is based on statements in Plan 2, pp. 1,037ff., Plan 3, p. 978, and Plan 4, pp. 499ff. In Plans 2 and 3, branch priorities are given very clearly. In Plan 4, priorities must be deduced from the context of the statements, and the relative growth rates envisaged by branches. Generally, however, the pattern of priorities in Plan 4 seems fully consistent with those established in the two preceding plans.

19. Mirkovich, *Postwar Reconstruction*, vol. 3, part 3; and Robert Lee Wolff, *The Balkans in Our Time* (Cambridge: Harvard University Press, 1956), p. 331.

20. For discussions of foreign trade problems, see Branko Horvat, *Privredni sistem i ekonomska politika Jugoslavije* (Belgrade: Institut ekonomskih nauka, 1970), pp. 68–76; idem, *The Yugoslav Economic System* (White Plains, N.Y.: International Arts and Sciences Press, 1976), pp. 188–205; Vinod Dubey, *Yugoslavia: Development with Decentralization* (Baltimore: Johns Hopkins University Press, 1975), chaps. 12 and 13; and Velimir Vasić, *Ekonomska politika Jugoslavije* (Belgrade: Savremena administracija, 1970), pp. 372ff.

21. Foreign exchange controls and bilateral clearing with the East make any effort to quantify precisely the relative shares of East and West in any aspect of Yugoslav foreign trade hopeless, especially where such heterogeneous items as machinery are involved. However, OECD data, cited in Dubey, clearly show the general proportions of the trade (*Yugoslavia*, p. 406). According to these data, in 1960 EEC, EFTA, and the United States accounted for 78 percent of total Yugoslav imports of nonelectrical machinery, 71 percent of electrical machinery, and 64 percent of transport equipment. In 1970, the percentages were 85, 82, and 72, respectively.

22. See, e.g., Nikola Čobeljić, *Privreda Jugoslavije: Rast, struktura i funkcionisanje* (Belgrade: Savremena administracija, 1974), p. 179; and Vasić, *Ekonomska politika*, p. 376.

23. Borijsav Srebrić, "Neki problemi usavršavanja metoda i mehanisma razvoja nerazvijenih područja u Jugoslaviji," in *Ubrzanje rasta Jugoslavenske priv-*

rede u uslovima stabilnosti, ed. Savez ekonomista Jugoslavije, Centralni odbor (Zagreb: Informator, 1969), p. 84. Prior to the 1957–61 Plan, no special emphasis was given to regional development, although issues pertaining to it were treated in the overall development plans.

24. In this context, to be less efficient means to have a higher incremental capital-output ratio. The question whether the less developed regions were, in fact, less efficient in this sense is controversial and is discussed in chapter 10. However, even if adjustments are made to take into account certain qualifications urged by defenders of the less developed regions, the statement in the text appears to hold true.

25. For evidence on this point, see chap. 6.

26. Transportation services and the activities of trade organizations are included directly in national income, but education and administrative, professional, personal, and housing services are included only indirectly. For explanation, see, e.g., SZS, *Privredni bilans Jugoslavije 1962–1965*, Studije, analize i prikazi, no. 29 (Belgrade: SZS, 1966). According to an estimate for 1956–67, aggregate national income computed by their methods was about the same as it would have been if computed by U.N. methods. See Gojko Grđić, *Sistem narodnoprivrednih bilansa* (Belgrade: Institut za ekonomiska istraživanja, 1967), pp. 29–30.

27. The actual shares of social product (national income plus depreciation) paid to the "nonproductive" sector were 33.7 percent in 1952, 29.4 percent in 1961, and 31.9 percent in 1971. These payments constituted about 70 percent of the total incomes of these sectors in the same years; the balance of the incomes came from direct payments by citizens and from intrasectoral transfers. The data were taken from SZS, *Privredni bilansi Jugoslavije 1952–1962*, Studije, analiza i prikazi, no. 19 (Belgrade: SZS, 1963), pp. 25–27; and idem, *Privredni bilansi Jugoslavije 1966–1971*, Studije, analize i prikazi, no. 61 (Belgrade: SZS, 1973), pp. 65–67. A second potential cause of incomparability lies in the foreign trade accounts, in which the trade balance was entered at the official rate of exchange. As that rate rarely reflected the actual rate of exchange at which transactions were made and since there was a complex multiple exchange-rate system in effect for much of that period and an almost equally complex tariff scheme for the rest of it, the treatment of foreign trade is inadequate. Since trade is relatively important in the Yugoslav economy, this shortcoming could have important repercussions on the sectoral distribution of net output. However, even an aggregate estimate of the effects of the methods for calculating foreign trade on the national income accounts is not possible in view of the complexities of the problem and the paucity of appropriate data with which to work.

28. Calculated from data in SZS, *Statistički godišnjak FNRJ 1957* (Belgrade: SZS, 1957), p. 131; idem, *Statistički godišnjak SFRJ 1965* (Belgrade: SZS, 1965), p. 118; and idem, *Statistički godišnjak SFRJ 1972* (Belgrade: SZS, 1972), p. 102.

29. In chap. 6, a measure of structural change in industrial output that has the same theoretical basis as conventional indexes of growth in output is presented.

30. See chap. 6 for a discussion of the difficulties of international comparisons with the new measure presented in that chapter.

31. According to the official index of agricultural production, the annual rate of growth between 1952 and 1969 (calculated between five-year averages centered on those two years in order to reduce the impact of harvest year fluctuations) was about 4.5 percent. The corresponding annual growth rate for industrial output, according to official indexes, was over 10 percent. See SZS, *Statistički godišnjak FNRJ* and *Statistički godišnjak SFRJ*, various issues.

32. The available data are not adequate for computing sectoral output shares for the prewar period, largely because comparable data for national income are not available. The ratio of the share of agriculture to that of industry and mining in 1939 can be estimated by multiplying the 1952 share ratio by the ratio of the agricultural and industrial output indexes for the period 1939 to 1952. For agriculture, a five-year average of the index values, centered on 1952, was used to reduce the influence of harvest year fluctuations. The actual ratio calculated in this manner was 2.39. The data for the agricultural index were obtained from SZS, *Jugoslavija 1945–1964: Statistički pregled* (Belgrade: SZS, 1965), p. 99; the data for the industrial output index were taken from SZS, *Statistički godišnjak SFRJ 1972* (Belgrade: SZS, 1972), p. 161.

33. The definition of active person is a broad one, including all persons in the usual occupations, persons working at home to augment family incomes, persons working part-time, and those doing odd jobs. There seems to be no way to convert the census data to something like full-time equivalents; so the data in the table are only rough estimates. Because industrial employment is more likely to be on a full-time basis than employment in other sectors, it is likely that its share is understated by these figures.

34. SZS, *Statistički godišnjak SFRJ 1971* (Belgrade: SZS, 1971), pp. 98–99.

35. SZS, *Statistički godišnjak SFRJ*, various issues.

36. Politically, the handicraft sector was undoubtedly viewed as a liability, both ideologically and strategically. Ideologically, there were many private producers operating small-scale enterprises. From a strategic point of view, the economic independence that might have been gained by the operators of these enterprises could have been viewed as potentially harmful to the regime.

37. In 1954, handicraft operations were carried out mainly by individual artisans employing single assistants; the average number of employees per handicraft firm was just over one. (SZS, *Statistički godišnjak FNRJ 1955* [Belgrade: SZS, 1955], p. 160). Despite the decline of this sector over the following years, the average size of the enterprises rose; in 1969, the corresponding figure was three. (SZS, *Statistički godišnjak SFRJ 1971*, p. 174.)

38. See chap. 9 for further discussion of scale economies in the industrial sector.

39. The handicraft sector includes cooperatives and private artisans, who may employ up to five persons. Although private handicraft sector shops must provide their own capital, cooperatives may have the use of capital provided by the state. The main practical distinction between social sector handicraft cooperatives and industrial enterprises is size. In 1969, the number of employees per industrial enterprise averaged just over 590, while the corresponding figure for the social handicraft sector was about 65 (calculated from SZS, *Statistički godišnjak SFRJ 1971*, pp. 153–54, 174.) The legal distinction between cooperatives and industrial enterprises lies in the form of organization; the rules under which cooperatives may be formed and operated effectively limit their size.

40. In social sector handicraft organizations, 78 percent of the employees in

metal products were employed in services; in electrical products, the corresponding figure was 82 percent. Similar data for private sector employment are not available. (See SZS, *Statistički godišnjak SFRJ 1973* [Belgrade: SZS, 1973], p. 186.)

CHAPTER THREE

1. For a description of the methodology, see SZS, *Indeks fizičkog obima industrijske proizvodnje: Metodologija i ponderacioni sistem*, Metodološki materijali, no. 82 (Belgrade: SZS, 1957).

2. SZS, *Nomenklatura proizvoda za godišnji izveštaj industrije*, Metodološki materijali, no. 192 (Belgrade: SZS, 1969).

3. Examples include managers' attitudes toward reporting output, sanctions for detected inaccuracies, probabilities of detection, and alternate uses of their time. Costs to the authorities of enforcing uniform reporting standards must be high.

4. Large variations exist in this respect. For example, in 1968 there were three enterprises in the petroleum and petroleum products branch; in that year, there were 243 enterprises in the building materials branch, and the two largest produced only 16 percent of branch value added. See SZS, *Industrijska preduzeća 1969*, Statistički bilten, no. 695 (Belgrade: SZS, 1971).

5. Branch priorities were established on the basis of investment priorities given in the 1957–61 and 1961–65 Five-Year Plans. See "Društveni plan privrednog razvoja Jugoslavije od 1957. do 1961. godine," *Službeni list* 1957, no. 53: 1,029–44; and "Društveni plan privrednog razvitka Jugoslavije od 1961. do 1965. godine," *Službeni list* 1960, no. 53: 969–97. The number of firms in each branch in 1961 was obtained from SZS, *Statistički godišnjak SFRJ 1963* (Belgrade: SZS, 1963), p. 177. Rough rankings of branches for degree of product uniformity and proportion of output produced within the branch were made by the author.

6. Numerically large changes also occurred in the electric power (decline), ferrous metallurgy (increase), metal products (increase), building materials (decrease), textiles (increase), and rubber (increase) branches, but in these cases the changes seemed unlikely to affect monitoring costs materially. Data were obtained from SZS, *Statistički godišnjak FNRJ 1954* (Belgrade: SZS, 1954), p. 149; and SZS, *Statistički godišnjak SFRJ 1973* (Belgrade: SZS, 1973), p. 179.

7. Probably more important for some industry branches was the decline of the handicraft (*zanatsvo*) sector. Apparently most affected were the food, leather, textiles, and metal and electric products branches. For further discussion, see chap. 2.

8. For discussion of Soviet practices, see Gregory Grossman, *Soviet Statistics of Physical Output of Industrial Commodities: Their Compilation and Quality* (Princeton: Princeton University Press, 1960).

9. In 1957, some 503 items were listed; in 1972, the list contained about 2,300 items. See SZS, *Indeks fizičkog obima*, p. 5; and SZS, *Nomenklatura proizvoda za godišnji izveštaj industrije*, Metodološki materijali, no. 203 (Belgrade: SZS, 1972).

10. SZS, *Indeks fizičkog obima.*

11. This point has often been emphasized by Yugoslav economists; see, e.g., Branko Suhina, *Amortizacija osnovnih sredstava*, 2d ed. (Zagreb: Informator, 1970), pp. 33–34. Capital revaluations were carried out in 1953, 1958, 1962, 1966, and 1971; see Nenad Butaš and Mihailo Puletić, *Priručnik o revalorizaciji sredstava organizacija udruženog rada* (Belgrade: Privredni pregled, 1971), pp. 114ff for a description. After 1966, depreciation rates were no longer specified by the central authorities; instead, minimum rates were established, and enterprises were given the authority to set their own rates subject to the minima.

12. For a summary of the evolution of the computation of personal incomes, see Ivan Paj, "The Development of the System of Distribution of the Social Product and Net Income," *Yugoslav Survey* new series 11 (1970): 65–88.

13. This has been true since the 1957 index was calculated. Before then, 1951 weights were used to compute the index for 1939 and for 1946–53, and 1953 weights were used for 1954–56. See SZS, *Indeks fizičkog obima*, pp. 9–11.

14. For example, in the Divisia index. See D. W. Jorgenson and Z. Griliches, "The Explanation of Productivity Change," *Review of Economic Studies* 34 (1967): 249–82; and W. E. Diewert, "Exact and Superlative Index Numbers," *Journal of Econometrics* 4 (1976): 115–45.

15. See G. Warren Nutter, "On Economic Size and Growth," *Journal of Law and Economics* 9 (1966): 163–88, for a development of these properties of fixed weight indexes.

16. As a final oddity, it might be noted that the weights used in the index for a particular year are not derived from the wage and depreciation data of that same year, but rather from the data of two years earlier. The reason for this is obscure.

17. The series used was *Industrija*, published annually by SZS since 1957.

18. Price data were obtained from the *CENE* series published by SZS.

19. Unit-value data were taken from the *Industrijski proizvodi* series published by SZS.

20. Full details on these and other computations made in deriving the weights are given in appendix A.

21. This well-known fact can be shown easily by the use of arc elasticities. If p_0 is the price of the product with no turnover tax and p_1 its equilibrium price after the imposition of the tax, the incidence of the tax can be measured by the ratio of p_1 to p_0. Let the tax rate be 100t percent and η_d denote the demand elasticity and η_s the supply elasticity; then,

$$\frac{p_1}{p_0} = (1 + t)\left[\frac{\eta_s - \eta_d}{\eta_s - \eta_d(1 + t)}\right]$$

The relevant partial derivatives of this ratio are:

$$\frac{\partial\left(\frac{p_1}{p_0}\right)}{\partial \eta_s} = (1 + t)\left\{\frac{-t\eta_d}{\{\eta_s - \eta_d(1 + t)\}^2}\right\} > 0 \quad \text{for } \eta_d < 0$$

and

$$\frac{\partial\left(\frac{p_1}{p_0}\right)}{\partial \eta_d} = (1 + t)\left\{\frac{-t\eta_s}{\{\eta_s - \eta_d(1 + t)\}^2}\right\} < 0 \quad \text{for } \eta_s > 0$$

Thus, the smaller the supply elasticity, or the greater the demand elasticity (i.e., the more negative it is), the smaller is the ratio of p_1 to p_0, and the more heavily does the turnover tax bear on the producer.

22. See Benjamin Ward, "Workers' Management in Yugoslavia," *Journal of Political Economy* 65 (1957): 373–86; and Jaroslav Vanek, *The General Theory of Labor-Managed Enterprises* (Ithaca: Cornell University Press, 1970).

23. During 1961, products whose rates were not otherwise specified were subject to a flat 0.5 percent tax. This flat rate was ignored in the computations.

24. The source used for this purpose is the series *Industrijska preduzeća* published irregularly by SZS.

25. The exception was rubber products, for which only a single ratio could be calculated.

CHAPTER FOUR

1. The 1961 direct weights index grew faster over the period 1952–71 than did the 1952 imputed weights index, in a seeming contradiction of the usual rule that a Laspeyres index grows faster than a Paasche index. This contradiction is only apparent. The samples in these two indexes are different, and those differences account for the difference in growth rates.

2. See appendix C for a rough comparison of the Yugoslav and American classifications.

3. Although the sample and official indexes differ in the growth rates for individual branches, there is considerable agreement between them as far as the ranking of the branches is concerned. Spearman rank correlation coefficients of 0.98, 0.95, and 0.94 were obtained for the branch rankings in the three periods shown in table 7.

4. See Fitzroy MacLean, *The Heretic* (New York: Harper & Row, 1957), p. 61, for Tito's early views on industrialization.

5. In part, the differences may be due to differences in coverage. Owing to lack of data for weights, the sample index coverage of organic chemicals and plastics is limited. Consequently, these relatively fast-growing products, many of which were introduced in the 1960s, may be underweighted in the sample index. On the other hand, the Yugoslav weighting system and the treatment of new products in the index may cause overweighting of the new, fast-growing products, underweighting of the slower-growing inorganic chemicals and more traditional products (paints, pigments, soaps, candles, etc.), and consequent overestimation of the growth rate of the chemicals branch. Although the methodological explanations do not explicitly specify how new products are entered in

the index, it may be inferred that they are introduced continuously, as they appear in the product mix.

6. The discrepancy in growth rates according to the sample and official indexes seems due to much the same set of causes as in the case of chemicals (see note 5, supra).

7. Some average annual growth rates for 1971–75 that indicate the growth in these products are: alumina, 23.1 percent; aluminum ingots, 37.9 percent; aluminum alloys, 13.4 percent; extruded aluminum products, 17.3 percent; zinc (crude and powder), 26.1 percent; refined zinc, 15.6 percent; ferromanganese, 19.3 percent; and ferrochrome, 30.7 percent.

8. The notes to table 8 give details of the product series that constitute each of its groups. Note that not all output series included in the sample indexes previously reported are included in these new groupings. The growth rates shown in tables 8, 9, and 10 are based on indexes calculated with 1961 unit-value weights.

9. The category of other machinery, tools, and equipment includes some machinery and equipment from the electric products branch, as the note to table 8 states. Transportation equipment does not include passenger automobiles because of the absence of output data in the early part of the period. Production of passenger automobiles grew very rapidly from an extremely small base in 1955; from 1961 to 1971 the average annual growth rate exceeded 20 percent. The omission of this series from the transportation equipment group means that this group's growth rate is understated. However, the omission has a relatively small impact on the overall rate for that group and an even less important impact on the industrial production index as a whole because of the small weight the series has in either total. Even by 1971, after a period of very rapid growth, total passenger car production was still only some 112,000 units, of which nearly one-fifth were produced by assembling parts imported from abroad. (See SZS, *Industrija 1973,* Statistički bilten, no. 847 [Belgrade: SZS, 1974], p. 32.)

10. At the end of 1951, there were 0.45 tractors per 1,000 hectares of agricultural land and 84 plows per 1,000 hectares. (See SZS, *Statistički godišnjak FNRJ 1957* [Belgrade: SZS, 1957], p. 163; and idem, *Statistički godišnjak FNRJ 1954* [Belgrade: SZS, 1954], p. 116.) By contrast, in the United States in 1969, there were about 13 tractors per 1,000 hectares of farmland and in 1940 about 7 per 1,000. (See U.S., Bureau of the Census, *Statistical Abstract of the United States: 1974,* 95th ed. [Washington, D.C.: Government Printing Office, 1974], pp. 597, 601, 612.) In making the estimates for the United States, the Bureau of the Census assumed that the number of tractors per nonreporting farm was the same as the number per reporting farm; this may bias the 1940 estimate upward relative to the 1969 estimate.

11. Because of lack of data for 1961 unit values, copper ore mining, whose output grew at an annual average rate of about 11.5 percent, could not be included. Its exclusion could, of course, cause understatement of the growth rate of the branch. However, this understatement is offset by the exclusion, for similar reasons, of chromium ore mining, whose output shrank to almost nothing (an average annual decline of 16.5 percent).

12. Simple regression of the proportional decline in growth rates by branch on the first decade growth rates produced poor results.

13. The growth rate and time periods covered were as follows: Egypt, 13.6 percent for 1953–69; Nicaragua, 10.3 percent for 1953–71; Panama, 10.2 percent for 1953–71; Ecuador, 10.9 percent for 1958–71; Syria, 10.0 percent for 1958–71; and Turkey, 11.1 percent for 1958–66. The coverages of the Nicaraguan and Panamanian indexes were substantially different from those in table 13. The time periods covered by the other four appeared too different from those in the table to warrant their inclusion.

14. An ordering of countries by this indicator produces some anomalies; e.g., in 1952, Canada ranks considerably ahead of the United States (4,581,000 kwh/person compared with 2,943,000), a result probably due to much higher use of other sources of energy in the United States (in fact, per capita consumption of energy in all forms in the two countries was just about the same in 1952). At the same time, the rankings that emerge are plausible; in Western Europe, the rank order was West Germany, Austria, Belgium/Netherlands (combined in the source), France, the Netherlands, Italy, and Denmark. The per capita figures ranged from 621,000 to 1,171,000 kwh/person. Electric power production data for all countries were obtained from United Nations, *World Energy Supplies, 1951–1954,* Statistical Papers, series J, no. 2 (New York: U.N., 1957), pp. 124–35. Population data for these countries were obtained from U.S., Bureau of the Census, *Statistical Abstract of the United States, 1954,* 75th ed. (Washington, D.C.: Government Printing Office, 1954), pp. 13, 955.

15. Population data for Yugoslavia were obtained from SZS, *Statistički godišnjak SFRJ 1973* (Belgrade: SZS, 1973), p. 82.

16. There is some evidence that this is the case for the countries included in table 13. Taking the logarithm of per capita electric power production as the indicator of initial stage of development, simple regression of the growth rates in table 13 and those reported in the text on that indicator yield a coefficient of −1.06 with a standard error of 0.47, significant at the 95 percent level. If India and Japan, the two outliers, are removed, the coefficient is −1.62 and the standard error is 0.37, again significant at the 95 percent level. It is interesting that Japan apparently achieved a growth rate greater than its 1952 per capita electric power production would suggest; the opposite was true of India.

17. For an excellent discussion of these distortions in connection with the official Soviet index, see Rush V. Greenslade, "Industrial Production in the USSR," in *Soviet Economic Statistics*, ed. Vladimir G. Treml and John P. Hardt (Durham, N.C.: Duke University Press, 1972), pp. 174–79.

18. According to Nutter's data, per capita electric power production was 163.6 kwh in 1935. This figure was calculated from data in G. Warren Nutter, *The Growth of Industrial Production in the Soviet Union* (Princeton: Princeton University Press, 1962), pp. 421, 519.

19. Ibid., p. 113.

20. Nutter's indexes include a variety of product coverages, with the three main ones defined so as to reflect different stages of fabrication. As the indexes presented in this book make no such effort to delineate stages of fabrication, Nutter's index for all civilian products is taken to be closest in coverage. The weights in the all-civilian-products index were derived from product unit values adjusted for costs of nonindustrial materials used in fabrication. Values so obtained were aggregated into industrial groups and the resulting groups combined by value added (in the case of the 1928 weight base) or employment (1955

weight base). The Nutter indexes provide both a Laspeyres and a Paasche index; our indexes are either Laspeyres (the 1952 imputed weights index) or "mixed" (the 1961 direct weights index). (See ibid., especially pp. 112–19.)

CHAPTER FIVE

1. Some of the series (12 of the more than 50) included in the sample using 1961 weights are for products that were not produced at all in 1952. Because these series tended to grow more rapidly than average, as is typical of new products, they were one source of the higher growth rate observed in the expanded sample.

2. A number of the series began after 1961; no measurement was attempted for any series whose coverage started after 1966. Twenty-six series were omitted from the expanded sample because they were obviously new products whose weights in the index would have been zero or nearly zero.

3. Actually, the procedure cannot directly employ the growth rates because combining branch growth rates by use of branch weights produces an aggregate growth rate that is not fully comparable to the aggregate growth rate obtained directly from the sample index. Instead, from the branch median growth rates, a set of branch growth relatives for 1961–71 can be calculated. From these relatives, an "index" for industry as a whole (i.e., for all unweighted products) can be calculated by use of branch weights. That index can then be combined with the sample index by using a set of weights, and from this combined index new growth rates can be calculated.

4. The weighting procedure involves a great oversimplification. Given the fact that data were unavailable to weight each product individually, the next best alternative would have been to weight each of the medians not with a constant fraction of the branch weight pertaining to the products included in the sample index, but rather with a variable fraction of it, the variation depending on the relation of branch value added already accounted for in the indexes to the total branch value added. However, this cannot be done with the available data, nor was there available a suitable approximation. The next best method is to assume a fraction of the branch weight that is the same for all branches. This, in effect, is what was done.

5. Calculated from SZS, *Statistički godišnjak SFRJ 1963* (Belgrade: SZS, 1963), p. 166; and idem, *Statistički godišnjak SFRJ 1973* (Belgrade: SZS, 1973), p. 171.

6. See SZS, *Industrija 1961,* Statistički bilten, no. 236 (Belgrade: SZS, 1962), p. 7; and idem, *Industrija 1971*, Statistički bilten, no. 730 (Belgrade: SZS, 1972), p. 8.

7. See chap. 3, note 9.

8. Define S_t^j as the weighted sum of j items in period t. Then the ordinary Laspeyres index with fixed sample size m for a two-year period is:

$$\lambda = \frac{S_2^m}{S_0^m} = \frac{S_2^m}{S_1^m} \cdot \frac{S_1^m}{S_0^m}$$

An index with changing coverage calculated as the product of annual relatives, where the new sample contains n additional items, can be written as

$$\hat{\lambda} = \frac{S_1^m}{S_0^m} \cdot \frac{S_2^m + S_2^n}{S_1^m + S_1^n}$$

Suppose $S_2^m = r^m\ S_1^m$ and $S_2^n = r^n\ S_1^n$, where r^m and r^n are average growth ratios of the products in the initial and next period bundles. Then

$$\frac{\hat{\lambda}}{\lambda} = \left(\frac{S_1^m}{S_2^m} \cdot \frac{S_0^m}{S_1^m}\right)\left(\frac{S_1^m}{S_0^m} \cdot \frac{S_2^m + S_2^n}{S_1^m + S_1^n}\right)$$

$$= \frac{1 + \dfrac{S_2^n}{S_2^m}}{1 + \dfrac{S_1^n}{S_1^m}} = \frac{S_1^m + \dfrac{r^n}{r^m} S_1^n}{S_1^m + S_1^n}$$

Obviously,

$$\frac{\hat{\lambda}}{\lambda} > 1 \text{ if } r^n > r^m .$$

9. In the chemicals branch, for example, the growth rates of products introduced after 1961 whose output is published in the sources for this study grew at annual rates ranging from 18 to 55 percent, while the average for established products in the branch was about 10 percent (according to the 1961 direct weights index).

10. According to the official explanation of the method (see SZS, *Indeks fizičkog obima . . .* , Metodološki materijali, no. 82 [Belgrade: SZS, 1957], pp. 6–8), the weight for each branch (through 1969) is total wages plus depreciation for the branch divided by the total of wages and depreciation for the industrial sector, the resulting fractions then converted to a basis of 10,000. However, the source of the data for calculating these weights is not clearly specified in the methodological explanation. They cannot be derived from the data for depreciation and personal incomes (net or gross) published in Yugoslav national income accounts. Since the weights are intended to represent "socially necessary labor time," they could be based on some combination of personal incomes paid to members of the producing enterprises and payments for services to outsiders. Alternatively, they could be simply the sum of all wage and depreciation payments reported by producing enterprises. The data available are inadequate to distinguish between these possibilities.

11. The standard deviation of the relative deviation of branch weights from social product shares (excluding shipbuilding and unclassified products) fell from

0.384 in 1952 to 0.261 in 1961 for the official weights and from 0.560 in 1952 to 0.196 in 1961 for the sample weights.

12. For example, social product is defined as gross value of sales (at producer prices, and including an imputation of the value of goods produced for direct consumption by the producer) less the cost of purchased materials and services (also at producer prices). Its value then is sensitive to the multitudes of price controls that have characterized the Yugoslav economy. Furthermore, as used here, branch distribution is done according to the organizational principle that all dealings of an enterprise are attributed to the branch in which it is classified on the basis of its principal activity. This would cause overweighting of any branch whose member enterprises engage in a relatively large amount of dealings in other branches.

13. Of fifteen regressions of the form $Y = a + bX$ where Y was the annual growth rate of a branch relative to the industry average and X was the annual relative of the growth of the branch weight, the coefficient b had a positive sign in fourteen and was statistically significant in all but three. The odd result (in 1966–67) does not appear to have been due to a fluke, but seems to represent a genuine readjustment. The reasons for this are not apparent, but it causes speculation about whether the sharp dip in the official index in 1967 is due partly to the readjustment of branch weights. The fact that the dip is echoed by the sample index, however, indicates that statistical reasons are not its entire cause.

14. Growth in a market economy normally would favor products whose relative costs fall; hence, if an annually linked index were constructed with relative cost weights, there should be an inverse correlation between the growth rates and the weights. Even in this case, it is not possible to show whether the annually linked index would grow at a faster or slower rate than one calculated with fixed base year weights.

15. Define

$$S_{pr} = \sum_{i=1}^{n} w_i^p q_i^r ,$$

the weighted sum of outputs q_i in year r, where p denotes the year from which the weights are drawn. Then the ordinary Laspeyres index (λ) would be, after t periods:

$$\lambda = \frac{S_{0t}}{S_{00}}$$

The corresponding index calculated as the product of a series of annual relatives would be:

$$\hat{\lambda} = \prod_{p=0}^{t-1} \frac{S_{p,p+1}}{S_{pp}}$$

Then it can be shown that:

$$\frac{\hat{\lambda}}{\lambda} = \left(\frac{\frac{S_{12}}{S_{11}}}{\frac{S_{02}}{S_{01}}}\right)\left(\frac{\frac{S_{23}}{S_{22}}}{\frac{S_{03}}{S_{02}}}\right)\cdots\left(\frac{\frac{S_{t-1,t}}{S_{t-1,t-1}}}{\frac{S_{0,t}}{S_{0,t-1}}}\right)$$

$$\triangleq \left(\frac{R_{12}}{R_{02}}\right)\left(\frac{R_{23}}{R_{03}}\right)\cdots\left(\frac{R_{t-1,t}}{R_{0t}}\right)$$

It is sufficient, but not necessary, for

$$\frac{\hat{\lambda}}{\lambda} > 1$$

that

$$\frac{R_{t-1,t}}{R_{0t}} > 1$$

for all t. Write

$$R_{t-1,t} = \sum_i \frac{S^i_{t-1,t-1}}{S_{t-1,t-1}}\left(\frac{q_i^t}{q_i^{t-1}}\right)$$

$$R_{0t} = \sum_i \frac{S^t_{0,t-1}}{S_{0,t-1}}\left(\frac{q_i^t}{q_i^{t-1}}\right)$$

and define

$$r_i = \frac{q_i^t}{q_i^{t-1}}, \quad \delta_i^t = \frac{S^i_{t-1,t-1}}{S_{t-1,t-1}}$$

Then

$$R_{t-1,t} - R_{0t} = \sum_i (\delta_i^t - \delta_i^0) r_i = \bar{r} \sum_i (\delta_i^t - \delta_i^0) \frac{r_i}{\bar{r}}$$

where $\bar{r}$ is the industry average growth rate. A positive correlation between the growth rates of branch outputs and branch weights means that $\delta_i^t - \delta_i^0 > 0$ when $r_i > \bar{r}$ which shows why these ratios may be positive. At the same time, it is clear that the positive correlation does not imply that the sum of the products is positive.

16. According to official sources, in 1973 some 95.5 percent of the output included in the official index was measured in physical terms, 1.8 percent in hours of labor, and 2.7 percent in value. In recent years, measurement in hours of labor was most important in shipbuilding and significant in the metal products branch; measurement in value was most important in chemicals and lumber and wood products. Values are generally expressed in current prices with no effort to correct for inflation; in itself, this practice would impart an upward bias to the official index. See SZS, *Industrija 1973*, Statistički bilten, no. 847 (Belgrade: SZS, 1974) pp. 6–7, for a discussion.

17. The following discussion is based on information drawn from SZS, *Industrijski proizvodi 1970*, Statistički bilten, no. 717 (Belgrade: SZS, 1972); and from SZS, *Industrija*, various issues.

18. Average size of trucks, buses, diesel engines for them, diesel and electric locomotives, freight cars, and other railroad coaches and vans rose between 1952 and 1971. Average sizes of tractors, motorcycles and motorcyle engines, and marine engines fell; those of passenger cars and their engines stayed about the same.

19. For these items, data are available only for 1959–71. During that period, in metalworking machinery, presses and bending and cutting machines became larger; average sizes of grinders, drills, lathes, and sharpeners fell or remained about the same. Woodworking drills, lathes, saws, and sanders all became larger or stayed about the same; combination woodworking machines became smaller. Average sizes of looms, spinning machines, leather-working machines, brick-and-tile–making machines, and dumpers rose, and those of rubber-working machines, dredges, concrete mixers, crushing and granulating machines, and bulldozers fell or remained about the same.

20. During the 1959–71 period, agricultural machines whose average size fell include barrows, horse-drawn plows, sowing machines, hammer mills, feed choppers, and incubators. The average sizes of fertilizer spreaders, grain combines, and cornhuskers rose. Those of tractor-drawn plows, rollers, rakes, elevators, sprinklers, and feed driers stayed about the same.

21. This includes sewing and accounting machines, typewriters, and clocks. Balances and medical and veterinary equipment are measured in tons, and no data are available for estimating changes in size.

22. The average power ratings of large (over 70 kw) rotating machines rose between 1952 and 1971; those of medium (1.6–70 kw) and small (less than 1.6 kw) rotating machines fell. No definite conclusion can be drawn on the basis of this information, but one might speculate that increases in size of already large motors and decreases in size of already small ones would both cause increases in unit costs, *ceteris paribus*. The change in power rating of medium-size motors could be assumed to have a negligible effect on unit cost.

23. For these items, measurement is in numbers of units. Between 1965 and 1971, the average power ratings rose for electric irons, electric ranges, hot water

heaters, and heater-ventilators; they fell for single-unit hot plates, ventilators, and vacuum cleaners and stayed about the same for boilers and hot plates with two or more units. Whether the changes observed over this short period of time are representative of longer-term trends is unknown. Between 1952 and 1971, the average size of clothes washers (in tons per unit) rose, as did that of compressor-type refrigerators (in liters per unit). The average size of clothes dryers (in tons per unit) and absorption refrigerators (in liters per unit) fell. Production of the last two items had virtually ceased by 1971.

CHAPTER SIX

1. Borijav Srebrić, "Neki problemi usavršavanja metoda i mehanisma razvoja nerazvijenih područja u Jugoslavija," in *Ubrzanje rasta Jugoslavenske privrede u uslovima stabilnosti*, ed. Savez ekonomista Jugoslavije, Centralni odbor (Zagreb: Informator, 1969), p. 84. Prior to the 1957-61 Five-Year Plan, no special emphasis was given to regional development, although issues pertaining to it were treated in the overall development plan.

2. Nikola Čobeljić, *Privreda Jugoslavije: Rast, struktura i funkcionisanje* (Belgrade: Savremena administracija, 1974), p. 287.

3. See Branko Horvat, *The Yugoslav Economic System* (White Plains, N.Y.: International Arts and Sciences Press, 1976), pp. 64-67, for further details about the classification of regions. At various times, parts of other republics—notably districts in southern Serbia and Croatia—were also made eligible for development aid.

4. Before 1957, Kosovo and Vojvodina were combined with Serbia proper in an aggregate for Serbia. This aggregate is reported in table 21 as Serbia (total). It is a conglomerate of the growth arising from quite different regions and must be interpreted with caution.

5. See, e.g., Čobeljić, *Privreda Jugoslavije*, p. 285.

6. This indicator was later criticized as too narrow by apologists for the regional policy. See the discussion in Horvat, *The Yugoslav Economic System*, p. 72.

7. Population growth rates were calculated from midyear estimates by SZS, as reported in *Demografska statistika 1971* (Belgrade: SZS, 1974), pp. 30-32. The rates were calculated as annual averages between terminal years by the compound interest formula. The actual rates for 1957-71 were, in percent per year: Serbia proper, 0.82; Croatia, 0.61; Slovenia, 0.79; Vojvodina, 0.63; Macedonia, 1.39; Montenegro, 1.24; Bosnia-Hercegovina, 1.44; Kosovo, 2.62.

8. Despite the arguments of some Yugoslav economists that the regional policy had, as one of its consequences, a tendency to autarkic policies by the regions, extensive interregional movement of goods and at least some movement of labor did occur.

9. Industrial growth in Kosovo was generally erratic, for reasons that are somewhat obscure and in any case beyond the scope of this study. Slovenia, the most advanced of the regions, also exhibited the steadiest industrial expansion during the period.

10. The actual values of the ratios $((r_{1957-71} - r_{1966-71}) \div (r_{1957-71}))$ are as follows:

Macedonia	0.34	Serbia proper	0.45
Montenegro	0.70	Vojvodina	0.83
Bosnia-Hercegovina	0.39	Croatia	0.46
Kosovo	0.21	Slovenia	0.18

11. Defining γ as the proportional decline in growth rate and X as the 1957 share of national income originating in industry and mining, the value of $\hat{\beta}$ in the regression $\gamma = \alpha + \beta X$ was −1.273, with a *t*-value of −2.18. This was not significant at the 95 percent level.

12. Defining γ as the 1957–71 growth rate and X as in the previous footnote, the value of $\hat{\beta}$ was −0.120, with a *t*-value of −1.47.

13. See Horvat, *The Yugoslav Economic System*, p. 73 and Čobeljić, *Privreda Jugoslavije,* pp. 313–14.

14. There are three official subindexes divided according to the use to which output is put: resources for labor (a collection of items used by workers in production, including machinery, equipment, tools, and energy consumed in production), semifabricates (all products destined for further fabrication), and final consumption goods. None of these categories corresponds closely to that wanted for the purpose of the text. In addition, indexes are published for goods grouped by economic and technical criteria. These indexes include measures of energy, mining, metallurgy, machine-building, chemical products, textiles and clothing, food and tobacco, and others. Again, none of these is fully satisfactory by itself, and weights for combining them are not available. In any case, they are not divided by republic and province in the standard sources.

15. No products were taken from the metal products, electrical products, chemicals, paper products, rubber products, and printing and publishing branches because all products in those branches represent more advanced degrees of fabrication than was deemed appropriate for an index of raw materials. For reasons discussed earlier, the shipbuilding branch was excluded from the sample indexes.

16. A complete list of the products included in the crude materials sample is provided in appendix D.

17. Specifically, the weighted sums for crude materials calculated for 1957, 1961, 1966, and 1971 were subtracted from the total weighted sums for those years and the differences taken as the basis for the index of the output of manufactured goods.

18. Branch growth rates according to the official index were calculated from indexes for the branches obtained by linking published indexes beginning in 1957. The data were obtained from SZS, *Industrija 1966*, Statistički bilten, no. 476 (Belgrade: SZS, 1967), pp. 12–13; idem, *Industrija 1970*, Statisticki bilten, no. 666 (Belgrade: SZS, 1971), pp. 12-13; and idem, *Industrija 1971*, Statistički bilten, no. 730 (Belgrade: SZS, 1972), pp. 12–13.

19. Growth rates were calculated from data underlying table 18.

20. SZS, *Statistički godišnjak FNRJ 1959* (Belgrade: SZS, 1959), p. 331.

21. Data were obtained from SZS, *Industrija 1967*, Statistički bilten, no.

528 (Belgrade: SZS, 1968), pp. 12–13; and idem, *Industrija 1971*, pp. 12–13.

22. In fact, in the summary tables of industrial production given in the statistical yearbooks, output of the chemicals and petroleum branches in 1962 was zero. The summary tables provide data only for selected products, but they are, presumably, the most important ones. (See SZS, *Statistički godišnjak SFRJ 1963* [Belgrade: SZS, 1963], pp. 397, 399.)

CHAPTER SEVEN

1. The index of change in output composition is described in appendix E.

2. For further details about the reforms, see chaps. 8 and 10.

3. See appendix E for description of this measure.

4. Except for the very limited applications reported later in this chapter, the structural change index has not yet been used for measuring change in any country except Yugoslavia. It is not known, therefore, whether secular decline is typical.

5. If the process of growth is depicted by movements of production possibility frontiers over time, this amounts to saying that the envelope frontier open to a system at any time is farthest from the existing frontier along the ray corresponding to the existing output bundle. (See G. Warren Nutter, "On Economic Size and Growth," *Journal of Law and Economics* 9 [1966]: 164–66, for the concept of the envelope frontier.) This is a very broad assertion about economic growth, and its evaluation is beyond the scope of this study. The test carried out here should be regarded only as a single instance in which it apparently is substantiated. The arguments in the text spell out necessary, not sufficient, conditions for the existence of the trade-off.

6. See Aleksander Bajt, "Investment Cycles in European Socialist Economies: A Review Article," *Journal of Economic Literature* 9 (1971): 53–63, for a summary of the work of economists in communist countries on business cycles.

7. Branko Horvat, "Business Cycles in Yugoslavia," *Eastern European Economics* 9 (1971), especially p. 45. Horvat's dating goes only as far as 1967. From 1967 through 1971, however, there were no clearly perceptible peaks or troughs in Yugoslav industrial activity.

8. The Durbin-Watson statistic was 1.28, lower than ideally desirable, but nevertheless in the indeterminate range. The null hypothesis of zero serial correlation cannot be rejected on this basis.

9. The bias in comparability is not directly proportional to the ratio of the coefficients of variation, but rather is proportional to the square root of one plus the square of that coefficient. In the case of the comparison of Japan (starting in 1950) with Yugoslavia (starting in 1952), this suggests a bias of less than 0.5 percent.

10. "Overstating change" means that the size of the angle between output vectors for the country to which the Yugoslav structural change is being compared overstates the relative extent of structural change in that country, and conversely.

CHAPTER EIGHT

1. As worded in the text, the statement implicitly takes one side of the dispute between Denison on the one hand and Jorgenson and Griliches on the other in which the latter argue that proper measurement of factor use, including adjustments for changes in quality, should fully account for increases in output. According to their reasoning, the existence of the famous residuals in growth accounting indicates errors in measuring factor usage. By the same reasoning, the estimation of technical change parameters in aggregate production functions, discussed in the next chapter, reflects the same errors; with proper measurement of inputs, according to Jorgenson and Griliches, these parameters should be zero. For Yugoslavia, this debate is moot because limitations in the data prevent the detailed measurements demanded by the Jorgenson-Griliches approach. (See D. W. Jorgenson and Z. Griliches, "The Explanation of Productivity Change," *Review of Economic Studies* 34 [1967]: 249–82; and Edward F. Denison, "Some Major Issues in Productivity Analysis: An Examination of Estimates by Jorgenson and Griliches," *Survey of Current Business* 49, part 2 [1969]: 1–27.)

2. The data are less detailed than those used by Carré, Dubois, and Malinvaud in their study of the French economy, in which only about half of French economic growth could be explained by the available data. The remainder was attributed to a number of unmeasureable factors, including technical change, economies of scale, attitudes of the participants in the economy, and the system of planning. (See J. J. Carré, P. Dubois, and E. Malinvaud, *French Economic Growth* [Stanford: Stanford University Press, 1975], especially pp. 177–221. For a discussion of the difficulties in separating technical changes from economies of scale, see George J. Stigler, "Economic Problems in Measuring Productivity," in *Output, Input, and Productivity Measurement,* ed. National Bureau of Economic Research, Studies in Income and Wealth, vol. 25 [Princeton: Princeton University Press, 1961], pp. 47–63.)

3. Yugoslav investment data include investments in "nonproductive" activities, which include capital spending by government for a variety of purposes. The U.S. budget does not include a capital account, and the national income accounts do not show government capital expenditures separately from government purchases of goods and services. Thus, total U.S. investment, if derived from gross private domestic investment in the national income accounts (as in definition 1 in table 28) understates U.S. investment relative to Yugoslavia. OECD estimates of capital expenditures partly rectify this shortcoming by separately estimating government capital expenditures. However, their estimates exclude governmental purchases of machinery and equipment, hence, there remains an unknown—but probably relatively small—understatement. A further shortcoming of the OECD data is that government capital consumption is considered to be equal to the value of new construction of public buildings.

The Yugoslav data for investment used in calculating the ratios in table 28 are based on data from the Social Accounting Service (Služba društvenog knjigovodstva). These data differ in coverage from those reported by the Federal Institute of Statistics (Savezni zavod za statistiku); the SZS data have a broader coverage, and if they had been used in table 28, the Yugoslav ratios would have been larger.

The denominators of the ratios in table 28 present similar difficulties. The denominator for Yugoslavia—social product less amortization—is roughly equivalent to net domestic national product (i.e., gross domestic product less capital consumption allowances) in Western terminology. It should be recalled that although Yugoslav national income accounts are based on Marxian concepts and therefore exclude "nonproductive" activities from social product, the taxes which largely pay for the nonproductive activities are included in social product; thus, the total is not much different from what gross domestic product would be using Western accounting principles. Deducting amortization gives something approximating net domestic national product; to go further and arrive at an aggregate comparable to national income according to Western definitions would require arbitrary adjustments of taxes.

In the definition 1 ratios for the United States, the denominator is net national product. Conceptually this is not identical with net domestic national product, the desired analog to the Yugoslav denominator, because of the inclusion of the foreign trade balance. But for the United States, the difference should be small. In the definition 2 ratios, the denominator is gross domestic product less capital consumption; so—apart from the differences noted in the previous paragraph—the concept is the same as that used for Yugoslavia.

4. This is because the denominators of the ratios were obtained by subtracting amortization from social product. For the gross ratios, it is easy to see why the unduly small amortization causes understatement. It is also easy to show that the net ratios are overstated. For comment on the understatement of depreciation, see Branko Suhina, *Amortizacija osnovnih sredstava*, 2d ed. (Zagreb: Informator, 1970).

5. In the regression $I_g/Y = \alpha + \beta t$, the estimate for $\hat{\beta}$ was –0.00744, and the 95 percent confidence interval ranged from –0.0171 to –0.0032.

6. In the regression $I_n/Y = \alpha + \beta t$, the $\hat{\beta}$ estimate was –0.00921, and the 95 percent confidence ranged from –0.0133 to –0.0051.

7. See Suhina, *Amortizacija osnovnih sredstava*; and Nenad Butaš and Mihailo Puletić, *Priručnik o revalorizaciji sredstava organizacija udruženog rada* (Belgrade: Privredni pregled, 1971). As noted above, depreciation rates were generally set too low, even after the reform mentioned in the text. As one result, capital revaluations were carried out in 1953, 1958, 1962, 1966, and 1971. This underestimation of capital consumption is one of the reasons that it is hard to make reliable estimates of the Yugoslav capital stock.

8. Data from SZS, *Statistički godišnjak FNRJ 1955* (Belgrade: SZS, 1955), p. 259; idem, *Statistički godišnjak FNRJ 1962* (Belgrade: SZS, 1962), p. 228; idem, *Statistički godišnjak SFRJ 1965* (Belgrade: SZS, 1965), p. 273; and idem, *Statistički godišnjak SFRJ 1972* (Belgrade: SZS, 1972), p. 256.

9. See Branko Horvat, "Business Cycles in Yugoslavia," *Eastern European Economics* 9 (1971): 45.

10. Regressing the ratio of net to gross investment on time, the coefficient was –1.66 with a *t*-value of –5.05.

11. Many price indexes are published, but none seems appropriate for this purpose. A weighted average of the indexes for capital goods (*sredstva rada*) and construction materials (*elementi i materijal za ugrađivanje*), if available over a sufficiently long period, could be calculated, but there would be little basis for choosing the necessary weights.

12. The growth rates were measured by SZS in its publication, *Osnovna sredstva društvene privrede SFRJ, SR i SAP 1952–1971* (Belgrade: SZS, 1973). The capital stock data given in this source are subject to all the misgivings associated with such estimates in any economy that has no capital market, but there is no alternative.

13. The model makes several simplifying assumptions; namely, that there is no technological change, that there exist linear and homogeneous production functions for each branch of industry, and that labor markets are in full competitive equilibrium. Thus, a two-factor production function for a branch producing, say, X, can be manipulated by well-known steps to obtain

$$\frac{\dot{X}}{X} = \alpha_X \left(\frac{\dot{K}}{K}\right)_X + \beta_X \left(\frac{\dot{L}}{L}\right)_X$$

where α_X and β_X denote the shares of payments to capital and labor, respectively, in branch output, and the dot denotes the time derivative. Data for α_X are not available, but Euler's theorem may be applied to convert this relation to:

$$\frac{\dot{X}}{X} = \left(\frac{\dot{K}}{K}\right)_X + \beta_X \left(\frac{\dot{L}}{L} - \frac{\dot{K}}{K}\right)_X \qquad (1)$$

Then, given data for the rates of growth of capital and labor and for the share of labor in output and assuming that the growth rates of the factors represent the intentions of the policymakers, the growth rate of output that would have resulted—and which can be taken as the expected growth rate—can be obtained.

This procedure requires some heroic assumptions. Besides those noted at the beginning of this note, the assumption that the reported share of labor in output corresponds to its marginal value product (as required by Euler's theorem) is open to serious question in the Yugoslav economy. Problems of this sort are part of the reason for not adopting such sophisticated techniques in the text.

14. For the subperiods of 1957–61, 1961–65, and 1966–71, wage shares for 1957, 1961, and 1966, respectively, were used as estimates of β in expression (1) of the preceding footnote. Spearman rank correlation coefficients of 0.994, 0.995, and 0.984 between rankings according to "expected" growth rates and according to capital stock growth rates were obtained for the three subperiods.

15. This conclusion rests on values of Spearman rank correlation coefficients for the branches ranked according to capital stock growth rates as follows: 1952–56/1957–61, 0.46; 1957–61/1961–65, 0.40; 1961–65/1966–71, 0.64.

16. However, the rankings of the branch by the more elaborate method described in note 13 were not substantially different from those by capital stock growth rate. The rapid growth in metal products remains something of a mystery; possibly technological change played an important role.

17. Hints about this matter may be obtained by examining the proportion of total investment in a branch accounted for by investment from the funds of the enterprise. If this proportion were systematically larger in the "traditional" branches, support would be rendered for the possibility expressed in the text. However, a superficial examination of investment data for benchmark years during the period revealed no such relation.

18. Norton T. Dodge and Charles K. Wilber, "The Relevance of Soviet Industrial Experience for Less Developed Economies," *Soviet Studies* 21 (1970): 330–49.

19. Albert O. Hirschman, *The Strategy of Economic Development* (New Haven: Yale University Press, 1958).

20. Hirschman's linkages were taken from the classic input-output study of Italy, Japan, and the United States by Chenery and Watanabe. (See Hirschman, *Strategy*, p. 105.)

21. This seems an inappropriate measure of development policy, for reasons explained in the text.

22. The computations were made by the method described in Hirschman, *Strategy*, p. 105.

23. See Nikola Čobeljić, *Privreda Jugoslavije: Rast, struktura i funkcionisanje* (Belgrade: Savremena administracija, 1974), pp. 290ff.; and Borijav Srebrić, "Neki problemi usavršavanja metoda i mehanisma razvoja nerazvijenih područja u Jugoslaviji," in *Ubrzanje rasta Jugoslavenske privrede u uslovima stabilnosti*, ed. Savez ekonomista Jugoslavije, Centralni odbor (Zagreb: Informator, 1969), p. 84.

24. According to official national income statistics, in 1957 some 14.6 percent of total Yugoslav industrial production originated in Bosnia-Hercegovina. The shares produced in the other three less developed areas—Macedonia, Montenegro, and Kosovo—totaled only 6.3 percent. (Data from SZS, *Statistički godišnjak FNRJ 1959* [Belgrade: SZS, 1959], p. 331.)

25. See chapter 10 for further discussion and data. Income is here measured by national income.

26. See Čobeljić, *Privreda Jugoslavije*, pp. 290ff.

27. At the end of 1963, when GIF funds were distributed among the specialized banks, GIF assets constituted some two-thirds of the total of all social investment funds; if republic investment funds are combined with the GIF funds (on the grounds that their use was probably closely controlled by the central authorities), nearly 90 percent of the total is accounted for. The remaining funds belonged to provincial and local investment funds. See Slobodan Sekulić, "Investment Capital of Socio-Political Communities," *Yugoslav Survey* new series 11 (1970): 3.

28. According to Sekulić, "The funds did not have the status of a juridic person, their assets being managed by banks in conformity with the plans of the socio-political communities involved" (ibid., p. 2).

29. "Zakon o bankama," *Službeni list* 1961, no. 10: 209–23.

30. Božidar Jovanović, "Reform of the Credit and Banking System," *Yugoslav Survey* 22 (1966): 3,219ff.

31. See "Zakon o upotrebi sredstava federacija za investicije u privredi," *Službeni list* 1963, no. 52: 978–79. For the requirement that the funds be administered according to the dictates of the federal plan, see ibid., p. 978.

32. Of the total transferred (21.996 billion new dinars), about 75 percent went to the Yugoslav Investment Bank, 18 percent to the Yugoslav Agricultural Bank, and 6 percent to the Yugoslav Foreign Trade Bank. The balance went to the Yugoslav National Bank. (Sekulić, "Investment Capital," p. 4.)

33. The most important were "Zakon o bankama i kreditnim poslovima" and

"Zakon o narodnoj banci Jugoslavije," both published in *Službeni list* 1965, no. 12. For discussion of the modifications in the banking system, see Sekulić, "Investment Capital"; and J. J. Hauvonen, "Postwar Developments in Money and Banking in Yugoslavia," *IMF Staff Papers* 17 (1970): 579ff.

34. Sekulić, "Investment Capital," p. 7.

35. "Zakon o izmjenama i dopunama zakona o bankama i kreditnim poslovima," *Službeni list* 1966, no. 4: 72.

36. 'Zakon o izmjenama i dopunama zakona o bankama i kreditnim poslovima," *Službeni list* 1966, no. 26: 460.

37. Sekulić, "Investment Capital," p. 8.

38. See Jakov Sirotković and Vladimir Stipetić, eds., *Ekonomika Jugoslavije* (Zagreb: Informator, 1967), p. 331. This point is also noted in the World Bank study of Yugoslavia; see Vinod Dubey, *Yugoslavia: Development With Decentralization* (Baltimore: Johns Hopkins University Press, 1975), p. 222.

39. Dušan Čobeljić, *Planiranje narodne privredne* (Belgrade: Rad, 1967), p. 284.

40. Dennison Rusinow, *The Yugoslav Experiment, 1948–1974* (Berkeley and Los Angeles: University of California Press, 1977), p. 209.

41. Ibid., p. 174.

42. Jovanović, "Reform of Credit," p. 3,233.

43. See Dubey, *Yugoslavia*, pp. 204ff.

44. The exact proportion is hard to determine, but, in 1971, the category "funds from the federation and other sociopolitical organizations," which included part of the FAD funds, accounted for about 13 percent of total investment in industry and mining (SZS, *Statistički godišnjak SFRJ 1972* [Belgrade: SZS, 1972], p. 257).

45. Dubey, *Yugoslavia*, p. 222.

46. The high ratio for enterprise funds in 1966 should be discounted because of several events in 1965 that caused the 1966 enterprise investment rate to be unusually high. First, there was a general increase in industrial prices decreed by the government, which inflated 1965 earnings; according to the regulations then in effect, 1965 earnings that enterprises wished to reinvest had to be reinvested in 1966. Second, the financial position of enterprises had been given a one-time boost by the shifting of the turnover tax from the enterprise to the retail level in 1965. Finally, there was a capital revaluation in 1965 that led to higher depreciation payments.

CHAPTER NINE

1. See SZS, *Statistički godišnjak FNRJ 1962* (Belgrade: SZS, 1962), p. 743.

2. SZS, *Zaposlenost 30.IX 1972*, Statistički bilten, no. 798 (Belgrade: SZS, 1973), p. 5.

3. SZS, *Zaposleno osoblje, April 1968*, Statistički bilten, no. 523 (Belgrade: SZS, 1968), p. 5.

4. From the methodological discussions in the references cited in notes 2 and 3, it appears that the reporting system does not provide a means for this adjustment.

5. These statements are based on data for average number of hours per year as reported in Yugoslav statistical yearbooks or calculated from monthly averages reported in the same sources. A fifty-week year was assumed in making the calculations.

6. Specifically, errors in the measurement of the labor input coupled with likely errors in measuring output and capital cause aggregate production function estimates to fall in the category of models with errors in variables and errors in equation. This means that estimators are inconsistent. If the errors in measurement of labor are systematically related to time (as the data in table 36 suggest), autocorrelation is also possible.

7. See D. W. Jorgenson and Z. Griliches, "The Explanation of Productivity Change," *Review of Economic Studies* 34 (1967): 249–82, for discussion of such a transformation of the stock of capital.

8. See Alan A. Walters, "Production and Cost Functions: An Econometric Survey," *Econometrica* 31 (1963): 1–66, for discussion of the use of the gross capital stock.

9. See Murray Brown, "The Measurement of Capital Aggregates—A Post Reswitching Problem," mimeographed (New York: National Bureau of Economic Research, 1976); and Edwin Burmeister, "Comments on Capital Aggregation," mimeographed (New York: National Bureau of Economic Research, 1976), for discussion of these problems.

10. SZS, *Osnovna sredstva društvene privrede SFRJ, SR i SAP 1952–1971* (Belgrade: SZS, 1973).

11. See ibid., pp. 161–62, for an explanation of the methods used.

12. Branimir Marković, *Kretanje narodnog dohotka, zaposlenosti i produktivnosti rada u privredi u Jugoslavije 1947–1967* (Belgrade: SZS, 1970).

13. Marković used the annual average number of persons employed, which is elsewhere reported by SZS (his monograph is a convenient source of these data for the period he covers). He noted that the data for number of persons employed are not fully comparable to those for national income because of differences in the definitions on which aggregation is based (ibid., p. 18). The explanations in the Yugoslav statistical yearbooks are not adequate for determining whether the index of persons employed used in the official labor productivity index is based on the same series as that used by Marković, but it probably is.

14. The employment index was the same as that used by Marković, but extended through 1971.

15. The 1952–67 average annual growth rates according to the official, Marković, and sample indexes were 4.6, 4.4, and 3.9 percent, respectively.

16. John W. Kendrick, *Productivity Trends in the United States* (Princeton: Princeton University Press, 1961), pp. 397–98, 465–66; G. Warren Nutter, *The Growth of Industrial Production in the Soviet Union* (Princeton: Princeton University Press, 1962), p. 172.

17. Marković, *Kretanje narodnog dohotka*, pp. 53, 58.

18. Kendrick, *Productivity Trends*, pp. 396–494. Kendrick's definitions of capital stock are not identical to those in the Yugoslav definition (principally

because Kendrick includes inventories), and there are important differences in measurement technique. As already discussed, his estimates of the number of persons engaged also differ in definition and method from the Yugoslav data. Thus, the figures mentioned in the text provide only a rough indication of relative rates of growth.

19. A slightly higher rate of growth occurred in manufacturing during the period 1869–89, but no data are available to calculate the corresponding growth rate for mining. It is interesting to note that the fastest ten-year growth rate of output per person in manufacturing (5.1 percent per year, 1919–29) was accompanied by a growth rate of the capital-labor ratio of less than 1 percent per year.

20. The incremental capital-output ratios were calculated from the formula:

$$\text{ICOR} = \frac{\frac{\dot{K}}{K}}{\frac{\dot{Q}}{Q}} \cdot \frac{K}{Q}$$

where K denotes capital, Q output, and the dot indicates the time derivative. In the calculations, K/Q was taken to be the simple average of the annual ratios for the years included in the subperiod involved.

21. The ratios reported are the simple averages of K/Q for the years included in the subperiods.

22. Technically, the procedure may be described by assuming a production function of the form $Q = Af(X_i)$, where A denotes a measure of the output that arises from elements other than the productive factors explicitly considered, or X_i. Differentiation with respect to time and rearrangement yields

$$\frac{\dot{A}}{A} = \frac{\dot{Q}}{Q} - \sum \beta_i \left(\frac{\dot{X}_i}{X_i}\right)$$

where the dot denotes the time derivative and $\beta_i = Af_iX_i/Q$ is the weight for the ith productive factor. $\dot{A}/A$ is the residual which consists of that part of the growth rate of output, $\dot{Q}/Q$, not explained by the weighted sum of the growth rates of the included productive factors.

23. In competitive equilibrium, each factor is paid a price or wage equal to the value of its marginal product: $w_i = Apf_i$, in the notation of note 22. Then $f_i = w_i/Ap$; substituting in the expression for β_i:

$$\beta_i = \frac{Af_iX_i}{Q} = \frac{Aw_iX_i}{ApQ} = \frac{w_iX_i}{pQ}$$

the factor's share in output.

24. See Howard M. Wachtel, "Workers' Management and Wage Differentials in Yugoslavia" (Ph.D. diss., University of Michigan, 1969), for evidence of imperfections.

25. In his study, Horvat constructed factor shares from data on the disposi-

tion of enterprise income by considering various payments made by enterprises to be factor payments. His return to capital, for example, was the sum of amortization, part of communal "contributions" (compulsory), and allocations to the enterprise and common consumption funds. The other part of the communal "contribution" was imputed to labor; the basis for the imputations was not made clear. In addition to the fact that the payments made were generally required or constrained by law (and thus not market-determined), the allocation of payments appears to have little theoretical justification. (See Branko Horvat, "Tehnički progres u Jugoslaviji," *Ekonomska analiza* 3 [1969]: 40–41.)

26. Ibid. Bajt has studied technological change for the economy as a whole, but not for the industrial sector separately. (See Aleksander Bajt, "Jugoslovenski društveni proizvod i njegovi činioci u razdoblju 1947–1964. godine," *Ekonomski pregled* 18 [1967]: 339–62.)

27. Martin L. Weitzman, "Soviet Postwar Economic Growth and Capital-Labor Substitution," *American Economic Review* 60 (1970): 676–92.

28. Ibid., p. 679.

29. Ibid., p. 681.

30. Calculated from data underlying tables 37 and 39.

31. But only roughly. Horvat's data show a steady trend in factor shares away from capital and toward labor; at a point within the time period of the study, the appropriate shares were paid, but whether this was an equilibrium point is questionable. (Horvat, "Tehnički progres," p. 41.)

32. This procedure is based on the same analysis as that given in note 22.

33. Some problems in the methods used merit secondary attention. First, as Horvat noted, there were difficulties with multicolinearity in version 3 of his estimates; hence, the parameter estimates from that equation, which were the basis for his conclusion that the production function was linear and homogeneous, were imprecise because of expected large variances. Second, although he made no mention of it, there is likely to be serial correlation in the residuals. No apparent attempt was made to adjust for this problem.

34. Ivo Vinski, "Rast fiksnih fondova Jugoslavije od reforme do početka 1967," *Ekonomski pregled* 18 (1967): 485–507, cited in Horvat, "Tehnički progres," p. 55.

35. Horvat, "Tehnički progres," pp. 33–36.

36. This may not, in fact, represent a serious problem for the period of Horvat's study. The downward trend in hours worked per employee shown in table 36 seems to have begun just at the end of that period. Whether there was an earlier trend cannot be established on the basis of available data.

37. For 1956–60, SZS published data for employment in industry by qualification level. The measurement was done according to the numbers of workers who had passed certain qualification tests; hence, the measure is imperfect. Whatever the difficulties in interpretation, the proportion of workers (as opposed to auxiliaries) rated as "qualified" or "highly qualified" rose from 44.7 to 47.2 percent of the total; the proportion of "unqualified" workers fell from 26.2 to 24.3 percent. The proportion of auxiliary workers and, within that group, the proportion of more highly skilled persons also rose during this period. Data for later in the period are on a different basis, making comparisons difficult, but it appears that the trend continued. (See SZS, *Statistički godišnjak*

FNRJ 1957 [Belgrade: SZS, 1957], p. 114; idem, *Statistički godišnjak FNRJ 1961* [Belgrade: SZS, 1961], p. 88; idem, *Statistički godišnjak SFRJ 1967* [Belgrade: SZS, 1967], p. 97; and idem, *Statistički godišnjak SFRJ 1973* [Belgrade: SZS, 1973], p. 100.)

38. Ivo Vinski, "Rast fiksnih fondova Jugoslavije od 1944 do 1964," *Ekonomist* 18 (1965): 677–79.

39. Assume that the instantaneous growth rates of nominal investment and the investment goods price index are μ and ρ, respectively. Then it can be shown that the growth rate of the real capital stock is given by

$$\frac{\dot{K}^*}{K^*} = (\mu - \rho)\left[\frac{e^{t(\mu-\rho)}}{e^{t(\mu-\rho)} - 1}\right]$$

The derivative of this expression with respect to ρ is negative if $\mu > \rho$.

40. The form of equation 3, table 40, may be represented as

$$\gamma = \beta_1 + \beta_2 X_2^* + \beta_3 X_3^* + \beta_4 X_4 + \epsilon$$

where X_2^* and X_3^* denote the measured labor and capital inputs and X_4 is time. The biases in the parameter estimates (for labor and capital) are given by

$$E(\hat{\beta}_2) = \beta_2 - \beta_2 d_{52} - \beta_3 d_{62}$$

$$E(\hat{\beta}_3) = \beta_3 - \beta_2 d_{53} - \beta_3 d_{63}$$

where the d_{ij} denote hypothetical regression coefficients in regressions of the unmeasured quantitative changes on the included variables. (Cf. Jan Kmenta, *Elements of Econometrics* (New York: Macmillan, 1971), pp. 392ff.) Positive correlation of the qualitative changes with the variables implies that the d_{ij} are positive. For the period studied by Horvat, β_2 and β_3 were positive. Hence, the bias is unequivocably downward.

41. Horvat, "Tehnički progres," pp. 36–37.

42. See, e.g., Miloš Bogdanović, *Ekonomika industrije SFRJ* (Belgrade: Privredno finansijski zavod, 1971), pp. 88–94. Bogdanović estimates that as early as 1967, output was 25 percent below its potential with full plan utilization.

43. For a valuable discussion of concepts of technical change, see Murray Brown, *On the Theory and Measurement of Technological Change* (Cambridge: Cambridge University Press, 1966).

44. Ibid., pp. 72–76, 114–18.

CHAPTER TEN

1. Nikola Čobeljić, *Privreda Jugoslavije: Rast, struktura i funkcionisanje* (Belgrade: Savremena administracija, 1974), pp. 285–87.

2. For discussion of so-called reserve labor in the less developed areas, see Lazar Sokolov, "Radna snaga u nedovoljno razvijenim područjima," in *Ubrzanje rasta Jugoslavenske privrede u uslovima stabilnosti*, ed. Savez ekonomista Jugoslavije, Centralni odbor (Zagreb: Informator, 1969), pp. 101–22.

3. See Čobeljić, *Privreda Jugoslavije*, p. 292.

4. The FAD was financed during 1966–70 by a levy of 1.85 percent on the social product of enterprises in the social sector; see Vinod Dubey, *Yugoslavia: Development with Decentralization* (Baltimore: John Hopkins University Press, 1975), p. 203. In 1966, this would have amounted to approximately 511 million new dinars, if the levy is assumed to have been assessed only on industrial enterprises in Croatia, Slovenia, Serbia proper, and Vojvodina (SZS, *Statistički godišnjak SFRJ 1968* [Belgrade: SZS, 1968], p. 364.)

5. Čobeljić, *Privreda Jugoslavije*, p. 306.

6. Ibid. For the situation in the most backward area, see Božidar Jovanović, *Privredni razvoj Kosova i problem formiranja komunalnih centara* (Priština: n.p., 1970), p. 87.

7. Jovanović, *Privredni razvoj Kosova*, p. 90.

8. See, e.g., Vladimir Farkaš et al., *Ekonomika Jugoslavije* (Zagreb: Informator, 1970), pp. 424–25; Šime Đođan, *Ekonomska politika Jugoslavije* (Zagreb: Školska knjiga, 1970), pp. 25ff.; Lazar Sokolov, *Dostignuti stepen i perspektiva privrednog razvoja nedovoljno razvijenih područja u Jugoslaviji* (Skopje: Ekonomski institut na univerzitetot "Kiril i metodij," 1973), pp. 18–21; Branko Horvat, *The Yugoslav Economic System* (White Plains, N.Y.: International Arts and Sciences Press, 1976), p. 73; Jovanović, *Privredni razvoj Kosova*, p. 88.

9. For example, the rank correlation coefficient between rankings in order of national income in industry per person employed and in order of total industrial fixed capital per person employed in 1971 was −0.524. Precisely the same correlation coefficient is obtained if national income in industry per capita is substituted for national income in industry per person employed.

10. Together these four branches accounted for over 75 percent of the total increase in industrial fixed capital; electric power production alone accounted for 37.9 percent.

11. The eight regional lists of five branches each that are the most important branches in capital growth for 1957–71 (those lists on which the first column of table 46 is based) contain a total of eleven branches. Electric power production is in every list and leads in all but one (Vojvodina). The other branches that appear in at least half the lists are metal products, chemicals, and textiles.

12. The measure of employment used in calculating average labor productivities in table 46 (number of employed persons as of September 30 of each year) is not the same as that used in the calculations of chapter 9 (annual average number of employed persons). Therefore, the growth rates in the two chapters are not fully comparable.

13. Simple regressions of the growth rates of output per person employed on contemporaneous growth rates of capital per person employed for the period as a whole and for the three subperiods show little evidence of a positive relation. Only in the 1957–61 period was the slope coefficient statistically significant (95 percent level). Lagged estimates were even less encouraging; in the only case in

which the slope coefficient was statistically significant (the 1966–71 productivity growth rate regressed on the 1961–65 capital-labor ratio growth rate), it had the wrong sign.

14. Miodrag Nikolić, *Nivo produktivnost rada u industriji po republikama 1952–1968* (Belgrade: SZS, 1970), pp. 47–60.

15. Ibid., pp. 49–51.

16. Ibid., p. 53.

17. Ibid., pp. 54–56.

18. Ibid., p. 58.

19. Ibid., p. 59.

20. See Đođan, *Ekonomska politika Jugoslavije*, pp. 17–24.

21. The year 1965 had to be omitted because required investment data are not available.

22. Cf. Dennison Rusinow, *The Yugoslav Experiment, 1948–1974* (Berkeley and Los Angeles: University of California Press, 1977), pp. 205–6.

23. That is, the reciprocal of the incremental capital-output ratio.

24. As observed in note 4, the FAD was actually financed by a levy on enterprise social product, which differs from national income by the amount of amortization. It proved convenient to use national income instead of social product, and the relative shares of the more developed regions are hardly affected by the use of one rather than the other.

25. The shares were computed for each year on the basis of national income in prices of that year.

26. In fact, the incremental capital-output ratios were calculated across three-year periods centered on individual years; hence, they are a form of moving average.

27. That is, if $\tilde{\lambda}$ denotes the estimated annual growth rate and λ the annual growth rate calculated from the sample index, the mean value of $(\tilde{\lambda}-\lambda)$ was 0.59 percent. The standard deviation of the differences was 3.2 percentage points.

28. See, e.g., Čobeljić, *Privreda Jugoslavije*, pp. 298–306; Sokolov, *Dostignuti stepen*, p. 7; Horvat, *The Yugoslav Economic System*, p. 71; and Pavle Sicherl, "Analiza nekih elemenata za ocenu stepene razvijenosti republika i pokrajina," *Ekonomska analiza* 3 (1969): 5.

29. SZS, *Statistički godišnjak SFRJ 1963* (Belgrade: SZS, 1963), pp. 339, 356.

30. Cobeljić, *Privreda Jugoslavije*, p. 306; Horvat, *The Yugoslav Economic System*, p. 72.

31. Horvat, *The Yugoslav Economic System*, p. 75.

32. Sicherl argues that national income per capita is an imperfect measure of development and that its use exaggerates interregional differences. According to him, regional policy was more successful than per capita national income figures indicate. But even with his more elaborate methods, which attempt to take a number of development indicators into account simultaneously, very little difference emerges in the rankings of the republics and autonomous provinces. Specifically, when Yugoslav regions are ranked according to Sicherl's more elaborate measures, no area that is considered less developed according to per capita

national income receives a ranking higher than any area designated more developed according to per capita national income. (See Sicherl, "Analiza nekih elemenáta," pp. 6, 24.)

33. Horvat, *The Yugoslav Economic System*, p. 73; Farkaš et al., *Ekonomika Jugoslavije*, pp. 424–25; Đođan, *Ekonomska politika Jugoslavije*, pp. 25ff.; Sokolov, *Dostignuti stepen*, pp. 18–21; and Jovanović, *Privredni razvoj Kosova*, p. 88.

34. Farkaš, et al., *Ekonomika Jugoslavije*, pp. 424–25.

35. Čobeljić, *Privreda Jugoslavije*, pp. 313–14.

36. See, e.g., Jovanović, *Privredni razvoj Kosova*, pp. 79ff.

37. Horvat, *The Yugoslav Economic System*, p. 73.

38. Đođan, *Ekonomska politika Jugoslavije*, pp. 25ff.

39. Jovanović, *Privredni razvoj Kosova*, pp. 79ff.

40. Horvat, *The Yugoslav Economic System*, p. 73; Čobeljić, *Privreda Jugoslavije*, pp. 313–14.

41. Sokolov, *Dostignuti stepen*, pp. 3–5.

42. Ibid., p. 21. The increase in the amounts paid out by enterprises in the less developed regions was, according to Sokolov, partly the result of the general inflation in Yugoslavia, which had an especially severe impact on the real incomes of the relatively low-income residents of those regions.

43. Ibid., pp. 18–21; Đođan, *Ekonomska politika Jugoslavije*, p. 25; Čobeljić, *Privreda Jugoslavije*, pp. 313–14.

CHAPTER ELEVEN

1. The following discussion is organized on lines developed by Edward F. Denison in his work on economic growth. See Denison, *Why Growth Rates Differ* (Washington, D.C.: Brookings Institution, 1969); and Denison and William K. Chung, *How Japan's Economy Grew So Fast* (Washington, D.C.: Brookings Institution, 1976). Denison's work concerns growth of the economy as a whole, of course, and not just the growth of the industrial sector upon which attention is focused in this study.

2. Denison and Chung, *Japan's Economy*, p. 33.

3. Ibid., p. 46.

4. Ibid., pp. 299–317.

5. Denison estimates much lower rates of growth for enterprise structures and equipment (the great bulk of the Yugoslav series for industrial capital) for the United States and Western Europe (see Denison, *Why Growth Rates Differ*, p. 139).

6. Branko Horvat, "Tehnički progres u Jugoslaviji," *Ekonomska analiza* 3 (1969): 29–57.

7. Denison and Chung, *Japan's Economy*, p. 48.

8. As examples, see Svetozar A. Pejovich, *The Market-Planned Economy of Yugoslavia* (Minneapolis: University of Minnesota Press, 1966); Deborah O.

Milenkovitch, *Plan and Market in Yugoslav Economic Thought* (New Haven: Yale University Press, 1971); and Vinod Dubey, *Yugoslavia: Development with Decentralization* (Baltimore: Johns Hopkins University Press, 1975). Of course, decentralization has not been the exclusive object of attention. In particular, much effort has been devoted to analyzing the implications of the system of property rights for performance in the self-management system.

9. Richard F. Staar, *The Communist Regimes in Eastern Europe*, rev. ed. (Stanford: Hoover Institution Press, 1971), pp. 200–205.

10. U.S., Bureau of the Census, *Statistical Abstract of the United States, 1974,* 95th ed. (Washington, D.C.: Government Printing Office, 1974), p. 377.

11. From SZS, *Privredni bilansi Jugoslavije 1965–1966* (Belgrade: SZS, 1968), fig. facing p. 10.

12. SZS, *Statistički godišnjak SFRJ 1970* (Belgrade: SZS, 1970), p. 106.

13. Between 1965 and 1966, net personal incomes as a percentage of social product in industry rose from 27.9 to 32.7 percent (calculated from SZS, *Statistički godišnjak SFRJ 1968* [Belgrade: SZS, 1968], p. 111). Later in the decade, when central control was reasserted, the percentage declined again.

14. Denison and Chung, *Japan's Economy*, p. 30.

15. Ibid., p. 68.

16. In 1974, for example, 68 percent of Yugoslav industrial workers were employed in enterprises with 500 or more members (SZS, *Industrijske organizacije 1974*, Statistički bilten, no. 955 [Belgrade: SZS, 1975], p. 35).

17. See Josip Obradović, *Workers' Participation in Yugoslavia: Theory and Research*, University of South Carolina, Institute of International Studies, Occasional Paper (Columbia: Institute of International Studies, n.d.).

18. Indeed, if it were not for the role played by the government, the high investment rate might appear paradoxical. According to the theory of the self-managed firm, there are disincentives for reinvesting net income in the enterprise. Workers do not have individual claims on enterprise capital, but do have rights in personal savings accounts. As a result, there is a wedge between the interest rate of savings accounts and anticipated returns to investment in the enterprise that implies a higher rate of payout of enterprise net income than would be the case if workers retained claims on enterprise capital (Eirik G. Furubotn and Svetozar A. Pejovich, "Property Rights and the Behavior of the Firm in a Socialist State: The Example of Yugoslavia," *Zeitschrift für Nationalökonomie* 30 [1970]: 431–54). By itself, this does not imply a lower aggregate rate of savings or investment since savings banks could loan their deposits to enterprises for investment; the aggregate investment rate then would depend on the level of voluntary savings and the behavior of socialist banks. The system would tend to be characterized by highly levered enterprise capital structures, and this would depress investment levels if banks behaved like risk-averse profit maximizers. It is not clear, however, how socialist banks would behave in such circumstances.

19. Although the policy carried out, in the relative emphasis put on various branches of industry, was not much different from that suggested by the plans laid down during the war by the government-in-exile (see Nicholas Mirkovich, ed., *Jugoslav Postwar Reconstruction Papers*, 4 vols., mimeographed [New York: Yugoslavia, Office of Reconstruction and Economic Affairs, 1942–43]).

20. Denison and Chung, *Japan's Economy*, chap. 7.

21. Ibid., p. 75.

22. U.S., Department of Commerce, *Projections of the Populations of the Communist Countries of Eastern Europe, by Age and Sex: 1975 to 2000* (Washington, D.C.: Government Printing Office, 1976), 28–29.

23. In 1931, the illiteracy rate in the population as a whole was 44.6 percent. By 1971, this figure was reduced to 15.1 percent (see SZS, *Statistički godišnjak FNRJ 1958* [Belgrade: SZS, 1958], p. 80; and idem, *Statistički godišnjak SFRJ 1973* [Belgrade: SZS, 1973], p. 84.)

24. In 1953, 35.5 percent of the economically active population had either no schooling (26.6 percent) or had completed less than four years (8.9 percent). In 1971, the corresponding total was 16.8 percent. In 1953, only 3.9 percent of the same group had completed the basic seven to eight years of schooling; in 1971, this figure was 13.4 percent. (Data from SZS, *Popis stanovništva 1953* [Belgrade: SZS, 1959], 3: 76–77; and idem, *Popis stanovništva 1971* [Belgrade: SZS, 1974], 2: 84.

25. This is a commonplace in the literature about the self-managed enterprise. For an elegant and penetrating analysis, see Eirik G. Furubotn, "The Long-Run Analysis of the Labor-Managed Firm: An Alternative Explanation," *American Economic Review* 66 (1976), especially pp. 105–8.

26. Denison and Chung, *Japan's Economy*, pp. 23, 85.

27. Ibid., pp. 85–86.

28. See table 3.

29. Calculated from Denison and Chung, *Japan's Economy*, p. 23; and from table 3.

30. According to the World Bank study, "almost all the investment on the peasant farms was from their own savings." (Vinod Dubey, *Yugoslavia*, p. 154.)

31. Ibid.

32. Ibid.

33. Technically, this statement is correct if the industrial sector production function is homothetic and the rate of capital growth exceeds the rate of labor growth, assuming no shifts in the production function such as could arise with technological change. See also Gary S. Becker, *Economic Theory* (New York: Alfred A. Knopf, 1971), pp. 202–4.

34. Ibid.

35. Specifically, if the elasticity of substitution between capital and labor is less than unity, unequal rates of growth of factors will result in a reduction in the growth rate of output (see Martin L. Weitzman, "Soviet Postwar Economic Growth and Capital-Labor Substitution," *American Economic Review* 60 [1970]: 679).

36. That is, it is not known whether the elasticity of substitution is less than 1.0 because the necessary statistical estimates have never been made.

37. See Denison and Chung, *Japan's Economy*, pp. 51, 78–83.

38. For an excellent exposition, see Armen A. Alchian and Harold Demsetz, "Production, Information Costs, and Economic Organization," *American Economic Review* 62 (1972): 777–95.

39. See chap. 9.

40. SZS, *Statistički godišnjak SFRJ 1972* (Belgrade: SZS, 1972), p. 79. The Yugoslavs working abroad were accompanied by almost 90,000 dependents; so the total number of Yugoslavs living outside the country was over 660,000.

41. For a recent discussion, see Dusko Doder, *The Yugoslavs* (New York: Random House, 1978), especially chap. 5.

42. Unemployment remained a serious problem throughout the sixties. In 1968, the number of persons seeking employment reached almost 330,000; in 1971, it was about 290,000 (SZS, *Statistički godišnjak SFRJ 1972*, p. 99), or nearly 5 percent of the economically active nonagricultural population (ibid., p. 79). These data are based on registrations at employment bureaus and probably understate the actual levels of unemployment.

APPENDIX E

1. This discussion and much of that in chapter 7 were reported in my paper, "A Measure of Structural Change in Output," *Review of Income and Wealth* 24 (1978): 105–18.

2. See G. Warren Nutter, "On Economic Size and Growth," *Journal of Law and Economics* 9 (1966): 163–88.

3. Zoltan Roman, "A Note on Measuring Structural Change," *Review of Income and Wealth* 15 (1969): 265–68. Algebraically, his measure is

$$V = \frac{1}{n} \sum_i |S_i|$$

where

$$S_i = \left(\frac{1 + \left(\frac{r_i}{100}\right)}{1 + \left(\frac{\bar{r}}{100}\right)} \right) 100 - 100.$$

$\bar{r}$ is the average of the percentage growth rates of the elements of the output bundle, r_i the percentage growth rate for element i, and n the number of elements. As written, V is an unweighted average, but Roman (ibid., p. 260) specified that this version of the formula was for "similarly important structural elements," clearly indicating that he meant a weighted average in the general case.

4. Oskar Kovać and Ljubomir Madžar, "Stope rasta i promene u privrednoj strukturi," *Ekonomist* 23 (1970): 5–31; and Marijan Korošić, *Strukturne promjene u industriji Jugoslaviji od 1960. do 1969. godine* (Zagreb: Ekonomiski institut, 1970). Algebraically, these measures can be represented by

$$S = \left(\frac{1}{n-1} \sum_i (r_i - \bar{r})^2 \right)^{1/2}$$

where the notation is the same as in the previous footnote.

5. But not in exactly the same way. The formula actually used by Kovać and Madžar for this purpose was

$$S_r = \sum_i W_{ri} \ln \left(\max \left(\frac{W_{r+1,i}}{W_{ri}}, \frac{W_{ri}}{W_{r+1,i}} \right) \right)$$

where W_{ri} denotes the share of the ith sector in the rth year. In contrast with the basic definition of entropy

$$\left(H = -\sum_i X_i \ln X_i \right),$$

the shares here enter nonsymmetrically. See Kovać and Madžar, "Stope rasta," and Henri Theil, *Economics and Information Theory* (Amsterdam: North-Holland, 1967), pp. 25–29.

6. This method was used by Kovać and Madžar, "Stope rasta."

7. The use of the cosine of the angle between commodity vectors was suggested by Linnemann in 1966, but in regard to the analysis of the commodity composition of foreign trade, where its theoretical basis is weak. Linnemann himself did not use the measure in his empirical work. (See Hans Linnemann, *An Econometric Study of International Trade Flows* [Amsterdam: North-Holland, 1966], pp. 141ff.) Kovać and Madžar, "Stope rasta," took the idea from Linnemann and used it as one of several measures in a study of the change in output composition in Yugoslavia. They did not, however, note the connection with the usual index numbers or the theoretical tie with the theory of economic growth.

8. By definition,

$$\cos\theta = \frac{a'b}{|a|\ |b|} = \frac{\Sigma a_i b_i}{(\Sigma a_i^2)^{1/2} (\Sigma b_i^2)^{1/2}} = \frac{\Sigma r_i a_i^2}{(\Sigma a_i^2)^{1/2} (\Sigma r_i^2 a_i^2)^{1/2}}$$

where a and b are the base- and given-period output vectors, respectively, and r_i designates the growth ratio for the ith commodity (i.e., $r_i = b_i/a_i$). It is evident that an equiproportional change in all growth rates, represented by multiplying each r_i by a constant k, leaves $\cos\theta$ unchanged.

9. This is easily shown. Let q_t denote the vector of quantities or values in period t, so that

$$\cos\hat{\theta} = \frac{\Sigma q_i^0 q_i^1}{(\Sigma (q_i^0)^2)^{1/2} (\Sigma (q_i^1)^2)^{1/2}}$$

Then let X_t denote the corresponding vector of output shares in period t, so that $X_t = q_i^t / \Sigma q_i^t$. (If physical quantities are used here, "share of output" loses its common sense meaning, but the principle remains the same.) Then the vector angle in terms of output shares is defined by

$$\cos \hat{\theta} = \frac{\Sigma X_i^0 \; X_i^t}{(\Sigma (X_i^0)^2)^{1/2} \; (\Sigma (X_i^t)^2)^{1/2}}$$

Substituting:

$$\cos \hat{\theta} = \frac{\Sigma \left(\frac{q_i^0}{\Sigma q_i^0}\right) \left(\frac{q_i^1}{\Sigma q_i^1}\right)}{\left(\Sigma \left(\frac{q_i^0}{\Sigma q_i^0}\right)^2\right)^{1/2} \left(\Sigma \left(\frac{q_i^1}{\Sigma q_i^1}\right)^2\right)^{1/2}} = \cos \theta$$

10. Let q_1^t denote the representative element in the output vector for the period t. Then the base year variance is given by

$$\sigma_0^2 = \frac{1}{n} \Sigma (q_i^0)^2 - (\bar{q}_0)^2$$

and the given year variance by

$$\sigma_1^2 = \frac{1}{n} \Sigma (q_i^1)^2 - (\bar{q}_1)^2$$

The covariance is given by

$$\sigma_{01} = \frac{1}{n} \Sigma q_i^0 \, q_i^1 - \bar{q}_0 \, q_1$$

Substituting in the formula for the cosine of the angle between the two vectors:

$$\cos \theta = \frac{\sigma_{01} + \bar{q}_0 \, \bar{q}_1}{(\sigma_0^2 + \bar{q}_0^2)^{1/2} \; (\sigma_1^2 + \bar{q}_1^2)^{1/2}}$$

As the sizes of the cosine of the angle and the angle itself are inversely related, the relationships in the text are obvious. It is this relation between θ and the covariance that provides the link to the rank correlation measure of structural change, but the link obviously is very weak.

11. In Nutter's terminology, this point is the boundary of the "normal" region of growth. If the output mix shifts "beyond" that defined by this limit, the value of the Laspeyres index recedes toward that corresponding to measurement along the original output ray. If the mix changes radically enough, the bias may be eliminated altogether. (See Nutter, "On Economic Size and Growth," p. 172.)

12. The normal relationship between Laspeyres and Paasche indexes holds over the normal region of production (see ibid., pp. 175–78).

13. Manipulation of the formula for the vector angle in terms of the variance and covariance gives:

$$\cos \theta = \frac{\left(\frac{\sigma_{01}}{\bar{q}_0 \bar{q}_1}\right) + 1}{(V_0^2 + 1)^{1/2} (V_1^2 + 1)^{1/2}}$$

where V_t denotes the coefficient of variation in the output vector for year t. The base year affects $\cos \theta$ in V_0 and $\bar{q}_0$. If the computation is carried out in terms of shares of several output branches, $\bar{q}_0 = 1/n$, where n is the number of branches; because $\cos \theta$ is the same whether shares or actual values are used in a computation in value terms, equality in the number of elements is sufficient to eliminate the influence of q_0 in the numerator. As can be seen, if the number of elements is the same and V_0 is the same for the two countries in some base period, differences in θ accurately reflect differences in structural change. If the number of elements is the same but V_0 is not, this is not the case; the extent of the error in θ is obviously a nonlinear function of the difference in the values of V_0 and θ, but can be computed readily.

14. As can be seen from the formula in the previous note, the relation is not linear in V.

Bibliography

SERBO-CROAT REFERENCES

Bajt, Aleksander. "Jugoslavenski društveni proizvod i njegovi činioci u razdoblju 1947–1964. godine." *Ekonomski pregled* 18 (1967): 339–62.

Bajt, Aleksander, and Mencinger, Jose. "Oživljavanje privredne djelatnosti u Jugoslaviji." In *Ubrzanje rasta Jugoslovenske privrede u uslovima stabilnosti*, edited by Savez ekonomista Jugoslavije, Centralni odbor, pp. 273–83. Zagreb: Informator, 1969.

Bogdanović, Miloš. *Ekonomika industrije SFRJ*. Belgrade: Privredno finansijski zavod, 1971.

Butaš, Nenad, and Puletić, Mihailo. *Priručnik o revalorizaciji sredstava organizacija udruženog rada*. Belgrade: Privredni pregled, 1971.

Čobeljić, Dušan. *Planiranje narodne privredne*. Belgrade: Rad, 1967.

Čobeljić, Nikola. *Privreda Jugoslavije: Rast, struktura i funkcionisanje*. Belgrade: Savremena administracija, 1974.

———. *Privreda Jugoslavije: Rast, struktura i funkcionisanje*. Belgrade: Savremena administracija, 1975.

Đodan, Šime. *Ekonomska politika Jugoslavije*. Zagreb: Školska knjiga, 1970.

"Dokumentacije uz zakon o društvenom planu federativne narodne republike Jugoslavije za godinu 1953," *Službeni list* 1953, no 5: 45–52.

Dragosavac, Dušan, et al., eds. *Aktuelni problemi privrednih kretanja i ekonomske politike Jugoslavije*. Zagreb: Informator, 1968.

"Društveni plan Jugoslavije za 1964. godinu." *Službeni list* 1963, no. 52: 943–61.

"Društveni plan Jugoslavije za 1965. godinu." *Službeni list* 1965, no. 5: 33–44.

"Društveni plan privrednog razvitka Jugoslavije od 1961. do 1965. godine." *Službeni list* 1960, no. 53: 969–97.

"Društveni plan privrednog razvoja Jugoslavije od 1957. do 1961. godine." *Službeni list* 1957, no. 53: 1,029–44.

"Društveni plan razvoja Jugoslavije od 1966. do 1970. godine." *Službeni list* 1966, no. 28: 473–524.

Dujšin, Uroš. "Sistem ekonomskih odnosa s inozenstvom." In *Aktuelni problemi privrednog razvoja i privrednog sistema Jugoslavije*, edited by Dragomir Vojnić, pp. 97–117. Zagreb: Informator, 1971.

Durovic, Dragoljub, ed. *Revalorizacija i amortizacija sredstava radnih organizacija*. Belgrade: Prosveta, 1966.

Farkaš, Vladimir, et al. *Ekonomika Jugoslavije*. Zagreb: Informator, 1970.

Grđić, Gojko. *Sistem narodno-privrednih bilansa*. Belgrade: Institut za ekonomiska istraživanja, 1967.

Horvat, Branko. *Privredni sistem i ekonomska politika Jugoslavije*. Belgrade: Institut ekonomskih nauka, 1970.

———. "Tehnički progres u Jugoslaviji." *Ekonomska analiza* 3 (1969): 29–57.

———. "Uzroci i karakteristike privrednih kretanja u 1961. i 1962. godini." *Ekonomist* 16 (1963): 3–15.

"Ispravak o izmjenama i dopunama tarife poreza na promet." *Službeni list* 1961, no. 33: 815.

Jovanović, Božidar. *Privredni razvoj Kosova i problem formiranja komunalnih centara*. Priština: n.p., 1970.

Korošić, Marijan. *Strukturne promjene u industriji Jugoslaviji od 1960. do 1969. godine*. Zagreb: Ekonomski institut, 1970.

Kovać, Oskar. "Spoljna trgovina kao faktor ubrzanja rasta." In *Ubrzanje rasta Jugoslavenske privrede u uslovima stabilnosti,* edited by Savez ekonomista Jugoslavije, Centralni odbor, pp. 161–85. Zagreb: Informator, 1969.

Kovać, Oskar, and Madžar, Ljubomir. "Stope rasta i promene u privrednoj strukturi." *Ekonomist* 23 (1970): 5–31.

Lang, Rikard. "Neki problemi privrednog sistema." *Ekonomist* 16 (1963): 133–42.

Marković, Branimir. *Kretanje narodnog dohotka, zaposlenosti i produktivnosti rada u privredi Jugoslavije 1947–1967*. Belgrade: SZS, 1970.

Mesarić, Milan, et al. *Problemi daljnjeg razvoja društvenog planiranja n Jugoslaviji*. Zagreb: Ekonomski institut, 1970.

"Naredbu o industrijskim proizvodima koji se ne mogo prodavati na kredit." *Službeni list* 1966, no. 17: 333.

"Naredbu o obaveznoj isporuci bakra, aluminija, olova, cinka, srebra, bizmuta, i žive određenim kategorijama potrošača u 1963. godinu." *Službeni list* 1963, no. 4: 71–72.

"Naredbu o obaveznoj isporuci bakra, aluminija, olova, cinku, srebra, bizmuta i žive određenim kategorijama potrošača u 1964. godinu." *Službeni list* 1964, no. 9: 221–22.

"Naredbu o obaveznoj isporuci elektrolitnog bakra, elektrolitnog cinku u bloku, kadmija, cink-lima, rafiniranog olova u bloku, srebra, alumunija u bloku i metalne žive za potrebe Jugoslavenske narodne armije u 1965. godinu." *Službeni list* 1965, no. 24: 1,060.

"Naredbu o privrednim djelatnosti koji se smatraju zanatskim djelatnostima." *Službeni list* 1963, no. 49: 901–2.

Nikolić, Miodrag. "Indeks fizičkog obima industriske proizvodnje." *Statistička revija* 6 (1956): 120–32.

———. *Nivo produktivnost rada u industriji po republikama 1952–1968*. Belgrade: SZS, 1970.

"Odluka o snijernicama za upotrebu sredstava općeg investicionag fonda za financiranje odredenih investicija." *Službeni list* 1963, no. 49: 413.

"Odluku o obaveznoj isporuci određenim korisnicima elektrolitnog bakra, elektrolitnog cinku u bloku, kadmija, cink-lima, rafiniranog olova u bloku, srebra, aluminija u bloku i metalne živa." *Službeni list* 1966, no. 8: 133.

"Odluku u odredivanju djelatnosti za koje privredne organizacija plaćaju kamate na poslovni fond po nižim stopama i djelatnosti za koje su oslobođenje od plaćanja tih kamata i doprinosa iz dohotka." *Službeni list* 1963, no. 25: 530–33.

"Odluku o stopama deprinosa iz dohotka privrednih organizacija." *Službeni list* 1961, no. 8: 102–3.

"Odluku o učesču investitora u troškovima investicija koje se financiraju iz općeg investicionog fonda." *Službeni list* 1955, no. 12: 1,968.

"Osnovni zakon o doprinosima i porezima gradana." *Službeni list* 1969, no. 13: 393–413.

"Osnovni zakon o društvenom planiranje." *Službeni list* 1970, no. 28: 725–28.

"Osnovni zakon o poduzećima." *Službeni list* 1965, no. 17: 813–39.

"Osnovni zakon o radnim odnosima." *Službeni list* 1965, no. 17: 797–811.

Popov, Sofija, and Jovičić, Milena. *Uticaj ličnih dohodaka na kretanje cena*. Belgrade: Institut ekonomskih nauka, 1971.

"Pravilnik o načinu obracunavanja i plaćanja doprinosa iz osobnog dohotka radnika." *Službeni list* 1965, no. 30: 1,186–91.

"Pravilnik o obračunavauju i plaćanju sredstava za zajedničke rezerve privrednih organizacija." *Službeni list* 1965, no. 57: 1,923–24.

"Pravilnik o utvrđivanju osnovica i o načinu obračunavanja i plačanja doprinosa za socijalno osiguranje." *Službeni list* 1966, no. 1: 30–39.

"Prečišćeni tekst: Tarife poreza na promet." *Službeni list* 1961, no. 19: 484–503.

"Preporuku o raspodjeli dohotka i osobnih dohodaka u radnim organizacijama." *Službeni list* 1965, no. 35: 1414–16.

"Privremena tarifa poreza na promet." *Službeni list* 1952, no. 9: 126–32.

Radulović, Milos. *Sistem i politika cijena u Jugoslaviji (1945–1965)*. Belgrade: Institut društvenih nauka, 1971.

"Savezni društveni plan za 1954. godinu." *Službeni list* 1954, no. 13: 258–71.

"Savezni društveni plan za 1955. godinu." *Službeni list* 1954, no. 56: 801–27.

"Savezni društveni plan za 1956. godinu." *Službeni list* 1956, no. 14: 205–27.

"Savezni društveni plan za 1957. godinu." *Službeni list* 1956, no. 54: 913–35.

"Savezni društveni plan za 1958. godinu." *Službeni list* 1957, no. 54: 1,121–42.

"Savezni društveni plan za 1959. godinu." *Službeni list* 1958, no. 50: 1,177–95.

"Savezni društveni plan za 1960. godinu." *Službeni list* 1959, no. 52: 1,201–18.

"Savezni društveni plan za 1961. godinu." *Službeni list* 1960, no. 53: 997–1,015.

"Savezni društveni plan za 1962. godinu." *Službeni list* 1961, no. 52: 1,033–49.

"Savezni društveni plan za 1963. godinu." *Službeni list* 1962, no. 53: 881–96.

Savezni zavod za statistiku (SZS). *CENE, Januar-Mart 1957*. Statistički bilten, no. 79. Belgrade: SZS, 1957.

———. *CENE, April-Jun 1962*. Statistički bilten, no. 243. Belgrade: SZS, 1962.

———. *CENE, Januar-Mart 1968*. Statistički bilten, no. 530. Belgrade: SZS, 1968.

———. *Demografska statistika 1971*. Belgrade: SZS, 1974.

———. *Indeks fisičkog obima industriske proizvodnje: Metodologija i ponderacioni sistem*. Metodološki materijali, no. 82. Belgrade: SZS, 1957.

———. *Industrija 1939 i 1946–1956*. Statistički bilten, no. 81. Belgrade: SZS, 1957.

———. *Industrija 1957*. Statistički bilten, no. 108. Belgrade: SZS, 1958.

———. *Industrija 1958*. Statistički bilten, no. 136. Belgrade: SZS, 1959.
———. *Industrija 1959*. Statistički bilten, no. 169. Belgrade: SZS, 1960.
———. *Industrija 1960*. Statistički bilten, no. 205. Belgrade: SZS, 1961.
———. *Industrija 1961*. Statistički bilten, no. 236. Belgrade: SZS, 1962.
———. *Industrija 1962*. Statistički bilten, no. 272. Belgrade: SZS, 1963.
———. *Industrija 1963*. Statistički bilten, no. 308. Belgrade: SZS, 1964.
———. *Industrija 1964*. Statistički bilten, no. 357. Belgrade: SZS, 1965.
———. *Industrija 1965*. Statistički bilten, no. 412. Belgrade: SZS, 1966.
———. *Industrija 1966*. Statistički bilten, no. 476. Belgrade: SZS, 1967.
———. *Industrija 1967*. Statistički bilten, no. 528. Belgrade: SZS, 1968.
———. *Industrija 1968*. Statistički bilten, no. 584. Belgrade: SZS, 1969.
———. *Industrija 1969*. Statistički bilten, no. 627. Belgrade: SZS, 1970.
———. *Industrija 1970*. Statistički bilten, no. 666. Belgrade: SZS, 1971.
———. *Industrija 1971*. Statistički bilten, no. 730. Belgrade: SZS, 1972.
———. *Industrija 1972*. Statistički bilten, no. 793. Belgrade: SZS, 1973.
———. *Industrija 1973*. Statistički bilten, no. 847. Belgrade: SZS, 1974.
———. *Industrija 1974*. Statistički bilten, no. 910. Belgrade: SZS, 1975.
———. *Industrija 1975*. Statistički bilten, no. 967. Belgrade: SZS, 1976.
———. *Industrijska preduzeća 1962*. Statistički bilten, no. 283. Belgrade: SZS, 1963.
———. *Industrijska preduzeća 1969*. Statistički bilten, no. 695. Belgrade: SZS, 1971.
———. *Industrijska preduzeća 1971*. Statistički bilten, no. 769. Belgrade: SZS, 1973.
———. *Industrijske organizacije 1974*. Statištički bilten, no. 955. Belgrade: SZS, 1975.
———. *Industrijski proizvodi 1968*. Statistički bilten, no. 634. Belgrade: SZS, 1970.
———. *Industrijski proizvodi 1970*. Statistički bilten, no. 717. Belgrade: SZS, 1972.
———. *Industrijski proizvodi 1971*. Statistički bilten, no. 775. Belgrade: SZS, 1973.
———. *Jugoslavija 1945–1964: Statistički pregled*. Belgrade: SZS, 1965.
———. *Konačni rezultati popisa stanovništva od 15 Marta 1948. godine*. Belgrade: SZS, 1954.
———. *Materijalni i društveni razvoj SFR Jugoslavije, 1947–1972*. Belgrade: SZS, 1973.
———. *Međusobni odnosi privrednih delatnosti Jugoslavije u 1955. godini*. Studije, analize i prikazi, no. 8. Belgrade: SZS, 1957.
———. *Međusobni odnosi privrednih delatnosti Jugoslavije u 1958. godini*. Studije, analize i prikazi, no. 15. Belgrade: SZS, 1962.
———. *Međusobni odnosi privrednih delatnosti Jugoslavije u 1962. godini*. Studije, analize i prikazi, no. 26. Belgrade: SZS, 1966.
———. *Međusobni odnosi privrednih delatnosti Jugoslavije 1962 i 1966: Uvoz po delatnostima porekla i namene*. Studije, analize i prikazi, no. 50. Belgrade: SZS, 1970.
———. *Međusobni odnosi privrednih delatnosti Jugoslavije u 1964*. Studije, analize i prikazi, no. 35. Belgrade: SZS, 1967.
———. *Međusobni odnosi privrednih delatnosti Jugoslavije u 1966*. Studije, analize i prikazi, no. 42. Belgrade: SZS, 1969.

———. *Međusobni odnosi privrednih delatnosti Jugoslavije u 1968*. Studije, analize i prikazi, no. 57. Belgrade: SZS, 1971.

———. *Metodologija za obračun narodnog dobotka u 1954. godini*. Metodološki materijali, no. 61. Belgrade: SZS, 1955.

———. *Nomenklatura proizvoda i sirovina za godišnji izveštaj industrijskih preduzeća za 1957. godinu*. Metodološki materijali, no. 90. Belgrade: SZS, 1958.

———. *Nomenklatura proizvoda za godišnji izveštaj industrije*. Metodološki materijali, no. 192. Belgrade: SZS, 1969.

———. *Nomenklatura proizvoda za godišnji izveštaj industrije*. Metodološki materijali, no. 203. Belgrade: SZS, 1972.

———. *Osnovna sredstva društvene privrede SFRJ, SR i SAP 1952–1971*. Belgrade: SZS, 1973.

———. *Popis stanovništva 1953*. Belgrade: SZS, 1959.

———. *Popis stanovništva 1961*. Belgrade: SZS, 1965.

———. *Popis stanovništva 1971*. Belgrade: SZS, 1974.

———. *Privredni bilans Jugoslavije 1952–1962*. Studije, analiza i prikazi, no. 19. Belgrade: SZS, 1963.

———. *Privredni bilans Jugoslavije 1962–1965*. Studije, analiza i prikazi, no. 29. Belgrade: SZS, 1966.

———. *Privredni bilansi Jugoslavije 1964–1968*. Studije, analiza i prikazi, no. 46. Belgrade: SZS, 1969.

———. *Privredni bilansi Jugoslavije 1965–1966*. Belgrade: SZS, 1968.

———. *Privredni bilansi Jugoslavije 1966–1969*. Studije, analize i prikazi, no. 54. Belgrade: SZS, 1971.

———. *Privredni bilansi Jugoslavije 1966–1971*. Studije, analize i prikazi, no. 61. Belgrade: SZS, 1973.

———. *Statistički godišnjak FNRJ 1954*. Belgrade: SZS, 1954.

———. *Statistički godišnjak FNRJ 1955*. Belgrade: SZS, 1955.

———. *Statistički godišnjak FNRJ 1956*. Belgrade: SZS, 1956.

———. *Statistički godišnjak FNRJ 1957*. Belgrade: SZS, 1957.

———. *Statistički godišnjak FNRJ 1958*. Belgrade: SZS, 1958.

———. *Statistički godišnjak FNRJ 1959*. Belgrade: SZS, 1959.

———. *Statistički godišnjak FNRJ 1960*. Belgrade: SZS, 1960.

———. *Statistički godišnjak FNRJ 1961*. Belgrade: SZS, 1961.

———. *Statistički godišnjak FNRJ 1962*. Belgrade: SZS, 1962.

———. *Statistički godišnjak SFRJ 1963*. Belgrade: SZS, 1963.

———. *Statistički godišnjak SFRJ 1964*. Belgrade: SZS, 1964.

———. *Statistički godišnjak SFRJ 1965*. Belgrade: SZS, 1965.

———. *Statistički godišnjak SFRJ 1966*. Belgrade: SZS, 1966.

———. *Statistički godišnjak SFRJ 1967*. Belgrade: SZS, 1967.

———. *Statistički godišnjak SFRJ 1968*. Belgrade: SZS, 1968.

———. *Statistički godišnjak SFRJ 1969*. Belgrade: SZS, 1969.

———. *Statistički godišnjak SFRJ 1970*. Belgrade: SZS, 1970.

———. *Statistički godišnjak SFRJ 1971*. Belgrade: SZS, 1971.

———. *Statistički godišnjak SFRJ 1972*. Belgrade: SZS, 1972.

———. *Statistički godišnjak SFRJ 1973*. Belgrade: SZS, 1973.

———. *Uputsva i nomenklatura za mesečni izveštaj industrijskih preduzeća*. Metodološki materijali, no. 129. Belgrade: SZS, 1962.

———. *Zaposleno osoblje, April 1968*. Statistički bilten, no. 523. Belgrade: SZS, 1968.

———. *Zapolenost 30.IX 1972*. Statistički bilten, no. 798. Belgrade: SZS, 1973.

Sharmo, Soumitra K. "Analiza faktora rasta poslijeratnog ekonomskog razvoja Jugoslavije (1947–1967)." *Ekonomist* 21 (1968): 381–97.

Sicherl, Pavle. "Analiza nekih elemenata za ocenu stepene razvijenosti republika i pokrajina." *Ekonomska analiza* 3 (1969): 5–28.

Sirotković, Jakov. *Planiranje u sistem samoupravljanje*. Zagreb: Informator, 1966.

Sirotković, Jakov, and Stipetić, Vladimir, eds. *Ekonomika Jugoslavije*. Zagreb: Informator, 1967.

Sokolov, Lazar. *Dostignuti stepen i perspektiva privrednog razvoja nedovoljno razvijenih područja u Jugoslaviji*. Skopje: Ekonomski institut na univerzitetot "Kiril i metodij," 1973.

———. "Radna snaga u nedovoljno razvijenim područjima." In *Ubrzanje rasta Jugoslavenske privrede u uslovima stabilnosti*, edited by Savez ekonomista Jugoslavije, Centralni odbor, pp. 101–22. Zagreb: Informator, 1969.

Srebrić, Borijav. "Neki problemi usavršavanja metoda i mehanisma razvoja nerazvijenih područja u Jugoslaviji." In *Ubrzanje rasta Jugoslavenske privrede u uslovima stabilnosti*, edited by Savez ekonomista Jugoslavije, Centralni odbor, pp. 83–100. Zagreb: Informator, 1969.

Stipetić, Vladimir. "Ekonomska odnosi s inozenstvom." In *Aktuelni problemi privrednog razvoja i privrednog sistema Jugoslavie*, edited by Dragomir Vojnić, pp. 232–57. Zagreb: Informator, 1971.

Suhina, Branko. *Amortizacija osnovnih sredstava*. 2d ed. Zagreb: Informator, 1970.

SZS: *see* Savezni zavod za statistiku.

"Tarifa poreza na promet." *Službeni list* 1952, no. 34: 1–12.

Turčić, Ivan. *Regonalni i granski aspekt efikasnosti uloženih sredstave Jugoslavenske industrije 1964. i 1967. godine*. Zagreb: Ekonomski institut, 1970.

"Uputsvo o postanjem određivanju djelatnosti za koje radne organizacije ne plaćaju doprinos iz dohotha po zakon o oslobađanju od plaćanje doprinosa iz dohotka ostvarenog vršenjem određenih delatnosti." *Službeni list* 1964, no. 33: 682–83.

"Uputsvo o provođenju nacela i općih mjerila za raspodjelu čistog prihoda u pravilnicima privrednih organizacija." *Službeni list* 1962, no. 16: 270–74.

"Uputsvo o provođenju načela raspodjeli vistog prihoda privrednih organizacija." *Službeni list* 1963, no. 19: 416–18.

"Uredbu o izmjenama i dopunama tarife poreza na promet." *Službeni list* 1961, no. 31: 798–800.

"Uredbu o izmjenama i dopunama uredbe o tarifi poreza na promet." *Službeni list* 1952, no. 58: 905–6.

"Uredbu o izmjenama i dopunama uredbe o tarifi poreza na promet." *Službeni list* 1952, no. 63: 983–84.

"Uredbu o izmjenama tarife poreza na promet." *Službeni list* 1961, no. 27: 737.

"Uredbu o raspodeli ukupnog prihoda privrednih organizacija." *Službeni list* 1957, no. 16: 265–80.

"Ustav socijalističke federativne republike Jugoslavije." *Službeni list* 1963, no. 14: 261–89.

Vajković, Teodosije. "Funkcije proizvodnije-problemi primjene i ocjenjivanju." *Ekonomist* 21 (1968): 775–90.

Vasić, Velimir. *Ekonomska politika Jugoslavije*. Belgrade: Savremena administracija, 1970.

Vinski, Ivo. "Rast fiksnih fondova Jugoslavije od 1944 do 1964." *Ekonomist* 18 (1965): 667–79.

———. "Rast fiksnih fondova Jugoslavije od reforme do početka 1967." *Ekonomski pregled* 18 (1967): 485–507.

Vojnić, Dragomir. *Investicije i ekonomski razvoj*. Zagreb: Ekonomski institut, 1970.

———. *Investicije i fiksni fondovi Jugoslavije*. Zagreb: Ekonomski Institut, 1970.

———, ed. *Aktuelni problemi privrednog razvoja i privrednog sistema Jugoslavije*. Zagreb: Informator, 1971.

Yugoslavia Federal Executive Council. Secretariat for Information. *The Five Year Plan of Economic Development of Yugoslavia 1961–1965*. Belgrade: Secretariat of Information, 1961.

Yugoslavia [Kingdom]. *Statistički godišnjak 1940*. Belgrade: Državna stamparija, 1941.

"Zakon o bankama." *Službeni list* 1961, no. 10: 209–23.

"Zakon o bankama i kreditnim poslovima." *Službeni list* 1965, no. 12: 392–407.

"Zakon o doprinosa iz dohotka privrednih organizacija." *Službeni list* 1961, no. 8: 96–99.

"Zakon o doprinosima fondu za obnovu i izgradnju Skoplja za 1964. godini." *Službeni list* 1963, no. 36: 806.

"Zakon o dopunama osnovnog zakona o porezu na promet." *Službeni list* 1967, no. 31: 900.

"Zakon o dopuni zakona o oslobađanje od plaćanja doprinos iz dohotka ostvarenog vršenjem odredenih delatnosti." *Službeni list* 1964, no. 52: 973.

"Zakon o dopuni zakona o tarifi Saveznog poreza na promet." *Službeni list* 1966, no. 4: 70.

"Zakon o društvenom planu federativne narodne republike Jugoslavije za godinu 1952." *Službeni list* 1952, no. 17: 277–98.

"Zakon o društvenom planu federativne narodne republike Jugoslavije za godinu 1953." *Službeni list* 1952, no. 62: 969–76.

"Zakon o izdvajanju sredstava za stambenu izgradnju." *Službeni list* 1965, no. 35: 1,396–97.

"Zakon o izmjenama i dopuna zakona o tarifi Saveznog poreza na promet." *Službeni list* 1968, no. 24: 445–46.

"Zakon o izmjenama i dopunama osnovnog zakona o doprinosa i porezima građana." *Službeni list* 1968, no. 32: 690–95.

"Zakon o izmjenama i dopunama osnovnog zakona o podūzećima." *Službeni list* 1968, no. 48: 982–86.

"Zakon o izmjenama i dopunama osnovnog zakona o porezu na promet." *Službeni list* 1965, no. 57: 1,893–4.

"Zakon o izmjenama i dopunama osnovnog zakona o porezu na promet." *Službeni list* 1966, no. 52: 1,098–1,103.

"Zakon o izmjenama i dopunama zakona o bankama i kreditnim poslovima." *Službeni list* 1966, no. 4: 72.

"Zakon o izmjenama i dopunama zakona o bankama i kreditnim poslovima." *Službeni list* 1966, no. 26: 460.

"Zakon o izmjenama i dopunama zakona o sredstvima privrednih organizacija." *Službeni list* 1967, no. 1: 10–11.

"Zakon o izmjenama i dopunama zakona o sredstvima privrednih organizacija." *Službeni list* 1965, no. 14: 608–11.

"Zakon o izmjenama i dopunama zakona o tarifi Saveznog poreza na promet." *Službeni list* 1965, no. 57: 1,894–5.

"Zakon o izmjenama i dopunama zakona o tarifi Saveznog poreza na promet." *Službeni list* 1967, no. 5: 117–8.

"Zakon o izmjenama i dopunama zakona o tarifi Saveznog poreza na promet." *Službeni list* 1968, no. 30: 609–10.

"Zakon o izmjenama i dopunama zakona o tarifi Saveznog poreza na promet." *Službeni list* 1968, no. 45: 913.

"Zakon o izmjenama i dopunama zakona o tarifi Saveznog poreza na promet." *Službeni list* 1968, no. 55: 1,298–1,300.

"Zakon o izmjenama i dopunama zakona o tarifi Saveznog poreza na promet." *Službeni list* 1969, no. 50: 1,223–4.

"Zakon o izmjenama i dopunama zakona o tarifi Saveznog poreza na promet." *Službeni list* 1970, no. 18: 581–2.

"Zakon o izmjenama i dopunama zakona o tarifi Saveznog poreza na promet." *Službeni list* 1971, no. 24: 413–4.

"Zakon o izmjenama i dopunama zakona o tarifi Saveznog poreza na promet." *Službeni list* 1971, no. 32: 620–1.

"Zakon o izmjenama zakona o tarifi Saveznog poreza na promet." *Službeni list* 1970, no. 52: 1,253.

"Zakon o izmjeni zakona o tarifi Saveznog poreza na promet." *Službeni list* 1966, no. 28: 545.

"Zakon o izmjeni zakona o tarifi Saveznog poreza na promet." *Službeni list* 1967, no. 18: 488.

"Zakon o narodnoj banci Jugoslavije." *Službeni list* 1965, no. 12: 408–12.

"Zakon o oslobađanju od plaćanja doprinosa iz dohotka ostvarenog vršenjem određenih djelatnosti." *Službeni list* 1964, no. 26: 481.

"Zakon o porezu na osobni prihod građana." *Službeni list* 1960, no. 24: 488–90.

"Zakon o republikama i pokrajni koje se smatraju privredno nedovoljno razvijenim." *Službeni list* 1971, no. 33: 641.

"Zakon o upotrebi sredstava federacija za investicije u privredi." *Službeni list* 1963, no. 52: 978–79.

"Zakon o upotrebi sredstava radnih organicacija u 1965. godini." *Službeni list* 1965, no. 19: 891.

"Zakon o Saveznom porezu na promet." *Službeni list* 1965, no. 33: 1251–85.

Živančević, Dragomir. *Zbirka propisa o sredstvima, utvrđivanju i raspodeli dohotka i knjigovodstvu u radnim organizacijama*. Belgrade: Savremena administracija, n.d.

OTHER REFERENCES

Adelman, Irma. *Theories of Economic Growth and Development*. Stanford: Stanford University Press, 1961.

Alchian, Armen A., and Demsetz, Harold. "Production, Information Costs, and Economic Organization." *American Economic Review* 62 (1972): 777–95.

Alton, Thad P. "Economic Structure and Growth in Eastern Europe." In *Economic Developments in Countries of Eastern Europe*, edited by U.S., Congress, Joint Economic Committee, pp. 41–67. Washington, D.C.: Government Printing Office, 1970.

Alton, Thad P., et al. "Economic Growth in Eastern Europe, 1965–1977." Research Project on National Income in East Central Europe, Occasional Paper no. OP-53. Mimeographed. New York: RPNIECE, 1978.

Alton, Thad P., et al. "Statistics on East European Economic Structure and Growth." Research Project on National Income in East Central Europe, Occasional Paper no. OP-48. Mimeographed. New York: RPNIECE, 1975.

Bacharach, Michael. *Biproportional Matrices and Input-Output Change*. Cambridge: Cambridge University Press, 1970.

Bajt, Aleksander. "Investment Cycles in European Socialist Economies: A Review Article." *Journal of Economic Literature* 9 (1971): 53–63.

Barna, Tibor. "On Measuring Capital." In *The Theory of Capital*, edited by F. A. Lutz and D. C. Hague, pp. 75–94. London: Macmillan & Co., 1963.

Bauer, P. T. *Dissent on Development*. London: Weidenfeld & Nicolson, 1971.

Becker, Gary S. *Economic Theory*. New York: Alfred A. Knopf, 1971.

Berlinguette, V. R., and Leacy, F. H. "The Estimation of Real Domestic Product by Final Expenditure Categories and by Industry of Origin in Canada." In *Output, Input, and Productivity Measurement*, edited by National Bureau of Economic Research, pp. 203–43. Studies in Income and Wealth, vol. 25. Princeton: Princeton University Press, 1961.

Bombelles, Joseph T. *Economic Development of Communist Yugoslavia, 1947–1964*. Stanford: Hoover Institution Press, 1968.

Brown, Alan A.; Licari, Joseph A.; and Neuberger, Egon. "Productivity Measurement in Socialist Economies Using Divisia Indexes and Adjusted Factor Shares." *Southern Economic Journal* 42 (1976): 482–85.

Brown, Murray. *On the Theory and Measurement of Technological Change*. Cambridge: Cambridge University Press, 1966.

———. "The Measurement of Capital Aggregates—A Post Reswitching Problem." Mimeographed. New York: National Bureau of Economic Research, 1976.

Burmeister, Edwin. "Comments on Capital Aggregation." Mimeographed. New York: National Bureau of Economic Research, 1976.

Carré, J. J.; Dubois, P.; and Malinvaud, E. *French Economic Growth*. Stanford: Stanford University Press, 1975.

Cohn, Stanley. "The Soviet Path to Economic Growth: A Comparative Analysis." *Review of Income and Wealth* 22 (1976): 49–59.

David, D. A., and Van de Klundert, Th. "Biased Efficiency Growth in the U.S." *American Economic Review* 55 (1965): 357–94.

Dedijer, Vladimir, et al. *History of Yugoslavia*. New York: McGraw-Hill, 1974.

Denison, Edward F. *Accounting for United States Economic Growth, 1929–1969*. Washington, D.C.: Brookings Institution, 1974.

———. "Some Major Issues in Productivity Analysis: An Examination of Estimates by Jorgenson and Griliches." *Survey of Current Business* 49, part 2 (1969): 1–27.

———. *Why Growth Rates Differ*. Washington, D.C.: Brookings Institution, 1969.

Denison, Edward F., and Chung, William K. *How Japan's Economy Grew So Fast*. Washington, D.C.: Brookings Institution, 1976.

Desai, Padma. "The Production Function and Technical Change in Postwar Soviet Industry: A Reexamination." *American Economic Review* 66 (1976): 372–81.

Diewert, W. E. "Exact and Superlative Index Numbers." *Journal of Econometrics* 4 (1976): 115–45.

Dirlam, Joel B., and Plummer, James L. *An Introduction to the Yugoslav Economy*. Columbus, Ohio: Charles E. Merrill, 1973.

Djilas, Milovan. *The Unperfect Society: Beyond the New Class*. New York: Harcourt, Brace & World, 1969.

Đ. M. "Yugoslavia's Plan of Economic Development." *Yugoslav Survey* 1/2 (1960/61): 468–77.

Doder, Dusko. *The Yugoslavs*. New York: Random House, 1978.

Dodge, Norton T., and Wilber, Charles K. "The Relevance of Soviet Industrial Experience for Less Developed Economies." *Soviet Studies* 21 (1970): 330–49.

Dubey, Vinod. *Yugoslavia: Development with Decentralization*. Baltimore: Johns Hopkins University Press, 1975.

Đurbabić, Marko. "Citizens' Contributions and Taxes." *Yugoslav Survey* 26 (1966): 3,793–3,802.

Eckstein, Alexander, ed. *Comparison of Economic Systems*. Berkeley and Los Angeles: University of California Press, 1971.

Fisher, Irving. *The Nature of Capital and Income*. New York: Macmillan, 1906.

Frankel, S. Herbert. *Some Conceptual Aspects of International Economic Development of Underdeveloped Territories*. Essays in International Finance, no. 14. Princeton: Princeton University Press, 1952.

Furubotn, Eirik G. "The Long-Run Analysis of the Labor-Managed Firm: An Alternative Interpretation." *American Economic Review* 66 (1976): 104–23.

Furubotn, Eirik G., and Pejovich, Svetozar A. "Property Rights and the Behavior of the Firm in a Socialist State: The Example of Yugoslavia." *Zeitschrift für Nationalökonomie* 30 (1970): 431–54.

———. "Tax Policy and the Investment Decisions of the Yugoslav Firms." *National Tax Journal* 23 (1970): 335–48.

Germany [Federal Republic]. Statistiches Bundesamt. *Statistiches Jahrbuch für die Bundesrepublik Deutschland 1974*. Stuttgart: Statistiches Bundesamt, 1974.

Gilbert, Milton, and Beckerman, Wilfred. "International Comparisons of Real Product and Productivity by Final Expenditures and by Industry." In *Output, Input, and Productivity Measurement,* edited by National Bureau of Economic Research, pp. 251–70. Studies in Income and Wealth, vol. 25, Princeton: Princeton University Press, 1961.

Greenslade, Rush V. "Industrial Production in the USSR." In *Soviet Economic Statistics,* edited by Vladimir G. Treml and John P. Hardt, pp. 155–94. Durham, N.C.: Duke University Press, 1972.

Greenslade, Rush V., and Robertson, Wade E. "Industrial Production in the U.S.S.R." In *Soviet Economic Prospects for the Seventies,* edited by U.S., Congress, Joint Economic Committee, pp. 270–82. Washington, D.C.: Government Printing Office, 1973.

Grossman, Gregory. *Soviet Statistics of Physical Output of Industrial Commodities: Their Compilation and Quality*. Princeton: Princeton University Press, 1960.

Hagen, Everett E. *The Economics of Development*. Homewood, Ill.: Richard D. Irwin, 1975.

Hamilton, F. E. I. *Yugoslavia: Patterns of Economic Activity*. New York: Praeger, 1968.

Hauvonen, J. J. "Postwar Developments in Money and Banking in Yugoslavia." *IMF Staff Papers* 17 (1970): 563–98.

Higgins, Benjamin. *Economic Development*. New York: W. W. Norton & Co., 1968.

Hirschman, Albert O. *The Strategy of Economic Development*. New Haven: Yale University Press, 1958.

Horvat, Branko. "Business Cycles in Yugoslavia." *Eastern European Economics* 9 (1971): 1–259.

———. *The Yugoslav Economic System*. White Plains, N.Y.: International Arts and Sciences Press, 1976.

Houthakker, H. "The Pareto Distribution and the Cobb-Douglas Production Function in Activity Analysis." *Review of Economic Studies* 23 (1955/56): 27–31.

Inter-Allied Reparation Agency. *Report of the Assembly of the Inter-Allied Reparation Agency to Its Member Governments*. Brussels: IARA, 1951.

———. *Report of the Secretary General for the Year 1949*. Brussels: IARA, 1950.

Japan. Bureau of Statistics. *Japan Statistical Yearbook 1971*. Tokyo: Bureau of Statistics, 1972.

Jorgenson, D. W., and Griliches, Z. "The Explanation of Productivity Change." *Review of Economic Studies* 34 (1967): 249–82.

Jovanović, Božidar. "Reform of the Credit and Banking System." *Yugoslav Survey* 22 (1966): 3,215–36.

———. "Taxation of Workers' Personal Incomes." *Yugoslav Survey* new series 9 (1968): 103–8.

Kendrick, John W. *Productivity Trends in the United States*. Princeton: Princeton University Press, 1961.

Kmenta, Jan. *Elements of Econometrics*. New York: Macmillan, 1971.

Knight, Frank H. "The Quantity of Capital and the Rate of Interest." *Journal of Political Economy* 44 (1936): 433–63, 612–42.

Lakočević, Ljubomir. "Printing and Publishing, 1963–1968." *Yugoslav Survey* new series 10 (1969): 99–118.

Lave, Lester B. *Technological Change: Concept and Measurement*. Englewood Cliffs, N.J.: Prentice-Hall, 1966.

Leontief, Wassily, et al. *Studies in the Structure of the American Economy*. New York: Oxford University Press, 1953.

Lewis, J. Patrick. "Postwar Economic Growth and Productivity in the Soviet Communications Industry." *Bell Journal of Economics* 6 (1975): 430–50.

Linnemann, Hans. *An Econometric Study of International Trade Flows*. Amsterdam: North-Holland, 1966.

Lutz, F. A., and Hague, D. C. *The Theory of Capital*. London: Macmillan & Co., 1963.

Macesich, George. *Yugoslavia: The Theory and Practice of Development Planning*. Charlottesville: University Press of Virginia, 1964.

Maclean, Fitzroy. *The Heretic*. New York: Harper & Row, 1957.

Milenkovitch, Deborah O. *Plan and Market in Yugoslav Economic Thought*. New Haven: Yale University Press, 1971.

Milošević, Miodrag. "The Chemical Industry." *Yugoslav Survey* new series 10 (1969): 55–64.

Mirkovich, Nicholas, ed. *Jugoslav Postwar Reconstruction Papers*. 4 vols., mimeographed. New York: Yugoslavia, Office of Reconstruction and Economic Affairs, 1942–43.

Moore, John H. "A Measure of Structural Change in Output." *Review of Income and Wealth* 24 (1978): 105–18.

———. "Industrial Production in Yugoslavia, 1952–1975." In *East European Economies Post-Helsinki,* edited by U.S., Congress, Joint Economic Committee, pp. 479–502. Washington, D.C.: Government Printing Office, 1977.

———. "Yugoslav Regional Development Policy, 1952–71." *Revue de l'est,* forthcoming.

Mundlak, Yair, and Razin, Assaf. "Aggregation, Index Numbers and the Measurement of Technical Change." *Review of Economics and Statistics* 51 (1969): 1,966–75.

Nadiri, M. Ishaq. "Some Approaches to the Theory and Measurement of Total Factor Productivity: A Survey." *Journal of Economic Literature* 8 (1970): 1,137–77.

Neal, Fred Warner. *Titoism in Action*. Berkeley and Los Angeles: University of California Press, 1958.

Nikolić, Miodrag. "Consumption of Industrial Materials." *Yugoslav Survey* new series 7 (1966): 3,611–16.

Noller, Carl W. "The Role of Money, Credit and Financial Intermediaries in an Evolving Economy: The Yugoslav Case, 1952–1968." Ph.D. dissertation, University of Virginia, 1975.

Nutter, G. Warren. *The Growth of Industrial Production in the Soviet Union*. Princeton: Princeton University Press, 1962.

———. "On Economic Size and Growth." *Journal of Law and Economics* 9 (1966): 163–88.

Obradović, Josip. *Workers' Participation in Yugoslavia: Theory and Research.* University of South Carolina, Institute of International Studies, Occasional Paper. Columbia: Institute of International Studies, n.d.

Organization for Economic Cooperation and Development. *Main Economic Indicators: Historical Statistics, 1955–1971.* Paris: OECD, 1973.

———. *National Accounts of OECD Countries, 1960–1971.* Paris: OECD, n.d.

———. *Socialist Federal Republic of Yugoslavia.* Paris: OECD, 1963.

———. *Socialist Federal Republic of Yugoslavia.* Paris: OECD, 1964.

———. *Socialist Federal Republic of Yugoslavia.* Paris: OECD, 1965.

———. *Socialist Federal Republic of Yugoslavia.* Paris: OECD, 1966.

———. *Yugoslavia, 1962.* Paris: OECD, 1962.

———. *Yugoslavia.* Paris: OECD, 1969.

———. *Yugoslavia.* Paris: OECD, 1970.

Organization for European Economic Cooperation. *General Statistics,* part 2, 1960, no. 1. Paris: OEEC, 1960.

Paj, Ivan. "The Development of the System of Distribution of the Social Product and Net Income." *Yugoslav Survey* new series 11 (1970): 65–88.

Pejovich, Svetozar A. "A Note on Bank Credit and the Investment Behavior of the Firm in Socialism." *Jahrbuch der Wirtschaft Osteuropas* 5 (1974): 155–70.

———. *The Market-Planned Economy of Yugoslavia.* Minneapolis: University of Minnesota Press, 1966.

"Resolution on the Socialist Development in Yugoslavia on the Basis of Self-Management and the Tasks of the League of Communists." *Yugoslav Survey* new series 10 (1969): 15–58.

Roman, Zoltan. "A Note on Measuring Structural Change." *Review of Income and Wealth* 15 (1969): 265–68.

Rusinow, Dennison. *The Yugoslav Experiment, 1948–1974.* Berkeley and Los Angeles: University of California Press, 1977.

Sekulić, Slobodan. "Investment Capital of Socio-Political Communities." *Yugoslav Survey* new series 11 (1970): 1–12.

Sims, Christopher A. "Theoretical Basis for a Double Deflated Index for Real Value Added." *Review of Economics and Statistics* 51 (1969): 470–71.

Sirc, Ljubo. "Lessons of Workers' Self-Management in Yugoslavia." Mimeographed. Glasgow, Scotland: University of Glasgow, 1975.

Staar, Richard F. *The Communist Regimes in Eastern Europe.* Rev. ed. Stanford: Hoover Institution Press, 1971.

Štajner, Rikard. "The System of Planning." *Yugoslav Survey* new series 12 (1971): 15–30.

Star, Spencer. "Accounting for the Growth of Output." *American Economic Review* 64 (1974): 123–35.

Stefanovich, Mileva. "Ferrous Mining and Metallurgy, 1963–1968." *Yugoslav Survey* new series 10 (1969): 57–66.

Stigler, George J. "Economic Problems in Measuring Productivity." In *Output, Input, and Productivity Measurement,* edited by National Bureau of Economic Research, pp. 47–63. Studies in Income and Wealth, vol. 25. Princeton: Princeton University Press, 1961.

Stone, Richard. *Quantity and Price Indexes in National Accounts.* Paris: Organization for European Economic Cooperation, n.d.

Terborgh, George. *Business Investment Management.* Washington, D.C.: Machinery and Allied Products Institute, 1967.

Theil, Henri. *Economics and Information Theory.* Amsterdam: North-Holland, 1967.

Tomasevich, Jozo. "Foreign Economic Relations, 1918–1941." In *Yugoslavia,* edited by Robert J. Kerner, pp. 169–214. Berkeley and Los Angeles: University of California Press, 1949.

———. "Postwar Foreign Economic Relations." In *Yugoslavia,* edited by Robert J. Kerner, pp. 387–426. Berkeley and Los Angeles: University of California Press, 1949.

Tucker, Robert C., ed. *The Marx-Engels Reader.* New York: W. W. Norton, 1972.

United Kingdom. Central Statistical Office. *Annual Abstract of Statistics, 1961.* London: Her Majesty's Stationery Office, 1961.

———. ———. *Annual Abstract of Statistics, 1968.* London: Her Majesty's Stationery Office, 1971.

United Nations. *Demographic Yearbook, 1948.* Lake Success, N.Y.: U.N., 1949.

———. *1972 Supplement to the Statistical Yearbook and the Monthly Bulletin of Statistics.* New York: U.N., 1973.

———. *Statistical Yearbook, 1972.* New York: U.N., 1973.

———. *The Growth of World Industry.* 1972 ed. New York: U.N., 1974.

———. *World Energy Supplies, 1951–1954.* Statistical papers, series J, no. 2. New York: U.N., 1957.

———. *Yearbook of National Accounts Statistics, 1973.* Vol. 3. New York: U.N., 1975.

United Nations Relief and Rehabilitation Administration. *Agriculture and Food in Jugoslavia.* Operational Analysis Papers, no. 23. London: UNRRA, European Regional Office, 1947.

United States. Board of Governors of the Federal Reserve System. *Industrial Production Measurement in the United States: Concepts, Uses, and Compilation Practices.* Washington, D.C.: Federal Reserve System, Board of Governors, Division of Research and Statistics, 1964.

———. Bureau of the Census. *Statistical Abstract of the United States, 1954.* 75th ed. Washington, D.C.: Government Printing Office, 1954.

———. ———. *Statistical Abstract of the United States, 1968.* 89th ed. Washington, D.C.: Government Printing Office, 1968.

———. ———. *Statistical Abstract of the United States, 1971.* 92d ed. Washington, D.C.: Government Printing Office, 1971.

———. ———. *Statistical Abstract of the United States, 1974.* 95th ed. Washington, D.C.: Government Printing Office, 1974.

———. Council of Economic Advisers. *Economic Report of the President, 1975.* Washington, D.C.: Government Printing Office, 1975.

———. Department of Commerce. *Projections of the Populations of the Communist Countries of Eastern Europe, by Age and Sex: 1975 to 2000*. Washington, D.C.: Government Printing Office, 1976.

Usher, Dan. *The Price Mechanism and the Meaning of National Income Statistics*. Oxford: Oxford University Press, 1968.

Vanek, Jaroslav. *The General Theory of Labor-Managed Enterprises*. Ithaca: Cornell University Press, 1970.

Vanek, Jaroslav, and Jovičić, Milena. "Capital Market and Income Distribution in Yugoslavia." *Quarterly Journal of Economics* 89 (1975): 432–43.

Vinski, Ivo. "The National Wealth of Yugoslavia at the End of 1953." In *The Measurement of National Wealth,* edited by Raymond Goldsmith and Christopher Saunders, pp. 16–92. Series on Income and Wealth, 8. Chicago: Quadrangle Books, 1959.

Vucinich, Wayne S. *Contemporary Yugoslavia: Twenty Years of Socialist Experiment*. Berkeley and Los Angeles: University of California Press, 1969.

Wachtel, Howard M. "Workers' Management and Interindustry Wage Differentials in Yugoslavia." *Journal of Political Economy* 80, part 1 (1972): 540–60.

———. "Workers' Management and Wage Differentials in Yugoslavia." Ph.D. dissertation, University of Michigan, 1969.

Walters, Alan A., "Incremental Capital-Output Ratios." *Economic Journal* 76 (1966): 818–22.

———. "Production and Cost Functions: An Econometric Survey." *Econometrica* 31 (1963): 1–66.

Ward, Benjamin. "Workers' Management in Yugoslavia." *Journal of Political Economy* 65 (1957): 373–86.

Waterson, Albert. *Planning in Yugoslavia: Organization and Implementation*. Baltimore: The Johns Hopkins Press, 1962.

Weitzman, Martin L. "Soviet Postwar Economic Growth and Capital-Labor Substitution." *American Economic Review* 60 (1970): 676–92.

Wolff, Robert Lee. *The Balkans in Our Time*. Cambridge: Harvard University Press, 1956.

Yugoslavia. Federal Executive Council. Secretariat for Information. *The Five Year Plan of Economic Development of Yugoslavia 1961–1965*. Belgrade: Secretariat for Information, 1961.

"Yugoslavia's 1966–1970 Social Development Plan." *Yugoslav Survey* new series 7 (1966): 3,869–914.

Zaleski, Eugene. *Planning for Economic Growth in the Soviet Union, 1918–1932*. Chapel Hill: University of North Carolina Press, 1971.

———. *Stalinist Planning for Economic Growth, 1933–1952*. Chapel Hill: University of North Carolina Press, 1980.

Index